W9-BPM-859

PRAISE FOR
ONE NATION UNDER GOD

"Illuminating. . . . A useful corrective to preacher-politicians who end-lessly call for a return to the nation's religious roots. As Kruse skillfully demonstrates, some of those roots took hold only yesterday."

—*Dallas Morning News*

"An illuminating addition to the growing field of the history of Amer-ican conservatism and capitalism, as well as a vibrant study of the way cultural influence works—one that will make it impossible to take for granted the small print on the back of a dollar bill ever again. . . . This is what's most interesting in the story Kruse is telling: the pattern of conti-nuity and change that links our own time with those that came before."

—*Nation*

"A fine new book. . . . Kruse's thoughtful book illustrates a kind of life cycle of American religious politics: fervent social movements rise up, crest with presidential support, and then slip away, leaving behind ritu-als, rhetoric, rules, and reforms." —*Foreign Affairs*

"An engaging and important book." —*Christianity Today*

"Kruse's book is a deft elaboration on the irony of the corporate involvement in the Christian America promotion: Supporters, be they of good or ill will, converged on the idea that they were producing or reproducing a nation united 'under God.' Frustrated in their attempts to change the Constitution, they had to settle for the insertion of 'under God' in the Pledge of Allegiance to the flag. Yet, as the author makes clear, they were, ironically, producing a new and enduringly conflicted and polarized America." —*America*

"A lucid narrative." —*Commonweal*

"It sheds new light on our tortured past and our abiding predicament."

—*Baptist News*

"*One Nation Under God* is an important book. We—Christians and Americans—need to understand our history. . . . Kruse offers us a potent reminder of where we have come from, and, perhaps more importantly, how far we still have to go."   —*Patheos*

"A thorough and fascinating treatment of a little known thread of US history."   —*Sojourners*

"A new, meticulous, and vital historical account that should be read by anyone who still scratches their head over whether the Tea Party is a religious movement, or wonders how the idealized conception of America as a 'Christian nation' was constructed. . . . Essential reading for anyone who wants to understand that uniquely American alliance between God and mammon."   —*National Memo*

"An engaging history of modern religious nationalism . . . briskly narrated and richly detailed"   —*Bookforum*

"Kruse's book will be an important resource for anyone who wonders why so many fundamentalist figureheads—clergy and politicians alike—promote fiscal conservatism alongside social conservatism."

—*Church and State*

"The author lays out a new mega-subdivision in our sprawling religious history. The result exposes a class of pulpit vipers who infect an insecure quarter of the population and who can never shake the feeling they are not as believed in as they believe they should be."   —*Humanist*

"As entertaining as it is revealing. . . . Kruse weaves a narrative that is quite funny, in an understated scholarly way."   —*Boston Review*

"Kruse has crafted a tight argument and marshaled a mountain of evidence to support it. His writing is sharp and clear, and his telling eye for detail makes this an engaging story. Simply put, *One Nation Under God* is an excellent book."   —*Marginalia*

"Fascinating, vividly drawn portraits."   —*American Prospect*

"*One Nation Under God* comes as something of a revelation (pardon the expression). Kruse makes the case that whatever the relationship between faith and the state in the nineteenth and early twentieth centuries, that connection went through a profound transformation in the 1950s."

—*Democracy: A Journal of Ideas*

"An eminently readable book, chock-full of lively and entertaining anecdotes."   —*Religion in American History*

"Both contributes decisively to an ongoing scholarly conversation and introduces its readers to a plethora of little-known documents, archives, organizations, and individuals. . . . A significant contribution to the history of the Christian Right, the Cold War, and the culture wars of the recent past."   —H-Net, H-AmRel

"A detailed history of the roots of the campaign arguing that the United States is a Christian nation."   —*Shelf Awareness for Readers*

"Kruse addresses how corporations used clergymen in their PR war against Roosevelt's New Deal and how evangelist Billy Graham helped Dwight Eisenhower and Richard Nixon use religion as the 'lowest-common denominator' to unite the public. I've yet to finish it, but I can already tell this will be an informative, insightful read."

—*Library Journal*, Editors' Spring Picks

"In a book for readers from both parties, Kruse ably demonstrates how the simple ornamental mottoes 'under God' and 'In God We Trust,' as well as the fight to define America as Christian, were parts of a clever business plan."   —*Kirkus*, starred review

"Thorough and thought-provoking scholarship. . . . Kruse reveals the marketing machine behind American godliness with authority, insight, and clarity. He illustrates key turning points along the way to provide a cohesive picture of a well-powered movement. He hands us the agenda behind the Pledge of Allegiance, 'in God we trust,' and other corner-stones of American patriotism. In short, he exposes the PR man behind the pious curtain."   —*Library Journal*, starred review

"Much has been written about the religious right, but Kevin Kruse has written a breakthrough book by describing the movement's pre-history in the 1930s and 1950s—and in fascinating detail. Engagingly written, *One Nation Under God* will provoke many arguments, but it will require all sides to come to terms with facts and events largely buried in our collective memory until Kruse bravely set out to challenge our assumptions."

—E. J. DIONNE JR., author of *Souled Out: Reclaiming Faith and Politics after the Religious Right*

"Kevin M. Kruse's startling *One Nation Under God* reveals the extraordinary Cold War politics that put 'under God' in America's Pledge of Allegiance, 'In God We Trust' on US stamps, and Cecil B. DeMille's *The Ten Commandments* on Hollywood's biggest movie list. The political warriors for a 'Christian America' made the Puritans look like pikers, and Kruse dissects their successes and foibles with grace, glowing research, and more than a little humor. A compelling read!"

—JON BUTLER, professor emeritus of American studies, history, and religious studies at Yale University

"In this riveting book, Kevin Kruse combines the history of religion with the history of capitalism to craft an original interpretation about America's religious identity. Revisionist in the best sense—bold, daring, and intelligent—it will change how we think about the American past."

—ANDREW PRESTON, author of *Sword of the Spirit, Shield of Faith: Religion in American War and Diplomacy*

"In this brilliant and iconoclastic book, Kevin M. Kruse shows how an unholy alliance of greedy businessmen, venal clergy, and conservative politicians exploited American spirituality for partisan gain. Kruse's research is extraordinary, his prose vivid, his argument profound. *One Nation Under God* is essential reading for anyone interested in understanding contemporary culture in the United States."

—ARI KELMAN, author of the Bancroft Prize–winning *A Misplaced Massacre*

"Prepare yourself for a startling and important discovery: 'Christian America' is not a legacy of the nation's founders or a construct of the Cold War era. Rather, as Kevin Kruse so powerfully shows, it was the deliberate invention of conservative corporate leaders who allied with like-minded clergymen in the 1930s to fight the antichrist they most feared: Franklin Roosevelt's New Deal. Kruse convincingly argues that the rise of the religious right over the next decades grew out of these anti-liberal politics, not the other way around. 'Church and state' in America has rarely had a better historian than Kruse."

—LIZABETH COHEN, author of *Making a New Deal: Industrial Workers in America, 1919–1939*

"Certain to be controversial, *One Nation Under God* persuasively reveals how business opponents of the New Deal joined forces with crusading ministers to place religious piety at the core of the American story. The book's redolent account of this underestimated midcentury point of inflection compels a reassessment of how and when the United States came to be regarded as a consecrated Christian nation."

—IRA KATZNELSON, author of *Fear Itself: The New Deal and the Origins of Our Time*

"The claim that the United States was founded and then flourished as a Christian nation turns out to be an all-American fraud, disseminated in the 1950s and after by an odd combination of reactionary businessmen, well-meaning political leaders, cranks, cynics, and dupes. Kevin M. Kruse's calm and devastating book more than debunks the fraud; it offers brilliant insight into our politics, then and now."

—SEAN WILENTZ, Bancroft Prize–winning author of *The Rise of American Democracy*

ONE NATION UNDER GOD

ONE NATION UNDER GOD

How Corporate America
Invented Christian America

KEVIN M. KRUSE

BASIC BOOKS
A Member of the Perseus Books Group
New York

Copyright © 2015 by Kevin M. Kruse

Hardcover first published in 2015 by Basic Books
A Member of the Perseus Books Group
Paperback first published in 2016 by Basic Books

All rights reserved. Printed in the United States of America. No part of this book may be reproduced in any manner whatsoever without written permission except in the case of brief quotations embodied in critical articles and reviews. For information, address Basic Books, 250 West 57th Street, New York, NY 10107.

Books published by Basic Books are available at special discounts for bulk purchases in the United States by corporations, institutions, and other organizations. For more information, please contact the Special Markets Department at the Perseus Books Group, 2300 Chestnut Street, Suite 200, Philadelphia, PA 19103, or call (800) 810-4145, ext. 5000, or e-mail special.markets@perseusbooks.com.

Designed by Brent Wilcox

The Library of Congress has cataloged the original edition as follows:
Kruse, Kevin Michael, 1972-
One nation under God : how corporate America invented Christian America /
Kevin M. Kruse.
pages cm
Includes bibliographical references and index.
ISBN 978-0-465-04949-3 (hardback : alkaline paper)—ISBN 978-0-465-04064-3 (ebook) 1. Christianity and politics—United States—History—20th century. 2. Church and state—United States—History—20th century. 3. New Deal, 1933–1939—Public opinion. 4. Corporations—Political activity—United States—History—20th century. 5. Conservatism—United States—History—20th century. 6. Political culture—United States—History—20th century. 7. Social conflict—United States—History—20th century. 8. United States—Religion—20th century. 9. United States—Politics and government—1933–1945. 10. United States—Politics and government—1945–1989. I. Title.
BR517.K78 2015
322'.10973—dc23
2014035883

ISBN 978-0-465-09741-8 (paperback)

LSC-C

Printing 5, 2021

For Maggie and Sam

CONTENTS

INTRODUCTION   ix

PART I: CREATION

  1 "Freedom Under God"   3

  2 The Great Crusades   35

PART II: CONSECRATION

  3 "Government Under God"   67

  4 Pledging Allegiance   95

  5 Pitchmen for Piety   127

PART III: CONFLICT

  6 "*Whose* Religious Tradition?"   165

  7 "Our So-Called Religious Leaders"   203

  8 "Which Side Are You On?"   239

  Epilogue   275

  ACKNOWLEDGMENTS   295

  NOTES   299

  INDEX   339

INTRODUCTION

THE INAUGURATION OF PRESIDENT DWIGHT D. Eisenhower was much more than a political ceremony. It was, in many ways, a religious consecration.

Though such a characterization might startle us today, the voters who elected Eisenhower twice by overwhelming margins would not have been surprised. In his acceptance speech at the 1952 Republican National Convention, he promised that the coming campaign would be a "great crusade for freedom." As he traveled across America that summer, Eisenhower met often with Reverend Billy Graham, his close friend, to receive spiritual guidance and recommendations for passages of Scripture to use in his speeches. Indeed, the Republican nominee talked so much about spirituality on the stump that legendary *New York Times* reporter Scotty Reston likened his campaign to "William Jennings Bryan's old invasion of the Bible Belt during the Chautauqua circuit days." On election day, Americans answered his call. Eisenhower won 55 percent of the popular vote and a staggering 442-to-89 margin in the Electoral College. Reflecting on the returns, Eisenhower saw nothing less than a mandate for a national religious revival. "I think one of the reasons I was elected was to help lead this country spiritually," he confided to Graham. "We *need* a spiritual renewal."[1]

The inaugural ceremonies on January 20, 1953, set the tone for the new administration. Some of Eisenhower's supporters tried to get Congress to designate it a National Day of Prayer, but even without such an official blessing, the day still had all the markings of one. In the past, incoming presidents had attended religious services on the morning of their inauguration, but usually discreetly. Before Harry Truman's inauguration in 1949, for instance, the president, his family, and a few cabinet officials made an unannounced visit to St. John's Episcopal Church for a brief fifteen-minute service, with only a few regular parishioners witnessing the moment. Eisenhower, in contrast, turned spirituality into spectacle. At a transition meeting with his cabinet nominees, he announced that they and their families were invited to a special religious service at National Presbyterian Church the morning of the inauguration. "He added hastily as an afterthought that, of course, no Cabinet member should feel under pressure to go to the Presbyterian services," remembered Sherman Adams, his chief of staff; "anybody could go instead to a church of his own choice." But given a choice between worshiping with the president or worshiping without him, almost all chose the former. More than 150 supporters joined the extended Eisenhower clan for the services. The event had been publicized widely in the press, so the attendees arrived to find the church completely full; a crowd of eight hundred more huddled outside in the morning chill. This presidential prayer service had echoes across Washington. All of the city's Catholic churches opened for the occasion, while many Jewish and Protestant houses of worship did the same, acting on their own initiative. St. John's Episcopal, for instance, offered a series of prayer services for the public, every hour on the hour. The *Washington Post* reported that even the city's first mosque, still under construction, would nevertheless be open "for all Moslems . . . who wish to invoke Allah's aid for the Republican administration."[2]

Public prayer highlighted the official inaugural festivities as well. Chief Justice Fred Vinson, on hand to deliver the oath of office, welcomed the religious emphasis. When he had risen to the high court a few years earlier, the Kentucky Democrat had taken part in a "consecration ceremony" sponsored by a new prayer breakfast group in the Senate. There, before a gathering of more than two dozen senators and the attorney general, the chief justice of the United States testified about "the importance of the Bible being the Book of all the people and how the whole superstructure of government and jurisprudence is built upon it." Now Vinson would watch Eisenhower do the same. As the chief justice delivered the oath, the new chief executive's left hand rested not on one Bible but on two, each opened to a selection suggested by Graham. A black leather-bound family Bible was opened to 2 Chronicles 7:14, a passage Graham regularly cited to urge a national religious revival: "If my people, which are called by my name, shall humble themselves and pray, and seek my face, and turn from their wicked ways; then I will hear from heaven, and will forgive their sin, and will heal their land." The second, a Masonic Bible used by George Washington at the first presidential inauguration, lay open to show a similar call for revival in Psalm 127: "Except the Lord build the house, they labour in vain that build it; except the Lord keep the city, the watchman waketh but in vain."[3]

Immediately after his oath, in his first official words as president, Eisenhower asked the 125,000 Americans in attendance—and the estimated seventy million more watching live on television—to bow their heads so that he might lead them in "a little private prayer of my own" he had composed that morning. "Almighty God," Eisenhower began, "as we stand here at this moment my future associates in the Executive branch of Government join me in beseeching that Thou will make full and complete our dedication to the service of the people in this throng, and their fellow citizens everywhere." The president's prayer caused a minor sensation—not because of anything said in it but simply because it had been said. A half mile from the Capitol ceremonies, crowds on Pennsylvania Avenue listened to the prayer over portable speakers strewn along the streets. "There was an electric something," an observer noted, "that seemed to summon the waiting multitudes to their knees." The "inaugural prayer" was quickly reproduced in countless newspapers and magazines. An oilman from Shreveport, Louisiana, printed the prayer as a pamphlet, with the cover showing the smiling president on the left, the American flag on the right, and the cross directly above. At the bottom ran the oilman's own prayer: "God Save Our President Who Saved Our Country and Our World!"[4]

Eisenhower's prayer was only the beginning of the day's spiritual emphasis. "Religion was one of the thoughts I had been mulling over for several weeks," he later reflected. "I did not want my Inaugural Address to be a sermon, by any means; I was not a man of the cloth. But there was embedded in me from boyhood, a deep faith in the beneficence of the Almighty. I wanted, then, to make this faith clear." Accordingly, his address was rife with references to the religious beliefs of the president and the people he sought to lead to revival. "We who are free must proclaim anew our faith," Eisenhower insisted. "This faith is the abiding creed of our fathers. It is our faith in the deathless dignity of man, governed by eternal moral and natural laws." Once he finished his speech, the new president retreated to a reviewing stand to watch the inaugural parade. The five-hour procession offered several remarkable sights for the record television audience, including a trio of elephants from Ohio and a cowboy named Monte Montana who threw a lasso around the president's head as Secret Service agents glowered nearby. For many viewers, though, the most memorable part of the parade was the very first float. Anointed "God's Float" by its creators, it consisted of a replica of a house of worship with large photos of churches and synagogues arrayed along the sides. Two phrases appeared in grand Gothic script at each end: "Freedom of Worship" and "In God We Trust."[5]

The inauguration and its immediate aftermath established the tenor for Eisenhower's entire presidency. On the first Sunday in February, he became the first president ever to be baptized while in office, taking the rite before the congregation of National Presbyterian Church. That same night, Eisenhower broadcast an Oval Office address for the American Legion's "Back to God" ceremonies, urging the millions watching at home to recognize and rejoice in what the president said were the spiritual foundations of the nation. Four days later, he was the guest of honor at the first-ever National Prayer Breakfast, which soon became an annual tradition. The initial event was hosted by hotel magnate Conrad Hilton, with more than five hundred dignitaries, including several senators, representatives, cabinet members, ambassadors, and justices of the Supreme Court, taking part. Fittingly, the theme was "Government Under God." The convening pastor led a "prayer of consecration" for Eisenhower, who then offered brief remarks of his own. "The very basis of our government is: 'We hold that all men are endowed by their Creator' with certain rights," the president asserted. "In one sentence, we established that every free government is embedded soundly in a deeply-felt religious faith or it makes no sense." Eisenhower made clear that he would personally turn those words into deeds. The next day, he instituted the first-ever opening prayers at a cabinet meeting. (It took some time before this innovation became a natural habit. His secretary recalled Eisenhower emerging from a cabinet session only to exclaim: "Jesus Christ, we forgot the prayer!")[6]

All this activity took place in just the first week of February 1953. In the months and years that followed, the new president revolutionized public life in America. In the summer of 1953, Eisenhower, Vice President Richard Nixon, and members of their cabinet held a signing ceremony in the Oval Office declaring that the United States government was based on biblical principles. Meanwhile, countless executive departments, including the Pentagon, instituted prayer services of their own. The rest of the Capitol consecrated itself too. In 1954, Congress followed Eisenhower's lead, adding the phrase "under God" to the previously secular Pledge of Allegiance. A similar phrase, "In God We Trust," was added to a postage stamp for the first time in 1954 and then to paper money the next year; in 1956, it became the nation's first official motto. During the Eisenhower era Americans were told, time and time again, that the nation not only should be a Christian nation but also that it had always been one. They soon came to believe that the United States of America was "one nation under God."

And they've believed it ever since.

AT HEART, THIS BOOK SEEKS to challenge Americans' assumptions about the basic relationship between religion and politics in their nation's history. For decades now, liberals and conservatives have been locked in an intractable struggle over an ostensibly simple question: Is the United States a Christian nation? This debate, largely focused on endless parsing of the intent of the founding fathers, has ultimately generated more heat than light. Like most scholars, I believe the historical record is fairly clear about the founding generation's preference for what Thomas Jefferson memorably described as a wall of separation between church and state, a belief the founders spelled out repeatedly in public statements and private correspondence.[7] This scholarly consensus, though, has done little to shift popular opinion. If anything, the country has more tightly embraced religion in the public sphere and in political culture in recent decades. And so this book begins with a different premise. It sets aside the question of whether the founders intended America to be a Christian nation and instead asks why so many contemporary Americans came to believe that this country has been and always should be a Christian nation.

As the story of the early months of the Eisenhower administration makes clear, part of the answer—though not all of it—can be found in the mid-1950s, when Americans underwent an incredible transformation in how they understood the role of religion in public life. Other historians have paid attention to the establishment of new religious mottos and ceremonies in these years, but most have misplaced their origins. Without exception, the works on the religious revival of the Eisenhower era attribute the rise of public religion solely to the Cold War. According to this conventional wisdom, as the United States fell into an anticommunist panic, its leaders suddenly began to emphasize the nation's religious traits as a means of distinguishing it from the "godless communists" of the Soviet Union.[8]

But as this book argues, the postwar revolution in America's religious identity had its roots not in the foreign policy panic of the 1950s but rather in the domestic politics of the 1930s and early 1940s. Decades before Eisenhower's inaugural prayers, corporate titans enlisted conservative clergymen in an effort to promote new political arguments embodied in the phrase "freedom under God." As the private correspondence and public claims of the men leading this charge make clear, this new ideology was designed to defeat the state power its architects feared most—not the Soviet regime in Moscow, but Franklin D. Roosevelt's New Deal administration in Washington. With ample funding from major corporations, prominent industrialists, and business lobbies such as the National Association of Manufacturers and the US Chamber of Commerce in the 1930s and 1940s, these new evangelists for free enterprise promoted a vision best characterized as "Christian libertarianism."

By the late 1940s and early 1950s, this ideology had won converts including religious leaders such as Billy Graham and Abraham Vereide and conservative icons ranging from former president Herbert Hoover to future president Ronald Reagan. The new conflation of faith, freedom, and free enterprise then moved to center stage in the 1950s under Eisenhower's watch. Though his administration gave religion an unprecedented role in the public sphere, it essentially echoed and amplified the work of countless private organizations and ordinary citizens who had already been active in the same cause. Corporate leaders remained central. Leading industrialists and large business organizations bankrolled major efforts to promote the role of religion in public life. The top advertising agency of the age, the J. Walter Thompson Company, encouraged Americans to attend churches and synagogues through an unprecedented "Religion in American Life" ad campaign. Even Hollywood got into the act, with director Cecil B. DeMille helping erect literally thousands of granite monuments to the Ten Commandments across the nation as part of a promotional campaign for his blockbuster film of the same name.

Inundated with urgent calls to embrace faith, Americans did just that. The percentage of Americans who claimed membership in a church had been fairly low across the nineteenth century, though it had slowly increased from just 16 percent in 1850 to 36 percent in 1900. In the early decades of the twentieth century the percentages plateaued, remaining at 43 percent in both 1910 and 1920, then moving up slightly to 47 percent in 1930 and 49 percent in 1940. In the decade and a half after the Second World War, however, the percentage of Americans who belonged to a church or synagogue suddenly soared, reaching 57 percent in 1950 and then peaking at 69 percent at the end of the decade, an all-time high.[9]

While this religious revival was remarkable, the almost complete lack of opposition to it was even more so. A few clergymen complained that the new public forms of faith seemed a bit superficial, but they ultimately approved of anything that encouraged church attendance. In political terms, both parties welcomed the popular new drive to link piety and patriotism; the only thing they fought over was which side deserved more credit for it. Legal scholars likewise claimed there was nothing to fear in these changes, arguing that the adoption of phrases and mottos such as "one nation under God" and "In God We Trust" did not impact America's commitment to the separation of church and state. Such acts of "ceremonial deism" were, according to Yale Law School dean Eugene Rostow, nothing but harmless ornamentation, "so conventional and uncontroversial as to be constitutional." The Supreme Court sanctioned most of these changes too. Even the outspokenly liberal Justice William O. Douglas concluded in 1952 that public invocations of faith were ironclad proof that Americans were "a religious people whose institutions presuppose a Supreme Being."[10]

Nor did civil liberties organizations take a stand, at least at first. The American Civil Liberties Union (ACLU), focused on the menace of McCarthyism, paid little attention to the new religious rhetoric and rituals of the Eisenhower era. Americans United for the Separation of Church and State, the most significant organization of its kind, focused elsewhere as well. As suggested by its original name, still used in that era—Protestants and Other Americans United for the Separation of Church and State—the organization was worried mainly about Catholics seeking public support for parochial schools. In general, these civil liberties groups accepted the then-common claim that the First Amendment mandated the separation of church and state but not the separation of religion and politics. They believed government support for a specific sect was wrong, but support for the generically sacred was fine.

Ultimately, then, present-day assumptions of conservative Christians do rest on a foundation of fact. There once was a time during which virtually all Americans agreed that their country was a Christian nation (or, in their more expansive expressions, a "Judeo-Christian nation"). To be sure, that period of consensus was much more recent and much more short-lived than most assume, but it existed all the same. And during that brief moment this new public religiosity succeeded in writing itself—literally, in some cases—into the very identity of the nation. It transformed the national motto and the Pledge of Allegiance. It became a central part of important ceremonies of civic life and created wholly new traditions of its own. It altered the course of American politics at the highest levels and transformed how ordinary citizens understood their country. Above all, it invented a new idea about America's fundamental nature, an idea that remains ascendant to this day. Yet, for all these revolutionary developments, its story has largely been forgotten.

This book recovers an important history that has been hiding in plain sight. Phrases such as "one nation under God" and "In God We Trust"— so seemingly simple, yet actually quite complex—are etched across our lives. They are woven into the pledge of patriotism our children say each morning; they are marked on the money we carry in our wallets; they are carved into the walls of our courts and our Congress. These are everyday things, often overlooked. But at a fundamental level they speak to who we are as a people—or at least who we think we might be or should be. It's time we stop taking them for granted.

PART I

CREATION

CHAPTER 1

"Freedom Under God"

In December 1940, more than five thousand industrialists from across America took part in their yearly pilgrimage to Park Avenue. For three days every winter, the posh Waldorf-Astoria Hotel welcomed them for the annual meeting of the National Association of Manufacturers (NAM). That year, the program promised a particularly impressive slate of speakers. Corporate leaders were well represented, of course, with addresses set from titans at General Motors, General Electric, Standard Oil, Mutual Life, and Sears, Roebuck, to name only a few. Some of the other featured attractions hailed from beyond the boardroom: popular lecturers such as noted etiquette expert Emily Post, renowned philosopher-historian Will Durant, and even Federal Bureau of Investigation director J. Edgar Hoover. Tucked away near the end of the program was a name that few knew upon arrival but everyone would be talking about by the week's end: Reverend James W. Fifield Jr.[1]

Ordinarily, a Congregationalist minister might not have seemed well suited to address the corporate luminaries assembled at the Waldorf-Astoria. But his appearance had been years in the making. For much of the 1930s, organizations such as NAM had been searching in vain for ways to rehabilitate a public image that had been destroyed in the crash and defamed by the New Deal. In 1934, a new generation of conservative industrialists took over NAM with a promise to "serve the purposes of business salvation." "The public does not understand industry," one of them argued, "because industry itself has made no effort to tell its story;

to show the people of this country that our high living standards have risen almost altogether from the civilization which industrial activity has set up." Accordingly, NAM dedicated itself to spreading the gospel of free enterprise, hiring its first full-time director of public relations and vastly expanding its expenditures in the field. As late as 1934, NAM spent a paltry $36,000 on public relations. Three years later, the organization devoted $793,043 to the cause, more than half its total income that year. Seeking to repair the image of industrialists, NAM promoted the values of free enterprise through a wide array of films, radio programs, advertisements, direct mail, a speakers bureau, and a press service that provided ready-made editorials and news stories for seventy-five hundred local newspapers. Ultimately, though, its efforts at self-promotion were seen as precisely that. As one observer later noted, "Throughout the thirties, enough of the corporate campaign was marred by extremist, overt attacks on the unions and the New Deal that it was easy for critics to dismiss the entire effort as mere propaganda."[2]

While established business lobbies such as NAM had been unable to sell free enterprise effectively in the Depression, neither had the many new organizations created specifically for that purpose. The most prominent, the American Liberty League, had formed in 1934 to "teach the necessity of respect for the rights of persons and property" and "the duty of government to encourage and protect individual and group initiative and enterprise." It benefited from generous financial support from corporate titans, particularly at DuPont and General Motors. But their prominence inadvertently crippled its effectiveness, as the Liberty League was easily dismissed as a collection of tycoons looking out for their own self-interest. Jim Farley, chairman of the Democratic Party, joked that it really ought to be called the "American Cellophane League" because "first, it's a DuPont product and second, you can see right through it." Even the president took his shots. "It has been said that there are two great Commandments—one is to love God, and the other to love your neighbor," Franklin D. Roosevelt noted soon after its creation. "The two particular tenets of this new organization say you shall love God and then forget your neighbor." Off the record, he joked that the name of the god they worshiped seemed to be "Property."[3]

As Roosevelt's quips made clear, the president delighted in using religious language to shame his opponents. A practicing Episcopalian, he shrewdly drew on spiritual themes and imagery throughout his career.[4] In the judgment of his biographer James MacGregor Burns, "probably no American politician has given so many speeches that were essentially sermons rather than statements of policy." During his two terms as governor of New York, Roosevelt frequently framed his earthly agenda in heavenly terms. Once, he introduced an otherwise dry speech criticizing Republican plans to privatize public utilities by saying, "This is a history and a sermon on the subject of water power, and I preach from the Old Testament. The text is 'Thou shalt not steal.'" Roosevelt's use of religious language was even more pronounced over his four presidential terms, especially when he condemned his enemies in the financial elite. In his acceptance speech at the 1932 Democratic National Convention, for instance, he placed blame for the Great Depression on the "many amongst us [who] have made obeisance to Mammon." Likewise, his first inaugural address was so laden with references to Scripture that the National Bible Press published an extensive chart linking his text with the "Corresponding Biblical Quotations." In the speech, Roosevelt reassured the nation that "the money changers have fled from their high seats in the temple of our civilization. We may now restore the temple to the ancient truths."[5]

In introducing the New Deal, Roosevelt and his allies revived the old language of the so-called Social Gospel to justify the creation of the modern welfare state. The original proponents of the Social Gospel, back in the late nineteenth century, had significantly reframed Christianity as a faith concerned less with personal salvation and more with the public good. They rallied popular support for Progressive Era reforms in the early twentieth century before fading from public view in the conservative 1920s. But the economic crash and the widespread suffering of the Great Depression brought them back into vogue. When Roosevelt launched the New Deal, an array of politically liberal clergymen championed his proposal for a vast welfare state as simply "the Christian thing to do." His administration's efforts to regulate the economy and address the excesses of corporate America were singled out for praise. Catholic and Protestant leaders hailed the "ethical and human significance" of New Deal measures, which they said merely "incorporated into law some of the social ideas and principles for which our religious organizations have stood for many years." The head of the Federal Council of Churches, for instance, claimed the New Deal embodied basic Christian principles such as the "significance of daily bread, shelter, and security."[6]

Throughout the 1930s, the nation's industrialists tried to counter the selflessness of the Social Gospel with direct appeals to Americans' self-interest but had little success. Accordingly, at the Waldorf-Astoria in December 1940, NAM president H. W. Prentis proposed that they try to beat Roosevelt at his own game. With wispy white hair and a weak chin, the fifty-six-year-old head of the Armstrong Cork Company seemed an unlikely star. But eighteen months earlier, the Pennsylvanian had electrified the business world with a speech to the US Chamber of Commerce that called for the recruitment of religion in the public relations war against the New Deal. "Economic facts are important, but they will never check the virus of collectivism," Prentis warned; "the only antidote is a revival of American patriotism and religious faith." The speech thrilled the Chamber and propelled Prentis to the top ranks of NAM. His presidential address at the Waldorf-Astoria was anticipated as a major national event, heavily promoted in advance by the *Wall Street Journal* and broadcast live over both ABC and CBS radio. Again, Prentis urged the assembled businessmen to emphasize faith in their public relations campaigns. "We must give attention to those things more cherished than material wealth and physical security," he asserted. "We must give more attention to intellectual leadership and a strengthening of the spiritual concept that underlies our American way of life."[7]

James W. Fifield Jr. was on hand to answer Prentis's call. Handsome, tall, and somewhat gangly, the forty-one-year-old Congregationalist minister bore more than a passing resemblance to Jimmy Stewart. (His politics resembled not those of the actor's famous character George Bailey, the crusading New Deal populist in *It's a Wonderful Life*, but rather those of Bailey's nemesis, the reactionary banker Henry Potter.) Addressing the industrialists at the Waldorf-Astoria, Fifield delivered a passionate defense of the American system of free enterprise and a withering assault on its perceived enemies in government. Decrying the New Deal's "encroachment upon our American freedoms," the minister listed a litany of sins committed by the Roosevelt administration, ranging from its devaluation of currency to its disrespect for the Supreme Court. He denounced the "rising costs of government and the multitude of federal agencies attached to the executive branch" and warned ominously of "the menace of autocracy approaching through bureaucracy." His audience of executives was stunned. Over the preceding decade, these titans of industry had been told, time and time again, that they were to blame for the nation's downfall. Fifield, in contrast, insisted that they were the source of its salvation. "When he had finished," a journalist noted, "rumors report that the N.A.M. applause could be heard in Hoboken."[8]

With his speech at the Waldorf-Astoria, Fifield convinced the industrialists that clergymen could be the means of regaining the upper hand in their war with Roosevelt in the coming years. As men of God, they could give voice to the same conservative complaints as business leaders, but without any suspicion that they were motivated solely by self-interest. In doing so, they could push back against claims that business had somehow sinned and the welfare state was doing God's work. While Roosevelt had joked that the Liberty League was concerned only with commandments against coveting and stealing, conservative clergymen now used their ministerial authority to argue, quite explicitly, that New Dealers were the ones violating the Ten Commandments. In countless sermons, speeches, and articles issued in the months and years after Fifield's address, these ministers claimed that the Democratic administration made a "false idol" of the federal government, leading Americans to worship it over the Almighty; that it caused Americans to covet what the wealthy possessed and seek to steal it from them; and that, ultimately, it bore false witness in making wild claims about what it could never truly accomplish. Above all, they insisted that the welfare state was not a means to implement Christ's teachings about caring for the poor and the needy, but rather a perversion of Christian doctrine. In a forceful rejection of the public service themes of the Social Gospel, they argued that the central tenet of Christianity remained the salvation of the individual. If any political and economic system fit with the religious teachings of Christ, it would have to be rooted in a similarly individualistic ethos. Nothing better exemplified such values, they insisted, than the capitalist system of free enterprise.

Thus, throughout the 1940s and early 1950s, Fifield and like-minded religious leaders advanced a new blend of conservative religion, economics, and politics that one observer aptly anointed "Christian libertarianism." A critic in the mid-1950s noted with sarcasm that "these groups do as much proselytizing for Adam Smith and the National Association of Manufacturers as they do for Christianity." But his targets would have welcomed that as a fair description of their work, even a compliment. For they saw Christianity and capitalism as inextricably intertwined and argued that spreading the gospel of one required spreading the gospel of the other. The two systems had been linked before, of course, but always in terms of their shared social characteristics. Fifield's important innovation was his insistence that Christianity and capitalism were political soul mates, first and foremost. The government had never loomed large in Americans' thinking about the relationship between Christianity and capitalism, but in Fifield's vision the state cast a long and ominous shadow. Accordingly, he and his colleagues devoted themselves to fighting back against the government forces that they believed were threatening capitalism and, by extension, Christianity. In the early postwar era, their activities helped reshape the national debate about the proper functions of the federal government, the political influence of corporations, and the role of religion in national life. They built a foundation for a new vision of America in which businessmen would no longer suffer under the rule of Roosevelt but instead thrive—in a phrase they popularized—in a nation "under God."[9]

JAMES W. FIFIELD JR. MADE his fame and fortune in Southern California. The frontier mythology of the region had long attracted Americans looking to reinvent both themselves and their nation, but that was never truer than during the depths of the Great Depression. In the early 1930s, the lush landscape and the allure of Hollywood held out promises of a fresh start for a people who had never needed it more. A continent away from the East Coast establishment that had dictated national norms for centuries, the region proved to be the perfect place for new modes of thought and action. This was especially evident in the otherwise staid worlds of religion and politics, as Southern California spawned new directions in both.[10]

As with many other Depression-era migrants to Los Angeles, Fifield came from the Midwest. Born in Chicago and educated at Oberlin, the University of Chicago, and Chicago Theological Seminary, he had been recruited in 1935 to take over the elite First Congregational Church in

Los Angeles. Located on a lush palm-shaded drive, the church boasted a sprawling complex that included a massive concrete cathedral with a 176-foot-tall Gothic tower, a full-size stage, a wedding chapel, a modern gymnasium, three auditoriums, and fifty-six classrooms. As the new pastor soon discovered, however, the church had an equally impressive debt of $750,000. While the deacons fretted about finances, Fifield launched a massive spending spree. A consummate organizer, he divided the church into four new divisions, hiring assistant ministers to run each of them with the help of their own complete staffs of secretaries, clerks, and organists, as well as five fully vested choirs shared between them. He recruited an instructor from Yale to launch a new drama club, while a new adult education series christened the College of Life started classes with a faculty of fourteen professors from nearby universities. Seeking to expand the church's reach even further, Fifield instituted five new radio programs and a speakers series, the Sunday Evening Club.[11]

Under Fifield's sharp direction, First Congregational rapidly expanded. The College of Life soon had twenty-eight thousand paying participants, while the Sunday Evening Club reported an average attendance of nine hundred each week, with collection plates bringing in twice as much as Fifield spent on programming. By 1942, the church was out of debt and turning a tidy profit. Its membership nearly quadrupled, making it the single largest Congregationalist church in the world and the church of choice for Los Angeles's elite. "Pushing four thousand," a reporter marveled, "its roster read like the *Wall Street Journal.*" The advisory board alone included rich and powerful figures such as Harry Chandler, a wealthy real estate speculator and conservative publisher of the *Los Angeles Times;* Dr. Robert A. Millikan, a Nobel Prize–winning chemist who had graced the cover of *Time* before becoming president of Cal Tech; Harvey Seeley Mudd, a mining magnate and prominent philanthropist; Alexander Nesbitt Kemp, president of the mammoth Pacific Mutual Life Insurance Company; and Albert W. Hawkes, a chemical industry executive who would soon become president of the US Chamber of Commerce and then a US senator. The mayor of Los Angeles regularly took part in the services, as did legendary filmmaker Cecil B. DeMille. Chronicling the achievements of Fifield and his flock, a friendly writer anointed him the "Apostle to Millionaires."[12]

To be sure, the minister was well matched to the millionaires in his pews. Fifield insisted that he and his wife always thought of themselves as simple "small-town folks," but they acclimated easily to their new life of wealth and privilege. Within a year of their arrival, they bought a mansion in an exclusive development on Wilshire Boulevard. "It had been built in the Twenties by a rich oil man for around a million dollars—using imported tile, special wood paneling, Tiffany stained glass windows, silk hand-woven 'wall paper' and many such luxuries," Fifield remembered. "The extensive lawn, colonnade archways, swimming pool and large main rooms on the first of three floors enabled us to entertain visiting speakers, dignitaries and important people from all over the world who could and did assist the church." The Fifields soon employed a butler, a chauffeur, and a cook, insisting that the household staff was vital in maintaining their "gracious accommodations" during the depths of the Depression. "The traditional image of a clergyman in those days [was] a man who has a hole in the seat of his pants and shoes run over at the heel," Fifield acknowledged. "It was quite a shock to a lot of people to see a minister driving around in a good car with a chauffeur at the wheel, who did not have to ask for a discount because he could afford to pay the regular price." Before long, Fifield was earning enough to pay full price even for luxury goods. First Congregational paid him $16,000 a year, a salary that, adjusted for inflation, would be roughly a quarter million dollars today.[13]

Fifield's connection to his congregation extended to their views on religion and politics too. In the apt words of one observer, Fifield was "one of the most theologically liberal and at the same time politically conservative ministers" of his era. He had no patience for fundamentalists who insisted upon a literal reading of Scripture. "The men who chronicled and canonized the Bible were subject to human error and limitation," he believed, and therefore the text needed to be sifted and interpreted. Reading the holy book should be "like eating fish—we take the bones out to enjoy the meat. All parts are not of equal value." Accordingly, Fifield dismissed the many passages in the New Testament about wealth and poverty and instead worked tirelessly to reconcile Christianity and capitalism. In his view, both systems rested on a basic belief that individuals would succeed or fail on their own merit. Although Fifield was not the first to suggest such connections, he put those theories into action in ways unlike any before him. At First Congregational and elsewhere, the minister reached out warmly to the wealthy, assuring them that their worldly success was a sign of God's blessings and brushing off the criticism of clergymen who disagreed. "I have smiled," he reflected later in life, "when critics of mine have called me the Thirteenth Apostle of Big Business or the St. Paul of the Prosperous."[14]

While Fifield took a loose approach to the Bible, he was a strict constructionist with the Constitution. Much like the millionaires to whom he ministered, Fifield had watched in alarm as Roosevelt convinced vast majorities of Americans that unfettered capitalism had crippled the nation and that the federal government now needed to play an important new role in regulating the free market's risks and redistributing its rewards. For Fifield and his flock, Roosevelt's actions violated not just the Constitution but the natural order of things. In December 1939, the minister placed a full-page ad in the *Los Angeles Times* decrying the New Deal as antithetical to the designs of the founding fathers. "From the beginning," the ad read, "America has built on the ideal of government which provides that the state is the servant of its citizens, that all just powers of government arise from consent of the governed, and that government's function is to provide maximum responsibility and maximum freedom to individual citizens. The opposite philosophy has been unwelcome in America until recently." The New Deal, it continued, posed a dire threat to the American way of life, and it was the duty of clergymen to save the nation's soul. In their crusade against the wanton growth of government, the church would find natural allies in corporate America because both were committed at their core to the "preservation of basic freedom in this nation." "Goodness and Christian ideals run proportionately high among businessmen," the ad assured. "They need no defense, for with all their faults, they have given America within the last decade a new world-high in general economic well-being."[15]

To lead his crusade in defense of freedom, Fifield offered the services of Spiritual Mobilization. He had founded the organization in the spring of 1935 with a pair of like-minded intellectuals, President Donald J. Cowling of Carleton College, a doctrinally liberal graduate of Yale Divinity School, and Professor William Hocking of Harvard University, a libertarian philosopher. The organization's founding goal was "to arouse the ministers of all denominations in America to check the trends toward pagan stateism, which would destroy our basic freedom and spiritual ideals." Soon Fifield took sole control, running its operations from his offices in Los Angeles. The organization's credo reflected the common politics of the minister and the millionaires in his congregation. It held that men were creatures of God imbued with "inalienable rights and responsibilities," specifically enumerated as "the liberty and dignity of the individual, in which freedom of choice, of enterprise and of property is inherent." Churches, it asserted, had a solemn duty to defend those rights against the encroachments of the state. Heeding this call, the First Congregational Church formally took charge of Spiritual Mobilization in 1938.[16]

With First Congregational now supporting it, Fifield brought the organization into national politics. He began by simply distributing copies of the political speeches he delivered from the pulpit. In one such pamphlet, Fifield detailed at great lengths the "grievous sin" of the New Deal state, which had wreaked havoc on the professional and personal lives of upstanding businessmen with its unwarranted meddling in their affairs. "The President of the United States and his administration are responsible for the willful or unconscious destruction of thrift, initiative, industriousness and resourcefulness which have been among our best assets since Pilgrim days," he charged. "I speak of the intimate, personal observations I have made of individuals who have lost their ideal, their purpose and their motive through the New Deal's destruction of spiritual rootage." It wasn't merely the rich who were suffering but all Americans. "Every Christian should oppose the totalitarian trends of the New Deal," he warned in another tract. Dismissing Roosevelt's promises of progress, Fifield called for a return to traditional values. "The way out for America is not ahead but back," he insisted. "How far back? Back as far as the old Gospel which exalted individuals, which placed responsibility for thought on individuals, and which insisted that individuals should be free spirits under God."[17]

These pamphlets from Spiritual Mobilization drew attention from leading conservatives across America, men who were eager to enlist the clergy in their fight against the New Deal. Former president Herbert Hoover, who had been deposed by Roosevelt and disparaged by his acolytes, encouraged Fifield in personal meetings and regular correspondence.

"If it would be possible for the Church to make a non-biased investigation into the morals of this government," Hoover wrote the minister in 1938, "they would find everywhere the old negation of Christianity that 'the end justifies the means.'" ("Aside from all that," he added, "I do not believe that the end they are trying to get to is any good either.") In October 1938, Fifield sent an alarmist tract to more than seventy thousand ministers across the nation, seeking to enlist them in the revolt against Roosevelt. "We ministers have special opportunities and special responsibilities in these critical days," it began. "America's movement toward dictatorship has already eliminated checks and balances in its concentration of powers in our chief executive." The New Deal undermined the spirit of Christianity and demanded a response from Christ's representatives on earth. "If, with Jesus, we believe in the sacredness of individual personalities, then our leadership responsibility is very plain." This duty was "not an easy one," he cautioned. "We may be called unpatriotic and accused of 'selling out,' but so was Jesus." Finding the leaflet to his liking, Hoover sent Fifield a warm note of appreciation and urged him to press on.[18]

As the 1930s drew to a close, these conservatives watched with delight as the New Deal stumbled. Though they had hoped to destroy the Roosevelt administration themselves, its wounds were largely self-inflicted. In 1937, the president's labor allies launched a series of sit-down strikes that secured union recognition at corporations such as General Motors and US Steel but also roused sympathy for seemingly beleaguered businessmen. At the same time, Roosevelt overreached with his proposal to "pack" the Supreme Court with new justices, a move that played into the hands of those who sought to portray him as dictatorial in intent. Most significant, though, was his ill-fated decision to rein in federal spending in an effort to balance the budget. The impressive economic recovery of Roosevelt's first term suddenly stalled, and the country entered a short but sharp recession in the winter of 1937–1938. As the New Deal faltered, Fifield began to look forward to the next presidential election—in "the critical year 1940"—when conservatives might finally rout the architects of the regulatory state. To his dismay, international tensions soon marginalized domestic politics and prompted the country to rally around Roosevelt again. "Our Mobilization program is developing somewhat," Fifield reported to Hoover in May 1941, "although, of course, under great difficulties in view of current tensions and trends." An ardent isolationist, Fifield argued strongly for neutrality in the coming conflict but found his prayers unanswered.[19]

Unable to keep America out of the Second World War, Fifield resolved to use it for his own ends. Pointing to the fascist dictatorships of the Axis powers as examples of "pagan stateism," he urged Americans to support Spiritual Mobilization as a bulwark against the coming threat. In a series of newspaper advertisements, the organization convinced nearly two million Christians to sign its official pledge. As originally written in June 1940, the pledge simply stated concern that the "rising tides of paganism and apostasy" around the globe were a threat to freedom. But as the war continued, Fifield began focusing on enemies at home. By 1944, the Spiritual Mobilization pledge had taken a more clearly partisan form: "Recognizing the anti-Christian and anti-American trends toward pagan stateism in America, I covenant to oppose them in all my areas of influence. I will use every opportunity to champion basic freedoms [of the] free pulpit, free speech, free enterprise, free press, and free assembly."[20]

As the distraction of the foreign war drew to a close, Fifield looked forward to renewing the fight against the New Deal. The minister now counted on the support of not just Hoover but an impressive array of conservative figures in politics, business, and religion. The advisory committee for Spiritual Mobilization's wartime pledge was, in the words of one observer, "a who's who of the conservative establishment." At mid-decade, its twenty-four-man roster included three past or present presidents of the US Chamber of Commerce, a leading Wall Street analyst, a prominent economist at the American Banking Association, the founder of the National Small Businessmen's Association, a US congressman, Dr. Norman Vincent Peale, a few notable authors and lecturers, and the presidents of the California Institute of Technology, Stanford University, the University of California, the University of Florida, and Princeton Theological Seminary.[21]

In Spiritual Mobilization's publications, these corporate leaders and conservative intellectuals strove to convince clergymen to reject the New Deal state. The organization's annual bulletin, distributed to seventy thousand "carefully selected ministers of all denominations," warned of the dangers of unchecked government power. The 1944 iteration, for instance, challenged Roosevelt's famous claim that Americans cherished "Four

Freedoms": freedom of speech, freedom of religion, freedom from want, and freedom from fear. "Within ever-narrowing limits, we still have freedom of speech, of the press, of assembly and worship," noted conservative author Channing Pollock, "but freedom of enterprise, of labor, and of the smallest concerns of our daily lives are gone with the wind from Washington. Instead we are offered the preposterous and impossible 'Four Freedoms' of slaves and convicts." The omens of a domestic dictatorship were clear, Senator Albert Hawkes agreed. "After careful examination of the records during the past ten years, one can only conclude that there is the objective of the assumption of greater power and control by the government over individual life. If these policies continue," he warned, "they will lead to state direction and control of all the lives of our citizens. That is the goal of Federal planners. That is NOT the desire of the American people!"[22]

The organization's national ambitions soon stretched its budget beyond even the ample resources of First Congregational, leading Fifield to search for new sponsors. In December 1944, Hawkes arranged a meeting with an elite group of industrialists at the Waldorf-Astoria in New York. Fifield found the audience to be just as receptive as the one he had addressed there four years before. After the meeting, the attendees dedicated themselves to raising funds for Spiritual Mobilization through corporate donations, personal checks, and solicitations from their friends and associates. Harvey Firestone, for instance, secured a donation at "the suggested maximum level" of $5,000 from his firm and promised to "work out a studied approach to two other rubber companies in Akron." H. W. Prentis Jr., meanwhile, sent Fifield the names of "twenty or twenty-five industrialists in this part of the country" from whom he could solicit funds. After Fifield wrote them, the former NAM president followed up with unsubtle messages of his own. Prentis noted that he personally had funded Spiritual Mobilization's work "in behalf of sound American Christian principles" and asked that they "give the movement some financial assistance" as well.[23]

FIFIELD WON A NUMBER OF powerful new patrons that year, but none was more important—not simply in terms of supporting Spiritual Mobilization financially but also in shaping its growth and effectiveness—than

J. Howard Pew Jr., president of Sun Oil. Tall and stiff, with bushy eyebrows, Pew had a stern appearance that was matched by his attitude. As a US senator once remarked, "He not only talks like an affidavit, he looks like one."[24] In theological terms, the doctrinally conservative Presbyterian had little in common with the liberal Congregationalist Fifield.[25] "He is far more modernistic in his religious views than I like," Pew confided to a friend, "and I am not sure his views on the divinity of Christ are sound." Politically, though, the two were in complete agreement, and that was what mattered most. During the 1930s, Pew had emerged as the voice of conservatism in corporate America, holding prominent positions in industrial organizations such as NAM and, more notably, serving as a driving force behind the American Liberty League. In his letter appealing for Pew's support, Fifield offered words of flattery that had the benefit of being true. "During the last decade I have been pretty active in connection with the fight to perpetuate our American way of doing things and have had contacts with most of the individuals and groups throughout the country who are working upon that same problem," he noted. "I just want to put in writing the fact that I have found no more steadfast, trustworthy, competent champion of our basic freedoms and spiritual ideals than J. Howard Pew."[26]

Pew believed the postwar era would see a new struggle for the soul of the nation. In a letter to Fifield at the end of 1944, he lamented that "the New Deal is in a much stronger position than it has been for the last several years. It is my judgment that within the next two years America will determine whether our children are to live in a Republic or under National Socialism; and the present Administration is definitely committed to the latter course." The oilman wanted to keep up the fight against Roosevelt, but after the "character assassination" he had suffered during his time in the Liberty League, he hoped others would take the lead. Fifield impressed him as a promising candidate. Looking over some material from Spiritual Mobilization, Pew believed the organization shared his understanding of what was wrong with the nation and what needed to be done generally. But to his dismay, the material offered no agenda for action whatsoever, merely noting that Spiritual Mobilization would send clergymen bulletins and place advertisements but ultimately "leave details" of what to do "to individual ministers." Pew thought this was no way to run a national operation. "I am frank to confess," he wrote a confidant, "that if Dr. Fifield has developed a concrete program and knows exactly where he is going and what he expects to accomplish, that conception has never become clearly defined in my mind."[27]

If Pew felt Fifield's touch with the ministers had been too light, he knew that a more forceful approach would likewise fail. NAM had been making direct appeals to ministers for years, targeting them with outreach campaigns and mass mailings in hopes of swinging them over to industry's side. For all the time and energy expended in these efforts, though, their campaign showed little sign of success. To understand just what had gone wrong, Pew reached out to his old friend Alfred Haake. Much like the oilman, Haake had an unshakable faith in the wonder-working powers of both Christianity and capitalism. Among other things, he credited prayer for curing a chronic childhood stutter and launching him on a lucrative career. Even though he had dropped out of high school, Haake worked hard enough later in life to earn a doctorate at Wisconsin and then chair the economics department at Rutgers. He moved on to battle the regulatory agencies of the New Deal as head of a manufacturers' organization and then serve as a famed industrial consultant for General Motors. Haake was a man, in short, who understood both the problems of big business and the solutions of spirituality.[28]

In February 1945, Haake explained to Pew why the NAM campaign to ministers and others like it had all failed. "Of the approximately thirty preachers to whom I have thus far talked, I have yet to find one who is unqualifiedly impressed," Haake reported. "One of the men put it almost typically for the rest when he said: 'The careful preparation and framework for the meetings to which we are brought is too apparent. We cannot help but see that it is expertly designed propaganda and that there must be big money behind it. We easily become suspicious.'" If industrialists wanted to convince clergymen to side with them, they would need a subtler approach. Rather than simply treating ministers as a passive audience to be persuaded, Haake argued, they should involve them actively in the cause as participants. The first step would be making ministers realize that they too had something to fear from the growth of government. "The religious leaders must be helped to discover that their callings are threatened," Haake argued, by realizing that the "collectivism" of the New Deal, "with the glorification of the state, is really a denial of God." Once they were thus alarmed, they would readily join Spiritual Mobilization as its representatives and could then be organized more effectively into a force for change both locally and nationally.[29]

Haake was so optimistic about the potential of a mass movement of ministers organized through Spiritual Mobilization that he signed on to become director of the Chicago office, with the entire Midwest as his domain. Together, Haake and Fifield resolved to build a real organization in the ranks of the clergy. "The goal," Haake stated, "should be at least one active and strong ministerial representative for every city in the United States, and even into the villages and towns." They worked quickly, increasing the number of ministers affiliated with the organization from little more than four hundred in June 1944 to over eighteen hundred in September 1945. Spread across all forty-eight states, these "minister-representatives" were largely concentrated in industrial regions, with New York, Pennsylvania, Ohio, and Illinois leading the way. They were overwhelmingly Protestant, with high numbers of Methodists, Baptists, Presbyterians, and Lutherans in particular. Still, a scattering of priests and rabbis among the ranks allowed the organization to present itself as part of the new spirit of "Judeo-Christianity" that was then coming into vogue in the United States. This innovative "interfaith" approach had taken shape in the previous decade as a way for liberal clergymen to unite Protestants, Catholics, and Jews in common social causes, and now, in the postwar era, conservative organizations such as Spiritual Mobilization shrewdly followed suit.[30]

The national campaign to enlist the clergy required even more funding. In May 1946, Senator Hawkes arranged for Fifield to meet with another prominent group of businessmen in New York that included Donaldson Brown, vice chairman of General Motors; Jasper Crane, a former DuPont executive; Harry L. Derby, president of the American Cyanamid and Chemical Corporation; and Leonard Read, a former head of the Los Angeles Chamber of Commerce (and another powerful member of Fifield's First Congregational Church), who had recently launched the Foundation for Economic Education, a pro-business think tank. Fifield easily sold them on Spiritual Mobilization, pointing to past accomplishments and noting rapid growth at the grassroots. "We have 3,517 committed representatives of our program in all the major cities and communities of the United States," he reported, "and we expect before Easter 1947 to have 10,000. The program is gaining favor." Duly impressed, the new Businessmen's Advisory Committee for Spiritual Mobilization took charge of its fund-raising efforts and promised to support an "expanded program and budget of $170,000" from then on.[31]

With the new financial support and sense of direction, Spiritual Mobilization underwent a massive overhaul. In February 1947, Fifield reported that he had already reached their goal for "the signing of ten thousand ministers as representatives." This national network of clergymen would be the primary channel through which the work and writings of Spiritual Mobilization would flow. In a new monthly publication that bore the organization's name, Fifield ran a column—with the businesslike heading "Director to Representatives"—devoted to marshaling these ministers to achieve their common goal of defeating the New Deal. Fifield repeatedly warned them that the growth of government had crippled not only individual initiative but personal morality as well. "It is time to exalt the dignity of individual man as a child of God, to exalt Jesus' concept of man's sacredness and to rebuild a moral fabric based on such irreducibles as the Ten Commandments," he urged his minister-representatives. "Let's redouble our efforts."[32]

Clergymen responded enthusiastically. Many ministers wrote the Los Angeles office to request copies of Friedrich Hayek's libertarian treatise *The Road to Serfdom* and anti–New Deal tracts by Herbert Hoover and libertarian author Garet Garrett, all of which had been advertised in *Spiritual Mobilization*. Some sought reprints of the bulletin itself. "I found your last issue of Spiritual Mobilization excellent," a Connecticut clergyman reported. "Could you send me 100 copies to distribute to key people in my parish? I am quite anxious to get my people thinking along this line." Others took more indirect routes in spreading the organization's message. "Occasionally I preach a sermon directly on your theme," a midwestern minister wrote, "but equally important, it is in the background of my thought as I prepare all my sermons, meet various groups and individuals." As it shaped his work inside his own church, the organization also helped him connect with like-minded clergymen nearby. "Being a representative," he wrote, "developed a real sense of fellowship and understanding between me and some other ministers in our community who share Mobilization's convictions and concerns."[33]

As local bonds between these ministers strengthened, national ones did as well. In October 1947, Spiritual Mobilization held a sermon competition on the theme "The Perils to Freedom," with $5,000 in total prize money. The organization had more than twelve thousand minister-representatives at that point, but it received twice as many submissions for the competition—representing roughly 15 percent of the entire country's clergymen. "I have profited from the materials you are sending," noted the minister of University Park Methodist Church in Dallas, "and am glad to add my bit to help the people of America recognize and accept the responsibilities of freedom as well as its privileges." The pastor at Pittsburgh's Trinity Lutheran Church agreed, calling the sermon competition "a concentrated and remarkable contribution to the cause of freedom." From Providence, Rhode Island, the minister of French Town Baptist Church echoed them: "I hope that this plan of Spiritual Mobilization, to have a great block of ministers in all parts of our great country in a concerted movement preaching upon the one subject, Perils [to] Freedom, will attract attention and cause a great awakening."[34]

Fifield's backers in the Businessmen's Advisory Committee were so pleased with his progress that they nearly doubled the annual budget. To raise funds, its members secured sizable donations from their own companies and personal accounts and, more important, reached out to colleagues across the corporate world for their donations as well. Pew once again set the pace, soliciting donations from officials at 158 corporations. "A large percentage of ministers in this country are completely ignorant of economic matters and have used their pulpits for the purpose of disseminating socialistic and totalitarian doctrines," he wrote in his appeal. "Much has already been accomplished in the education of these ministers, but a great deal more is left to be done." Many of the corporations he contacted—including General Motors, Chrysler, Republic Steel, National Steel, International Harvester, Firestone Tire and Rubber, Sun Oil, Gulf Oil, Standard Oil of New Jersey, and Colgate-Palmolive-Peet—were already contributing the maximum allowable annual donation. Other leading businesses, from US Steel to the National Cash Register Company, had donated in the past, but Pew hoped they would commit to the limit as well. Recognizing that there were many conservative groups out there "fighting for our American way of life," Pew assured a colleague in the oil industry that Spiritual Mobilization deserved to be "at the top of the list" when it came time to donate, "because recent polls indicated that of all the groups in America, the ministers had more to do with molding public opinion."[35]

The success of Spiritual Mobilization brought increased funding, but also the scrutiny and scorn of progressives. In February 1948, journalist Carey McWilliams wrote an acidic cover story on it for *The Nation*. "With the 'Save Christianity' and the 'Save Western Capitalism' chants becoming almost indistinguishable, a major battle for the minds of the clergy, particularly those of the Protestant persuasion, is now being waged in America," he began. "For the most part the battle lines are honestly drawn and represent a sharp clash in ideologies, but now and then the reactionary side tries to fudge a bit by backing movements which mask their true character and real sponsors. Such a movement is Spiritual Mobilization." McWilliams explained to his readers the scope of its operations, noting that it now had nine organizers working in high-rent offices in New York, Chicago, and Los Angeles and had distributed hundreds of thousands of pamphlets by pro-business authors for free. But no one knew who was funding the operation, McWilliams warned. There had only been vague statements from Fifield that "non-ministers who have a common stake in the American and Christian traditions cannot contribute service" and that it was "only natural that they give substance instead." In McWilliams's withering account, Fifield came off as a charlatan who prostrated himself before the "apostles of rugged individualism" to secure his own fame and fortune and, in return, prostituted himself for their needs.[36]

In response, Spiritual Mobilization's sponsors redoubled their efforts. Charles White, president of the Republic Steel Corporation in Cleveland, sent out a mass mailing defending Fifield as "one of my personal friends." The relationship was not surprising. Republic Steel had long led corporate resistance to the New Deal's expansion of labor rights, most dramatically in the 1937 "Memorial Day Massacre," when ten striking workers were gunned down by policemen outside one of its factories in Chicago. "Our company has supported his Crusade, generously, for some years," White wrote, "and we believe in it deeply—the more so since I have read this irresponsible article and see how 'the opposition' feels about Spiritual Mobilization." The group "ought to have more support." "Why don't you send a cheque at once," he all but ordered. "I consider this very important and suggest prompt and generous action on your part." By all appearances, the appeal worked. In just a few months, Spiritual Mobilization had an additional $86,000 in hand from thirty-nine corporate donors, with expectations of nearly $39,000 more to come from another nineteen. In August, the board of directors decided to accept even greater levels of corporate giving, doubling the maximum allowable donation to $10,000 a year.[37]

These corporate leaders increased their commitment to Spiritual Mobilization because they believed there was a fast-expanding totalitarian threat that endangered the nation. Although these were the early years of the Cold War panic, these businessmen were alarmed less by the foreign threat of the Soviet Union and more by the domestic menace of liberalism, which had been recently reinvigorated by President Truman's surprising reelection in 1948. In their private correspondence, Fifield and his funders made it perfectly clear that the main threat to the American way of life, as they saw it, came from Washington, not Moscow. "There is a very much accelerated response to the efforts of Spiritual Mobilization," Fifield confided, "because it is so obvious that the battle to collectivize America is really on, and on in earnest since the announcement of President Truman's legislative program." Pew wholeheartedly agreed. "According to my book there are five principal issues before the country: The socialization of industry, the socialization of medicine, the socialization of education, the socialization of labor, and the socialization of security," he noted. "Only through education and the pressure which the people exert on their politicians can we hope to prevent this country from becoming a totalitarian state."[38]

To educate Americans about the impending threat, Spiritual Mobilization took an even more aggressive approach to public relations in 1949. First it launched *The Freedom Story,* a fifteen-minute radio program consisting of a dramatic presentation and brief commentary from Fifield. The broadcasts were marketed to stations as a means of fulfilling their public service requirements in a way that would attract listeners. This allowed the organization to secure free airtime for the program, but it also dictated significant changes in its content. In the original scripts, Fifield had directly attacked the Democrats, but his lawyer warned him about being "too plain spoken." "I admire your determination not to side-step the issues," he wrote, but "you can only go so far with respect to currently controversial and specific issues without disqualifying the program as a public service feature." As a solution, his counsel suggested that Fifield use "from time to time a horrible example from current experience in the socialist and communist countries of Europe and Asia. We could go as far as we want in that field in the dramatic part of the program," he continued, "and your speech could be developed in such a way as to make it plain enough to your radio audience that we are heading for the same kind of situation here."[39]

Accordingly, the topics dramatized and discussed on *The Freedom Story* varied considerably, even as the underlying message about the dangers of "creeping socialism" remained a constant. Heeding the advice of his legal counsel, Fifield relied on foreign examples to illustrate the issue, decrying the impact of collectivism in communist lands. But the minister tackled domestic subjects as well. One week, the show explored Reconstruction, claiming that southern states had thrived without federal policies or subsidies after the Civil War; the next, it celebrated the history of the Boy Scouts, arguing that the private organization's success stemmed directly from a lack of government meddling.[40] Fifield's financial backers helped secure free airtime for these programs across the nation. "Republic Steel is taking steps to get them on radio stations in every town where they have a factory or office," Fifield noted in March 1949. "We are expecting to be on one hundred fifty radio stations by June." A year later, *The Freedom Story* was broadcast on a weekly network of over five hundred stations; by late 1951, it aired on more than eight hundred.[41]

Meanwhile, Spiritual Mobilization launched a new monthly magazine, *Faith and Freedom,* edited by veteran journalist William Johnson. The publication printed the work of an expanding network of libertarian and conservative authors, including Ludwig von Mises, leader of the Austrian School of economics; Leonard Read, founder of the Foundation for Economic Education; Henry Hazlitt, a founding member of the American Enterprise Association (later renamed the American Enterprise Institute); Clarence Manion, a former dean of Notre Dame's College of Law who became a noted right-wing radio host in the 1950s; Felix Morley, founder of the far-right journal *Human Events;* and Rose Wilder Lane, who had cowritten the Little House on the Prairie series with her mother before attacking the "creeping socialism" of the New Deal in her own work.[42]

While libertarian and conservative laymen dominated the pages of *Faith and Freedom*, the journal purposely presented itself as created *by* ministers *for* ministers. Spiritual Mobilization had long operated on the principle that clergymen could not be swayed through crude propaganda. "The articulation should be worked out before-hand, of course, and we should be ready to help the thinking of the ministers on it," Haake noted in one of his early musings on Spiritual Mobilization, "but it should be so done as to enable them to discover it for themselves, as something which they really had believed but not realized fully until our questions brought it out so clearly. I am sure we may not TELL them: not as laymen, or even as fellow clergymen. We must help them to discover it themselves." The new magazine embraced this approach wholeheartedly. "We know there are countless questions unanswered about individual liberty," Johnson announced in the first issue. "We want a magazine which will serve the ministers who will shape the answers to these questions, a magazine which will stimulate them, a magazine which will challenge them, a magazine which will earn a place in their busy schedules." *Faith and Freedom* sought input from subscribers, not simply printing letters but soliciting sermons that expounded on "the moral and spiritual significance of individual liberty" for publication in a monthly feature called "The Pulpit and Liberty." Ultimately, Johnson argued, the magazine would receive a great deal of its direction from the clergymen who read it. "We shall," he wrote, "depend heavily on ministerial guidance and criticism in developing a useful periodical for you."[43]

Faith and Freedom thus presented itself as an open forum in which ministers could debate a wide variety of issues and disagree freely. But there was an important catch. "Clergymen may differ about politics, economics, sociology, and such," Fifield stated, "but I would expect that in matters of morality all followers of Jesus speak in one voice." Because Fifield and Johnson insisted that morality directly informed politics and economics, they were able to cast those who disagreed with them on those topics as essentially immoral. For his part, Fifield claimed he approached all issues with an open mind and a desire to follow God's will. "There have been many solutions suggested for meeting today's and tomorrow's problems, and there will be more," he noted in his first column. "Before we accept any proposal or remedy, we have the obligation to measure it, not only as to its probable effectiveness, but as to whether the proposal does not conflict with Christian principle and the spiritual values of liberty and personal responsibility." Not surprisingly, when Fifield held liberal proposals to this standard, they always fell short. Time and time again, he condemned a variety of "socialistic laws," such as ones supporting minimum wages, price controls, Social Security pensions for the elderly, unemployment insurance, veterans' benefits, and the like, as well as a wide range of federal taxation that he deemed to be "tyrannical" in nature. In the end, he judged, such policies violated "the natural law which inheres in the nature of the universe and is the will of God."[44]

Indeed, for all of its claims about encouraging debate, *Faith and Freedom* did little to hide its contempt for liberal ministers. The magazine repeatedly denounced the Social Gospel and, just as important, clergymen who invoked it to advocate for the establishment and expansion of welfare state programs. Johnson even devoted an entire issue to the subject. "The movement is directed by a small, unusually articulate minority who feel political power is the way to save the world," he warned in his opening comments. "Unclothed, their gospel is pure socialism—they wish to employ the compulsion of the state to force others to act as the social gospelers think they should act." Irving Howard, a Congregationalist minister, darkly noted the "pagan origin of the Social Gospel" in nineteenth-century Unitarianism and Transcendentalism, claiming it was part of a larger "impetus to a shift in faith from God to man, from eternity to time, from the individual to the group, [from] individual conversion to social coercion, and from the church to the state." Other contributors drew ominous comparisons between the Social Gospel and similarly suspect ideologies. "Communism aims to destroy the capitalist minority no matter what killing, stealing, lying, and covetousness are required," argued one. "The Social Gospel calls for the destruction of this minority by the more peaceful means of the popular vote, to put it bluntly, by *socialized* covetousness, stealing, and the bearing of false witness."[45]

Consistently libertarian, the contributors to *Faith and Freedom* varied only in terms of style and sophistication. The June 1950 issue, for
instance, featured four articles, each advancing the same message from
different angles. In the first, George S. Benson, president of conservative
Harding College, offered a folksy parable about a group of seagulls who
let themselves be fed by shrimp boats and soon forgot how to care for
themselves. "The moral," the author noted for those who somehow missed
it: "A welfare state, for gull or man, always first destroys the priceless attribute of self-reliance." Next, Ludwig von Mises advanced a sophisticated
argument to disprove "the passionate tirades of Marx, Keynes and a host
of less well-known authors." Prominent missionary R. J. Rushdoony then
explained how "noncompetitive life" on a Native American reservation,
which he called "the prime example in America today of a functioning
welfare society," inevitably reduced its residents to a state of "social and
personal irresponsibility." The fourth and final article, "Human Rights
and Property Rights," by industrial relations author Allen W. Rucker, asserted that any effort to take control of private property was "in direct violation of the Commandment, 'Thou shalt not steal.' That Commandment
is not limited in the slightest degree; it is an adjuration laid upon all men,
whether acting as individuals, as an organization, or as a state."[46]

Conservatives concerned about the "creeping socialism" of the welfare
state under Truman were emboldened by the Republican gains in the
midterm elections of 1950. In an upbeat letter to Alfred Sloan, the head
of General Motors and an ardent supporter of his work, Fifield reflected
on the recent returns. "We are having quite a deluge of letters from across
the country, indicating the feeling that Spiritual Mobilization has had
some part in the awakening which was evidenced by the elections," he
wrote. "Of course, we are a little proud and very happy for whatever good
we have been able to do in waking people up to the peril of collectivism
and the importance of Freedom under God." But the battle was far from
won. "I do not consider that we can relax our efforts in any way or at any
point," Fifield noted. "It is still a long road back to what was and, please
God, will again be America."[47]

For Fifield and his associates, the phrase "freedom under God"—in
contrast with what they saw as oppression under the federal government—
became an effective new rallying cry in the early 1950s. The minister

pressed the theme repeatedly in the pages of *Faith and Freedom* and in his radio broadcasts of *The Freedom Story*, but he soon found a more prominent means of spreading the message to the American people.[48]

IN THE SPRING OF 1951, Spiritual Mobilization's leaders struck upon an idea they believed would advance their cause considerably. To mark the 175th anniversary of the signing of the Declaration of Independence, they proposed for the week surrounding the Fourth of July a massive series of events devoted to the theme of "Freedom Under God." According to Fifield's longtime ally William C. Mullendore, president of the Southern California Edison Company, the idea originated from the belief that the "root cause of the disintegration of freedom here, and of big government, is the disintegration of the nation's spiritual foundations, as found in the Declaration of Independence. We want to revive that basic American credo, which is the spiritual basis of our Constitution."[49]

To that end, in June 1951, the leaders of Spiritual Mobilization announced the formation of a new Committee to Proclaim Liberty to coordinate their Fourth of July "Freedom Under God" celebrations. The committee's name, they explained to a crowd of reporters, came from the tenth verse of the twenty-fifth chapter of the Book of Leviticus, in which God instructed Moses that the Israelites should celebrate the anniversary of their arrival in the Promised Land and "proclaim liberty throughout all the land and to the inhabitants thereof." This piece of Scripture, organizers noted, was also inscribed on the crown of the Liberty Bell in Philadelphia. The committee originally had just fifty-six members, equal to the number of signers of the Declaration, but the list quickly expanded as others clamored for a place. Although the committee claimed to seek a spiritual emphasis for the upcoming holiday, very few religious leaders actually served in its ranks. Indeed, aside from Fifield and his longtime friend Norman Vincent Peale, the founding ministerial members of the committee included only a liberal Methodist bishop, G. Bromley Oxnam; the Catholic bishop of the Oklahoma City–Tulsa diocese; and a rabbi from Kansas City.[50]

The true goal of the Committee to Proclaim Liberty was advancing conservatism. Its two most prominent members had been brought low by Democratic administrations: former president Herbert Hoover, driven from the White House two decades earlier by Franklin Roosevelt, and General Douglas MacArthur, removed from his command in Korea two months earlier by Harry Truman. These conservative martyrs were joined by military leaders, heads of patriotic groups, conservative legal and political stars, right-wing media figures, and outspoken conservatives from the realm of entertainment, such as Bing Crosby, Cecil B. DeMille, Walt Disney and Ronald Reagan. But the majority came from corporate America. J. Howard Pew was joined by other business titans, such as Conrad Hilton of Hilton Hotels, B. E. Hutchinson of Chrysler, James L. Kraft of Kraft Foods, Hughston McBain of Marshall Field, Admiral Ben Moreell of Jones & Laughlin Steel, Eddie Rickenbacker of Eastern Airlines, and Charles E. Wilson of General Motors. The interest of leading businessmen in the endeavor was so strong that the committee was forced to expand its ranks to make room for the others clamoring for a spot, including household names such as Harvey Firestone, E. F. Hutton, Fred Maytag, Henry Luce, and J. C. Penney, as well as the less well-known heads of US Steel, Republic Steel, Gulf Oil, Hughes Aircraft, and United Airlines. The presidents of both the United States Chamber of Commerce and the National Association of Manufacturers served, as did the heads of free enterprise advocacy organizations such as the Foundation for Economic Education and the Freedoms Foundation. As a token counterweight to this overwhelming corporate presence, the Committee to Proclaim Liberty included a single labor leader: Matthew Woll, a vice president with the American Federation of Labor, but more important, a lifelong Republican well known for his outspoken opposition to industrial unions and New Deal labor legislation.[51]

As the Fourth of July drew near, the Committee to Proclaim Liberty focused its attention on encouraging Americans to mark the holiday with public readings of the preamble to the Declaration of Independence. The decision to focus solely on the preamble was in some ways a natural one, as its passages were certainly the most famous and lyrical in the document. But doing so also allowed organizers to reframe the Declaration as a purely libertarian manifesto, dedicated to the removal of an oppressive government. Those who read the entire document would have discovered, to the consternation of the committee, that the founding fathers followed the high-flown prose of the preamble with a long list of grievances about the *absence* of government and rule of law in the colonies. Among other things, they lambasted King George III for refusing "his Assent to Laws, the most wholesome and necessary for the public good," for forbidding his governors from passing "Laws of immediate and pressing importance," for dissolving the legislative bodies in the colonies, and for generally enabling a state of anarchy that exposed colonists to "all the dangers of invasion from without, and convulsions within." In the end, the Declaration was not a rejection of government power in general but rather a condemnation of the British crown for depriving the colonists of the government they needed. In order to reframe the Declaration as something rather different, the Committee to Proclaim Liberty had to edit out much of the document they claimed to champion. Even their version of the preamble was truncated. They excised a final line about the specific plight of the colonists and ended instead on one that better resonated with their contemporary political aims: "When a long train of abuses and usurpations, pursuing invariably the same Object evinces a design to reduce them under absolute Despotism, it is their right, it is their duty, to throw off such Government, and to provide new Guards for their future security."[52]

The committee's corporate sponsors took out full-page newspaper ads to promote this pinched interpretation of the Declaration. The San Diego Gas & Electric Company, for instance, encouraged its customers to reread the preamble, which it presented with its editorial commentary running alongside:

> These words are the stones upon which man has built history's greatest work—the United States of America. Remember them well!
>
> "... **all men are created equal** ... " That means you are as important in the eyes of God as any man brought into this world. You are made in his image and likeness. There is no "superior" man anywhere.
>
> "... **they are endowed by their Creator with certain unalienable rights** ... " Here is your birthright—the freedom to live, work, worship, and vote as you choose. These are rights no government on earth may take from you.

" . . . **That to secure these rights, governments are instituted among men** . . . " Here is the reason for and the purpose of government. Government is but a servant—not a master—not a giver of anything.

" . . . **deriving their just powers from the consent of the governed** . . . " In America, the government may assume only the powers you allow it to have. It may assume no others.

The ad urged readers to make their own declaration of independence in 1951. "Declare that government is responsible TO you—rather than FOR you," it continued. "Declare that freedom is more important to you than 'security' or 'survival.' Declare that the rights God gave you may not be taken away by any government on any pretense." Other utilities offered similar ads. The Detroit Edison Company, for instance, quoted at length from a Clarence Manion piece first published by the original Heritage Foundation. "Despotism never advertises itself as such," Manion warned. "By its own sly self-definition it may label itself 'democratic,' 'progressive,' 'liberal,' 'humanitarian,' or 'fraternal.' Those who oppose it will be called reactionaries, fascists, and other 'bad names.'" The Utah Power & Light Company, meanwhile, cut right to the chase in a full-page ad with the alarmist headline "How many 'Independence Days' have we left?" The utility company implored readers to "pray for help in maintaining man's closeness to God, in preserving man's God-given rights and responsibilities against those who would make you dependent upon a socialistic, all-powerful government."[53]

The Committee to Proclaim Liberty also enlisted the nation's ministers to promote the "Freedom Under God" festivities. Those on the Spiritual Mobilization mailing list received a suggested press release that merely needed clergymen to fill in the blanks with their personal information ("'The purpose of the Committee,' the Reverend _____ declared, 'is to revive a custom long forgotten in America—spiritual emphasis on the 4th of July'"). The committee also established a sermon contest, modeled on the wildly successful "Perils to Freedom" competition that Spiritual Mobilization had held in 1947. The seventeen thousand minister-representatives of the organization were encouraged to compete for cash prizes and other rewards by writing an original sermon on the

Utility companies such as the Utah Power & Light Company ran full-page advertisements that promoted the "Freedom Under God" celebrations of Spiritual Mobilization and, more important, its underlying message of Christian libertarianism.

theme of "Freedom Under God" and delivering it to their congregations on "Independence Sunday," July 1, 1951. They could also order, for a penny each, special worship calendars prepared by the committee, adorned with illustrations and messages supporting the festivities' theme. The interior was intentionally left blank so that the minister could mimeograph the details of his particular service and then literally wrap the Committee to Proclaim Liberty's message around it.[54]

On "Independence Sunday," the organization reported, "tens of thousands" of clergymen offered sermons on the topic of "Freedom Under God." Because the contest was limited to official minister-representatives of Spiritual Mobilization, the sermons invariably sounded its themes. "The effort to establish socialism in our country has probably progressed farther than most of us fully realize," asserted a Lutheran minister in

Kansas. "It would be well to remember that every act or law passed by which the government promises to 'give' us something is a step in the direction of socialism." A clergyman from Brooklyn agreed. "Today our homes are built for us, financed for us, and the church is provided for us. Our many services are in danger of robbing us of that which is most important," he warned, "the right to our own kingdom of self." "The growing acceptance of the philosophy of the Welfare State is a graver peril to freedom in America today that the threat of military aggression," cautioned a Missouri Baptist. A Congregationalist minister in Illinois advanced the same argument: "People have been encouraged to believe that a benevolent government exists for the sole purpose of ministering to the selfish interest of the individual. We have achieved the four freedoms: Freedom to ask; freedom to receive; freedom to be a leech; and freedom to loaf."[55]

First place in the sermon competition went to Reverend Kenneth W. Sollitt, minister of the First Baptist Church of Mendota, Illinois. Published in the September issue of *Faith and Freedom*, his sermon bore the title "Freedom Under God: We Can Go on Making a God of Government, or We Can Return Again to the Government of God." As the title suggested, it was an extended jeremiad about the sins of the welfare state. Reverend Sollitt decried the national debt, growing federal payrolls, corporate taxation, government bureaucracy in general, and Social Security in particular, while still finding the time and imagination to use the parable of the Good Samaritan as grounds for a diatribe about the evils of "socialized medicine." "For 175 years we have focused our attention so much on 'the enjoyment of *our* liberty' that we have been perfectly willing to pass all kinds of legislation limiting the other fellow's liberty for our benefit," he argued. "'Government of the people, by the people, for the people' has become government of the people by pressure groups for the benefit of minorities. 'Give me liberty or give me death' has been shortened to just plain 'Give me.'" In the dire tones of an Old Testament prophet, he warned that "America stands at the cross roads." "The one road leads to the slavery which has always been the lot of those who have chosen collectivism in any of its forms," he said, be it "communism, socialism, the Welfare State—they are all cut from the same pattern. The other road leads to the only freedom there is"—free enterprise.[56]

The sermons delivered on "Independence Sunday" were amplified by a program broadcast that same evening over CBS's national radio network. The committee had originally hoped to schedule the broadcast for the Fourth of July itself, but all airtime on the holiday had been reserved. As organizer James Ingebretsen noted, "Even if we had the Lord Himself making a return appearance, we couldn't get the time." He quickly warmed to the idea of holding a special program on Sunday instead, both to highlight the spiritual emphasis of the festivities and to build on the momentum of the day's sermons. The national advertising agency J. Walter Thompson officially promoted the program, but organizers believed that a word-of-mouth campaign from the pulpit would be even more effective. "There will be a couple of hundred thousand ministers across the country who will have had direct word about this program and many of them will definitely be cooperative," Ingebretsen said in a telephone call with the head of public affairs at CBS. "There will be thirty to forty million people in church that Sunday as usual . . . and we will pick them up just a few hours afterwards instead of three days later."[57]

The program itself lived up to the organizers' expectations. Cecil B. DeMille worked with his old friend Fifield to plan the production, giving it a professional tone and attracting an impressive array of Hollywood stars. Jimmy Stewart served as master of ceremonies, while Bing Crosby and Gloria Swanson offered short messages of their own. The preamble to the Declaration was read by Lionel Barrymore, who had posed for promotional photos holding a giant quill and looking at a large piece of parchment inscribed with the words "Freedom Under God Will Save Our Country." The program featured choral performances of "America" as well as "Heritage," an epic poem composed by a former leader of the US Chamber of Commerce. The keynote came from General Matthew Ridgway, who interrupted his duties leading American forces in Korea to send an address from Tokyo. He insisted that the founding fathers had been motivated, in large part, by their religious faith. "For them there was no confusion of thought, no uncertainty of objectives, no doubt as to the road they should follow to their goals," he said. "Theirs was a deep and abiding faith in God, a faith which is still the great reservoir of strength of the American people in this day of great responsibility for their future and the future of the world."[58]

The "Freedom Under God" festivities reached a crescendo with local celebrations on the Fourth of July. The Committee to Proclaim Liberty coordinated the ringing of church bells across the nation, timed to start precisely at noon and last for a full ten minutes. Cities and small towns across the country scheduled their own events around the bell ringing. In Los Angeles, for instance, the city's civil defense agency sounded its air raid sirens, in the first test since their installation, resulting in what one newspaper described as "a scream as wild and proud as that of the American eagle." As bells chimed across the city, residents were encouraged by the committee "to open their doors, sound horns and blow whistles and ring bells, as individual salutes to Freedom." After the ten minutes of bell ringing, groups gathered in churches and homes to read the preamble to the Declaration together.[59] Both Mayor Fletcher Bowron and Governor Earl Warren, like their counterparts in many other cities and states, issued official proclamations that urged citizens, in Warren's words, to spend the day reflecting upon "the blessings we enjoy through Freedom under God."[60] That night, fifty thousand residents attended a massive rally at the Los Angeles Coliseum. Organized under the theme "Freedom Under God Needs You," the night featured eight circus acts, a jet plane demonstration, and a fireworks display that the local chapter of the American Legion promised would be the largest in the entire country. Reverend Fifield had the honor of offering the invocation for the evening ceremonies, while actor Gregory Peck delivered a dramatic reading of the Declaration's preamble.[61]

In the end, the Committee to Proclaim Liberty believed, rightly, that its work had made a lasting impression on the nation. "The very words 'Freedom Under God' [have] added to the vocabulary of freedom a new term," the organizers concluded. "It is a significant phrase to people who know that everybody from Stalin on down is paying lip service to freedom until its root meaning is no longer apparent. The term 'Freedom Under God' provides a means of identifying and separating conditions which indicate pseudo-freedom, or actual slavery, from those of true freedom." Citing an outpouring of support for the festivities, the committee resolved to make them an annual tradition and, more important, keep the spirit of its central message alive in American life. The entire nation, its members hoped, would soon think of itself as "under God."[62]

CHAPTER 2

The Great Crusades

O N SEPTEMBER 25, 1949, ROUGHLY five thousand residents of Los Angeles huddled together downtown beneath a massive "canvas cathedral tent" at the corner of Washington and Hill. They had come to this place, in the shadow of the metropolitan courthouse, to hear an evangelical preacher tell them about a judgment that would be handed down by God rather than man. Only thirty years old and still largely unknown, Billy Graham nevertheless made a commanding impression as he strode onto the stage. Dressed sharply in a trim double-breasted suit with his wavy blond hair swept back, he set his square jaw and locked his eyes on the crowd. Drawing on the biblical story of Sodom and Gomorrah, the preacher told them that their so-called City of Angels shared many of the "wicked ways" of those infamous cities—sexual promiscuity, addictions to drink and "dope," teenage delinquency, rampant crime—and it would inevitably share their fate of destruction unless its citizens repented and reformed. In many ways, Graham's sermon that day was a preacher's perennial, a warning of God's wrath and a call for penitence. But his message took on unusual urgency because of an event then dominating the news. Just two days earlier, Americans had learned that the Soviet Union now had the atomic bomb.[1]

The energetic young Graham seized on the headlines to make the Armageddon foretold in the New Testament seem imminent. "Communism," he thundered, "has decided against God, against Christ, against the Bible, and against all religion. Communism is not only an economic interpretation of life—communism is a religion that is inspired, directed, and motivated by the Devil himself who has declared war against Almighty God." He urged his audience to get religion not simply for their own salvation but for the salvation of their city and country. Without "an old-fashioned revival," he warned, "we cannot last!" A virtual unknown when he began this "Christ for Greater Los Angeles" evangelistic campaign, the charismatic preacher rode the rising wave of nuclear anxiety to national prominence. Initial reports in the Hearst papers and wire services were soon followed by longer, glowing stories in *Time, Life,* and *Newsweek*. With crowds soon swarming to the outdoor revival, Graham had to extend his stay from the original three weeks to eight in all. When the Los Angeles revival finally came to a close in November 1949, organizers reported that a total of 350,000 people had attended. And Billy Graham had transformed himself into a rising star: a servant of God ready to fight the Cold War.[2]

In the conventional historical narrative, Graham's dramatic debut on the national stage has been presented as part of a broader story of action and reaction: the Soviet Union discovered the bomb, and the United States rediscovered God. There are, to be sure, some grounds for the argument that the tensions of the early Cold War era helped fuel the religious revival of midcentury America.[3] As Americans confronted the reality that nuclear war might destroy the nation, countless people were certainly driven to prayer. But the spiritual revival of the postwar era was much more than fallout from the nuclear age. Its roots predated the Cold War, and its importance and impact stretched well beyond the concerns of that conflict. Despite all the attention Graham gave foreign threats in his "canvas cathedral" debut, his public ministry—especially in these early years—was much more concerned with domestic matters. He was not alone. Three important movements in the 1940s and early 1950s—the prayer breakfast meetings of Abraham Vereide, Graham's evangelical revivals, and the presidential campaign of Dwight D. Eisenhower—encouraged the spread of public prayer as a political development whose means and motives were distinct from the drama of the Cold War. Working in lockstep to advance Christian libertarianism, these three movements effectively harnessed Cold War anxieties for an already established campaign against the New Deal.

Just as Spiritual Mobilization used faith to defend free enterprise, these movements called for a return to prayer to advance the same ends. Graham was the most prominent of the new Christian libertarians, a charismatic figure who spread the ideas of forerunners such as Fifield to even broader audiences. In 1954, Graham offered his thoughts on the relationship between Christianity and capitalism in *Nation's Business,* the magazine of the US Chamber of Commerce. "We have the suggestion from Scripture itself that faith and business, properly blended, can be a happy, wholesome, and even profitable mixture," he observed. "Wise men are finding out that the words of the Nazarene: 'Seek ye first the kingdom of God and His righteousness, and all these *things* shall be added unto you' were more than the mere rantings of a popular mystic; they embodied a practical, workable philosophy which actually pays off in happiness and peace of mind. . . . Thousands of businessmen have discovered the satisfaction of having God as a working partner."[4]

Billy Graham partnered with a number of businessmen himself. Following the lead of Methodist minister Abraham Vereide, Graham helped introduce captains of industry to the incredible power of prayer. In his hands, prayer was not simply a means of personal salvation but also, and just as important, a tool to improve the public image of their companies. In 1951, for instance, the Chicago & Southern Airline invited him to preach a dedicatory sermon aboard a four-engine airplane that had been outfitted with a pulpit and an electric pump organ. As the crew and congregation circled above Memphis, Graham led them in a solemn prayer that "the great C&S Airline may be blessed as never before." Years later, the minister would touch down in Memphis again to speak before a convention of hotel owners, where he furnished a similar sort of benediction. "God bless you and thank you," Graham said earnestly, "and God bless the Holiday Inns."[5]

Graham's warm embrace of business contrasted sharply with the cold shoulder he gave organized labor. The Garden of Eden, he told a rally in 1952, was a paradise with "no union dues, no labor leaders, no snakes, no disease." The minister insisted that a truly Christian worker "would not stoop to take unfair advantage" of his employer by ganging up against him in a union. Strikes, in his mind, were inherently selfish and sinful. In 1950, he worried that a "coal strike may paralyze the nation"; two years later, he

warned that a looming steel stoppage would hurt American troops fighting in Korea. If workers wanted salvation, they needed to put aside such
thoughts and devote themselves to their employers. "The type of revival
I'm calling for," Graham told a Pittsburgh reporter in 1952, "calls for an
employee to put in a full eight hours of work." On Labor Day that same
year, he warned that "certain labor leaders would like to outlaw religion,
disregard God, the church, and the Bible," and he suggested that their
rank and file were wholly composed of the unchurched. "I believe that
organized labor unions are one of the greatest mission fields in America
today," he said. "Wouldn't it be great if, as we celebrate Labor Day, our
labor leaders would lead the laboring man in America in repentance and
faith in Jesus Christ?"[6]

His hostility to organized labor was matched by his dislike of government involvement in the economy, which he invariably condemned as
"socialism." Graham warned that "government restrictions" in the realm
of free enterprise threatened "freedom of opportunity" in America. In
April 1952, he stood outside the Texas state capitol and insisted, "We
must have a revolt against the tranquil attitude to communism, socialism,
and dictatorship in this country." The next month, Graham spoke at a
businessmen's luncheon in Houston, warning that socialism was on the
march around the world as well. "Within five years we can say good-by
to England," he insisted. "Japan could go communist within two years.
The United States is being isolated." Two years later, Graham's thoughts
on the dangers of socialism became a bit of an international scandal after
the Billy Graham Evangelical Association sent followers a free calendar.
A page on England noted that "when the war ended a sense of frustration
and disillusionment gripped England and what Hitler's bombs could not
do, socialism with its accompanying evils shortly accomplished. England's
historic faith faltered. The churches still standing were gradually emp-
tied." Learning of the slight, a columnist for the London *Daily Herald*
denounced Graham with a new nickname: "the Big Business evangelist."[7]

As preachers like Billy Graham helped to popularize public prayer, they
thus managed to politicize it as well. They shared the Christian libertarian
sensibilities of Spiritual Mobilization but were able to spread that gospel
in much subtler—and much more effective—ways than that organization ever could. At the same time, their work helped to democratize the

phenomenon of public prayer. Spiritual Mobilization focused its attention largely on ministers, but these contemporaneous campaigns attracted a much broader swath of laypeople. Though they tended to target the rich and powerful, the changes they instituted ultimately made the movement more accessible to ordinary Americans and thereby set the stage for a larger revival to come. In the political ascendancy of Dwight D. Eisenhower, the prayers of Christian libertarians were finally answered.

FRANKLIN D. ROOSEVELT'S FIRST INAUGURAL address had been filled with scriptural references, but in his second inaugural in January 1937 religion was even more pronounced. Reflecting on the record of progressive legislation and economic progress in the first four years of his administration, the president portrayed himself, rather unsubtly, as a modern-day Moses leading his people out of the wilderness. "Shall we pause now and turn our back upon the road that lies ahead? Shall we call this the promised land?" he asked rhetorically. "Or shall we continue on our way?" There was still much to be done, he warned, but the nation would soon reach "our happy valley" if it stayed on the present path. The Exodus theme of the inaugural address, speechwriters insisted, had come entirely from Roosevelt. But others still sought credit. In February 1937, Abraham Vercide sent the president a letter reminding him of a meeting they had had more than four years earlier, when Roosevelt was still governor of New York. "You may recall," the Seattle minister wrote, "that I reminded you about the story of Moses and the Israelites, stating that you were our Moses and we were Israel who needed to be led out of the bondage of Egypt, into the Promised Land. You may recall your own statement at that time and your pledge. Your efforts have been true to that pledge."[8]

While Vereide's praise for the president's religious rhetoric was sincere, his claim that he saw Roosevelt as a modern-day Moses most certainly was not. The Methodist clergyman was thoroughly conservative in his politics and, by the time of his letter, had long abandoned any belief in the worth of either private charity or public welfare. A deeply pious Norwegian, he had immigrated to America in 1905 and, a decade later, begun work as a minister in Seattle. During the 1920s, he ran Goodwill Industries' operation in the city with efficiency, organizing forty-nine thousand housewives into thirty-seven districts to collect used goods for the needy. While his approach to running the charity was businesslike, so too was his attitude toward the underlying idea. "Promiscuous charity pauperizes," he insisted in 1927, "and the average person seeking aid . . . does not want to work for it." Nevertheless, his success in Seattle led to promotions at Goodwill and, ultimately, consideration by Roosevelt for a role leading the federal relief effort, consideration that led to their 1933 meeting in Albany. But as Vereide became more involved with charity work, he became less sure of its worth. "In conference with heads of governments and unemployment committees in New England and New York," he later remembered, "I became convinced that [the] depression was moral and spiritual as well as material. The country needed a spiritual awakening as the only foundation for economic stability." In 1934, Vereide resigned from Goodwill and began searching for a new career.[9]

Nearly fifty at the time, with trim white hair and a perpetually serious gaze, Vereide found the turmoil of his professional life mirrored in the nation. When the Methodist minister returned to the West Coast, he found businessmen and labor unions embroiled in an epic struggle that helped give him a new sense of purpose. First he spent three months in San Francisco, where the Industrial Association had recently retaliated against a dockworkers' strike by assembling a private army to open the port by force, killing two strikers in the process. In response, the longshoremen convinced the rest of the city's unions to join them in a general strike that effectively shut down San Francisco for days. Highways were blockaded, shipments of food and fuel turned away. As the city's elite holed up in the posh Pacific Union Club, debating how to handle the largest labor uprising they had ever seen, Vereide ministered to them in regular prayer meetings.[10]

When the clergyman returned to Seattle soon after, he found it in a similar state of chaos. The city's stevedores went on strike, and the Waterfront Employers Association prepared for a massive struggle. They put three ships in port to serve as barracks for an army of strikebreakers recruited from wherever they could be found, including fraternities at the University of Washington. Strikers kept control of the port, leaving dozens of ships idling in the harbor. Local newspapers gave voice to the worries of the business community. "Strike Costing City a Million a Day!" screamed the *Seattle Times*. The *Post-Intelligencer* grumbled that "a mob of striking longshoremen" had "paralyzed Seattle shipping." As pressure mounted, the mayor personally led three hundred policemen, armed with tear gas and submachine guns, down to the docks to break the strike. In the ensuing struggle, both sides suffered serious injuries before calling an uneasy truce. The next spring, in April 1935, union leaders from all over the West Coast descended on Seattle to make plans for an even greater wave of strikes that summer.[11]

That same month, Vereide had an important meeting of his own. On a downtown street corner he ran into Walter Douglass, a former Army major and a prominent local developer. The two soon began commiserating about how the entire country was, in Douglass's words, "going to the bow-wows." "The worst of it is you fellows aren't doing anything about it!" he snapped at the minister. "Here you have your churches and services and a merry-go-round of activities, but as far as any actual impact and strategy for turning the tide is concerned, you're not making a dent." The wealthy developer said clergymen needed to "get after fellows like me" and motivate them to get involved. He offered Vereide a suite of offices in the downtown Douglass Building and "a check to grubstake you" if only he would take the job. Vereide readily accepted. The two men immediately made their way to the offices of William St. Clair, president of Frederick and Nelson, the largest department store in the Pacific Northwest, and one of the richest men in Seattle. "He made a list of nineteen executives of the city then and there," Vereide later remembered, and invited them for breakfast at the Washington Athletic Club. The men at that first prayer meeting included the presidents of a gas company, a railroad, a lumber company, a hardware chain, and a candy manufacturer, as well as two future mayors of Seattle. Only one belonged to a church at the time, but even he had little use for religion, joking that the others knew him only as a gambler, a drinker, and a golfer—someone who swore so much "the grass burns when I spit." But like the others, he rallied to Vereide's call and joined what became a regular prayer breakfast for businessmen called the City Chapel. Their services were nondenominational, but the message that came from their meetings was one that called for a return to what they saw as basic biblical principles.[12]

That summer, the City Chapel held a retreat for Seattle's elite at the Canyon Creek Lodge in the Cascade Mountains. With labor unrest still simmering on the city's docks, the business leaders were worried. "Subversive forces had taken over," Vereide recalled. "What could we do?" After a great deal of prayer, city councilman Arthur Langlie rose from his knees and announced, "I am ready to let God use me." Others were ready to use him as well. The president of a securities corporation immediately offered financial support for a Langlie mayoral campaign, and others soon followed. On his first run for the office in 1936, the Republican came up short. His opponent secured the backing of the city's powerful unions and ominously warned voters about Langlie's affiliation with "a secret society," by which he meant not the City Chapel but a right-wing organization called the New Order of Cincinnatus. In 1938, however, labor split evenly between two competing candidates, allowing Langlie to win in what was understood nationally as a major coup for conservatism. "Seattle Deals Radicals Blow," read the headline in the *Los Angeles Times;* "Left-Wing Nominees Decisively Beaten in Mayoralty Election." The *New York Times* likewise called Langlie's election "a sweeping victory for conservatism," while the *Wall Street Journal* argued that the victory of the candidate who "promised industrial peace" had helped boost the market value of Seattle's municipal bonds considerably. From the mayor's office, Langlie's star continued to rise. Only two years later, he won election as governor of Washington, ultimately serving three terms, first from 1941 to 1945 and then again from 1949 to 1957. Now a nationally prominent Republican, Langlie made the short list for Dwight Eisenhower's running mate in the 1952 presidential campaign and then delivered the keynote address at the 1956 Republican National Convention.[13]

After establishing the breakfast group in Seattle, Vereide looked to expand his efforts to the rest of the nation. "Business and social leaders throughout the country are recognizing that economic reconstruction must begin with an individual recovery from within," he noted in 1935. "They are beginning to realize that we cannot solve all the problems of our present-day civilization by our wits, but must rely on a higher power to help. They hope to revive the spiritual life in commerce, to aid the churches and to get back to a real American home life." Accordingly, when they filed articles of incorporation, the founders of City Chapel announced their intention "to foster and promote the advancement of Christianity and develop a Christian nation." As the Seattle group flourished, businessmen in other communities reached out to Vereide in hopes of starting ones of their own. The minister informed them that the organization followed "a non-political and non-denominational" program, but quickly added a line that suggested a political leaning akin to that of Spiritual Mobilization. "We believe with William Penn: 'Men must either be governed by God or ruled by tyrants,'" he said. Through personal visits and correspondence, Vereide created a network of prayer groups across the nation. In San Francisco, a former secretary of the navy established one at the Olympic Club. The head of a wool trading business started another at the Boston City Club. A set of businessmen convened at the Lake Shore Club in Chicago to begin their own group, while an oilman did likewise with associates in Los Angeles. In New York City, Republican mayor Fiorello LaGuardia was so taken with the idea he sought Vereide's assistance in getting a group started there too. The minister traveled tirelessly around the country to organize and mobilize new meetings. In a letter home that seemed routine for these years, Vereide noted in passing that he had "just returned from a visit with some of these groups in St. Paul, Minneapolis, Chicago, St. Louis, Miami, Palm Beach and Daytona Beach, and before that at Philadelphia and Baltimore."[14]

Of all the cities enamored by the prayer breakfasts, none was more important than Washington, D.C. Vereide had not only national ambitions from the beginning but political ones as well. Even though businessmen had taken the lead in forming the City Chapel in Seattle, their meetings quickly became an important political rite of passage. A typical session in January 1942, for instance, attracted more than sixty business and civic leaders, including a national director of J. C. Penney, the president of the Seattle Gas Company, a railroad executive, a municipal court judge, and two naval officers. Notably, representatives of both political parties were on hand and, despite their different partisan affiliations, showed unanimity when it came to the rites of public prayer. A Democratic contender for the governor's office gave the opening prayer, with the brother of the incumbent Republican offering comments; the closing prayer, meanwhile, came from the Republican candidate for the US Senate. The same month as that gathering in Washington State, Vereide held an organizational meeting for new breakfast groups in Washington, D.C. In the midst of a massive blizzard, he brought together seventy-four prominent men—mostly congressmen, but with a few business and civic leaders as well—for a luncheon at the Willard Hotel. They heard testimonials to his work from Howard B. Coonley, the far-right leader of the National Association of Manufacturers, and Francis Sayre, former high commissioner to the Philippines and Woodrow Wilson's son-in-law. "I told the story of the Breakfast Groups," Vereide remembered, "and suggested to members of Congress that they begin to meet in a similar fashion and set the pace for our national life, in order that we might be a God-directed and God-controlled nation." The next week, the House of Representatives breakfast group began with Thursday morning meetings held in the Speaker's dining room; a regular Senate group soon met as well, on Wednesday mornings in a private room in that chamber's restaurant.[15]

These congressional breakfast meetings quickly became a fixture on Capitol Hill. Each month, Vereide printed a program to guide the groups in their morning meditations, offering specific readings from Scripture and providing questions for discussion. The groups were officially nonpartisan, welcoming Republicans and Democrats alike, but that was not to say they were apolitical. Most of the Democratic members of the House breakfast group, for instance, were conservative southerners who held federal power and the activism of the New Deal state in as much contempt as the average Republican did.[16] Political overtones were lightly drawn but present nonetheless. "The domestic and the world conflict is the physical expression of a perverted mental, moral and spiritual condition," noted a program for a House session. "We need to repent from our unworkable way and pray." The congressional prayer meetings gave Vereide immediate access to the nation's political elite. In January 1943, just a year after his introductory meeting at the Willard Hotel, the minister marveled to his wife how he was not simply mingling with important political figures but actively enlisting them in his crusade. "My what a full and busy day!" he began. "The Vice President brought me to the Capitol and counseled with me regarding the program and plans, and then introduced me to Senator Brewster, who in turn [introduced me] to Senator Burton—then planned further the program and enlisted their cooperation," he continued. "Then to the Supreme Court for visits with some of them, and secured their presence and participation—then back to the Senate, House—and lunch with Chaplain Montgomery." The rest of the day, and the ones that followed, were packed with meetings, but Vereide pressed ahead. "The hand of the Lord is upon me," he noted in closing. "He is leading."[17]

Having won over political leaders in Washington, D.C., Vereide used their influence to establish even more breakfast groups across the nation. Businessmen in Cleveland had been interested in forming a regular prayer meeting, for instance, but they told Vereide that there was "a class of men we have not been reaching" and asked for help. "I am told that our own Senator Harold Burton is a member of one of your groups in Washington," wrote an organizer. "He is very favorably known in Cleveland as a church man and we are just wondering whether an invitation or other promotion material might carry considerable more weight if it could go out over his name as an honorary chairman or some such title." Vereide arranged for an immediate meeting with the Republican senator and secured his support. The very next day, Burton sent the organizers a list of prominent Clevelanders whom they should recruit. "You perhaps might also wish to quote some portion of this letter as indicating my interest in the movement," the senator volunteered. "It is important that there be deep-seated, moral convictions which shall form the basis for our daily decisions in business and in government."[18]

The contacts Vereide made in congressional prayer groups also gave him access to corporate leaders across the country. NAM president Howard Coonley had helped launch the breakfast meetings, and by 1943, both the past president and the current president of the US Chamber of Commerce were regular participants at the Senate sessions. Corporate titans followed their lead, inviting Vereide to join them for private meetings in their offices or small dinners with fellow executives. "The big men and real leaders in New York and Chicago," he wrote his wife, "look up to me in an embarrassing way." In Manhattan, Thomas Watson of IBM gathered together "a few of New York's top men" for a luncheon at the Bankers Club to meet Vereide and hear about his work. J. C. Penney took the minister to lunch at New York's Union League Club, arranged for a meeting with Norman Vincent Peale, and then promised to set up "a retreat for key business executives" soon after. In Chicago, Vereide lunched at its Union League Club with "fifteen top leaders," including Hughston McBain, president of the Marshall Field department store chain. Other corporate titans sought more intimate audiences. The head of Quaker Oats spent an hour with Vereide in his Chicago office, while the president of Chevrolet spent more than three with him in Detroit. Given his travels, Vereide inevitably won support from the Pew family as well. While James Fifield had found a patron in J. Howard Pew, Vereide won support from his brother Joseph Newton Pew Jr., head of the massive Sun Shipbuilding Company and a powerful force in the Republican Party in Pennsylvania. As the minister shuttled back and forth between the private and public sectors of power in America, his success quickly became a self-fulfilling prophecy. The more politically connected he became, the more leading businessmen sought time with him. And the more backing he secured from corporate titans, the more eager politicians were to count themselves as his friend. Vereide believed he was bringing these influential people closer to God—but he was also bringing them closer to one another, and in a forum that seemed as pure and patriotic as possible.[19]

During the war, Vereide brought together his newfound political and corporate supporters to serve on the board of directors for the new national version of City Chapel, which he called the National Council for Christian Leadership (NCCL). By 1946, the forty-five members of the board represented an impressive range of public and private power in America. From the political arena, its number included eight members of the US Senate and ten representatives in the US House. Drawn in equal numbers from the Republican and Democratic parties, the congressmen were almost universally conservative in their politics. (Former senator Harold Burton, by then appointed to the Supreme Court, still served on the board with his former congressional colleagues.) These political leaders were joined by a number of prominent businessmen, including NAM president Coonley, timber titan F. K. Weyerhauser, earthmoving equipment manufacturer R. G. LeTourneau, and steel magnate Roy Ingersoll. The National Council for Christian Leadership made its headquarters in Washington, D.C., where Vereide had relocated during the war. In November 1945, with considerable help from a wealthy patron, the organization had bought a four-story mansion on Embassy Row, which became its official base of operations. "This," Vereide announced with pride, "is God's Embassy in Washington."[20]

Despite the seeming hyperbole, Vereide's organization did reach into the highest levels of politics. In 1946, for instance, when President Truman appointed treasury secretary Fred Vinson to become the new chief justice of the United States, Vereide invited Vinson to join the Senate breakfast group for a "dedication" of his new position on the Supreme Court. A devout Methodist, Vinson readily accepted and brought along attorney general Tom Clark. Before a gathering of twenty-eight senators, the Presbyterian attorney general offered his own religious testimony, and then the new chief justice followed suit. As Vereide remembered, Vinson spoke warmly about the influence the Bible had not just on his own life but on all of American government and law. After a silent prayer, Missouri senator Forest Donnell led the dedicatory prayer, "invoking God's blessing on the Chief Justice and dedicating him in the name of the Father, the Son, and the Holy Spirit to his exalted and important position." Afterward, Vinson told Vereide that he wished the morning meeting had been "broadcast to all the American people, for he felt that it would do more than anything else to restore the confidence of the people in their government and to unite the nation in a common faith."[21]

The "consecration" of the chief justice of the United States was not an aberration. Indeed, when Tom Clark and Sherman Minton were appointed to the Supreme Court in late 1949, Vereide arranged for another ceremony dedicating their new roles as well. The two new justices joined Chief Justice Vinson and a bipartisan set of senators for a special ceremony in early 1950. Virginia senator A. Willis Robertson, father of the evangelist Pat Robertson, led the group in an opening prayer, after which they polished off plates of toast and eggs. In the discussion that followed, these leaders from the judicial and legislative branches reflected on the role of prayer in political life. Senator John Stennis, a Mississippi Democrat, spoke of how America often focused on material issues, but "we must balance our planning with spirituality." Chief Justice Vinson agreed. "I am not a preacher or even the son of a preacher," he reflected. "But I know we must adhere to the ideals of Christianity." Past civilizations, Vinson warned darkly, had crumbled from within as decadence removed them from their founding principles. Justice Clark wholeheartedly agreed. "No country or civilization can last," he said, "unless it is founded on Christian values."[22]

At the end of his "dedication" ceremony, Justice Sherman Minton urged those gathered to work for a closer brotherhood with the people of Europe. But Vereide had already begun just such an effort. In 1947, he unveiled a new International Council for Christian Leadership (ICCL). In theory, the ICCL was simply an extension of the NCCL, working alongside it in a common effort directed both at home and abroad. But in practice, many of Vereide's allies worried it meant that foreign issues would take priority over domestic ones. Republican congressman John Phillips, a member of the NCCL board of directors, sent Vereide an impassioned letter in August 1948 reminding him that he had "repeatedly been told by your executive committee that there must be no connection between the two movements until the home-grown movement is stronger on its feet." Phillips felt so strongly about the matter that he resigned from the board and asked that his name be removed from the group's literature and letterhead. Responding with deep regret, Vereide insisted that he had never neglected their domestic priorities. "I have given myself unstintingly for the development in our nation of an appreciation for the protection of our form of government and private enterprise," he asserted. Furthermore, the minister reasoned, any program to protect capitalism at home had to protect capitalism everywhere. "Our own economy will crack without the right relationship to [the] world economy," Vereide argued, "and that whole structure is built on moral foundations." The minister pressed ahead in his drive to give the organization an international presence, with quick success. Within a few years, Christian Leadership breakfast groups were meeting regularly in thirty-one foreign countries. England, France, West Germany, the Netherlands, and Finland represented the bulk of the initial growth of the group, but the ICCL made its presence felt in nations as varied as China, South Africa, and Canada, with isolated operations in localities such as Havana and Mexico City as well.[23]

Vereide recognized that the tensions of the Cold War could be exploited to win more converts to his cause. "The Time is Now!" he wrote members of the House breakfast group in August 1949. "On all sides today we hear people speaking fearfully of the spread of atheistic communism. Is there really anything we can do about it? Yes!" He urged the congressmen to stand up to communism in three ways—by maintaining their personal relationship with Jesus Christ; by "cultivating 'intensive

fellowships,' i.e. the spread of small groups or cells," back in their congressional districts patterned on their breakfast group in Congress; and
by working with like-minded Christians across the country to present
"a united front against the forces of the anti-Christ." "The choice," he
insisted, "boils down to this: 'Christ or Communism.' There is really no
other. Those in between—playing neutral—are literally playing into the
hands of the enemy."[24]

Just two weeks later, Americans learned that the Soviet Union now
had nuclear weapons. The paranoia over the dangers posed by "godless
communism" increased dramatically in the coming months and years, and
so too would the campaign to Christianize America. Abraham Vereide
and his associates worked tirelessly to win more converts to their cause,
moving on to ever greater successes over the course of the coming decade.
They would not be alone.

IN BOTH MEANS AND MOTIVES, Billy Graham's ministry represented a continuation of Abraham Vereide's. Fresh from his success in
Los Angeles in late 1949, the sensational young preacher toured the
country in a series of revivals that seemed, in the words of one biographer, "like a long Palm Sunday procession of celebration and arrival." He
began in 1950 in Boston. There, a single, lightly advertised New Year's
Eve service at Mechanics Hall attracted a crowd of more than six thousand, forcing stunned organizers to throw together a series of additional
revivals at the opera house, the Park Street Church, Symphony Hall, and
finally Boston Garden, where more than twenty-five thousand tried to
get in. That spring, Graham held his first "crusade" in Columbia, South
Carolina. Governor Strom Thurmond made regular appearances onstage
at the services, as did Senator Olin Johnston and Supreme Court justice
James Byrnes. Henry Luce, a devout missionary's son who had become
publisher of Time Inc., came to see Graham preach to a record crowd at
the University of South Carolina football stadium. Deeply impressed, he
afterward returned with Graham to the governor's mansion, where the
two stayed up late into the night discussing their faith. In the summer,
the crusade came to Portland, Oregon. Frustrated by seating shortages in
the earlier revivals, Graham convinced local organizers to craft a special

"tabernacle" of wood and aluminum that would seat twelve thousand worshipers. Nearly twice as many tried to get into the opening night's service; a half million more came over the next six weeks. Graham ended the year with a similar six-week revival in Atlanta, where organizers converted the Ponce de Leon baseball park to seat twenty-five thousand, ultimately drawing in another half-million worshipers. Between these extended crusades in 1950, Graham scheduled one-off revivals wherever he could, ranging from an overflow audience of twenty-five hundred at the State Auditorium in Providence, Rhode Island, to an estimated one hundred thousand at the Rose Bowl in Los Angeles. In early 1951, Billy Graham's travels took him to Fort Worth, Texas. The four-week crusade there was an unqualified success, with a total attendance of nearly 336,000, making it the largest evangelistic campaign in the history of the state or, for that matter, the entire Southwest.[25]

Of Graham's legion of admirers during the Fort Worth crusade, Sid Richardson stood out. A crusty, barrel-chested oilman, Richardson was by then one of the wealthiest men in the entire nation, if not *the* wealthiest. Not even the reclusive Richardson knew for sure; much of his immense fortune was buried underneath the Texas soil in his vast oil fields. Still, the journalist Theodore White declared him "far and away the richest American" in a 1954 article, suggesting that fellow Texas oilman H. L. Hunt might be "his only rival in the billion-dollar bracket." In one of the earliest attempts to rank America's wealthiest citizens, *Ladies' Home Journal* gave Richardson the top honors in its inaugural 1957 list, estimating his overall net worth at $700 million. For his part, Richardson wore his wealth uncomfortably, like the rumpled suits that had to be custom-made for his stocky frame. For most of the year, the "billionaire bachelor" lived in two modest rooms at the downtown Fort Worth Club. But he also owned a private island in the Gulf of Mexico, a twenty-eight-mile-long retreat he purchased for a million dollars and then adorned with a luxurious hunting lodge.[26]

The oilman was a collector of sorts. He had started purchasing pieces of art from the American West at an associate's suggestion, soon amassing an unrivaled array of Remingtons and Russells. He also collected political clients. By 1951, he was already a generous backer of both Speaker of the House Sam Rayburn and Senator Lyndon B. Johnson. That year, he hired

John Connally as his executive secretary, launching the career of another talented young politician. Believing Graham had similar potential, Richardson befriended the evangelist, introducing him to other leaders in the state and offering help whenever he could. Graham, for his part, adored the oilman, whom he always called "Mr. Sid." When the preacher started his film production company, the first two features seemed to be tributes to Richardson, or men like him. Filmed during the Fort Worth crusade, *Mr. Texas* (1951) chronicled the conversion of a hard-drinking rodeo rider; *Oiltown, U.S.A.* (1954) told a similar tale about an oil tycoon from Houston who made his way to Christ. The second film cost $100,000 to produce and was advertised as "the story of the free-enterprise system of America, the story of the development and use of God-given natural resources by men who have built a great new empire." Years later, when Richardson passed away, Billy Graham flew down to his private island to preside over the funeral. The preacher offered the highest praise he could imagine for his longtime patron: "He was willing to go to any end to see that our American way of life was maintained."[27]

The earthy Richardson had little use for Graham's religion, but the two shared a common faith in free enterprise. "When Graham speaks of 'the American way of life,'" an early biographer noted, "he has in mind the same combination of economic and political freedom that the National Association of Manufacturers, the United States Chamber of Commerce, and the *Wall Street Journal* do when they use the phrase." Indeed, during the early years of his ministry, Graham devoted himself to spreading the gospel of free enterprise. In his 1951 crusade in Greensboro, North Carolina, he spoke at length about the "dangers that face capitalistic America." The nation was no longer "devoted to the individualism that made America great," he warned the crowd. If it hoped to survive, it needed to embrace once again "the rugged individualism that Christ brought" to mankind. Not surprisingly, Graham saw that individualistic spirit in self-made millionaires such as Richardson and, therefore, made no apologies for ministering to him and men like him. "Whether the story of Christ is told in a huge stadium, across the desk of some powerful leader, or shared with a golfing companion," the preacher reasoned, "it satisfies a common hunger."[28]

Much like his patron, and much like Abraham Vereide and James Fifield, the preacher hungered to make his presence felt in Washington,

D.C. His network of political contacts gave him easy access to the Capitol, where he led a congressional prayer service in April 1950. "Our Father, we give thee thanks for the greatest nation in the world," he offered. "We thank thee for the highest standard of living in the world." Although Graham was delighted to make new friends in the legislature, he had a bigger target. During the Boston crusade, he told a reporter that his real ambition was "to get President Truman's ear for thirty minutes, to get a little help." He peppered the president with letters and telegrams for months but had no luck winning an invitation until House majority leader John McCormack intervened. To Graham's lasting embarrassment, their July 1950 meeting was an utter disaster. He and his three associates arrived at the Oval Office wearing brightly colored suits, hand-painted silk ties, and new white suede shoes. They looked, Graham remembered with a grimace, like a "traveling vaudeville team." The president received them politely. A devout but reserved Baptist who was wary of public displays of piety, he held the foursome at some distance. When Graham asked if he could offer a prayer, Truman shrugged and said, "I don't suppose it could do any harm." The preacher wrapped his arm around the president, clutching him uncomfortably close. As he called down God's blessing, an associate punctuated the prayer with cries of "Amen!" and "Tell it!"[29]

After their visit, reporters pressed Graham's group to divulge details while a row of photographers shouted at them to kneel down for a photo on the White House lawn. To their later regret, they agreed to both requests. In sharing details with the press and posing for the picture, Graham had made a significant, if innocent, mistake. The president now viewed the preacher with suspicion, dismissing him as "one of those counterfeits" only interested in "getting his name in the paper." Feeling used and furious as a result, Truman instructed his staff that Graham would never be welcome at the White House again as long as he was president, a decision leaked to the public by political columnist Drew Pearson. Graham continued to send unrequited letters to Truman, but he sensed that he had overstepped his bounds. "It began to dawn on me a few days later," he wrote, "how we had abused the privilege of seeing the president. National coverage of our visit was definitely not to our advantage."[30]

While Graham was dismayed at how the meeting went, Truman's coldness toward him made it much easier for him to express his true feelings about the president. "Harry is doing the best he can," he joked at one revival. "The trouble is that he just can't do any better." In a more serious tone, Graham soon ventured to criticize the administration from the pulpit. In January 1951, he warned that "the vultures are now encircling our debt-ridden inflationary economy with its fifteen-year record of deficit finance and with its staggering national debt, to close in for the kill." He chided Democrats for wasting money on the welfare state at home and the Marshall Plan abroad. "The whole Western world is begging for more dollars," he noted that fall, but "the barrel is almost empty. When it is empty—what then?" He insisted that the poor in other nations, like those in his own, needed no government assistance. "Their greatest need is not more money, food, or even medicine; it is Christ," he said. "Give them the Gospel of love and grace first and they will clean themselves up, educate themselves, and better their economic conditions."[31]

In January 1952, Graham returned to Washington, determined to make a better impression than he had two years before. This time, his team planned a five-week revival in the capital. The focus of the Washington crusade was a series of regular meetings at the National Guard Armory, but it also featured daily local broadcasts on both radio and television, weekly coast-to-coast broadcasts of his *Hour of Decision* TV show on Sunday nights, and a network of prayer services coordinated over the radio. Graham led prayer meetings all over town, including daily sessions in the Pentagon auditorium. On Monday mornings, he held "Pastor's Workshops" with local clergymen; on Tuesdays, there were luncheons at the Hotel Statler to discuss religion with "the men who have so much a part in shaping the destiny of the Capital of Western Civilization: the business men of Washington." Graham courted congressmen as well, of course. When he first announced the crusade, he did so with a senator and ten representatives standing alongside him. Abraham Vereide, who had helped conceive the Washington crusade and served on its executive committee, invited members of his congressional prayer breakfast groups to attend a special luncheon with Graham for "a discussion on 'The Choice Before Us.'" Despite the rift between them, Graham hoped to convince President Truman to attend the first service and, if possible, offer some opening remarks. Truman steered clear. A staff memo noted the president "said very decisively that he did not wish to endorse Billy Graham's Washington revival, and particularly, he said, he did not want to receive him at the White House. You remember what a show of himself Billy Graham made the last time he was here. The President does not want it repeated."[32]

As the Washington crusade began in January 1952, Graham made clear his intent to influence national politics. If Congress and the White House "would take the lead in a spiritual and moral awakening," he said, "it would affect the country more than anything in a long time." Those who supported the revival were given cards to place in their Bibles, reminding them to pray daily "for the message of [the] Crusade to reach into every Government office, that many in Government will be won for Christ." Although the president remained aloof, many congressmen embraced Graham. Virginia senator A. Willis Robertson secured unanimous Senate approval of the crusade, as well as a prayer that "God may guide and protect our nation and preserve the peace of the world." Several congressmen took roles in the revival, including four who regularly served as ushers. Many more attended, with roughly one-third of all senators and one-fourth of all representatives requesting special allotments of seats to the Armory services. "As near as I can tell," Graham bragged to a reporter, "we averaged between 25 and 40 Congressmen and about five Senators a night." Congressional attendance was noteworthy, but so too was the overall turnout. Despite the Armory's official seating capacity of 5,310, more than 13,000 people packed the venue on opening night, with crowds exceeding 7,000 allowed on subsequent evenings. Even with such limitations, the total attendance for the Washington crusade ultimately reached a half million. As Vice President Alben Barkley marveled to Graham, "You're certainly rockin' the old Capitol."[33]

Interest proved to be so high that Graham soon staged a huge rally at the Capitol itself. At first, the idea seemed impossible. But a call to his patron Sid Richardson—who, in turn, called Speaker of the House Sam Rayburn—prompted Congress to push through a special measure authorizing the first religious service ever to be held on the steps of the Capitol Building. "This country needs a revival," Rayburn explained, "and I believe Billy Graham is bringing it to us." Even though it took place in a cold drizzling rain, the February service drew a crowd estimated to be as large as forty-five thousand. (The gathering, the House sergeant at arms noted, was larger than the one for Truman's inauguration.) Graham reveled in the

In January 1952, Reverend Billy Graham launched the Washington crusade, staging religious revivals at the National Armory and, in a first for the city, on the steps of the Capitol Building itself. If Congress and the White House "would take the lead in a spiritual and moral awakening," he said, "it would affect the country more than anything in a long time." *Mark Kauffman, The LIFE Premium Collection, Getty Images.*

turnout, taking off his tan coat to address them in a powder-blue double-breasted suit with a polka-dot tie. To those assembled, and to the millions more listening over the ABC radio network, he called for Congress to set aside a national day of prayer as a "day of confession of sin, humiliation, repentance, and turning to God at this hour." The minister noted that a formal return to God would benefit not just the American people but also the political representatives who had the faith to make such a cause their own. "If I would run for President of the United States today on a platform of calling people back to God, back to Christ, back to the Bible, I'd be elected," Graham insisted. "There is a hunger for God today."[34]

The proposal for a national day of prayer was nothing new; several presidents, including Abraham Lincoln, had called for similar religious observances in the past. Graham himself had tried to convince Truman of the need for a national day of prayer during their July 1950 meeting.

The idea generated considerable interest at the time, as ministers across the nation picked up Graham's proposal and urged Americans, in sermons delivered in their own churches and over the radio, to lobby the president. Thousands did. "The minds of the people must be directed more toward spiritual values," a Cincinnati woman wrote. "The time is NOW for *spiritual mobilization.*"[35] Despite the outpouring of public pressure, Truman had not been swayed. The second time around, however, the president gave in. He still had reservations about public displays of prayer—in his diary that month, he noted that he abided by "the V, VI, & VIIth chapters of the Gospel according to St. Matthew," which were often cited for their injunctions against the practice—but he read the national mood and decided to acquiesce.[36] As Congress took up the proposal in February 1952, House majority leader John McCormack let it be known that Truman now supported the plan.[37]

Congress resolved, by the unanimous consent of both House and Senate, "that the President shall set aside and proclaim a day each year, other than a Sunday, as a National Day of Prayer, on which the people of the United States may turn to God in prayer and meditation." The language of the legislation was significant, as all previous congressional proclamations for days of prayer "requested" that the president designate a day, while this one alone "required" him to do so. Truman was thus bound by the law, just as every one of his successors in the White House has been to this day. In an apparent nod to the previous year's "Freedom Under God" observance, which was set to be repeated in 1952, Truman selected the Fourth of July as the date for the first National Day of Prayer. The choice, he explained, was intended to coincide "with the anniversary of the adoption of the Declaration of Independence, which published to the world this Nation's 'firm reliance on the protection of Divine Providence.'" In the official proclamation, Truman encouraged all Americans to ask God for strength and wisdom and to offer thanks in return "for His constant watchfulness over us in every hour of national prosperity and national peril." For his own part, the president observed the day of prayer by taking in a doubleheader between the Washington Senators and the New York Yankees. His critics noted with satisfaction that the Yankees beat the home team in both games and that Truman had to leave early when the second was called on account of rain.[38]

While Billy Graham welcomed the adoption of the National Day of Prayer, he saw it as merely the beginning of the political and moral transformation needed to save the nation. In late 1951, he insisted that "the Christian people of America will not sit idly by during the 1952 presidential campaign. [They] are going to vote as a bloc for the man with the strongest moral and spiritual platform, regardless of his views on other matters." By that time, Graham believed he had already found the man who fit the description: General Dwight D. Eisenhower.[39]

EISENHOWER SEEMED AN UNLIKELY CANDIDATE to lead the nation to spiritual reawakening. For decades he had remained distant from religion and could not even claim a specific denominational affiliation. During his childhood, however, his family had been deeply devout. His grandfather had been a minister for the River Brethren, an offshoot of the Mennonites, and his father maintained that faith. His mother traveled a more circuitous spiritual path: born and raised a Lutheran, she joined the River Brethren at marriage but was later baptized as a Jehovah's Witness when Dwight was eight years old. While denominations may have varied, the family's commitment to a literal reading of the Bible remained constant, and a constant presence in their lives. In their white clapboard home in Abilene, Kansas, the Bible was a source of inspiration read each morning in prayers and a source of authority to be quoted again and again. "All the Eisenhowers," one of Dwight's brothers later explained, "are fundamentalists."[40]

Dwight Eisenhower certainly bore the imprint of this upbringing—he had been named after Dwight Moody, a popular nineteenth-century evangelist who was, in essence, a forerunner of Billy Graham—but for much of his adult life he showed little of it publicly. The River Brethren required strict observance of the Sabbath, but Eisenhower rarely attended services during his military career. The Brethren demanded abstinence from tobacco, but he became a heavy smoker, going through four packs of Camels a day during the climax of the Second World War. The Brethren were also strongly committed to pacifism on religious grounds; Eisenhower's mother condemned war as "the devil's business" and believed those waging it were sinners. While most members of the River Brethren and the Witnesses sought to secure a conscientious-objector exemption from military service during times of war, Eisenhower actively pursued a military career during a time of peace, leaving home in 1911 to enroll at West Point and then rising through the ranks over the course of two global conflicts.[41]

In spite of his outward indifference to the faith of his family, Eisenhower insisted that its lessons still resonated with him. "While my brothers and I have always been a little bit 'non-conformist' in the business of actual membership of a particular sect or denomination," he wrote a friend in 1952, "we are all very earnestly and very seriously religious. We could not help being so considering our upbringing." Indeed, while he lacked ties to any specific denomination, Eisenhower remained firmly committed to the Bible itself. Like his parents, he considered it an unparalleled resource. One of his aides during the Second World War remembered that Eisenhower could "quote Scripture by the yard," using it to punctuate points made at staff meetings. After the war, his sense of religion's importance only grew stronger. In an interview before he assumed the presidency of Columbia University in 1948, Eisenhower declared himself "the most intensely religious man I know." Faith, he believed, was important not just for him personally but also for the entire country. "A democracy cannot exist without a religious base," he told reporters. "I believe in democracy."[42]

Comments such as these led Billy Graham—and many other Americans—to believe that their democracy needed Dwight Eisenhower. In a letter to Sid Richardson in late 1951, Graham wrote that "the American people have come to the point where they want a man with honesty, integrity, and spiritual power. I believe the General has it. I hope you can persuade him to put his hat in the ring." Richardson had been friendly with Eisenhower since just after the attack on Pearl Harbor, when they met by chance on a train trip through Texas. He urged Graham to "write General Eisenhower some good reasons why he ought to run for the presidency." "Mr. Sid, I can't get involved in politics," Graham demurred. But his patron was set on the idea. "There's no politics," he insisted. "Don't you think any American ought to run if millions of people want him to?" When Graham replied, "Yes, Mr. Sid, I agree he should—" the oilman cut him off with a brusque "Well, then, say that in a letter!" Doing as instructed, the minister exhorted Eisenhower to run. During the crusade in the capital, Graham related, a district court judge had "confided in me that if Washington were not cleaned out in the next two or three years, we were going to enter a period of chaos or downfall." The stakes were high. "Upon this decision," he concluded, "could well rest the destiny of the Western World." Eisenhower told Richardson that it was "the damnedest letter I ever got. Who is this young fellow?"[43]

Richardson arranged for the two to meet, sending Graham to the general's offices in Paris shortly after the Washington crusade. Eisenhower made a powerful impression on the preacher. "Although he was in uniform," Graham later remembered, "his office looked like that of a corporate executive, with walnut-paneled walls, a walnut desk, and green carpeting to match his chair." The two began talking about their mutual friend, but much of the two-hour meeting served as a chance for Graham to make his case for an Eisenhower candidacy. The minister would later downplay the importance of his visit in the ultimate decision, aware that other Americans—including a congressional delegation led by Senator Frank Carlson of Kansas, a close ally of Abraham Vereide—had likewise made the pilgrimage to Paris. But Graham's spiritual support was surely influential in the general's decision, as was the financial support Richardson promised. Once Eisenhower announced his intentions, the oilman put his vast fortune to work for him. Richardson's direct contribution to the campaign was reportedly $1 million, but he also paid for roughly $200,000 in expenses at the Commodore Hotel in New York, where the general had established offices after returning home, and then covered most of his expenditures during the Republican National Convention in Chicago as well.[44]

In June 1952, Eisenhower launched his campaign for the presidency in Abilene. The town staged a massive parade in his honor, with a series of floats depicting events in his life, ending with one carrying a replica of the White House with him inside. His parents had long since passed away, but the candidate made an appearance at their old clapboard home, using it as a shorthand for his humble upbringing, his family, and his faith. In his comments, he condemned a set of "evils which can ultimately throttle free government," which he identified as labor unrest, runaway inflation, "excessive taxation," and the "ceaseless expansion" of the federal government. These were commonplace conservative positions, but Eisen-hower presented them in religious language that elevated them for his audience. Scotty Reston of the *New York Times* was reminded of William Jennings Bryan, the great evangelist for old-time religion and plain-folks politics. "He appealed to the virtues of a simpler era that this town sym-bolizes," Reston wrote. "He appealed not to the mind but to the heart, and his language was filled with the noble words of the old revivalists: frugality, austerity, honesty, economy, simplicity, integrity." Referring to Eisenhower's memoirs of the war, the journalist noted, "His 'Crusade in Europe' over, he opened up a second front here as if he intended to start a second crusade in America."[45]

Eisenhower encouraged the perception that his candidacy was a reli-gious cause. In his acceptance speech at the Republican National Con-vention, he declared the coming presidential campaign to be "a great crusade for freedom in America and freedom in the world." He appropri-ated not only Graham's "crusade" brand but also Graham himself. Shortly after Eisenhower secured the nomination in July 1952, the preacher re-ceived an urgent call from Senator Carlson, whom he had met months earlier during the Washington crusade, asking him to come to Eisen-hower's hotel in Chicago. There the candidate asked if Graham might be able to "contribute a religious note" to some of his speeches for the election season. "Of course, I want to do anything I can for you," Graham agreed, with the caveat that "I have to be careful not to publicly disclose my preferences or become embroiled in partisan politics." Soon after, the minister spent a few days with the campaign staff at the Brown Palace Hotel in Denver, offering scriptural references and spiritual observations that could be used to sanctify the secular positions of the candidate. Be-fore leaving, Graham gave Eisenhower a gift of a silk-sewn red-leather Bible—red because, as one of his associates liked to joke, "a Bible should be read"—which the preacher had painstakingly annotated with his inter-pretations. Eisenhower treasured the gift, keeping it close at hand during the campaign and placing it on his bedside table at the White House. He seemed to value sincerely Graham's advice, but he also understood the po-litical benefit of his public association with the popular preacher. In a let-ter to Governor Arthur Langlie, who had been propelled to prominence in large part by Vereide's breakfast groups and had served as cochairman of Graham's 1951 Seattle crusade, Eisenhower noted with delight that the minister had praised the Republican "crusade for honesty in government" before his radio audience of millions. But Eisenhower wanted more if possible. "Since all pastors must necessarily take a nonpartisan approach," he acknowledged, "it would be difficult to form any formal organization of religious leaders to work on our behalf. However, this might be done in an informal way."[46]

While Graham insisted he could never reveal his political leanings, he spent much of the campaign dropping what seemed to be considerable hints. On domestic matters, Graham had long been sounding Republican themes of rolling back the welfare state and liberating business leaders to operate on their own. But on foreign policy too, Graham closely followed the Republican script for those issues, summed up by South Dakota senator Karl Mundt as the "K_1C_2," formula for its component elements of "Korea, communism, and corruption." "The Korean War is being fought," he told a Houston congregation in May, "because the nation's leaders blundered on foreign policy in the Far East." He called the Truman administration "cowardly" for not following the advice of General Douglas MacArthur and pursuing "this half-hearted war" rather than unleashing the full powers of the American military. On domestic issues, meanwhile, Graham condemned the "tranquil attitude to communism" in the country, warning that "Communists and left-wingers" posed a danger to the nation and that there already might be "a fifth column in our midst." As for corruption, Graham pressed the issue early and often, so much so that his comments became indistinguishable from the official Republican slogans. The GOP insisted, "We must clean up the mess in Washington"; at the same time, Graham asserted, "We all seem to agree there's a mess in Washington." Time and time again, the preacher made a clear political attack from the pulpit, only to walk it back slightly with a shrug and a smile. Once, for example, he made a disparaging comment about Truman, only to cut himself short: "I won't say anything more about that. Except," he immediately added, "that I have found that after my car has run for a long time, it needs a change of oil. That's the strongest political statement I'm going to make, now."[47]

Though the Eisenhower campaign made use of Graham as much as possible, the campaign of his Democratic rival, Illinois governor Adlai

Stevenson, refused to conduct religious outreach of its own. There were plenty of opportunities. In 1951, a group of leading clergymen formed Christian Action, which intended "to draw together Protestants on the non-communist left for the implementation of the implications of the Gospel in social, economic, and political affairs."[48] It was, in essence, a liberal counterpart to James Fifield's Spiritual Mobilization. The theologian Reinhold Niebuhr, who frequently traded barbs with Fifield in the press, served as one of its two national cochairmen.[49] In a response to Graham's involvement in the Eisenhower campaign, Niebuhr suggested that Christian Action could counter his work by assembling "an inter-faith committee of ministers for Stevenson." The group lined up 124 Protestant religious leaders and drafted a statement announcing their support for Stevenson as the candidate who could best lead "the free world in resisting the dread peril of communism." The Stevenson campaign was divided on the proposal, but ultimately chose not to pursue it due to fears of a negative reaction in the press. Billy Graham had no such reservations. A few days before the election, he announced that he had conducted his own personal survey of 220 religious editors and clergymen and found that they favored Eisenhower over Stevenson by an overwhelming margin of six to one. Graham still insisted that, personally, he was neutral in the race. "I believe, however, it is the duty of everyone who calls himself a Christian to go to the polls and vote," he asserted. "Every Christian should be in much prayer that God will have his way."[50]

While Graham's support was influential, Eisenhower's campaign received similar endorsements from other Christian libertarian leaders. During the Republican National Convention in Chicago, for instance, Vereide's International Council for Christian Leadership held a special breakfast meeting for nearly a hundred convention delegates at the Board of Trade Building. They prayed for the success of the Republican convention and, moreover, "for God's man to be elected this fall, praying that America may become aroused and led by God in the coming election and that God's grace and power may rest upon our country, preparing it for service at home and abroad as a nation under God." In September 1952, Vereide sent a mass mailing to his national network of more than two hundred breakfast groups. He urged the members of the business and civic elite who participated to devote all their energies to the cause of raising "alertness to the right choice and vote in the November elections."[51]

Likewise, Spiritual Mobilization's *Faith and Freedom* published a manifesto, titled "The Christian's Political Responsibility," in its September 1952 issue. Advancing arguments that would later be made by the religious right, the magazine sought to convince Christian voters that they had a duty to bring their religious convictions to bear in the ballot box. "The Christian may keep aloof from politics because it is 'dirty,'" the magazine's editor observed. "In that event, he may be sure the non-Christian cynic will take full advantage of his apathy. Politics will then be 'played' not according to the principles of Christ, but according to the principles of the anti-Christ. This is precisely what happened in our country to an extent that has shaken the foundations of our Republic. Action *must* be taken, and now." *Faith and Freedom* followed the lead of Graham and Vereide, claiming it would never endorse one party or the other. But it offered a "political checklist for Christians" that nudged readers rather strongly toward the Republicans. When considering the Christian merits of a particular candidate, party, or law, the editor noted, readers should ask themselves a series of questions: "If it proposes to take the property or income of some for the special benefit of others, does it violate the Commandment: 'Thou shalt not steal'? If it appeals to the voting power of special interest groups, or to those who have less than others, does it violate the Commandment: 'Thou shalt not covet thy neighbor's house'?" As Spiritual Mobilization made the case for Eisenhower, others noted the connections between them as well. "America isn't just a land of the free in Eisenhower's conception," journalist John Temple Graves observed that same month. "It is a land of freedom under God."[52]

In the end, Eisenhower's "great crusade" for the presidency proved to be every bit as popular as Graham's own crusades. He took more than 55 percent of the popular vote, with even more impressive margins in the Electoral College, where he won 442 to 89. Stevenson only managed to win nine states, all in the still solidly Democratic South, but even there Eisenhower made historic inroads by taking Texas, Tennessee, Virginia, and Florida. Outside the region, he won every single state west of Arkansas and virtually every state north of it, including his opponent's home state, Illinois. "Earthquake, landslide, tidal wave," marveled Marquis Childs in the *Washington Post*, "whatever it was it worked with the overpowering completeness resembling a natural force." The famous columnist Walter Lippmann agreed, asserting that the president-elect's "mandate from the people is one of the greatest given in modern times."[53]

Reflecting on the election returns, Eisenhower resolved to put that mandate in the service of a national religious revival. He asked Graham to meet with him in the suite Sid Richardson had provided at the Commodore Hotel in New York, to discuss plans for his inauguration and beyond. "I think one of the reasons I was elected was to help lead this country spiritually," the president-elect confided. "We *need* a spiritual renewal." Graham, moved nearly to tears, responded with an excited exclamation: "General, you can do more to inspire the American people to a more spiritual way of life than any other man alive!" For the next eight years, Eisenhower would attempt to do precisely that. Working with Graham, Vereide, and countless others both inside and outside his administration, the new president endeavored to lead the nation back to what he understood to be its religious roots. In doing so, however, he would actually transform America into something altogether new.[54]

PART II

CONSECRATION

CHAPTER 3

"Government Under God"

A FEW DAYS BEFORE CHRISTMAS in 1952, Dwight Eisenhower addressed the crowded ballroom of the Waldorf-Astoria Hotel. As reporters hurriedly took notes, the president-elect asserted that "the great struggle of our times is one of spirit" and, therefore, "if we are to be strong, we must be strong first in our spiritual convictions." With members of his new administration looking on, including Secretary of State John Foster Dulles and Attorney General Herbert Brownell, Eisenhower explained that Americans "have got to go back to the very fundamentals of all things. And one of them is that we are a religious people. Even those among us who are, in my opinion, so silly as to doubt the existence of an Almighty, are still members of a religious civilization, because the Founding Fathers said it was a religious concept that they were trying to translate into the political world." In the crucial passage in his speech, Eisenhower called the crowd's attention to the invocation of "the Creator" in the preamble of the Declaration of Independence. He then insisted, in what quickly became a famous line, that "our form of government has no sense unless it is founded in a deeply-felt religious faith, and I don't care what it is."[1]

That single sentence from Eisenhower, more than any other during the campaign or perhaps even his presidency, resonated with observers across the political spectrum.[2] For William Lee Miller, a liberal theologian at Yale Divinity, Eisenhower's reference to a "deeply-felt religious faith"—a phrase to which he would repeatedly return as president—signaled an immaturity in his thinking. "Depth of feeling is the important thing, rather than any objective meaning," Miller wrote. "One might say that President Eisenhower, like many Americans, is a very fervent believer in a very vague religion." Other critics agreed. "Is this not just another indication that in America religion is considered vaguely to be a good thing," the sociologist Robert Bellah asked, "but that people care so little about it that it has lost any content whatsoever?" Conservative scholars, however, believed that liberals entirely missed the point. Though he shared their concerns about the shallowness of Americans' civil religion, the sociologist Will Herberg appreciated its essential power and effectiveness. "The President was saying something that almost any American could understand and approve," he noted. "Eisenhower's apparent indifferentism ('and I don't care what it is') was not indifferentism at all, but the expression that at bottom the 'three great faiths' [Judaism, Catholicism, and Protestantism] were really 'saying the same thing' in affirming the 'spiritual ideals' and 'moral values' of the American Way of Life."[3]

Indeed, for Eisenhower, the most important thing about religion was its power to unite Americans around a common understanding of their past and to dedicate them to a common plan for their future. While critics mocked the president for being "a very fervent believer in a very vague religion," that was exactly his intent. He understood that, in a diverse nation long divided along doctrinal lines, religion could serve a public role only if it was reduced to its lowest common denominator—or, perhaps, its lowest common denomination. In this respect, the president was perfectly matched to the moment. On the surface, the postwar period witnessed a tremendous revival in religious faith that clearly distinguished that era from the past. The percentage of Americans who claimed membership in a church had remained fairly constant in the early twentieth century, barely rising from 43 percent in 1910 to 49 percent in 1940. The decade and a half after the Second World War, however, saw a significant surge: the percentage claiming a church membership climbed to 57 percent in 1950 and then spiked to an all-time high of 69 percent at the end of the decade. Even though studies revealed the revival to be a bit light on substance—a Gallup Poll in 1950, for instance, found that while 80 percent of Americans believed the Bible was "the revealed word of God," only 47 percent could name even a single author of the gospels—the shift was nonetheless remarkable. The American people, like Eisenhower, had become very fervent believers in a very vague religion.[4]

While this broader picture helps contextualize Eisenhower's call for a "deeply felt religious faith," the specific setting for his remarks is even more revealing. The gathering at the Waldorf-Astoria in late 1952 was the annual meeting of the board of the Freedoms Foundation. "These days I seem to have no trouble filling my calendar," the president-elect told them. "But this is one engagement that I requested. I wanted to come and do my best to tell those people who are my friends, who are support-ers of the idea that is represented in the foundation, how deeply I believe that they are serving America." The basic idea of the Freedoms Founda-tion was that those who promoted "a better understanding of the Ameri-can way of life" should be singled out for awards and attention, especially those who celebrated the central role played by "the American free en-terprise system" in making the nation great. Fittingly, for an organization devoted to the promotion of big business, its president was Don Belding, head of a national advertising agency whose clients included Walt Disney and Howard Hughes. The board of directors, meanwhile, included lead-ers at General Foods, Maytag, Republic Steel, Sherwin Williams, Union Carbide and Carbon, and US Rubber, as well as individuals such as Sid Richardson and Mrs. J. Howard Pew. The corporate presence was so pro-nounced that one honoree sent his award back, grumbling that the Free-doms Foundation was "just another group promoting the propaganda of the National Association of Manufacturers."[5]

More accurately, the Freedoms Foundation promoted Christian lib-ertarianism. Belding was a close ally of James Fifield, whom he person-ally praised as "Freedom's Crusader" in a ceremony honoring the minister in 1950. The advertising executive was deeply involved in the work of Spiritual Mobilization, regularly attending events in Los Angeles and serving as a founding member of the Committee to Proclaim Liberty. Many members of the Freedoms Foundation board, including E. F. Hut-ton, Fred Maytag II, and Charles White, were likewise active in the same movements. Not surprisingly, the foundation these men created looked favorably upon those groups. Early recipients of Freedoms Foundation awards included Fifield, several regular contributors to *Faith and Freedom*, producers of *The Freedom Story* radio program, and, notably, all the mem-bers of the Committee to Proclaim Liberty, who were honored as a group and, in several instances, honored once again as individuals. Presiding over the first awards ceremony in 1949, Eisenhower told the winners they had "become marked as among America's disciples. You have issued your defiance to all who would destroy the American dream."[6]

Eisenhower's relationship with the Freedoms Foundation ran back to its founding. In his first meeting with Belding in September 1948, he discovered that the ad man shared his belief that the free enterprise system was in desperate need of defense. "We thoroughly agreed that it is absolutely essential to the security of this country in the years ahead that a coordinated effort, well organized, well disciplined, and well staffed, be created to intelligently direct the education of the American people," Belding wrote soon after. "It must present the basic principles of our economy, the advantages of the American system, and the dangers inherent in the lack of unity of the American people." The Freedoms Foundation was the result. Belding led the organization, but Eisenhower established its mission by joining with Herbert Hoover to write its charter. In March 1949, "The Credo of the American Way of Life" appeared in the pages of *Reader's Digest*. It was depicted as a soaring monument whose upper reaches included references to the Bill of Rights and an equal number of rights especially designed for business, including the "right to own private property," the "right to engage in business, compete, make a profit," the "right to bargain for goods and services in a free market," the "right to contract about our affairs," and, last but not least, the "right to freedom from arbitrary government regulation and control." Together, these political and economic rights rested on a pedestal inscribed "Constitutional Government designed to *Serve* the People." And that, in turn, stood on a more substantial foundation: "Fundamental Belief in God."[7]

For the Freedoms Foundation, "The Credo of the American Way of Life" was more than a list of political and economic rights. It was rather, as its name indicated, a *creed*—a statement of religious belief and commitment to a sanctified cause. When Eisenhower launched his "crusade" for the White House in 1952, he pointedly made the credo part of his campaign. For starters, the Republican nominee led a drive to have a monument in its likeness erected in the nation's capital, to honor the American ideal of "permitting the creative spirit of man made in the image of his Maker to reach its highest aspirations, to seek its own destiny, and to serve in the cause of freedom for its fellow man." While the credo monument never materialized, its message was spread widely in a massive get-out-the-vote campaign coordinated by the Freedoms Foundation

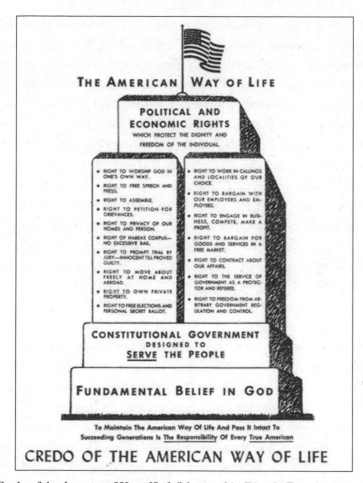

THE AMERICAN WAY OF LIFE

POLITICAL AND
ECONOMIC RIGHTS
WHICH PROTECT THE DIGNITY AND
FREEDOM OF THE INDIVIDUAL.

- RIGHT TO WORSHIP GOD IN ONE'S OWN WAY.
- RIGHT TO FREE SPEECH AND PRESS.
- RIGHT TO ASSEMBLE.
- RIGHT TO PETITION FOR GRIEVANCES.
- RIGHT TO PRIVACY OF OUR HOMES AND PERSON.
- RIGHT OF HABEAS CORPUS— NO EXCESSIVE BAIL.
- RIGHT TO PROMPT TRIAL BY JURY—INNOCENT TILL PROVED GUILTY.
- RIGHT TO MOVE ABOUT FREELY AT HOME AND ABROAD.
- RIGHT TO OWN PRIVATE PROPERTY.
- RIGHT TO FREE ELECTIONS AND PERSONAL SECRET BALLOT.

- RIGHT TO WORK IN CALLINGS AND LOCALITIES OF OUR CHOICE.
- RIGHT TO BARGAIN WITH OUR EMPLOYERS AND EMPLOYEES.
- RIGHT TO ENGAGE IN BUSINESS, COMPETE, MAKE A PROFIT.
- RIGHT TO BARGAIN FOR GOODS AND SERVICES IN A FREE MARKET.
- RIGHT TO CONTRACT ABOUT OUR AFFAIRS.
- RIGHT TO THE SERVICE OF GOVERNMENT AS A PROTECTOR AND REFEREE.
- RIGHT TO FREEDOM FROM ARBITRARY GOVERNMENT REGULATION AND CONTROL.

CONSTITUTIONAL GOVERNMENT
DESIGNED TO
SERVE THE PEOPLE

FUNDAMENTAL BELIEF IN GOD

To Maintain The American Way Of Life And Pass It Intact To
Succeeding Generations Is The Responsibility Of Every True American

CREDO OF THE AMERICAN WAY OF LIFE

"The Credo of the American Way of Life," designed by Dwight Eisenhower and Herbert Hoover for the pro-business Freedoms Foundation, illustrated their belief that all political and economic rights in America rested on a "fundamental belief in God." *Courtesy of Freedoms Foundation at Valley Forge.*

and the Boy Scouts of America. Together, the two organizations put up a million posters in store windows and plastered another ninety thousand cards on trains and buses. On November 1, 1952, the Saturday before the election, they placed more than thirty million additional pieces of literature on doorknobs across the country. Shaped like the Liberty Bell, the door hangers featured the image of the credo on one side and a plea from earnest-looking Scouts to "*Think* when you *Vote*" on the other.[8]

Eisenhower's appearance before the Freedoms Foundation in December 1952 thus served as a chance to thank those who had stood by him in the election and to promise that his administration would stand by its credo. The businessmen assembled at the Waldorf-Astoria already knew that the president-elect agreed with their goals, and now they heard him embrace their means as well. Whether he ever linked the means with the ends as explicitly as men such as Fifield, Vereide, or Graham did was ultimately irrelevant, for the members of the Freedoms Foundation believed that the latter would naturally follow the former. What was truly important was the simple fact that Eisenhower vowed to take the vague religion of the late 1940s and early 1950s and make it a concrete fixture in the federal government. But this apparent triumph of the Christian libertarians would involve a significant transformation of their arguments. After Eisenhower, religion would no longer be used to tear down the central state but instead to prop it up. Piety and patriotism became one and the same, love of God and love of country conflated to the core.

THE RELIGIOUS THEMES THAT EISENHOWER highlighted throughout the transition period and his inauguration ceremonies were repeated throughout the early weeks of the administration. On Sunday, February 1, 1953, he became the first president ever to be baptized while in office. Despite his upbringing, the president had remained uncommitted to any single denomination for most of his adult life. During the campaign, he had explained the rationale for his rootlessness to his friend Cliff Roberts, an investment banker and chairman of Augusta National Golf Club. "While I have no objection whatsoever to belonging to a particular group," he wrote, "the fact remains that the only reason for doing so from my viewpoint is the ease it provides in answering questions. It is much easier to say, 'I am a Presbyterian' than to say 'I am a Christian but I do not belong to any denomination.'" But Eisenhower soon decided he had little choice in the matter. Billy Graham urged him to choose a denomination, if only for appearances. "Frankly," the preacher warned, "I don't think the American people would be happy with a president who didn't belong to any church." Eisenhower agreed but said he would wait until after the election, to avoid seeming "to use the church politically." The denomination he would pick was almost an afterthought. "I suppose Presbyterian," he said offhandedly, "because Mamie is Presbyterian." And so, a week and a half after his inauguration, President Eisenhower was baptized at the National Presbyterian Church in Washington.[9]

His new denominational affiliation seemed little more than a formality, however, and the president sought to downplay it at all costs. He had agreed to join National Presbyterian only after Reverend Edward L. R. Elson promised to be discreet. But, as Eisenhower wrote angrily in his diary, "we were scarcely home before the fact was being publicized, by the pastor, to the hilt."[10] The president screamed to his press secretary, Jim Hagerty, "You go and tell that goddam minister that if he gives out one more story about my religious faith I won't join his goddam church!" His rage stemmed not simply from the broken promise but also from his desire not to be constrained by any one denomination. As the press secretary later explained, even though the president "did actually *physically* join the Presbyterian Church," he never wanted to be held back by its doctrine. In Hagerty's telling, Eisenhower remained committed to "a very basic spiritual strength" that transcended the teachings of any one church and thereby gave him "great rapport" with all faiths.[11]

In fact, on the very same day as his baptism, Eisenhower continued to publicize his embrace of nondenominational faith, taking part in a televised program for the American Legion's "Back to God" movement. The Legion had conceived the ecumenical campaign in the fall of 1951, just months after Spiritual Mobilization's "Freedom Under God" program. Expanding on the growing movement for public religion, the "Back to God" campaign sought to foster faith in individual homes, schools, churches, and synagogues. Though they emphasized private sites of worship, organizers believed their efforts served a public need. In October 1952, Father John E. Duffy, national chaplain for the Legion, insisted that its campaign for religious revival "should be based fundamentally upon Americanism" because faith was "the foundation for our government." "After all," he told the executive committee, "belief in God was the essential tenet of the Founding Fathers, and the bond that kept our people together, that enabled this nation to grow, to flourish and triumph." As they encouraged Americans to pray in their own lives, the Legionnaires insisted that such prayers would benefit the country as a whole. Tabletop prayer cards for restaurants made the connection clear. "The American Legion, pledged for service 'for God and country,' has continually emphasized the spiritual foundations of our Freedom," the card read. "It believes that a spiritual awakening of the people of the United States is needed in order to preserve that freedom."[12]

The centerpiece of the "Back to God" movement was its nationally televised "patriotic presentation" on February 1, 1953. The National Council of Churches secured free airtime on NBC for the television broadcast, but the special aired simultaneously on the ABC, NBC, CBS, and MBS radio networks and was rebroadcast abroad through the Voice of America and the Armed Forces Radio Network. The program itself took place at the Center Theatre in New York City, with a crowd of fifteen hundred in attendance. A choir of 160 cadets from West Point, dressed in their formal gray uniforms, performed choral versions of "The Star-Spangled Banner" and "America." They also provided backup vocals for a somewhat unwieldy musical rendition of the preamble to the American Legion's constitution. The main lyrics were delivered by Morton Downey, a popular tenor whose son and namesake would later become an outspoken right-wing television host.[13]

Billed as "a half-hour inter-faith religious program," the "Back to God" special commemorated the tenth anniversary of the sacrifice made by four army chaplains on the USS *Dorchester* who gave their life preservers to soldiers when the ship was sunk by the Germans. Importantly, the four chaplains who sacrificed their lives on the *Dorchester*—a pair of Protestant ministers, a Catholic priest, and a Jewish rabbi—personified the postwar emphasis on ecumenical religious sentiment. The Legion replicated that denominational diversity in its memorial program. Father Duffy served as master of ceremonies, while another past national chaplain, Rabbi David Lefkowitz Jr., gave the invocation. "May our program," he asked, "be blessed with holy strength and purpose and promote a spiritual awakening in the hearts of our people, serving to symbolize for all nations and creeds, the individual responsibility of free men, one to the other, in God, Amen." Meanwhile, two Protestant ministers—Reverend Norman Vincent Peale and Chaplain John B. Williams—offered contributions of their own, with the former reading a passage from Longfellow and the latter offering the benediction.[14]

The featured speakers, President Eisenhower and Vice President Nixon, repeated the program's call for a patriotic return to prayer. "If we study history," Nixon observed, "we will find that more great civilizations, more great nations, have been destroyed because of moral decay from within than have been destroyed because of armed attack from without." The vice president assured the audience that the new administration would lead a new revival. Nixon noted the importance of military and economic strength in the nation's survival, but insisted—pumping his fist for emphasis—that "above all, the greatest advantage we have over the slave world is the spiritual strength which should be ours and which, I am sure, will be ours, and is ours under our leadership." The president, meanwhile, offered a similar message in an Oval Office address. Americans enjoyed a number of material comforts, he observed. "But when we think about the matter very deeply, we know that the blessings that we are really thankful for are a different type," he said. "They are what our forefathers called our rights—our human rights—the right to worship as we please, to speak and to think, and to earn, and to save. Those are the rights that we must strive so mightily to merit."[15]

For Eisenhower, the "Back to God" program would offer an annual forum for his thoughts on the nation's need for religion. "In our fundamental faith, we are all one," he noted in his 1954 address. "Together, we thank the Power that has made and preserved us as a nation. By the millions, we speak prayers, we sing hymns—and no matter what their words may be, their spirit is the same—'In God is Our Trust.'" In 1955, the president ratcheted up his rhetoric, arguing that the founding fathers had recognized that all rights came from God and it was merely the state's duty to defend those rights rather than grant new ones of its own. "If the State gives rights, it can—and inevitably will—take away those rights," he warned. "Without God, there could be no American form of Government, nor an American way of life. Recognition of the Supreme Being is the first—the most basic—expression of Americanism."[16]

The "Back to God" programs that began on February 1, 1953, became an important touchstone in Eisenhower's drive to promote prayer in public life. But they paled in comparison to another annual tradition that began that same week.

MORE THAN ANY OTHER INDIVIDUAL, Senator Frank Carlson deserved credit for creating the National Prayer Breakfast. With a deeply tanned face, pointed ears, and white wings of hair, the Kansan looked, in the words of an unkind observer, "like a sunburned Bela Lugosi." Carl-son had long been active in Republican politics, serving six terms in the House and one as governor before winning a seat in the Senate in 1950. An outspoken opponent of the New Deal, he denounced Franklin Roo-sevelt as the "destroyer of human rights and freedom" for his adminis-tration's interventions in the economy. He held Harry Truman in similar contempt. "Little Caesars walk the highways of our nation, trying to tell us what to wear, eat, plant, sow and reap," Carlson complained in 1947. "It was such a time, two thousand years ago, when Rome's vaunted legions were setting up their despicable Herods over the civilized world. Let us shake this dream of conquest by lustful men from our eyes before another Pontius Pilate nails civilization to another Roman cross." When his fellow Kansan Dwight Eisenhower mulled a run for the presidency, Carlson became an early backer, helping convince the general to run and coining a campaign slogan for him: "No Deal."[17]

Senator Carlson also enthusiastically supported the growing campaign to bring religion to Washington. A devout Baptist with an ecumenical streak, he quickly became a faithful participant in the Senate prayer break-fast meetings and emerged as one of Abraham Vereide's closest confi-dants in that chamber. In December 1952, he met with Eisenhower at the president-elect's transition offices and invited him to attend one of their breakfast meetings after his inauguration. Eisenhower accepted, but Carlson soon discovered that a presidential visit would be more compli-cated than he had assumed. Their usual meeting spot, the Vandenberg Room in the Senate, only held a few dozen people, and as word spread, more and more clamored for invitations. Searching for a solution, Carlson remembered a chance encounter with hotel magnate Conrad Hilton at the Republican campaign headquarters. Although a devout Catholic, Hilton had long wanted to meet Billy Graham, who happened to be there visiting Eisenhower that day. Carlson made introductions, and a grateful Hilton promised to repay the favor. "Senator," he said, "if there ever comes a time I can be of help in a Christian or religious cause, you call me." Months later, Carlson did just that in a blunt phone call. "Mr. Hilton," the senator said, "you own the Mayflower Hotel and I'd like to have the use of your ballroom there for a breakfast, a prayer breakfast that the President of the United States will attend, and I'd like to have you pick up the check."[18]

Conrad Hilton was thrilled to host the first National Prayer Breakfast—which would be more commonly, if inaccurately, known as the Presidential Prayer Breakfast—on Thursday, February 5, 1953. Above the speaker's dais in the Mayflower ballroom, Hilton hung a large painting of a kneeling Uncle Sam, an image he had designed himself. "I visualized the portrait of Uncle Sam," he later reflected, "not weak, not knocked to his knees, but freely and confidently kneeling, knowing how to do battle for peace." While some were surprised by the gesture, it had been years in the making. The hotel magnate had worked as a member of the Committee to Proclaim Liberty to encourage religious celebrations for Independence Day in 1951; in the same spirit, he had commissioned the painting, titled "America on Its Knees," and then arranged for its publication in full-page, full-color pictorials in national magazines on Independence Day in 1952. "I felt the need of re-expressing the belief of America's founders in prayer as a vital force in national life," he remembered. To his delight, the painting proved a hit. Eisenhower soon hung a copy in the Oval Office, and Hilton distributed more than four hundred thousand others upon request. Later that year, the hotel chain president was honored with an award from the Freedoms Foundation for spreading the image across the nation.[19]

The hotel magnate Conrad Hilton commissioned this image, "America on Its Knees," for publication in newspapers and magazines on July 4, 1952. When he hosted the first National Prayer Breakfast the following February, a copy was displayed above the speaker's table. Soon after, Dwight Eisenhower hung a copy of his own in the Oval Office.

Fittingly, the official theme for the inaugural National Prayer Breakfast was "Government Under God." The crowd of more than five hundred included senators, representatives, cabinet members, ambassadors, and Supreme Court justices. So many Washington dignitaries were present that the usual rules of protocol were thrown out in the confusion. "Chief Justice Fred Vinson had to look around for a seat like everyone else," Vereide later recalled. Senator Carlson presided, with leaders of the congressional prayer breakfast groups—Representative Katharine St. George of New York and Senator Alexander Wiley of Wisconsin, both Republicans—offering the opening prayer and the scripture lesson. Vereide then led the "prayer of consecration" for the new president before Eisenhower offered brief remarks of his own. "The very basis of our government is: 'We hold that all men are endowed by their Creator' with certain rights," the president said. "In one sentence, we established that every free government is embedded soundly in a deeply-felt religious faith or it makes no sense. Today if we recall those things and if, in that sense, we can back off from our problems and depend upon a power greater than ourselves, I believe that we begin to draw these problems into focus."[20]

For the participants, the National Prayer Breakfast was both revelatory and revolutionary. Chief Justice Vinson, who had spent three decades in the capital, in all three branches of government, marveled that he had "never felt or seen anything like this in all my years here in Washington." Dr. Frederick Brown Harris, chaplain of the Senate, was equally enthusiastic in his account of the day's proceedings for the *Washington Star*. "The Return-to-God movement is more than a slogan," he insisted. "There are signs that once again, as in the former days of the Nation's true glory, America is once again bending its knees. There are increasing numbers of those in high places of governance and industry whose solemn and serious attitude is: 'I want to be a Christian, in my heart.'" The event, Reverend Harris noted excitedly, was further evidence of a "new under-God consciousness" sweeping the nation. Billy Graham certainly agreed. "This conference," he raved, "could very well be the turning point in the history of western civilization."[21]

Carlson had been the prime architect of the National Prayer Breakfast, but Vereide benefited most from the new tradition. He was thrilled at how successful the event had been and how broadly its message had been heard. "Front page publicity was given the conference by practically every newspaper throughout the United States," he reflected with pride, noting that the prayer breakfast had been reported in ninety-eight foreign countries too, with the Voice of America securing a full recording for later use. "The question now comes to me," he wrote to the White House counsel: "How may we make this event a springboard for further advances and a continuous teamwork for God and country?" For Vereide, the immediate answer was obvious, as he capitalized on the publicity by starting more prayer groups of government workers. By the following year, he had established seventeen new groups, meeting weekly at the Pentagon and the State Department, as well as the House and Senate. Vereide sought to spread the gospel of breakfast meetings to every conceivable corner of the federal government. In 1959, one of his deputies told a friendly congressman about the next stage in their expansion plans. "We would like to see new groups started soon," he specified, "in the Atomic Energy Commission, National Labor Relations Board, and the Federal Communications Commission."[22]

Vereide established prayer breakfast groups at private organizations as well, though these too were used to advance the mission of "Government Under God." For instance, after Chief Justice Vinson died in the fall of 1953 and Earl Warren was confirmed as his replacement, Vereide arranged for a "dedication ceremony" with the Army and Navy Club Breakfast Group. The event, held a few weeks after Warren's appointment, followed in the same tradition used in recent years to consecrate Vinson as well as Associate Justices Harold Burton and Tom Clark. For Warren, the gathering was nothing new. He had spoken to the Senate Prayer Breakfast years earlier and promised Vereide he would work closely with the prayer groups involved in the government of his home state of California. "I have always had an admiration for the purposes of this organization and for those men who have had the conviction to associate themselves with the movement," Warren now told the crowd of judges, politicians, and businessmen. "I think there is nothing more important in government than to keep the spirit of Christianity and the very firm belief that in these troubled times, and even if the times become more troubled, there is no problem, domestic or international, that cannot be solved by the simple principles of Christianity."[23]

While Vereide cultivated these prayer breakfast groups in official and unofficial halls of power, he worked to make the National Prayer Breakfast an enduring tradition. Interestingly, Eisenhower had originally intended to make just one visit. Billy Graham remembered the president indicating that "he would come to the first one but would not promise to come to another one; he did not want to set a precedent." But Eisenhower was so pleased with his first experience that he returned repeatedly, helping create the misconception that the National Prayer Breakfast was officially "presidential" instead. In February 1954, Eisenhower, Nixon, and several cabinet members returned to the Mayflower ballroom, along with nearly six hundred figures from government and business. Chief Justice Warren offered the main address of the morning. Speaking at length on the role of religion in American political life, he concluded that "no one can read the history of our country without realizing that the Good Book and the spirit of the Savior have, from the very beginning, been our guiding genius." Looking forward, the chief justice urged the crowd to adhere to "the spirit of Christian religion" to ensure that the country remained strong both in spirit and substance in the days and years to come. In the end, Warren stated emphatically: "We are a Christian nation."[24]

The following year, Billy Graham gave the keynote, stressing the same themes. "In the last 25 years," he said, in an unsubtle swipe at the Roosevelt and Truman administrations, "we have had a spiritual drought." During the trials of the Great Depression and the Second World War, "we departed from God and we departed from this book called the Holy Bible. . . . But during the past five years," he marveled, "something has happened. This has been an era of unprecedented religious renaissance and resurgence in the United States." As he finished, the crowd of nearly a thousand rose in a standing ovation. After Vereide delivered the closing prayer, Vice President Nixon, Chief Justice Warren, assorted members of the cabinet and the judiciary, several hundred senators and representatives, and a host of business leaders joined together, loudly singing a hymn. The lyrics were on their programs, but most knew the words by heart: "Onward Christian Soldiers, marching as to war / With the Cross of Jesus going on before. / Christ our royal Master, leads against the foe / Forward into battle, see his banner go."[25]

President Eisenhower had been unable to attend in 1955, but he made his third appearance at the February 1956 event. To commemorate the occasion, Conrad Hilton prepared a special gift: the exact desk from the Statler Hotel at which Eisenhower had written his inaugural prayer. The hotel magnate treated the desk with reverence worthy of a relic, adding a silver plaque engraved with the text. Deeply moved by the gesture, Eisenhower offered some extemporaneous remarks about his "little prayer" and the early days of his administration. "I was seeking to impress upon the audience at that moment that all of us realized a new chief executive would be inaugurated over a nation that was founded on religious faith," he explained. "Our founding documents so state in explaining our Government and what we intended to do." Immediately after the breakfast, Eisenhower had the desk placed in the Oval Office. Harold Stassen, the special assistant to the president, was so moved that he insisted that "the breakfast this morning, the words he spoke, the entire ceremony and the subsequent consequences following, will be one of the high points when future historians record this period."[26]

FOR EISENHOWER, THE "GOVERNMENT UNDER God" theme of the first prayer breakfast became a blueprint for his entire administration. The very next day, February 6, 1953, he instituted a new practice of opening all of his administration's cabinet meetings with prayer. Unlike the spontaneous prayer at the inaugural, this came as no surprise to the department heads. A few weeks earlier, they had met for a luncheon at the Commodore Hotel in New York. Ezra Taft Benson, a member of the ruling Council of Twelve Apostles of the Church of Jesus Christ of Latter-Day Saints and Eisenhower's pick to lead the Department of Agriculture, proposed that they begin with prayer. Eisenhower welcomed the suggestion and asked him to lead them in a brief moment of worship. "When the press discovered that our meeting had begun with a prayer," Benson later remembered, "reporters badgered James Hagerty, Eisenhower's press secretary, so much that he telephoned me the next day in Washington, D.C., to see if I could provide a copy." Benson had improvised the prayer and had no text to share, but after repeated pleas from the press secretary, he reconstructed it from memory and wrote it down for the press—"the only prayer I've ever written out in my life," Benson stressed. As printed, it ran for nine long paragraphs.[27]

When the president neglected to open their first formal cabinet meeting with a similar prayer, Benson asked him to institute the practice as a regular feature. "I know that without God's help we cannot succeed," he wrote. "With His help, we cannot fail." Eisenhower's new pastor encouraged the innovation as well. He reminded the president that House and Senate sessions routinely opened with prayer but, for some reason, meetings in the executive branch had rarely done the same. "Since you symbolize today a moral resurgence and spiritual counter-offensive in our world," Elson suggested, "the establishment at this time of the practice of prayer as the initial act at Cabinet meetings would have a tremendous effect upon the Cabinet and the Country." Thus persuaded, Eisenhower polled his department heads about the proposal, suggesting that "this would be a splendid and helpful habit *provided* that we unanimously— or practically unanimously—have the same desire." He included a crude ballot with choices for a spoken prayer, a silent prayer, or "no ceremony of any kind." Everyone wanted some form of prayer, with "silent" beating "spoken" by nearly a two-to-one margin, perhaps due to fears that Benson might again engage in a spiritual filibuster. Thus, at the February 6, 1953, cabinet meeting, the president announced that all their meetings would begin with a silent prayer, though individuals could request a spoken one on special occasions.[28]

The cabinet's unanimous embrace of prayer was not surprising. With only one exception, they were all conservative Protestants; several had already demonstrated their own commitment to religion in public life. Benson was not the only cabinet member who held a leadership position in his church. Secretary of State John Foster Dulles, for instance, served as an elder in the Presbyterian Church and was also a prominent leader of the National Council of Churches. The son of a minister, Dulles piously carried his religious convictions to his new post, making so many references to religion and spirituality in his official speeches that the president called him "an Old Testament prophet" while the White House press secretary likened him to a Puritan.[29] Though none of the other department heads played as prominent a role in formal church structures as Benson and Dulles, many found their own ways to embrace religion in public life. For instance, Secretary of Defense Charles Wilson and Oveta Culp Hobby, who served as administrator of the Federal Security Agency and then the first-ever secretary of health, education, and welfare, were both founding members of the Committee to Proclaim Liberty. Responding to the prayer proposals, Hobby added a handwritten note for the president: "This kind of leadership will make government service rewarding."[30]

It was natural, then, that the cabinet members made the theme of "Government Under God" manifest in their agencies. At the Department of Agriculture, Benson had his top aides pull their chairs into a semicircle around his desk to join him in "a prayer for divine blessing and guidance" before meetings. Dulles brought a similar religious sensibility to the State Department. Clergymen from a variety of faiths and political persuasions had praised his appointment, and he in turn did not disappoint them. In January 1954, for instance, the State Department published an official government pamphlet titled *The Secretary of State on Faith of Our Fathers.* "Our American political institutions are what they are because our founders were deeply religious people," Dulles wrote. "If ever the political forces in this country became irreligious, our institutions would change. The change might come about slowly, but it would come surely. Institutions born of faith will inevitably change unless they are constantly nurtured by faith."[31]

The Pentagon underwent a similarly dramatic transformation. As a new employee explained in February 1954, when he first arrived to work for the Department of Defense "I was immediately struck by signs all over the building urging employees to attend religious services held daily in the building. These services are held for the three major faiths on government time and officiated over by an Army chaplain." During the Christmas season, hymns were sung in the Pentagon's main corridors; on Good Friday, a religious service was held in the inner court. "I have worked in many federal buildings," this employee continued, "but have never seen such open and active support of religious groups and practices by federal authorities on federal property as exists at the Pentagon." Several organizations concerned about the separation of church and state confirmed the facts of his complaints but ultimately decided not to intervene. The American Jewish Congress believed "our limited energies should be expended in more significant areas," while the ACLU decided "it was not worth starting a row." The counsel for the American Jewish Committee agreed, noting he had "little doubt" that such religious activities "would not be frowned on in an administration where cabinet meetings are opened with prayer."[32]

As Eisenhower's cabinet focused its attention on spiritual rewards yet to come, its members faced the danger that the press and the public might focus more on the earthly riches they had already amassed. Secretary of Defense Charles Wilson had been the country's highest-paid executive as president of General Motors, the world's largest private corporation. Wilson's initial refusal to divest his holdings in the corporation, which had nearly $5 billion worth of contracts with the same federal department he would now lead, had delayed his confirmation and tarnished his image. When asked whether his GM holdings would tempt him to favor his corporation over his nation, Wilson famously answered that he always thought "what was good for our country was good for General Motors, and vice versa." The auto tycoon eventually agreed to release his shares, but he was not the only top Defense Department official whose business associations gave the appearance of impropriety. Deputy Secretary Roger Kyes had been in charge of procurement for General Motors; Secretary of the Army Robert Ten Broeck Stevens's family textile company made uniforms for that branch of the military; Secretary of the Air Force Harold Talbott had ties to both Chrysler and North American Aviation; and Secretary of the Navy Robert Anderson—put in the post at Sid Richardson's recommendation—had previously managed a major facility for Associated Refineries. There were so many apparent conflicts of interest for the businessmen now running the Pentagon that, in his first official act, Wilson banned department officials from dealing with any companies in which they had any financial stake.[33]

Though he attracted a considerable deal of scrutiny, Wilson was by no means the only corporate titan in the Eisenhower cabinet. Treasury Secretary George Humphrey, for instance, had long served as president of the Mark A. Hanna Company of Cleveland, a sprawling conglomerate with interests in coal, oil, natural gas, iron, steel, copper, rayon, plastics, shipping, and banking. (A fellow cabinet member called him "the Ohio Tycoon" for the sake of brevity.) Commerce Secretary Sinclair Weeks, a

New England financier and banker, was such a zealous advocate for business that Eisenhower privately worried that he "seems so completely conservative in his views that at times he seems to be illogical." Postmaster General Arthur Summerfield ran one of the nation's largest automobile agencies but also found success in real estate, oil, and insurance, while Hobby had made her fortune as a Texas newspaper publisher. Although not businessmen themselves, both Dulles and Brownell had close ties to the corporate world from their time at two of New York's oldest law firms; Dulles had reportedly earned more in billings than any other corporate attorney in America. The glaring exception in the cabinet's cast of business figures was Secretary of Labor Martin Durkin, who was not only the sole Catholic in the group but also an avowed Democrat and union man. At the group's first meeting, Benson observed that "Durkin seemed a little uncomfortable, as though he felt a Democratic labor leader was out of place in this conservative gathering from the world of American business and finance." Others noticed as well. In a famous quip, Richard Strout of the *New Republic* joked that "Ike has picked a cabinet of eight millionaires and a plumber." An awkward fit from the beginning, Durkin lasted just eight months before he resigned.[34]

The presence of the corporate elite in the Eisenhower cabinet was so pronounced that some observers wondered if the Republicans had changed direction from the New Deal a bit *too* abruptly. "There is bigness all around the White House: General Motors, the Chase bank, Dillon Reed, Continental Can," noted *The Nation*. "We wish President Eisenhower well, but fear that in surrounding himself with Big Dealers he has cut himself off from the millions of little people who elected him." Such complaints might have been expected from a liberal magazine, but corporate leaders were equally worried. Accordingly, several enlisted the Opinion Research Corporation of Princeton, New Jersey, to determine whether the American people thought the new administration was too attuned to the needs of big business. Not surprisingly, Republicans were wholly supportive of the presence of corporate leaders in the cabinet, with 90 percent approving; independents and Democrats, however, were not far behind, with 79 and 68 percent satisfied, respectively. Americans did worry about the abilities of these officials to root out corruption in their departments and to understand the plight of ordinary people, but in general they were willing to give the business leaders in charge of their government a chance to prove themselves. In a personal letter to his friend Sinclair Weeks, Opinion Research's president, Claude Robinson, suggested that there was a "strong feeling that business leadership is a package which can be merchandised successfully if we would but use our imaginations on it."[35]

Business leaders, of course, had long been working to "merchandise" themselves through the appropriation of religion. In organizations such as Spiritual Mobilization, the prayer breakfast groups, and the Freedoms Foundation, they had linked capitalism and Christianity and, at the same time, likened the welfare state to godless paganism. After decades of work, these businessmen believed their efforts had finally paid off with the election of Dwight Eisenhower. Watching him enthusiastically embrace public faith, these supporters assumed that the national religious revival was largely a means to a more important end: the rollback of the New Deal state. But they soon realized that, for all his sympathies for and associations with business leaders, Eisenhower saw the religious revival itself as his essential domestic duty. To their amazement, once in office he gave relatively little thought to the political and economic causes that his backers had always seen as the real reason for that revival.

Eisenhower did agree with his supporters about the need to reduce the regulatory role of the federal government, especially its oversight of the business world. "I believe this country is following a dangerous trend when it permits too great a degree of centralization of government functions," he wrote his brother in 1954. "When we came into office there were Federal controls exercised over prices, wages, rents, as well as over the allocation and use of raw materials. The first thing this Administration did was to set about the elimination of those controls." But he refused to go further, especially when it came to the welfare state that his supporters had long worked to destroy. Despite his personal sympathies with their position, the president believed "the mass of the people" disagreed. "Should any political party attempt to abolish social security, unemployment insurance, and eliminate labor laws and farm programs, you would not hear of that party again in our political history," he warned. "There is a tiny splinter group, of course, that believes you can do these things. Among them are H. L. Hunt . . . , a few other Texas oil millionaires, and an occasional politician or business man from other areas. Their number is negligible and they are stupid."[36]

Even though Eisenhower's rise to power had depended on support from "Texas oil millionaires" such as Sid Richardson, he refused to roll back the welfare state they despised. In fundamental ways, he ensured the longevity of the New Deal, giving a bipartisan stamp of approval to its continuation and significantly expanding its reach. Notably, Eisenhower pushed Congress to extend Social Security coverage to another ten million Americans and increase benefits as well. In his first term, the president repeatedly resisted calls from conservatives to cut education spending; in his second, he secured an additional $1 billion for the cause. On a much larger scale, Eisenhower established the single largest public works project in American history with the interstate highway system, a massive undertaking whose costs soon exceeded the original estimate of $101 billion. As government spending increased, meanwhile, the president did little to bring down tax rates for the wealthy; the top bracket barely dipped, declining from 94 percent to 92 percent over the course of his two terms in office. By then, more of Eisenhower's former admirers from the business world agreed with Senator Barry Goldwater's assessment that his presidency had offered Americans little more than a cheap imitation of the Democratic agenda. The Eisenhower administration seemed, in the conservative champion's memorable phrase, just a "dime-store New Deal."[37]

Eisenhower had, however, accomplished one of the goals he ostensibly shared with his supporters from the business world. His administration succeeded in sacralizing the state, swiftly implementing a host of religious ceremonies and symbols and thereby inscribing—quite literally, in many ways—an apparently permanent public religion on the institutions of American government. Unlike Christian libertarians, who had long presented God and government as rivals, Eisenhower had managed to merge the two into a wholesome "government under God." In doing so, he ironically undercut the key argument of many of his earlier backers, making their old claims about the "pagan" origins of statism seem suddenly obsolete. The state was now suffused with religion, and so it would remain.

FOR CONSERVATIVES WHO HAD ASSUMED that the success of "under-God consciousness" during the Eisenhower administration would naturally lead to tangible reductions in the welfare state, his time in office was a disappointment. But for those who welcomed the religious revival on its own terms, the Eisenhower administration was a turning point. In April 1953, for instance, an official with the National Association of Evangelicals (NAE) praised the president for the pious example he had set. "With you, the churches and Christian leaders in these United States have a profound belief in Almighty God and the freedom of all men under Him," noted Clyde Taylor. "Religious congregations all over America have been greatly strengthened by the simple, unabashed, public stand which you have taken, demonstrating your belief in God, especially in your inaugural prayer to Him for strength and guidance." As the NAE's representative in Washington, Taylor informed the president about its plan to hold a "Capital Crusade Day" on Independence Day that year and requested his participation in ceremonies held at the base of the Washington Monument. The event would feature prominent Christian leaders drawn from the ranks of government, education, industry, and entertainment. Gathered together, they would launch a yearlong "March of Freedom," which would be heavily promoted across the nation. The goal, Taylor noted, was "rekindling the fires of enthusiasm of the American people for freedom under God."[38]

The National Association of Evangelicals was a relatively new organization, little more than a decade old, and White House staffers who were unfamiliar with it were initially inclined to reject the request. A check with the Library of Congress, however, revealed that the association represented more than ten million Americans from thirty-five different Protestant denominations and was, in fact, "thoroughly reputable," with "some of the finest preachers in the country included in its membership." Accordingly, Eisenhower's staff brought the matter to his attention. (As they passed along the NAE proposal, they clipped to it a note about a separate request from Fifield, seeking a presidential proclamation for the third annual "Freedom Under God" ceremony scheduled for the same day. "While it is an entirely separate undertaking from that of the National Association of Evangelicals," an official noted, "it seems to me that it is a similar movement.") The president's staff recommended avoiding making any commitment, but Eisenhower decided it was a cause that deserved his time.[39]

In a dramatic show of support, Eisenhower took part in a signing ceremony for a religious manifesto that organizers called the "Statement of Seven Divine Freedoms." Derived from Psalm 23, the seven freedoms formed what an NAE official called "a simple basic scriptural statement of the Spiritual source of Freedom" in the United States of America. Promotional posters detailed the list of freedoms and the specific verses of the psalm that supported them:

1. FREEDOM FROM WANT:
   "The Lord is my shepherd, I shall not want" (v. 1)
2. FREEDOM FROM HUNGER:
   "He maketh me to lie down in green pastures:" (v. 2a)
3. FREEDOM FROM THIRST:
   "He leadeth me beside the still waters" (v. 2b)
4. FREEDOM FROM SIN:
   "He restoreth my soul: he leadeth me in the paths of righteousness for His name's sake." (v. 3)
5. FREEDOM FROM FEAR:
   "Yea, though I walk through the valley of the shadow of death, I will fear no evil: for thou art with me; thy rod and thy staff they comfort me." (v. 4)
6. FREEDOM FROM ENEMIES:
   "Thou preparest a table before me in the presence of mine enemies." (v. 5)
7. FREEDOM TO LIVE ABUNDANTLY:
   "Thou anointest my head with oil; my cup runneth over. Surely goodness and mercy shall follow me all the days of my life; and I will dwell in the house of the Lord forever." (vv. 5–6)

In all, the Seven Divine Freedoms were intended both to reflect and to reject the famous Four Freedoms advanced by Franklin Roosevelt more than a decade before. They were clearly patterned on that precedent, closely echoing Roosevelt's quartet of freedom of speech, freedom of worship, freedom from want, and freedom from fear, with the last two repeated verbatim. But the Seven Divine Freedoms, with their invocation of biblical authority, were meant to trump the "human freedoms" that Roosevelt had enumerated.[40]

As with earlier drives to supplant the secular authority of the welfare state with the higher power of the Almighty, the Seven Divine Freedoms

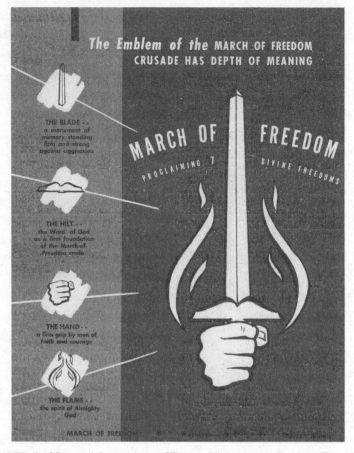

In July 1953, the National Association of Evangelicals arranged to have Eisenhower, Nixon, and other high-ranking officials sign a statement declaring that the United States government was based on biblical principles. In this promotional poster for this "March of Freedom" event, the Washington Monument is joined to the Holy Bible to symbolize the fusion of freedom and faith. *Courtesy of Wheaton College, Archives & Special Collections.*

ultimately served an earthly purpose. Organizers made the political aims of the project explicit in their plans. "There is a growing realization that the enemies of freedom are not foreign powers," observed R. L. Decker, the NAE's executive director, "but that there are forces at work within the nation which are just as dangerous and more sinister than any foreign foe. These forces take advantage of the natural desires of the people for unity and security and material prosperity to propose panaceas for our social, economic, and political problems which, if accepted, would rob us of our

freedom as effectively as defeat in warfare," he continued. "Our only protection against such forces is a real revival of the spiritual life from which
freedom flowed through our founding fathers into the very essence of
American life." A promotional pamphlet noted that the March of Freedom
was designed "to change the pattern of thinking about our nation from the
present prevailing socialistic, collectivist, secularist, agnostic pattern to the
original God-centered freedom ideal as expressed in the Declaration of
Independence and the Preamble to the United States Constitution."[41]

As the Fourth of July approached, the NAE promoted the event thoroughly. The Jaeger and Jessen advertising agency of Chicago blanketed
the country with publicity that stressed Eisenhower's involvement in, and
inspiration for, the movement. An early promotional booklet, for instance,
repeatedly referenced the prayer he offered at his inauguration. "Our President touched a deep need of each heart when one day he voiced these
words: 'At such a time in history we who are free must proclaim anew
our faith,'" it read. "President Eisenhower's spark of faith set the fires of
hope burning in the hearts of Christian people throughout the country."
Moreover, these materials stressed how other "leading Christian citizens"
would be involved. Senator Carlson agreed to lead the national sponsoring committee, which had 177 members, one for "each year of freedom
since the signing of the Declaration of Independence." The group would
encourage public and private leaders to sign the "Statement of Seven Divine Freedoms" and thereby signify that the United States of America had
been founded on the principles of the Holy Bible.[42]

Eisenhower was the first to sign, in an Oval Office ceremony on July
2, 1953. "This is the kind of thing I like to do," he said afterward. "This
statement is simple and understandable, and sets forth the basic truth
which is the foundation of our freedoms." Nixon added his name next,
as did members of the cabinet. The administration's support was just the
beginning of the document's journey. "It is being carried in a real MARCH
OF FREEDOM to each Justice of the Supreme Court, and then the MARCH
will include each state capitol, to be signed by the Governors," the NAE
reported. "As each capitol is reached, MARCH OF FREEDOM rallies will be
held all through that state." The document would travel across the nation,
they promised, gaining support as it went, ultimately returning to the nation's capital for a major event at the base of the Washington Monument

on the following Fourth of July. "By means of the radio, motion pictures, television, newspaper and periodical advertisements, signboards and posters, essay contests and amateur dramatics as well as community rallies, sermons and editorials," Decker insisted, "this theme 'Freedom is of God and we must have faith in him' can constantly be dinned into the consciousness of America."[43]

The March of Freedom campaign was an unparalleled success, but the movement's underlying emphasis on framing Independence Day festivities as a religious event was, by this point, nothing new. In 1953, the "Freedom Under God" movement of Spiritual Mobilization entered its third year, beginning with a monthlong series of radio specials on the program *The Freedom Story*, local speeches and sermons on the theme, and festivities on the Fourth. Ever more popular with the public, the third annual festivities were sponsored by organizations such as the Amvets, the American Legion, Kiwanis clubs, Moose lodges, the Boys' Clubs of America, and the USO. Governors and mayors across the nation once again issued proclamations attesting that "our government is a government under God."[44]

At the same time, Eisenhower declared—like Truman before him—that Independence Day would be officially designated as a National Day of Prayer. He had apparently planned on doing so from the start of his administration, but found himself following through after prompting from Bishop Fulton Sheen on his popular television show. In a May broadcast, the Catholic prelate reminded his millions of viewers of Eisenhower's inaugural address, in which "God was not an after-thought, but a pre-thought and a dedication." "For this reason," he wrote the president, they knew "you would be sensitive to the appeals of the American people for such humbling of ourselves before God, that we may be exalted as a nation." The White House received so many letters urging the president to make the holiday a holy day that it issued what aides called "a blanket acknowledgment" in a press conference. A formal proclamation from the president soon followed, again designating "July 4, 1953—the one hundred and seventy-seventh anniversary of the adoption of the Declaration of Independence in firm reliance on God's transcendent power—as a National Day of Prayer." The president formally requested that "all of our people turn to Him in humble supplication on that day, in their homes or in their respective places of worship."[45]

For his part, Eisenhower spent the day at the presidential retreat at Camp David. Though he had already done much to revive religion in national life in his first few months in office, critics seized upon his vacation as a sign of insincerity. "The greatest demonstration of the religious character of this administration came on July Fourth, which the President told us all to spend as a day of penance and prayer," noted radio commentator Elmer Davis. "Then he himself caught four fish in the morning, played eighteen holes of golf in the afternoon, and spent the evening at the bridge table." In truth, Eisenhower had gone to great lengths to find a place of worship near Camp David. "I sent out a scout to search the countryside," he wrote a few days later, "to find for me a church that I could go for a short service. He visited six towns, only to discover that none of them was holding a special service on the 4th," which that year fell on a Saturday. "I did get to church on the 5th, but it struck me that it was odd that the ministers in that region did not feel they could develop enough interest among their parishioners to make it worth while to have a short service on the 4th." Despite everything Eisenhower had done to encourage a religious revival in the nation, much more work was needed.[46]

CHAPTER 4

Pledging Allegiance

T HERE ARE FEW QUIET DAYS in Washington, D.C., but Monday, May 17, 1954, was particularly frantic. For nearly a month, some twenty million Americans had been watching the dramatic showdown between Senator Joseph McCarthy and the United States Army in congressional hearings broadcast live on ABC and the DuMont network. But that morning, President Eisenhower stunned the nation by barring all Pentagon officials from testifying, and suddenly McCarthyism's climactic battle came to an abrupt halt. Then, only hours later and a block away, the United States Supreme Court issued its long-awaited ruling in the school desegregation case of *Brown v. Board of Education*. At 12:52 p.m., Chief Justice Earl Warren began delivering the unanimous opinion that tore down the constitutional foundation for racial segregation, speaking slowly but surely in awareness of the moment's importance. When he finished at 1:20 p.m., wire services sent the news across the nation as the Voice of America trumpeted it around the globe in thirty-four languages. Riveted by these events, reporters gave little thought to the hearings taking place that afternoon in Room 424 of the Senate Office Building, where a subcommittee of the Judiciary Committee sat to consider a proposed amendment to the Constitution of the United States. If passed, it would have declared, "This Nation devoutly recognizes the authority and law of Jesus Christ, Saviour and Ruler of nations through whom are bestowed the blessings of Almighty God."[1]

The campaign for this "Christian amendment" had been under way, in fits and starts, for nearly a century. Like most efforts to add religious elements to American political culture, the idea originated during the Civil War. In 1861, several northern ministers came to believe that the conflict was the result of the godlessness of the Constitution. "We are reaping the effects of its implied atheism," they warned, and only a direct acknowledgment of Christ's authority could correct such an "atheistic error in our prime conceptions of Government." These clergymen banded together to create the National Reform Association, an organization that was single-mindedly dedicated to promoting the Christian amendment. It won the support of prominent governors, senators, judges, theologians, college presidents, and professors. "It can never be out of season to explain and enforce mortal dependence on Almighty God," Senator Charles Sumner of Massachusetts applauded. Despite his own frequent invocations of faith, however, Lincoln ignored the calls for an amendment, and the effort stalled. Campaigns devoted to the cause appeared sporadically in the decades that followed, but they all failed to find traction.[2]

The religious revival of the Eisenhower era, however, gave this long-frustrated movement its best chance yet. In 1954, Republican senator Ralph Flanders of Vermont advanced a new version of the amendment in what would be its latest and greatest campaign. Bald with a short, sandy-colored mustache, wire-rimmed glasses, and a pipe perpetually in hand, the soft-spoken seventy-three-year-old did not look the part of a conservative firebrand. But his convictions ran deep. A former industrialist and head of the Federal Reserve Bank in Boston, Flanders had been an outspoken opponent of the New Deal, which he believed was designed "to establish permanent Federal control over business." "A fundamentalist on free enterprise," in the words of a *Saturday Evening Post* profile, Flanders was no different when it came to his faith. Soon after his arrival in Washington, he became a loyal ally of Abraham Vereide, serving as a regular participant in the Senate prayer breakfasts and then chair of his International Council for Christian Leadership. Spurred on by these associations, the senator revived the Christian amendment and advanced it further along the legislative process than ever before. Though overlooked at the time, the 1954 Senate hearings represented a major milestone.[3]

Despite such progress, advocates of the Christian amendment still faced an inherently difficult challenge in the Senate. By its very nature, their proposal to change the Constitution forced them to acknowledge that the religious invocation was something new for the document. The founding fathers had felt no need to acknowledge "the law and authority of Jesus Christ," and neither had subsequent generations of American legislators. Some of the more imaginative advocates of the Christian amendment at the Senate hearings simply waved away this history and argued that leaders such as Washington and Lincoln had supported the idea even if they never acted upon it. For evidence, they repeatedly made reference in their testimony to letters and meetings in which these presidents allegedly had lent support to their cause. At the hearings, the presiding senator kindly offered to have these documents inserted into the official transcript once they were found. But the published record provided a quiet rebuke to such claims, noting that inquiries to the Library of Congress and other authoritative sources showed that the alleged documents did not, in fact, exist.[4]

Other supporters of the Christian amendment took a different, if equally imaginative, approach to the issue of original intent. R. E. Robb, a newspaper columnist from South Carolina, compiled a collection of religious invocations from American history, stretching from the Mayflower Compact of 1620 to early twentieth-century America. From them, he testified, "we are warranted in stating categorically that this is in fact basically and fundamentally a Christian nation." However, Robb admitted, "the Nation itself does not say so. Its official spokesman, its written or enacted Constitution, is silent on the subject." No matter; there was another "unwritten and vital" constitution whose authority superseded the written one. "The vital, the actual Constitution of this Nation is and always has been Christian, from the first settlers down to the present," Robb argued. "But the written Constitution, which should accurately reflect the vital Constitution, is sadly lacking in respect to its acknowledgment of Jesus Christ as the Supreme Ruler and His law as the supreme authority of the Nation." Therefore, it needed to be amended.[5]

There was, according to advocates of the Christian amendment, ample evidence of the religious intent of this unwritten constitution, intent that had been expressed in a variety of official and unofficial ways. The head of the National Reform Association, a Presbyterian minister from Los Angeles named J. Renwick Patterson, presented the Senate with a litany of examples showing how "the spiritual has been woven into the fabric of American life" as part of the "unwritten law of the land." He singled out the public prayers given in presidential inaugurations and congressional sessions, the chaplains employed by the military and Congress whose salaries were paid with public funds, the tax-exempt status of churches, and the traditional notion of Sunday as a day of rest. "All of these things testify to the place Christianity had had in the past and continues to have in our national life," Patterson noted. "But when it comes to our Constitution, our fundamental law, there is complete silence regarding God. He isn't even mentioned. There is no recognition, no acknowledgment. In our Constitution there is absolutely nothing to undergird and give legal sanction to the religious practices mentioned above." Recognizing there was no constitutional authority for these activities, he argued not that these practices should be abandoned but rather that the Constitution should be rewritten to support them.[6]

The 1954 campaign for the Christian amendment failed, as had all the previous ones. Nevertheless, Patterson's observations about religious references in American political life remained an important point. Two years earlier, in a unanimous opinion for the Supreme Court case of *Zorach v. Clauson*, Justice William O. Douglas had taken note of some of these same examples of public religiosity—"prayers in our legislative halls; the appeals to the Almighty in the messages of the Chief Executive; the proclamations making Thanksgiving Day a holiday; 'so help me God' in our courtroom oaths"—and asserted that they did not represent a violation of the First Amendment doctrine of separation of church and state. Notably, the liberal Douglas used these examples exactly as the conservative Patterson would in 1954: to draw a stark conclusion. "We are," Douglas stated matter-of-factly, "a religious people whose institutions presuppose a Supreme Being." The Constitution, the Court seemed to say, might not officially acknowledge the authority and law of God, but neither would it object to any government official who did.[7]

A decade later, in a 1962 lecture at Brown University, the dean of Yale Law School, Eugene Rostow, referred to these extraconstitutional religious practices in American political life as "ceremonial deism." His choice of words captured the conventional wisdom on these issues well. The invocation of "deism" called to mind the specific religious practice of many of the founding fathers, of course, but it also reflected the ways in which public acknowledgments of a deity tended to be vague and divorced from any particular sect. "God" was regularly invoked; "Jesus Christ" rarely, if ever. While other crusades for public religiosity had stressed a Christian identity—often an implicitly Protestant Christian identity, as seen in the work of Spiritual Mobilization or the International Council for Christian Leadership—the God celebrated in acts of ceremonial deism was more easily embraced by other faiths. Indeed, during the 1950s, Catholics played pivotal roles in spreading such religious symbolism, especially with the twin mottos that represented the pinnacle of the phenomenon: "In God We Trust" and "one nation under God." Catholic congressmen wrote much of the key legislation that enabled these changes, Catholic fraternal organizations lobbied for their passage, and leaders in the Catholic clergy lent their support. Jews, for the most part, were supportive as well, with prominent rabbis and leading Jewish congressmen sanctioning the changes. Much like the public statements of President Eisenhower, the "deism" of such invocations welcomed a wide range of religious worship.[8]

Rostow's framing of these religious references as "ceremonial" in nature was also telling. In the eyes of the law—even a stalwart liberal such as Justice Douglas—these invocations were ceremonial in the sense that they were merely ornamental. They had no meaningful substance, and as a result, courts routinely held that those who objected to their use had no standing to challenge them. Legal scholars likewise dismissed the importance of these issues, as Rostow did when he characterized them as "so conventional and uncontroversial as to be constitutional." Surprisingly, this attitude was echoed by the era's most vigilant guardians of the wall separating church and state. The American Civil Liberties Union, for instance, paid practically no attention to these issues when they were considered before Congress. As McCarthyism consumed the country, the ACLU focused its energies there. Protestants and Other Americans United for the Separation of Church and State (POAU), the most significant organization of its kind, worried largely about Catholic organizations seeking public money for parochial schools. Although they raised a few pro forma objections, these civil liberties organizations largely acceded to the argument, made often by proponents of ceremonial deism, that the First Amendment mandated the separation of church and state, not the separation of religion and politics. Support for a specific sect, especially when it came to the use of taxpayer money or government policy, was beyond the pale. But general support for the sacred was perfectly fine. Like many others, these civil liberties organizations believed official invocations of a vague "God" had no substance or significance.[9]

And yet the "ceremonial" nature of public religious invocations did not diminish their importance. Quite the contrary—it vested them with incredible weight. In the eyes of many Americans, the official embrace of religion by the nation's leaders was, in effect, as politically significant and legally binding as any formal amendment to the Constitution possibly could have been. This religious revival in government, which had begun in earnest with Eisenhower's innovations, rapidly expanded as legislators got into the spirit. Though Congress dismissed the 1954 Christian amendment, during that very same session legislators enthusiastically and, indeed, effortlessly adopted the religious mottos "In God We Trust" and "one nation under God," as well as a host of other changes that echoed and amplified this theme. These measures may not have had the legal impact of a constitutional amendment, but they were, for all intents and purposes, formal acknowledgments that the United States government recognized the law and authority of Almighty God. In the end, the "unwritten constitution" was written into American law and life after all.

THE ORIGINAL PLEDGE OF ALLEGIANCE, much like the Constitution itself, did not acknowledge the existence of God. Its author, Francis Bellamy, a Baptist minister from Rome, New York, was a decidedly religious man, but when he wrote the pledge in the 1890s he described himself as something that would seem an oxymoron in Eisenhower's America: a "Christian socialist." A first cousin of Edward Bellamy, author of the 1888 socialist utopian novel *Looking Backward*, Francis Bellamy helped found the Society of Christian Socialists a year later in order "to show that the aim of socialism is embraced in the aim of Christianity" and "to awaken members of Christian Churches to the fact that the teachings

of Jesus Christ lead directly to some specific form or forms of Socialism."
He became so busy spreading the gospel of Christian socialism that he
left the ministry in 1891. Soon after, he went to work for *Youth's Companion* magazine, touring America to promote a commemoration of the four
hundredth anniversary of Christopher Columbus's arrival. In his public
lectures, Bellamy promoted "a new Americanism." The old interpretations
of liberty, he said, "had meant liberty for great corporations to oppress the
people" and "liberty for the atoms on the top of the sand heap to press
down harder and harder on the atoms below." But America had "had
enough of that kind of liberty." Instead, the nation needed liberty for all
Americans, a true equality that would ensure that "every man shall have
the equal right to work and earn bread for his family; that every child
shall be taken and given as good a chance as the government can afford."[10]

In that spirit, Bellamy organized a national program of public school
celebrations for Columbus Day in 1892. His plans centered on a then-
novel proposal for every schoolhouse in the nation to display the American flag and lead students through a brief ceremony celebrating it and the
country it represented. The idea quickly caught on. After a White House
meeting with President Benjamin Harrison, Bellamy secured a congressional resolution making Columbus Day a national holiday. The next step
was arranging for the program, which in Bellamy's mind would involve
"an original Carol, an original Address, [and] an original Ode, prepared
by the best American writers." With his attention fixed on these matters,
Bellamy paid little attention to the comparatively minor details of the flag
salute. A colleague who had been assigned that duty was unable to come
up with anything suitable, however, and Bellamy had to tackle it himself.
He spent only two hours drafting the pledge, but he was satisfied with the
result: "I pledge allegiance to my Flag and to the Republic for which it
stands—one Nation indivisible—with Liberty and Justice for all."[11]

Though widely used in the 1892 Columbus Day ceremonies, Bellamy's
pledge did not officially become *the* pledge until after the Second World
War. Indeed, at the turn of the century, a number of different pledges
competed for the loyalty of American schoolchildren. In New York State,
schools that held flag ceremonies had a choice of five pledges, none of
which made any reference to a deity. In San Francisco, the sixty different
public schools followed their own preferences, resulting in a considerable

range of pledges. Only after the First World War was there any real effort to select a single pledge for the entire nation, a movement that peaked with a pair of National Flag Conferences in 1923 and 1924. Concerns over labor radicalism and new immigration from southern and eastern Europe were widespread at the time, and Bellamy, by this point in his late sixties and much more conservative, offered his pledge as the solution. He argued that it would dispel the influence of a wide variety of domestic radicals, "including direct action communists and revolutionary socialists who are boring into the labor unions and are inciting revolt among all classes of working people." To ensure the loyalty of new immigrants, his pledge was altered in 1923 to change the somewhat vague "my flag" to "the flag of the United States." (In case the country in question remained unclear, "of America" was added the following year.) "This pledge," *Time* later noted, "rapidly became a fixture of U.S. school life, as standard as Palmer penmanship and chewed erasers." In December 1945, an act of Congress finally made it the official Pledge of Allegiance to the American flag.[12]

Through all these various revisions, the pledge remained godless. But as the Christian libertarian movement of "under-God consciousness" swept the nation in the early 1950s, a campaign to add that phrase to the pledge began in earnest. The idea originated with the Knights of Columbus, a leading Catholic fraternal organization. In April 1951, its Supreme Board of Directors adopted a resolution requiring its Fourth Degree Assemblies—divisions devoted to the promotion of patriotism, of which there were 750 in all—to insert "under God" after the words "one nation" when reciting the pledge at their meetings. As the phrase gained greater prominence during the "Freedom Under God" festivities held on the Fourth of July that year and the next, the Knights decided all Americans would benefit from their revision. In 1952, the national board of the organization called on Congress to add "under God" to the pledge, with copies of the resolution sent to President Harry Truman, Vice President Alben Barkley, and Speaker of the House Sam Rayburn. Moreover, the Knights of Columbus urged its nearly six hundred thousand members to write their representatives in Congress about it as well.[13]

In April 1953, Representative Louis C. Rabaut, a Democrat from suburban Detroit, received one such letter. While "outwardly brusque," a newspaper profile noted, the elderly congressman consistently displayed a "soft spot" for children's issues, perhaps because he had nine children and twenty-nine grandchildren of his own. A devout Catholic—one son was a Jesuit priest and three of his daughters were nuns—Rabaut was immediately taken with the arguments for adding "under God" to the Pledge of Allegiance. He soon introduced a bill to do just that, saying that the words would serve as "public proclamation of our religious traditions and our dependence on divine providence." The congressman noted in passing that an acknowledgment of God in the pledge would serve as a "bulwark against communism," but his argument focused on the relationship between religion and individual freedom. "It is my hope that the recitation of the pledge, with this addition, 'under God,' by our schoolchildren will bring to them a deeper understanding of the real meaning of patriotism," Rabaut said. "Love of country is a devotion to an institution that finds its origin and development in the moral law and commands our respect and allegiance so long as it provides that liberty and justice for all in which freemen can work out their own immortal destinies. Our country was born under God," the congressman insisted, "and only under God will it live as a citadel of freedom."[14]

Rabaut's emergence as chief congressional champion of the pledge proposal demonstrated how quickly the campaign for "under-God consciousness" had spread beyond the original intentions of its creators. In its early years, Protestant leaders—ministers such as Fifield, Vereide, and Graham and laymen such as Eisenhower and Pew—had championed a slate of events and ideas that, while nominally ecumenical, were in practical terms overwhelmingly Protestant in composition and character. Soon enough, however, Catholics such as the Knights of Columbus and Rabaut had joined the cause. Over the previous decade, Catholic politicians and lay organizations had been on the defensive, as Protestants complained about their ambition to secure public funding for parochial schools. But Rabaut was evidence that Catholics could blend religion and politics in ways that Protestants not only accepted but applauded. And if his religion was notable, his politics were too. In 1953, the Michigan congressman received a perfect rating from Americans for Democratic Action (ADA), the progressive organization founded by prominent liberals including Reinhold Niebuhr, Walter Reuther, and Eleanor Roosevelt. The involvement of liberal Democrats such as Rabaut demonstrated that the "under-God" campaign had moved well beyond the original intent of Christian libertarians who hoped it would undermine the New Deal.[15]

The popular reaction to Rabaut's proposal showed how support for the campaign of "under-God consciousness" now spread across the spectrum of both religion and politics. In May 1953, a Gallup poll reported that 69 percent of Americans favored adding "under God" to the pledge, with only 21 percent opposed and 10 percent undecided. Catholics and Protestants overwhelmingly favored the idea, with a majority of Jews supporting it as well. At the grass roots, Democrats and Republicans alike rallied around the idea. Yet the House initially made no effort to act on Rabaut's bill. The Knights of Columbus renewed their campaign, while other fraternal organizations, including the American Legion, announced their support as well. Yet Congress still failed to act.[16]

It ultimately took a sermon from a Presbyterian to prompt action. Reverend George M. Docherty, a tall Scotsman with thinning brown hair, had been recruited in 1950 to take over New York Avenue Presbyterian Church in Washington, D.C. Known as "the church of the presidents" because fourteen chief executives, including Lincoln, had worshiped there, it held a prominent position both within Presbyterian circles and in popular culture at large. (Reverend Peter Marshall, Docherty's predecessor in the pulpit, had been a world-renowned minister and author. The 1955 film based on his life, *A Man Called Peter*, was nominated for an Academy Award.) Docherty took over the pastorate of New York Avenue Presbyterian before he turned forty, and he was immediately marked as a rising star. Though he did not become an American citizen for another decade, he was an early convert to the campaign to merge religion and patriotism in the nation he now called home. When Billy Graham held services at the Capitol in February 1952, for instance, Docherty sat at a place of honor on the platform and offered his full-throated support to the endeavor. "I am certain," he told a reporter from the *Post*, "that this young man is being used by God in the Nation's Capital to remind all of us of the sovereignty of God."[17]

A few months later, Docherty had his own chance to be used by God, when he addressed the Washington Pilgrimage of American Churchmen. As its name suggested, the Pilgrimage involved hundreds of leading laymen and church figures, representing several faiths from across the country, converging on the capital. Believing that "faith is the foundation of freedom," they visited various shrines and monuments in order "to demonstrate to the world that belief in God has served as the basis of American government and the democratic way of life." As he mulled his thoughts on that theme, Docherty was drawn to the Gettysburg Address, especially Lincoln's hope that "this nation, under God, shall have a new birth of freedom." When a chance conversation with his second-grader son turned to the Pledge of Allegiance, Docherty realized that the flag salute failed to follow Lincoln's example of acknowledging God. He decided to make the omission the central theme of his May 1952 address. "It was received by the Washington Pilgrims with acclamation," he later remembered. "But after the congratulations and the ceremonies of presentation, the Washington Pilgrimage did nothing about it." According to the *Post,* "several of Dr. Docherty's colleagues in this city declared it would violate the principle of separation of church and state" and therefore "dropped the idea" of pursuing it further. The minister remained undeterred and held on to the sermon.[18]

Docherty found an opportune chance to deliver it again when Dwight Eisenhower attended the annual "Lincoln Sunday" service at New York Avenue Presbyterian on February 7, 1954. That morning, the president and First Lady sat in the same pew where Lincoln had once prayed, with the remainder of the fourteen-hundred-seat sanctuary filled to capacity. "At this season of anniversary of the birth of Lincoln," Docherty began, "it will not be inappropriate to speak about freedom, and what is called 'the American way of life.'" That phrase was at once intimately familiar yet fairly vague, the Scotsman noted, so he illustrated its meaning with images that might have come from Madison Avenue: baseball games, popcorn, Coca-Cola, Sears, Roebuck, and so on. "And where did all this come from?" Docherty asked. "It was brought here by people who laid stress on fundamentals. They called themselves Puritans." While it is easy to scoff at the idea that postwar America's obsession with consumer goods could be traced back to the staid Puritans, Docherty's argument resonated with an audience accustomed to such rhetoric. These "Fathers of a Mighty Nation," he continued, had carried to the New World certain "fundamental concepts of life" taken from the teachings of Moses and Jesus Christ, and those religious concepts still represented the true heart of the nation. "This," he concluded, "is the 'American Way of Life.'"[19]

Even though religious principles were central to the nation's character, Docherty believed there was little evidence of them in public professions of patriotism. Turning to the Pledge of Allegiance, the Scotsman told the assembled that he had an advantage over American parents who listened to the "noble words" of their flag salute with rote familiarity. "You have learned them so long ago," he said, "like the arithmetic table or the Shorter Catechism, something you can repeat without realizing what it all really means. But I could sit down and brood upon it." Having done so, he had concluded "there was something missing in this Pledge, and that which was missing was the characteristic and definitive factor in the 'American Way of Life.' Indeed, apart from the mention of the phrase, the United States of America, this could be the pledge of any Republic. In fact," he added ominously, "I could hear little Muscovites repeat a similar pledge to their hammer and sickle flag in Moscow with equal solemnity." To distinguish their national pledge from all others, Americans needed to stress the issue that distinguished their nation from all others—the fundamental role of religion. "It should be 'one nation, indivisible, Under God,'" the minister insisted. "To omit the words 'Under God' in the Pledge of Allegiance is to omit the definitive character of the 'American Way of Life.'"[20]

Docherty addressed the question of the separation of church and state directly. "What the Declaration [*sic*] says, in effect, is that no state church shall exist in this land," he said. "This is separation of Church and State; it is not, and never was meant to be, a separation of religion and life." He believed that his proposal was broad enough to encompass all Americans. "It must be 'UNDER GOD' to include the great Jewish Community, and the people of the Moslem faith and the myriad of denominations of Christians in the land," he said. "What then of the honest atheist? Philosophically speaking, an atheistic American is a contradiction in terms." The Presbyterian praised atheists for being "fine in character" and "good neighbors" but suggested they were "spiritual parasites." "I mean no term of abuse in this," the minister added. "A parasite is an organism that lives upon the life force of another organism without contributing to the life of the other. These excellent ethical seculars are living upon the accumulated Spiritual Capital of a Judaio-Christian civilization, and at the same time, deny the God who revealed the divine principles upon which the ethics of this Country grow." And whether atheists admitted it or not, those divine principles were in evidence all around them, in the prayers offered before presidential inaugurations and sessions of Congress. Like the supporters of the Christian amendment testifying before the Senate that year, Docherty invoked an ever-expanding list of religious references in American public life as a rationale for creating yet another.[21]

Docherty's sermon elicited a tremendous reaction. As the minister later reflected, "One of the advantages—and dangers—of being a preacher in the nation's capital is the ease with which a given sermon, such as one preached when the president is in church, can be given front-page headlines in the press." Eisenhower lit the fuse, endorsing the minister's proposal as he left the church. The next morning, the offices of senators and representatives phoned the pastor to request copies of his sermon; it was soon reprinted in the *Congressional Record* and distributed widely. A Paramount Pictures recording of the event played in newsreel segments in theaters across the country for weeks afterward. The Hearst newspaper chain launched a major editorial campaign in favor of the change, while several radio commentators pressed the issue as well. Resolutions supporting the proposal were issued by organizations ranging in size and significance from a Brooklyn club for retired policemen to the Massachusetts state legislature. Veterans' groups, fraternal clubs, labor unions, and trade associations joined the cause as well. "Congress is being flooded with mail," the *New York Times* soon reported. "The letter writers by the thousands daily are demanding that Congress amend the pledge of allegiance so that the pledge is made to read 'one nation under God.'"[22]

Passage of a bill based on Rabaut's proposal now seemed inevitable. As an editorial in the *Christian Century* noted, "This is the sort of proposal against which no member of Congress would think of voting, any more than against a resolution approving of motherhood." Opposition was light. The ACLU, for instance, decided not to intervene. "If some outstanding religious leaders would speak out on the basis of the church-state separation point, it might hold up action," an official noted. But he immediately added, "I doubt whether any such leaders would make this statement." Objections from clergymen were indeed few, with the most notable coming from the Unitarian Ministers Association, which passed a resolution opposing the proposal at its annual convention in May 1954.

A speaker warned that the measure was a sign that religion was becoming little more than a fad. "If you don't bring God into every Cabinet meeting, political convention or other assembly," she noted sarcastically, "it is bad public relations."[23]

If anything, the proposal to add "under God" to the Pledge of Allegiance was perhaps *too* popular, with legislators scrambling to claim credit for the idea. The House of Representatives found itself in a state of chaos as multiple bills calling for the change competed for attention. The idled proposal that Representative Rabaut had introduced the previous April was still pending, but it was soon joined by another sixteen bills: seven from Democrats, eight from Republicans, and one from an independent.[24] Notably, the congressmen behind these bills had agreed on little else that year. As the ADA's voting scorecards made clear, the Democrats and the lone independent had been reliably liberal, while the Republicans had been just as consistently conservative. Only the broad concept of "one nation under God" proved elastic enough to bring them together.[25]

But liberals and conservatives had wildly different interpretations of the phrase's meaning. For Republicans, "one nation under God" simply extended old Christian libertarian arguments. When Michigan representative Charles Oakman introduced his proposal, for instance, he spoke at length about how the nation's founders "recognized the inherent truth that any government of and by the people must look to God for divine leadership in order to protect itself from tyranny and despotism." For Democrats, in contrast, "one nation under God" signaled not opposition to government power but an alliance with it. "This country was founded on theistic beliefs, on belief in the worthwhileness of the individual human being which in turn depends solely and completely on the identity of man as the creature and son of God," noted Representative Rabaut. While groups such as Spiritual Mobilization stopped there, using the concept of "freedom under God" to wage war against the welfare state, the liberal Democrat stressed the common good, in an echo of the Social Gospel. "Children and Americans of all ages," he insisted, "must know that this is one Nation [in] which 'under God' means 'liberty and justice for all.'"[26]

Democrats and Republicans were able to set aside partisanship in this instance, largely due to Eisenhower's successful rebranding of the federal government as a "government under God." Now that the political system was so suffused with prayer, the state no longer seemed "pagan," as Christian libertarians had once argued, and liberals could present themselves as acting in accord with God's will too. And much as Eisenhower helped bring right and left together, Docherty also encouraged their cooperation by pointing to a common enemy in the Soviet Union. Though only a brief passage in his sermon, his line about the "little Muscovites" had been singled out in news reports and reprinted over and over again, a development that did a great deal to further the cause of "one nation under God." For two decades, those advocating the ideology of "freedom under God" had wanted to discredit and dismantle the New Deal state, only referencing the Soviet Union occasionally. But as the entire American political spectrum rallied around the phrase "one nation under God," the New Deal state was no longer the counterpoint to godly politics. The Soviet Union now took its place.

So as Democratic and Republican congressmen argued for their various proposals to change the pledge, they loaded their speeches with approving references to Docherty's "little Muscovites" line. Oakman, for instance, read long passages from the sermon into the *Congressional Record*, purposely ending on that very passage. "I think Mr. Docherty hit the nail squarely on the head," he said. "One of the most fundamental differences between us and the Communists is our belief in God." Rabaut, opposed to his Michigan colleague on most every issue, also quoted Docherty's sermon, though he focused even more narrowly on the "little Muscovites" part. "Dr. Docherty and I are not of the same Christian denomination, but I may say that in this matter he has hit the nail right on the head," Rabaut said. "You may argue from dawn to dusk about differing political, economic, and social systems, but the fundamental issue which is the unbridgeable gap between America and Communist Russia is a belief in Almighty God." These comments gave the public at the time—and scholars ever since—the mistaken idea that the pledge change was largely, or even solely, a result of Cold War anticommunism. But in reality it was the result of nearly two decades of partisan fighting over domestic issues. The Cold War contrasts were largely a last-minute development, one that helped paper over partisan differences.[27]

As the House sorted through its seventeen separate bills, the Senate moved with uncharacteristic speed. Senator Homer Ferguson, a conservative Republican from Michigan, introduced the first and only pledge proposal in that chamber just days after Docherty's sermon. A fellow Presbyterian, Ferguson claimed that the minister's advice needed to be followed to remind Americans that "our Nation is founded on a fundamental belief in God and the first and most important reason for the existence of our Government is to protect the God-given rights of our citizens." Speeding through the Senate, his resolution won passage on May 11 and went to the House. But Rabaut, who had fought his House colleagues to secure credit for changing the pledge, refused to step aside for the Senate. The two proposals were virtually identical, with only the placement of a single comma distinguishing one from the other, but Rabaut refused to cede his ground. In a violation of congressional etiquette, he convinced the House to ignore the Senate resolution, pass his own measure in its place, and force the Senate to adopt the House law instead. Because supporters of the change wanted to have the bill signed into law by Flag Day, then quickly approaching, Ferguson graciously ignored the breach of protocol and urged his colleagues to pass Rabaut's resolution. On June 8, they did.[28]

On Flag Day, June 14, 1954, President Eisenhower signed the bill into law. Congressional advocates had hoped to televise the moment, but the president decided instead to sign the bill privately and issue a public statement. "From this day forward," Eisenhower announced, "the millions of our school children will proclaim daily in every city and town, every village and rural school house, the dedication of our nation and our people to the Almighty." Members of Congress held an event of their own on the steps of the Capitol. Most of the congressional leadership attended, including Senate majority leader Bill Knowland of California and Senate minority leader Lyndon B. Johnson of Texas. A flag given to Vice President Nixon by the American Legion during that year's "Back to God" ceremonies was raised over the Capitol building. Rabaut and Ferguson jointly led the assembled in reciting the new Pledge of Allegiance, which was followed by a lone bugler's rendition of "Onward, Christian Soldiers." CBS broadcast the event live on television, with Walter Cronkite leading the coverage of what he called "a stirring event." "'New glory for Old Glory'—a wonderful idea," he said. "Maybe if we all remember to display our flags today and every special day, we will remember more clearly the traditions of freedom on which our country is founded."[29]

Celebrations of the new Pledge of Allegiance continued into the following year. To mark the first anniversary, Rabaut convinced a composer best known for writing the song "Tea for Two" to set the words of the new pledge to music. On Flag Day 1955, the twenty-man Singing Sergeants choral group performed the patriotic tune on the floor of the House, accompanied by the full United States Air Force Band. More significantly, the National Conference of Christians and Jews (NCCJ) made "One Nation Under God" the principal theme of its Brotherhood Week. Some ten thousand cities and towns across the country took part in the ceremonies, celebrating the theme with special religious observances, speeches at civic clubs, and film shorts in theaters. Separate from the NCCJ events, local communities highlighted the message in events of their own design. In October 1955, for instance, the annual Burbank on Parade festival featured hundreds of marching majorettes, fifteen marching bands, and seventeen parade floats, all devoted to the theme "One Nation Under God: A Portrait of American History." By 1957, the phrase had become so popular that the Washington Pilgrimage, the group that originally rebuffed Docherty's pledge proposal as too radical, revised its stance. Not only did the Pilgrims travel to Washington under the banner of "This Nation Under God," but they also secured a formal proclamation from the commissioners of the District of Columbia attesting that their group had been the first to hear Docherty's revolutionary idea.[30]

In short order, the phrase "one nation under God" quickly claimed a central position in American political culture. It became an informal motto for the country, demonstrating the widespread belief that the United States had been founded on religious belief and was sustained by religious practice. Although its creation depended a great deal on the groundwork of the Christian libertarian movement, the new pledge moved well beyond that original base of conservative Protestants to unite Americans from across the religious and political spectrum. Soon this unofficial motto was joined by an official one.

MUCH LIKE "ONE NATION UNDER GOD," "In God We Trust" had its origins in the bloodier chapters of nineteenth-century American history. Francis Scott Key's "The Star-Spangled Banner," composed during the shelling of Fort McHenry in the War of 1812, originally contained an often-forgotten fourth stanza with the couplet "Then conquer we must, when our cause it is just / And this be our motto: 'In God is our trust.'" A half century later, the Civil War inspired Americans to rediscover the phrase. In 1861, a Pennsylvania minister wrote an urgent plea to Secretary of the Treasury Salmon Chase. "From my heart I have felt our national shame in disowning God as not the least of our present national disasters," mourned Reverend M. R. Watkinson. He urged the secretary to secure "recognition of the Almighty God in some form on our coins" as penance. Chase seized on the idea. "Trust in God should be declared on our national coins," he instructed the director of the US Mint. "You will cause a device to be prepared without unnecessary delay with a motto expressing in the fewest and tersest words this national recognition." The mint offered several suggestions, but Chase ultimately selected "In God We Trust" and lobbied for legislation authorizing the new slogan. It soon appeared, on bronze 2¢ pieces, in 1864.[31]

Soon after, proposals to add the phrase to paper currency were made as well. Lincoln, aware that the gold supply supporting "greenbacks" was dwindling, joked that a more appropriate motto might be found in the words of the apostle Peter: "Silver and gold have I none, but such as I have give I thee." In the end, Lincoln dismissed the idea. Still, the motto quickly began to grace a wide variety of coins: the gold double eagle, eagle, and half eagle—pieces valued at $20, $10, and $5, respectively—as well as the dollar, half-dollar, quarter, and nickel. While Chase applied the motto enthusiastically, many of his successors lacked his passion. In 1883, the motto was removed from the nickel and would not return for another fifty-five years. In 1907, designs were commissioned for new $10 and $20 gold coins, accompanied by instructions from Theodore Roosevelt to drop the phrase. "My own firm conviction," the president reasoned, "is that such a motto on coins not only does no good, but positive harm and is in effect, irreverence, which comes close to sacrilege." By this time, however, the words had become fixed in the public's mind, and an outcry led to a quiet reversal of Roosevelt's order. From that point on, the phrase was inscribed on most of the nation's coins.[32]

The fortunes of "In God We Trust" took a new turn during the religious revival of the postwar era. In 1952, Ernest Kehr, the Catholic author of a popular newspaper column for stamp collectors, came up with the idea of creating new postage bearing the phrase. Such a stamp, he argued, would be a strong warning to America's enemies that "before they can attack democracy and freedom, they first must destroy a people's faith in God." He recruited other newspapers, magazines, and television and radio stations to spread the idea and convinced national organizations such as the American Legion to pass resolutions of support as well. The campaign soon secured Congress's attention. In the Senate, two bills were introduced in late March 1953, with Democrat Mike Mansfield, a Montana Catholic, and Republican Charles Potter, a Michigan Methodist, offering nearly identical measures calling for "In God We Trust" to be added to all future stamps. (In yet another sign of the broad political support for ceremonial deism, these senators stood at opposite ends of the ideological spectrum. According to ADA voting guides that year, Mansfield sided with the progressive organization on thirteen of fifteen key votes; Potter, only two.) Three days later, Representative Rabaut sought to link his name to the cause as well, introducing a bill in the House requiring that all mail be postmarked with the phrase. With Congress on board, proponents of the plan then turned their attention to postal officials. "Putting it mildly," the *Washington Post* reported in April 1953, "Post Office Department officials have been harassed in recent weeks by a flood of letters urging that the national motto 'In God We Trust' be placed on all future postage stamps." This "deluge of letters," the *New York Times* added, was so unprecedented in the history of the postal service that officials suspected a coordinated campaign lay behind it all.[33]

Although the press reported that Postmaster General Arthur Summerfield was "not happy" about the campaign, he responded dutifully to the requests. In April 1954, he unveiled a new 8¢ stamp, a red-white-and-blue image of the Statue of Liberty with the words "In God We Trust" arrayed as a halo around the statue's head. As one account noted, the stamp claimed "a number of 'firsts'": the first regular-issue stamp with a religious theme and the first low-price stamp with a multicolor design. Most notably, it was the first stamp to be officially introduced by a sitting president, in what postal officials called "the biggest ceremony of its kind in the history of the United States Post Office Department." Eisenhower, Summerfield, and Secretary of State Dulles all offered their thoughts on the stamp, with a tri-faith selection of religious leaders—Dr. Roy Ross, executive secretary of the National Council of Churches, a leading Protestant umbrella organization; Francis Cardinal Spellman, Catholic archbishop of New York; and Dr. Norman Salit, president of the Synagogue League of America—offering blessings as well. Interest in the event was so high that Vice President Nixon hosted a luncheon for an overflow crowd of three hundred government officials and guests at the Shoreham Hotel.[34]

NBC carried the proceedings live on TV. "The issuance of this stamp," Summerfield proclaimed, "symbolizes the rededication of our faith in the spiritual foundations upon which our Government and our Nation exist." Because the postage had been issued in an amount used for international letters, he called it a "Postal Ambassador" that would travel abroad at an estimated rate of two hundred million letters a year. "We want men of good will everywhere to know that America will always remain a God-fearing, God-loving nation, where freedom and equality for all are living and imperishable concepts," Summerfield added. In his extemporaneous remarks, Eisenhower sounded the same themes. "Throughout its history, America's greatness has been based upon a spiritual quality," he said, noting that the new stamp offered every American a chance to spread that message far and wide. "Regardless of any eloquence of the words that may be inside the letter," Eisenhower reflected, "on the outside he places a message: 'Here is the land of liberty and the land that lives in respect of the Almighty's mercy to us.' And to him that receives that message, the sender can feel that he has done something definite and constructive for that individual."[35]

The response to the new "In God We Trust" stamp was overwhelming. On its first day of availability, nearly nine hundred thousand stamps were sold; within weeks, twenty-five million more were distributed to post offices across the country to answer the still-growing demand. "Will the stamp set the precedent for others embodying religious belief," worried the editors of *Church and State*, "and for other acts of government in aid of religion?" Many believed that the first regularly issued, religiously themed postage set a clear precedent. "The Post Office Department is to be complimented on the issuance of this stamp," Rabaut noted after its unveiling, "and I hope it witnesses the adoption of a policy with regard to new issues which will make our postage stamps true symbols of the history and

The phrase "In God We Trust," used on many American coins since the Civil War, became an important touchstone of religious nationalism during the Eisenhower administration. In 1954, Secretary of State John Foster Dulles, President Dwight Eisenhower, and Postmaster General Arthur Summerfield helped introduce a popular new postage stamp with the phrase. *Corbis Images.*

traditions of our Nation." The Catholic congressman proposed a "world peace prayer" stamp to commemorate the first-ever Marian Year that Pope Pius XII had declared for 1954. Meanwhile, his colleagues offered ideas of their own, including two Christmas stamps, a Jewish synagogue tercentenary stamp, and postage depicting the Second Assembly of the World Council of Churches taking place that year in Evanston, Illinois.[36]

At the same time, Rabaut continued his campaign to have the motto of "In God We Trust" used as the postmark on all mail. "The new 8-cent stamp is, of course, a step in the direction of proclaiming our national belief," he told the House. "Use of the motto as a cancellation mark would give it a wider distribution and bring it more constantly to the attention of our people." When that proposal failed to progress, Rabaut tried a slightly different approach the next year, suggesting that a new canceling stamp be issued with the words "Pray for Peace." The measure sped through the House, though it met some resistance in the Senate. Supporting the idea, Senator John Pastore of Rhode Island pointed to the recent precedent of adding "under God" to the Pledge of Allegiance and suggested this would be another way to get an "inspirational element" into American life. "What harm does it do?" the Catholic senator asked. Senator Clifford Case, a New Jersey Republican and a Presbyterian, responded that "it is a question of who does it. I don't think the government has any business to tell anybody to do anything in a religious way and this in a sense is that." Pastore protested, "We are not telling anybody to do anything." "If we authorize it," Case replied, "we are." Such concerns were in the minority, however, and the Senate soon passed the measure. Despite reservations about the $250,000 cost of creating a new canceling stamp, the president swiftly signed the proposal into law. Taking note of the revival at the Post Office, the theologian William Lee Miller joked that now "the devout, in place of daily devotions, can just read what is stuck and stamped all over the letters in their mail."[37]

Following the enthusiastic reaction to the arrival of the "In God We Trust" stamp in April 1954 and the addition of "under God" to the pledge in June 1954, the public clamored for religious language to be placed on paper currency as well as coins. On August 21, 1954, the American Numismatic Association passed a resolution at its annual convention in Cleveland calling for the inscription of "In God We Trust" on all forms of American money; just nine days later, the American Legion passed an almost identical resolution at *its* annual convention in Washington, D.C. Donald Carroll, the state commander of the Florida American Legion, who offered the resolution, insisted he arrived at the idea independently, following a talk he had given in Gainesville. "I had been talking on the subject of this government being based upon a belief in God," Carroll told a friend, "and the fact that the pledge to the flag has been recently amended to include the words 'under God,' and the fact that all our coins and also two recent issues of an eight-cent stamp and a three-cent stamp bore the motto 'In God We Trust.'" After the speech, a man asked why paper currency did not carry the same inscription. It struck Carroll as an excellent question, one he raised at the Legionnaires' convention in August and then again in a letter to his congressman that December.[38]

Congressman Charles E. Bennett was the perfect champion for the proposal. The Jacksonville representative was, if anything, a fighter. He had resigned a seat in the state legislature to enlist in the Second World War, earning distinction as a guerrilla in the Philippines before contracting polio and losing use of his legs. Returning home, he won a congressional seat as a Democrat in 1949 and held it, long past the point when the rest of his region became reliably Republican, until he finally decided to resign in 1993, after forty-four years of service. Despite his many accomplishments, Bennett constantly felt the need to prove himself. To convince constituents that his handicap did not hold him back, for instance, he never missed a single roll call in the House. A devout member of the Disciples of Christ, he served as the chamber's conscience. In 1951, he proposed a new code of ethics—he called them "the Ten Commandments"—which then became the nation's first ethical code for government employees seven years later. Seeking to set a good example, Bennett refused to accept his congressional salary, his veteran's disability checks, and his Social Security benefits. Not surprisingly, one colleague grumbled that the Floridian was perhaps "a little too pious."[39]

All these traits recommended Bennett as a champion of Carroll's idea, but Carroll believed another stood out. "You would be a most natural one to sponsor Federal legislation to require the addition to our paper money of these words," he wrote, "for you are (unless the position has recently been changed) Chairman of the House ICCL Group." As it turned out, Bennett's one-year term as the leader of Vereide's prayer breakfast group had concluded the previous spring. But during his tenure as chair, he had proven himself to be committed to the ICCL cause of bringing religious revival to the political world. In January 1954, Bennett attended a major conference for government officials at the Fellowship House, where he offered both a scripture lesson and his thoughts on the need for public faith. "The minds and hearts of people are being challenged as never before in the last fifty years," Bennett said. "The future is in the hands of those who really have a strong faith in God." Not surprisingly, his fellow ICCL members agreed. Senator Homer Ferguson said they needed to "remember the words carved above the door in the Senate, 'In God We Trust.'" (Ironically, Ferguson, whose greatest claim to fame would be adding "under God" to the pledge a few months later, added, "We cannot do this by only repeating those words or carving them in concrete and stone. Each of us as we go about our tasks must live those words.")[40]

For Bennett, religious organizations such as the ICCL offered not just inspiration for action but assistance as well. In January 1955, soon after he introduced the bill calling for the motto's addition to all paper currency, he searched for supporters. "Perhaps some of your Representatives or Senators in ICCL might put in a good word for it," Carroll suggested. Actually, they already had. Senator Carlson, for instance, had been blanketing his colleagues with letters to recruit them for the currency proposal in particular and the larger ICCL cause in general. By all appearances, the letters were effective. "I am very much interested in your movement to put God back into the government of this great nation," responded Representative Philip J. Philbin, a Catholic Democrat from Massachusetts. "I think there is much room in this country for restoring those great spiritual values which lie at the very base of our great government and our great free system of enterprise."[41]

As congressional support grew, Bennett sought endorsements from the executive branch. Secretary of the Treasury George Humphrey demurred at first, claiming that "a clear precedent appears to have been set in past years for Congressional action in such a matter." But once Eisenhower expressed his support, the Treasury Department came on board, adopting a role that was both supportive and supporting. Its officials let congressional advocates take the lead but offered assistance at every turn. They explained that the cost of changing the design of currency was usually prohibitively high, but as luck had it, the department was already installing a new procedure for printing currency that required the creation of brand-new dies, rolls, and plates. "We find that, in connection with this redesigning, the inscription 'In God We Trust' can be included in the design with very little additional cost," a Treasury official reported. Eisenhower authorized the plan in late April 1955 and then reviewed draft designs for the new money, ultimately choosing one that located the motto most prominently on the back of the bill.[42]

A few weeks later, the House Committee on Banking and Currency convened to consider the proposal. Democrat Herman Eberharter, a liberal Catholic from Pittsburgh, was so enthusiastic about the idea that he cut short a three-month convalescence from a major illness and returned to the House for the hearing. To his delight, he found his colleagues virtually unanimous in their support. The lone objection came from Representative Abraham Multer from Brooklyn. As a Jew, he was wary of dissenting too strongly on issues of faith. "I want it made crystal clear on this record that I think I am as religious as any man in the House," the liberal Democrat began. "We may differ in our forms, but I respect every other person's form or ritualistic observance, and I know they do mine, too." But, he added, "I feel very strongly that it was a mistake to put it on coins in the first place, and this is perpetuating a grievous error." The inscription debased God, Multer argued, and brought no one closer to Him. "I don't believe it has inspired one single person to be more religious because we have these words on our currency," he said. "If we are going to have religious concepts—and I am in favor of them—I don't think the place to put them is on our currency or on our coins." Despite these sentiments, Multer indicated he would do nothing to oppose the bill. Accordingly, the Banking and Commerce Committee gave its unanimous support to the measure. Its official report asserted that the phrase "In God We Trust" best expressed "the spiritual basis of our way of life," and the committee therefore urged the House of Representatives to mandate its use on all coins and currency. The House did so, with almost no debate and a quick vote, on June 7.[43]

The bill's movement through the Senate was even easier. Earlier that term, Senator William Fulbright of Arkansas introduced a proposal that was virtually identical to the one Representative Bennett had ushered through the House, and now, in his role as chairman of the Senate Banking and Commerce Committee, the liberal Democrat moved the bill through his chamber with ease. Fulbright knew his colleagues were on board. "We thought it was so nearly in unanimity in the subcommittee, I didn't call hearings," reported Oklahoma's Mike Monroney, a moderate Democrat. "In fact, we didn't even have a meeting." Instead, he canvassed members of the subcommittee and, finding them all in favor, passed the proposal on to the full committee. The senators were unanimously in favor but felt duty-bound to mention the few complaints they had received. Monroney reported receiving a telegram that morning, "the first adverse comment we have had," while his colleague Wayne Morse of Oregon, a liberal Republican, added that there had been, "to my utter surprise," a half dozen notes of protest sent to his office from ethical and humanist groups. Although the committee acknowledged these complaints, it never bothered to discuss their content. Despite their own political and religious differences—Fulbright was a Disciple of Christ, Monroney an Episcopalian,

Morse a Baptist—the senators came together in their common embrace of the motto and passed it unanimously. The full Senate followed, passing the measure in another unanimous voice vote on June 29.[44]

As the bill moved to the White House, supporters hoped they might secure a public ceremony for the signing. "The National Association of Evangelicals asked about it," a presidential aide noted, "and are very much interested in the bill." But Eisenhower begged off, noting that so many important bills had passed at the end of the congressional session that he wanted to keep such ceremonies, in the words of his aide Bryce Harlow, "to a bare minimum." He signed the bill privately on July 11, making sure Bennett received one of the pens. Even without a ceremony, White House officials still hoped they could use the new law for political gain. In March 1956, the deputy press secretary, Murray Snyder, reported that he had been in contact with the Treasury Department about their progress in adding "In God We Trust" to the redesigned dollar and had asked them "to consult with the White House on the timing of the launching of this new bill." To his delight, he learned that "it might be summer or perhaps early fall, which would be wonderful for our purposes. It seems to me it should be timed to coincide with a major holiday so that the full benefits of a 'non-political' ceremony might be derived—all the coverage the traffic will bear."[45]

Due to delays in the installation of the new high-speed printing presses at the Treasury Department, however, the first batch of bills with "In God We Trust" were not produced until the following year. Even as the printing began, Treasury officials explained to an eager public that "placing of the notes in circulation would have to be delayed until October to permit the production of an adequate supply for all sections of the country." The bureau had to work nonstop, "twenty-four hours a day, seven days a week for three months," in order to produce some forty million new bills with the motto. Adding another souvenir to his collection, Bennett arranged to have a picture taken of him turning in an old dollar bill to Treasury Secretary Robert Anderson in exchange for a new one. The White House staffers who had hoped to capitalize on the bills' release did not make out as well. "America must have a trust in God," the *Oregonian* observed, "but the motto might be better inscribed on our hearts than on our bank notes." The *Chicago Tribune*, meanwhile, sarcastically saw some benefit in the change, noting that the motto's addition coincided with a government announcement that the cost of living had gone up once again, the fifteenth hike in sixteen months. "In these days of inflation," the paper joked, "politicians turn thankfully to a spiritual anchor."[46]

Even as the motto was added to currency, its supporters looked to increase its presence in other ways. Bennett sought to clear up the popular confusion over whether the phrase—or any phrase—was the official national motto. He asked the Legislative Reference Service at the Library of Congress for insight. "Four mottoes have been adopted by law for various purposes," its researchers reported. "The earliest well-known motto is *E Pluribus Unum*, 'One out of many,' on the obverse of the seal of the United States." Next, there were the two mottoes that were "adopted for the reverse of the seal: *Annuit Coeptis*, 'God has favored our undertakings' and *Novus Ordo Seclorum*, 'a new order of the ages.'" However, because the reverse of the seal had never been cut or used publicly, the researchers noted, "these two mottoes could hardly compete with *E Pluribus Unum*, which has been in use since 1782. They do, however, appear on our current one dollar bills." The fourth and final motto, of course, was "In God We Trust," which through its usage on coins and now currency had emerged as the strongest rival. Still, the report concluded, "if one motto were to be designated as being more clearly 'the' motto than any other, it would seem to be *E Pluribus Unum*. This has priority in time, having been officially chosen in 1782 and confirmed by the new Government under the Constitution in 1789; and it is the only motto on the obverse of the Seal of the United States, the seal that has been used throughout our history as a nation. The motto on the seal of a government is generally considered to be the motto of that government."[47]

Bennett nevertheless believed that "In God We Trust" should be the official motto. In July 1955, just days after Eisenhower signed into law the currency change, Bennett barraged his colleagues with letters announcing plans for another congressional resolution: that "the national motto of the United States is hereby declared to be 'In God We Trust.'" He noted his recent findings, with a slight interpretative twist that placed his preferred motto on an even plane with the one on the seal. "The Library of Congress, after research, has stated that there is no officially recognized motto of the United States," he reported, "although 'E Pluribus Unum' and 'In God We Trust' have been at various times and places used where a national motto would be appropriate." The latter, he added, had a distinct advantage: it "would keep us constantly reminded of the spiritual and moral values upon which our Country was founded and upon which it depends for survival." On July 21, he introduced the measure on the floor of the House, where it was referred to the Judiciary Committee.[48]

The measure languished for a short while before picking up speed the following winter. In February 1956, a House Judiciary subcommittee held hearings with Bennett as its sole witness. "In sponsoring this legislation," he told his colleagues, "it is my position that it would be valuable to our country to have a clearly designated national motto of inspirational quality and in plain popularly accepted English." The members of the subcommittee agreed, passing the proposal along to the full Judiciary Committee. Hoping to enlist the support of its powerful chairman, Representative Emanuel Celler of New York, Bennett resorted to flattery. The inspiration for the motto proposal, he wrote Celler, "comes from your own leadership in the 71st Congress in the congressional adoption of 'The Star Spangled Banner' as our national anthem, which contains the phrase, 'And this be our motto, In God is our trust.'" He referenced Celler's argument for the anthem in 1930. "It is my belief that similarly legalizing 'In God We Trust' as our national motto is"—and here he cited the chairman's own words—"a 'method of further increasing the patriotism of the people of our country.'" The approach worked. Celler brought the bill before the full committee in a matter of days and quickly secured its approval. After a few weeks, the House passed the resolution on April 17 and sent it on to the Senate.[49]

Only after the House vote did civil libertarians raise objections, and even then halfheartedly. As in the campaign to add "under God" to the pledge, the ACLU was largely preoccupied with other matters and unable to devote any sustained attention to matters of church and state. When Democratic senator Thomas Hennings held major hearings on the state of civil liberties in fall 1955, for instance, the organization's officials noted in internal memos that "the ACLU should not testify in the religion area because we will be making an appearance on other more important matters." The organization paid so little attention to the motto developments, in fact, that its leaders apparently only heard about the bill three weeks *after* its passage in the House, even though it had been widely reported in the press. On May 6, 1956, ACLU associate director Alan Reitman issued a memorandum noting that the head of their Philadelphia chapter had "heard that a bill has passed the House of Representatives to change the U.S. motto from 'E Pluribus Unum' to 'In God We Trust'" and asking for additional information. Even after learning more, though, Reitman remained largely ambivalent. "I know that we are pressed on all fronts with crises, but we do not have many separation of church-state cases, and this appears to be an important one," he wrote. "I do not suggest that we drop all other project[s], but perhaps we can place a few stumbling blocks in the way of the bill, even by talking with some other organizations." As they looked around, however, ACLU officials found that other organizations had also ignored the measure. "The P.O.A.U. is taking no stand on the bill," an aide reported. The American Humanist Association complained about it in a press release, he added, but that was about it.[50]

The ACLU did draft a polite letter of protest to members of the Senate. "In our opinion, this change would be at the very least an approach toward the infringement upon the Constitutional guarantee that there shall be no establishment of religion in this country," it read. "It would also, through the implicit authority of the national motto, constitute a religious test for government employees." The organization acknowledged that most Americans were religious, "but the place for that act of devotion is to be found in their house of worship or in their hearts. They should not, through their Congress, require one other person who is a non-believer to link his civic loyalty with their doctrinal belief." The letter concluded by requesting a public hearing on the matter and asking for an invitation to testify if one was held. The organization mailed the protest to members of the Senate Judiciary subcommittee when it first considered the bill in May 1956. When they ignored the request, the ACLU sent the same letter to members of the full committee in June.[51]

These actions were, in the end, both timid and tardy. Months earlier, when the first hints of opposition had emerged, supporters of the proposal rushed to action. In late April, Bennett wrote Senator Spessard L. Holland, a fellow Floridian, to warn that "there have recently been received some letters which apparently come from atheists or agnostic organizations." He suggested that "it would seem to be a good thing to have this bill passed before the mail creates any problems. As I understand it, the members of the Committee are favorably disposed toward the legislation, and a prompt disposal of it would eliminate a lot of unnecessary correspondence." Despite Bennett's best efforts, however, the Senate took its time. These fears were unfounded, though; no significant opposition ever materialized. The Judiciary Committee reported favorably on the House resolution on July 20, and the full Senate voted it into law three days later. The White House political office checked to see if any departments had objections, but found none, and so the president signed the measure into law on July 30, 1956.[52]

In little more than two years' time, "In God We Trust" had surged to public notice, first taking a place of prominence on stamps and currency, and then edging its way past "E Pluribus Unum" to become the nation's first official motto. The concept of unity from diversity could not compete with that of unity from divinity. "In God We Trust," along with its counterpart in the Pledge of Allegiance, "one nation under God," quickly emerged as the twin pillars of the ceremonial deism sweeping through the Capitol. The Eisenhower administration had already done a great deal to put religion into politics, ranging from the religious elements in the inauguration ceremonies and cabinet meetings to more formal events such as the "Back to God" broadcasts and the National Prayer Breakfasts. As important as those developments were, however, such initiatives were tied closely to the president and, like any administration's policy, might not have lasted longer than his term. In contrast, the changes to the Pledge of Allegiance and the national motto, initiated and authorized by Congress, could claim a much broader parentage. Protestants, Catholics, and Jews had all played a part in their creation, and so had members of both political parties from across the ideological spectrum.

As central expressions of patriotism, these changes guaranteed that religious sentiment would be not just a theme pressed by a transitory administration but rather a lasting trait of the nation. The addition of "one nation under God" to the Pledge of Allegiance ensured that the new fusion of piety and patriotism that conservatives had crafted over the past two decades would be instilled in the next generation of children and beyond. From then on, their interpretation of America's fundamental nature would have a seemingly permanent place in the national imagination.

And with "In God We Trust" appearing on postage stamps and paper currency, the daily interactions citizens made through the state—sending mail, swapping money—were similarly sacralized. The addition of the religious motto to paper currency was particularly important, as it formally confirmed a role for capitalism in that larger love of God and country. Since then, every act of buying and selling in America has occurred through a currency that proudly praises God.

CHAPTER 5

Pitchmen for Piety

O N THE AFTERNOON OF JULY 17, 1955, ABC television broadcast a live special event called *Dateline Disneyland*. For more than a year, the famed entertainer Walt Disney had made weekly appearances on the network to promote a colossal theme park he was building on roughly 168 acres of former farmland in Anaheim, California. Now that it was ready, ABC marked its opening with considerable pomp and pageantry. Its hour-and-a-half program began in the spacious pressroom at Disneyland, which, an announcer noted, was "equipped to service over one thousand members of the worldwide press here to cover this truly great event." Host Art Linkletter told the audience that the network had twenty-nine cameras installed across the park, along with "dozens of crews and literally miles and miles of cables," to capture the magic. Thanks to ABC's efforts, Linkletter claimed, millions watching at home would share the experience of the thirty thousand who had the fortune to be there in person to witness the grand opening of "the eighth wonder of the world."[1]

The amiable Linkletter quickly turned things over to "Ronnie"—his cohost, Ronald Reagan, who had the honor of introducing the dedication ceremonies from a perch above Main Street, U.S.A., the park's idyllic reproduction of a nineteenth-century town. Wearing an oversized white sports coat, starched dress shirt, and thin black bow tie, the actor flashed a beaming smile and pointed viewers to a clutch of political and religious figures in the town square. "Walt Disney, Governor Knight, the mayor of Anaheim, and other dignitaries," he said, "are talking to three chaplains representing the Protestant, Catholic and Jewish faiths." Disney then strode to the microphone to read the inscription from the dedicatory plaque: "Disneyland is dedicated to the ideals, the dreams, and the hard facts that have created America, with the hope that it will be a source of joy and inspiration to the world." His nephew, Reverend Glen D. Puder, offered an opening prayer that stressed the religious motivations behind the theme park. "I have known Walt Disney for many years, and have long been aware of the spiritual motivation in the heart of this man who has dreamed Disneyland into being," the Presbyterian pastor said. "Beyond the creeds that would divide us, let us unite in a silent prayer, that this and every worthy endeavor may prosper at God's hand." Governor Goodwin Knight followed with similar thoughts on the godly nature of both Disneyland and the nation it would entertain. "This is a wonderful place," the Republican said, "just like your hometown, all built by American labor and American capital under the belief that this is a God-fearing and a God-loving country. And as we dedicate this flag now, we do it with the knowledge that we are the fortunate ones to be Americans, and that we extend to everyone everywhere the great ideals of Americanism: brotherhood, and peace on earth, goodwill towards men." A drumroll began, and the US Marine Corps Band played "The Star Spangled Banner" as four uniformed servicemen raised the flag. Disney peered up to the clear blue sky, where a formation of fighter jets from the California Air National Guard soared past in salute.[2]

Disneyland's dedication testified to how deeply piety and patriotism were intertwined in its creator's worldview. Disney, a Congregationalist, relied on Christianity as a constant guide. His faith in his country was equally strong, though his political beliefs changed considerably over the course of his life. During the 1930s, he had been a strong supporter of Franklin Roosevelt and the New Deal. His cartoons during the Depression helped establish the so-called "sentimental populism" of the era's popular culture, always championing "little guys"—Mickey Mouse, the Three Little Pigs, the Seven Dwarves—in their struggles against stronger foes. But in the 1940s, Disney's politics took a sharp turn to the right. In 1941, a bitter strike at his company led him to denounce "Communist agitation" in a full-page ad in *Variety*. The day after Pearl Harbor, Disney was stunned when the US Army abruptly commandeered his studio for seven months' use as a supply base. During the war, the government never paid him for some propaganda shorts he made, and his overseas profits dwindled to a trickle. Disney emerged from the conflict a staunch conservative. He helped bring the House Un-American Activities Committee to Hollywood in October 1947 and, in his appearance as a friendly witness, condemned communist influence in labor unions, pointedly naming names. When fellow Congregationalist James Fifield organized the Committee to Proclaim Liberty a few years later, Disney readily signed on to support its "Freedom Under God" festivities.[3]

Disneyland represented a subtle extension of Disney's postwar politics, but within a few years he began to worry that the theme park was perhaps *too* subtle. Therefore, in 1958, he began planning a new addition, a second major thoroughfare to run parallel to Main Street, U.S.A. The new Liberty Street would celebrate colonial America, with its architecture and storefronts reflecting eighteenth-century life. The avenue would lead visitors into Liberty Square, where they would find a replica of Independence Hall. Inside, they would be dazzled by a film depicting American history through the Civil War, shown in Circarama, a two-hundred-degree screen that encompassed their entire field of vision. At the film's conclusion, the curtain would drop and then rise again to reveal life-size versions of a half dozen American presidents. "The visitor will see all the chief executives modeled life-size," the lead designer explained. "He'll think it's waxworks—until Lincoln stands up and talks." Disney was sure that the advanced "audio-animatronics" would make the exhibit the central attraction of the entire park. Accordingly, he gave it a grand name: One Nation Under God.[4]

Due to developmental problems, the entire plan was never realized at Disneyland. (The exhibit lived on elsewhere, first in a smaller-scale Mr. Lincoln animatronic feature at the 1964 World's Fair and then as a new Hall of Presidents attraction at Walt Disney World in Florida a few years later.) But the underlying spirit of the One Nation Under God attraction remained a vital part of Disneyland nonetheless. In a 1957 interview with the columnist Hedda Hopper, Disney stressed the "American theme" that ran through the theme park. "I believe in emphasizing the story of what made America great and what will keep it great," he said. Free enterprise, in his mind, was an essential element of the nation's success. As a reporter for the *Wall Street Journal* enthusiastically recorded, more than sixty-five corporations advertised their products at the park, with seemingly unlikely partners such as Richfield Oil and Monsanto Chemical sponsoring entire rides. But as the One Nation Under God plans illustrated, the patriotism and capitalism on display at Disneyland were merely manifestations of a deeper foundation of faith. "It was," as Disney biographer Neal Gabler noted aptly, "a modern variant on the City on a Hill of Puritan dreams."[5]

In its conflation of piety and patriotism, Disneyland embodied larger currents in American popular culture during the postwar era. Political leaders and religious reformers led the way in fomenting the religious revival of the Eisenhower era, but their counterparts in Hollywood and on Madison Avenue proved to be indispensable allies. Prompted by both patriotism and an eye for profits, entertainers and advertisers did a great deal to promote public expressions of faith in the era. Prominent advertising agencies promoted religious observance as a vital part of American life and religion as an essential marker of the national character. In the same spirit, the era's biggest film emphasized the foundational role of religion in American institutions, while prominent movie and television stars banded together in a Christian "crusade" to defend America. When it came to the role of religion in American life, political culture and popular culture sang from the same hymnal.

LIKE MUCH OF CORPORATE AMERICA, the advertising industry discovered religion as a means of professional salvation in the aftermath of the Great Depression. The industry had fallen into turmoil when ad revenues plummeted along with corporate profits in the crash of the late 1920s and early 1930s. More ominously for advertising executives, the New Deal represented the first real efforts to regulate their work, as it empowered the Federal Trade Commission to fight false claims about food and drugs. As the nation prepared itself for the Second World War, further growth of the federal government seemed guaranteed. Thus, in November 1941, hundreds of ad executives gathered at a spa in Hot Springs, Virginia, to discuss the danger of "those who would do away with the American system of free enterprise" or who might "modify the economic system of which advertising is an integral part." Marketing legend James Webb Young of the J. Walter Thompson Company urged the assembled admen to close ranks with corporate America, to defend its interests as if they were their own. "Let us ask ourselves whether we, as an industry, do not have a great contribution to make in this effort to regain for business the leadership of our economy," Young said. "We have within our hands the greatest aggregate means of mass education and persuasion the world has ever seen—namely, the channels of advertising communication. We have the masters of the techniques of using these channels. We have the power. Why do we not use it?" He argued that the advertising industry should work tirelessly on behalf of "a belief in a dynamic economy," particularly through the use of public service campaigns.[6]

The Advertising Council was the result. Founded in 1942 as the War Advertising Council, the organization brought together representatives from major ad agencies and their corporate clients to promote bond drives, material conservation campaigns, and similar programs on the home front. When the war ended, the council continued identifying campaigns for the industry as a whole and coordinating contributions from specific agencies that did the work. The Advertising Council classified its projects as acts of public service, but in truth they were acts of public relations, meant to sell the American people on the merits of free enterprise. In 1946, for instance, the council launched a campaign titled "Our American Heritage." On the surface, it seemed wholly nonpartisan, simply intended to raise Americans' awareness of their rights and responsibilities as citizens. Internally, though, organizers described it as a conservative-minded effort that would help Americans resist becoming "pawns of a master state." The admen persuaded corporations that their sponsorship would offer "an unparalleled opportunity to build public goodwill for themselves and enhance respect for American business at the same time that they make an important contribution to the country's welfare when, because of both world and internal conditions, that contribution is most needed." A second campaign promoting the "American Economic System" was even more explicit in championing corporate interests. Begun in late 1948, a week after Truman's reelection, it focused on fighting collectivization. "If people really understand what our private enterprise system had done for us and exactly how it had done it," an Ad Council official explained, "they will not be very good prospects for swapping this system for government ownership and control."[7]

In 1949, the Advertising Council launched what would be its most influential effort, the "Religion in American Life" campaign. The stated purposes of RIAL, its creators claimed, were "(1) to accent the importance of all religious institutions as the basis of American life" and "(2) to urge all Americans to attend the church or synagogue of their choice." While RIAL seemed more altruistic than the other postwar drives, it served the interests of corporate America as much as the others. ("In fact," Ad Council chairman Stuart Peabody later noted, "when you stop to figure it out, there is hardly any Council campaign which doesn't make some contribution to the health of American business.") Major corporations and ad firms rushed to take part. Charles E. Wilson, head of General Electric, served as RIAL chairman; Robert W. Boggs of the Union Carbide and Carbon Corporation coordinated its work with the Advertising Council. Launched the same year as the print and radio programs of Spiritual Mobilization, their program advanced an almost identical message about the foundational role of religion in American political and social institutions. While RIAL refrained from arguing explicitly that the free enterprise system was the only rightful result of that religious heritage, it nevertheless did much to advance the fundamental arguments of Christian libertarianism.[8]

The J. Walter Thompson Company (JWT), the largest advertising firm in the world, handled the practical work of the campaign. Its RIAL advertisements had a simple message for Americans: go to church. Copywriters drew on their conventional strategies, pitching religion as a path to personal improvement and self-satisfaction. "Find yourself through *faith,*" the 1949 RIAL campaign urged; "come to church this week." Ads typically dramatized the concerns of a frantic father or an anxious housewife and then, in the same tones used to hawk antacid or mouthwash, promised that faith would cure their problems quickly. Some ads, however, took a different approach, framing faith as something that transcended individual concerns and affected the nation as a whole. One magazine piece, for instance, depicted a dozen children singing together, open hymnals in their hands. Beneath the picture ran a banner: "Democracy starts

In 1949, the Advertising Council launched a massive "Religion in American Life" campaign to encourage attendance at churches and synagogues. Its ads urged ordinary Americans to embrace religion for their own salvation and the salvation of the nation. *Courtesy of the Ad Council Archives at the University of Illinois, Ad Council Historical File, RS 13/2/207.*

here . . . " "The way I see it," the copy began, "when you're a father you're automatically a Founding Father, too. It's up to you to found America in the heart and mind of every young citizen you add to the census. Because a nation isn't history—it's what's going on right now in your own children's minds and spirits."[9]

The new advertising drive proved incredibly popular, prompting a steady expansion of the "Religion in American Life" campaign during the next decade. Newspapers ran more and more of the ads each year, from about twenty-two hundred in 1949 to over ninety-seven hundred in 1956. Along with the ads, these papers published more than a thousand stories promoting national and local RIAL campaigns that same year. Meanwhile, popular magazines such as *Reader's Digest, TV Guide, Sports Illustrated,* and *Ladies' Home Journal* ran full-color advertisements and stories of their own. Radio played a vital role as well, with the Ad Council distributing program kits to twenty-nine hundred radio stations across the country, with a variety of scripts ready to air. In 1955, for instance, station owners could choose from eight different topics and then, on each topic, select scripts written for one minute, thirty seconds, twenty seconds, or ten seconds in length. Of course, RIAL took its message to television too, soon producing a full-length program each year. In 1956, bandleader Vaughn Monroe interviewed celebrities, including Olympic champion Jesse Owens and Miss America Lee Meriwether, about the role religion played in their lives. NBC devoted its *Wide, Wide World* program to the special, with sponsor General Motors covering all expenses and broadcasting it live on 143 stations nationwide.[10]

The "Religion in American Life" campaign succeeded, in large part, because its creators linked it to the religious revival in the political sphere. In a 1955 letter to radio stations, Ad Council officials explained that their work was meant to remind Americans that "religious faith, cultivated by our churches and synagogues, is one of the foundations of our nation and of our dedication to human rights and individual liberty, as suggested in our national motto, 'In God We Trust.'" To publicize this idea, the letter offered talking points: "What to Tell Your Audience." Again, the council stressed that stations should "point out that our nation was founded on faith in God and that freedom to worship God constitutes a precious national heritage."[11] As it pressed these themes, RIAL increasingly seemed an unofficial extension of the work done by the Eisenhower administration in the same sphere. This was no accident, of course, as many of the admen involved in RIAL were also working on Republican presidential campaigns at the same time, using the same themes. "Faith in God and Country," blared a 1956 billboard: "That's Eisenhower! How about you?"[12] The Ad Council, meanwhile, linked its work explicitly to the president. In a letter describing its activities, it cited Eisenhower as its authority, quoting at length his claim that "all free civilization rests upon a basis of religious faith." The 1957 RIAL television special made such links between the program and politics clear. Aired simultaneously on ABC, NBC, and CBS, it featured a speech from Eisenhower and a roundtable discussion on religion that included Republican congressman Walter Judd, a prominent figure in Abraham Vereide's organization.[13]

RIAL's message about the union of piety and patriotism echoed themes pressed by the president, but on a scale that would have seemed repulsive to most Americans if it had been officially tied to him. In 1956 alone, the RIAL venture erected 5,412 billboards along major highways, with another 9,857 posters featured at bus, train, and railroad stations and 59,590 ad cards highlighted inside buses, trains, subways, and streetcars. Taken together, organizers bragged, the transportation advertising would stretch more than forty-one miles long if it were laid end to end. They described their goal as nothing less than total saturation with the RIAL message:

> Tom Smith gets up, turns on the radio, hears an announcer say: "Worship together every week." On the bus he looks up and sees a car card urging him to "Build a stronger, richer life." He opens his newspaper and reads an ad about "Faith and the Atomic Age." In his office he opens his company magazine to an ad giving him "Food for Thought." Going home he pauses in the bus station before a seven-foot poster picturing a family emerging from a house of worship. Along the highway he sees the same scene on a billboard. Home, he turns to his Reader's Digest and reads a RIAL page about "The Look On Their Faces." He turns on the TV . . . to a one-minute film on religion.

And that was only the national campaign:

> If Tom Smith lives in a community observing Religion in American Life Month, he might also go to a restaurant and use a RIAL table prayer card for his grace. At his service club he might hear a talk about spiritual strength. In his mail he might find a card on "Faith and Football." He might find someone has placed on his car a bumper sticker urging him to attend worship. In the bank a miniature billboard urges him, once again, "Build." It does happen.

Indeed, local communities found imaginative ways to elaborate on the message of the national campaign. Sometimes these efforts took place on a relatively small scale. In Longmont, Colorado, for instance, eighty-two hundred pieces of RIAL material were distributed, mostly left on doorsteps with milk deliveries or tucked into grocery bags. Likewise, in Albany, Oregon, supporters placed two thousand prayer cards on restaurant tables. At times, though, local ingenuity took on impressive proportions, as when bread-wrapping businesses in Columbus, Ohio, and Menasha, Wisconsin, multiplied the RIAL message considerably by placing labels for the campaign on thirty million loaves.[14]

"Religion in American Life" had broad reach at the local level because of the strong support from social clubs and community organizations. In some places, the list of local groups sponsoring the RIAL program reached almost absurd lengths. The local campaign in the Los Angeles suburb of Culver City, for instance, was backed by business organizations such as the Chamber of Commerce, the Realty Board, and the Business and Professional Women's Club; service groups like the Exchange Club, Rotary International, the Kiwanis Clubs, and the YMCA; veterans' groups including the American Legion, Veterans of Foreign Wars, Disabled American Veterans, and Jewish War Veterans; fraternal clubs such as the Lions, Elks, Moose, and Optimists; women's leagues like Soroptimist, Opti-Mrs., and the Palms Women's Club; children's activities such as the Boy Scouts, Girl Scouts, Campfire Girls, and Brownies; religious organizations ranging from the mainline Council of Churches to the evangelical Sky Pilots of America; and community-wide organizations including Parent-Teacher Associations, the Civic Improvement League, and the Coordinating Council.[15]

While this grassroots support for the campaign seemed impressive, it was, to a great degree, another creation of the advertisers. A few years earlier, the J. Walter Thompson agency had put its powers of persuasion to work promoting the "Freedom Under God" celebrations organized by the Committee to Proclaim Liberty; now it applied those same techniques to this new cause. The agency distributed a blueprint detailing the "Seven Steps to a Successful Local Religion in American Life Program." The kit instructed local leaders about which organizations should be recruited for the campaign, how the central committee should be organized, what specific sorts of citizens were best suited to each leadership position, how the various subcommittees should be composed, and what duties each should handle. No detail was ignored. The kit set forth a role for everyone, ensuring that ordinary Americans would be not simply recipients of the

"Religion in American Life" message but participants in its propagation. Their involvement guaranteed a wider dissemination of the RIAL theme, of course, but also a broader acceptance of the message than would have resulted from a simple top-down approach. In an echo of the "minister-representative" model of Spiritual Mobilization, the admen understood that ordinary Americans would be much more likely to buy an idea that they were themselves selling.[16]

The ad agency not only taught local participants how to organize themselves; it told them precisely what to do and say. The "Seven Steps" kit, for instance, included a proclamation to be issued by the mayor. Spaces were left blank so that the mayor could add his name and his town's, but the rest was spelled out for him. "The freedoms we enjoy today are the gift of God, no matter in what terms or creed we worship Him," the mayor was instructed to say. "Faith in Divine power was stamped on this nation's first [sic] money with the words, 'In God We Trust.' Our religious beliefs have steadfastly endured as the foundation of our way of life." The kit also provided a news release that called attention to the proclamation. ("Be sure to make [this form] your copy," the packet instructed, "filling in names and facts. Deliver your release by hand to local editors.") Meanwhile, newspapermen who received that press release had already been issued a prefabricated editorial that they, in turn, were supposed to run as their own. Beginning with a quotation on religion in politics from George Washington, the editorial argued the "ringing declaration of faith by the first President of the United States marks religion as the cornerstone of American democracy. Similar avowals have been made by our presidents right down through history. In fact," the editors were instructed to say, "democracy is a system of government derived from religious principles."[17]

The Advertising Council reported that its efforts had been wildly successful. There was a marked increase in religious observances each year as the annual campaigns reached their peak. "According to the Gallup Poll report of Dec. 31, 1956," the council bragged, "attendance at worship services was highest in America during November, RIAL Month, than at any other time during the year." More important, religious observance had significantly increased from year to year over the life of the campaign. Naturally, the council implied there had been a direct correlation between the two, noting in its 1957 report that "51% of Americans attend worship regularly, compared with 39% in 1949, the year of the first RIAL campaign." Executives at J. Walter Thompson used a different metric, relying on softer claims about religious "affiliation" rather than the harder data on regular attendance, almost surely because it led to more impressive numbers. "Today, for the first time in history, more than 100 million persons in the U.S. are affiliated with some church or synagogue," a JWT newsletter claimed in 1956. "This is 60.9% of the total U.S. population."[18]

As the admen boasted about their own effectiveness, outside observers agreed. In 1957, Eisenhower's secretary of the interior, Fred Seaton, said, "I have only praise for this movement which takes the message of religion and morality out of the cloistered area of church and synagogue and carries it right into the heart of the everyday world, puts it up on streetcars and busses and carries it into millions of homes over radio and television." He admitted that it was impossible to say with certainty if any one factor had been the key to the surge in religious observance. But he thought RIAL deserved credit, pointing to a man-on-the-street interview in the *Toledo Blade* that summed up his own view. "Churches are beginning to advertise their product," an Ohio man said, "and the result is that they are selling it."[19]

The "Religion in American Life" campaign permeated every space in the United States—public and private, national and local, sacred and secular. Its twin messages, about the role of religion as a founding principle in American society and the need for all Americans to employ faith to help themselves and their nation, proved inescapable. But while the admen of Madison Avenue were highly effective in spreading that message, they were not alone. Thousands of miles away in Hollywood, conservative figures in the entertainment industry were working just as hard to install the messages of "under-God consciousness" in popular culture as well.[20]

IN MANY WAYS, THE TELEVISION, radio, and print advertisements put out by the "Religion in American Life" campaign were barely distinguishable from the content surrounding them. Newspapers at the time related biblical stories not simply in religion columns but on the comics page and elsewhere. A writer for *Reader's Digest* rewrote the Bible in the magazine's informal style, syndicating it as a series carried by hundreds of newspapers. Weekly magazines joined the cause as well. In 1953, for instance, an observer of the *Saturday Evening Post* was struck by the "emphatically moral and even religious" themes in the magazine. "If the *Post* was once an emporium of entertainment," he noted, "we must now judge from these stories that it now sees itself as a citadel of faith, and even— such is its intensity of tone—faith's last outpost." In the same vein, *Good Housekeeping* published a small paperback titled *Dwight D. Eisenhower's Favorite Poetry, Prose and Prayers.* (The uncanny resemblance between Ike's little red-and-white-striped book and Mao's "little red book" was, one imagines, entirely coincidental.)[21]

The era's most popular books also focused on religion, representing a shift in consumer interests that was as significant as it was sudden. Reverend Halford Luccock of Yale Divinity marveled that it was "one of the most striking changes in feeling, mood and taste which have occurred in centuries, [taking place] not as changes in literary trends have usually occurred, over a generation or a half century, but telescoped into a very few years." By 1953, one out of every ten texts sold in America was religious in nature. Sales of the Holy Bible neared ten million copies that year, with the new Revised Standard Version outselling all other books. *Publishers Weekly* reported that "the theme of religion dominates the non-fiction best sellers," with spiritual titles including *Angel Unaware, Life Is Worth Living, A Man Called Peter, This I Believe,* and *The Greatest Faith Ever Known* all in the top eight. Reverend Norman Vincent Peale's *The Power of Positive Thinking* ranked second on the nonfiction list, right behind the Bible, for three straight years. Meanwhile, the two most popular works of fiction from 1953, *The Robe* and *The Silver Chalice,* likewise had religious themes. Clergymen were ecstatic. "We believe this has never happened before in American publishing," exclaimed Edward Elson, the president's pastor. "When religion takes over in the field of best-sellers, something is happening in the American mind!"[22]

Television and film followed the religious trend throughout the 1950s. Billy Graham's *Hour of Decision* program was televised by three different networks, on some 850 stations, to an estimated audience of twenty million viewers. Roman Catholic bishop Fulton Sheen, whom actress Loretta Young hailed as "the finest ham in the business," proved almost as strong an attraction, with a weekly audience of ten million. "He is easily the strongest letter-puller on TV," noted one observer; "better than 8,000 letters come in from his audience each week." Recognizing the rising interest in religious programming, Hollywood rushed to produce mainstream films on spiritual or biblical themes. The 1955 film version of *A Man Called Peter,* for example, was intended to show that "religion can be fun." Its protagonist was Peter Marshall, Reverend George Docherty's predecessor at New York Avenue Presbyterian. Ads for the film assured audiences: "He was everybody's kind of guy. . . . He was God's kind of guy." Even as Hollywood brought religion down to earth in this movie and others, it also used biblical stories as the basis for its biggest blockbusters, including *Samson and Delilah* (1949), *David and Bathsheba* (1951), *Solomon and Sheba* (1959), and *The Story of Ruth* (1960). At the same time, filmmakers used the Bible as inspiration for fictional epics, from *Quo Vadis?* (1951) to *Ben-Hur* (1959). By far, however, the most important of the biblical blockbusters was Cecil B. DeMille's *The Ten Commandments* (1956).[23]

A deeply devout and outspoken conservative, the legendary director followed a familiar path to religious nationalism in the postwar era. As with other Christian libertarians, DeMille despised the New Deal. "At the beginning," his son remembered, "he was sucked in by Roosevelt's false promises, but then [the president] proceeded to a very systematic socialist program and DeMille turned against him." The government's growth during the Second World War and DeMille's own conflicts with Hollywood labor organizations only hastened his turn to the right. "When a Union can literally shackle a citizen by forbidding and actually preventing him from working at his trade," DeMille complained to the House Un-American Activities Committee in 1945, "a situation is created which is un-American and unendurable, and the people of the United States are in the grip of tyranny as all-out as Fascism or Nazism or Communism." After the war, DeMille became even more outspoken in his conservatism. "Increasingly," his granddaughter recalled, "he made a distinction between a good American and a liberal. He hated communism with such a passion, thought it was godless tyranny; he thought anyone who was a fellow traveler was a traitor." In private, he expressed even angrier views. "The happiest man in the world to see a continuance of the Truman regime," he wrote, "would be Joseph Stalin."[24]

Not surprisingly, DeMille became a close ally of James Fifield. Although raised an Episcopalian, the director was deeply impressed with the pastor of First Congregational. He often attended services there and lectured to the Sunday Evening Club. In January 1950, when the church celebrated the fifteenth anniversary of Fifield's arrival, DeMille was a featured speaker. The service began with a processional; DeMille dutifully marched into the church alongside Don Belding, the advertising executive who led the Freedoms Foundation, and Fletcher Bowron, the mayor of Los Angeles. DeMille's address, broadcast live on KMPC and KFAC radio, praised Fifield's work in Spiritual Mobilization. "Like all good Americans, he believes in maintaining the separation of church and state," he said. "But, like the Founders of America, he does not believe in the separation of God and government." Pointing, as Fifield often did, to the Declaration's assertion that man's rights were "endowed by their Creator," the director insisted that God alone could restrict those rights. "True Americans," DeMille asserted, "believe that the people own the government. But certain groups have grown strong in the past two decades who believe that the government owns the people. Which side you are on depends to a great extent on how you answer the old question 'What is man?' The Church answers, as the Declaration of Independence answers, that man is the child of God with God-given rights that the State cannot touch."[25]

At the end of his speech, DeMille urged his listeners—the eighteen hundred packed into First Congregational's pews and all those following on the radio—to join in Fifield's crusade. "The honor I know he covets most," he said in conclusion, "is not our words tonight, but our deeds tomorrow." For his own part, the director personally enlisted in Spiritual Mobilization's program, serving as a founding member of the Committee to Proclaim Liberty and helping plan its radio broadcast for the first "Freedom Under God" celebration. Meanwhile, DeMille lent his support to other major figures in the postwar religious revival. During Billy Graham's 1949 Los Angeles crusade, for instance, the director leaked word that he had offered the charismatic preacher a formal screen test at Paramount Studios, thereby providing more publicity for Graham's cause.[26]

The director also worked in the political realm on his own. In 1945, he formed the DeMille Foundation for Political Freedom. A result of his wartime fight against the American Federation of Radio Artists, the foundation worked to weaken labor unions across the country. Fifield helped steer some of his more generous donors to his "admired friend," recommending that individuals and corporations who had already made the maximum allowable contribution to Spiritual Mobilization channel their remaining charitable giving to DeMille. "His organization seeks to secure legislation protecting the 'right to work,' which is basic to Freedom," Fifield advised his allies. "It needs and, assuredly, deserves the consideration and support of all corporations and individuals who wish to be counted in Freedom's fight." As a result, many of the same interests that had generously supported Spiritual Mobilization donated to DeMille's foundation too. General Motors gave $20,000, for instance; Chrysler, $10,000 more.[27]

Despite his political activism, DeMille believed he could best serve the conservative religious revival with his considerable talents as a filmmaker. In August 1952, he announced that his next film would be an epic production of *The Ten Commandments*. The director had already produced a film on the topic three decades earlier, but he wanted to tackle it again. "I feel that this subject is particularly timely today," he announced to the press. "There is a spiritual resurgence throughout the world. I want to do my part in furthering this spiritual mobilization both in countries where the state has not tried to replace God and in countries where it apparently has." (Reporters did not ask into which category the director believed his own country fell.) In later interviews, DeMille often described the story in tones strikingly similar to those in his speech for Fifield. "The great clash between two beliefs is dramatized," the director explained to the *Los Angeles Times*. "Rameses II represents the ruler governing only by his own whims and caprices, whereas Moses brought to the people a rule of life which was eternal and right because it came from the Supreme Being." "It is the story of human freedom," he told the *Washington Post*, "whether men are to be ruled by law or by the whims of dictators, whether they are to be free souls under God or whether they belong to the state."[28]

In promoting the film, DeMille and his crew presented *The Ten Commandments* as a true story grounded in the hard facts of history and the holy truths of the Bible. A year before its premiere, the film's screenwriter Aeneas MacKenzie vouched for its accuracy in a lengthy piece for the

New York Times. He recalled how DeMille made his "team of scenarists" aware of the solemnity of their duty. "There is no place for the usual fiction in a picture that deals with the interpretations and circumstances from which not one—but three!—of the world's great religions have sprung," the director had instructed. "You may dramatize the scenes in any way you wish, but whatever episodes you employ must be justified to me in terms of recognized authorities. You are to invent nothing out of your own talented imaginations. " (At this, MacKenzie remembered, DeMille had added a flourish from the pharaoh: "So let it be written, gentlemen! So let it be done!") The director, however, had issued an impossible demand, for there simply was no record for much of Moses's life. The biblical account introduced Moses as a baby along the Nile and then returned to him three decades later, with no mention of his life in between. For a film that claimed simply to reveal God's words, much of its script would have to be written by man.[29]

To preserve the illusion of historical accuracy, DeMille instructed his head of research, Henry Noerdlinger, to find the documentation that would be needed to fend off religious and academic critics. Noerdlinger cast his net broadly, drawing on ancient rabbinical texts, early Christian narratives, and the Koran. Most of these accounts had been composed centuries after the Book of Exodus, leading the researcher to refer to them cautiously as "traditions" rather than "histories." But he used them all the same, filling in the missing decades of Moses's life with a story quite literally made for Hollywood. In his telling, the Hebrew prophet who defiantly challenged the pharaoh had grown up with him as a fellow prince of Egypt. This was a version of events that had eluded biblical scholars in three major faiths for millennia, but DeMille's team insisted it was true, or true enough. For proof they pointed not to the quality of Noerdlinger's work but to the quantity, noting repeatedly that he had consulted some 1,644 sources in his research. Such claims helped keep critics of the film at bay. But more important, they gave DeMille the necessary cover to advance his own subjective interpretation as objective fact.[30]

DeMille went to great lengths to ensure that the audience saw the film as he did. A ten-minute trailer for the blockbuster, for instance, showed the director in an elegantly furnished room that overflowed with original works and reproductions of classical art, leather-bound Bibles, reference books, and assorted historical documents. With the care of a curator, DeMille examined the evidence and instructed moviegoers on its meaning. "All this happened three thousand years ago," he said, "but we're still fighting the same battle that Moses fought. Are men to be ruled by God's laws? Or are they to be ruled by the whims of a dictator, like Rameses II? Are men property of the state? Or are they free souls under God?" Shortly before its premiere, the director filmed a special introduction to be shown before the film. In it, DeMille parted a gold and white curtain, strode toward the audience, and informed them they were about to witness "the story of the birth of freedom." He then repeated, virtually verbatim, his lines from the trailer about the film's depiction of the timeless struggle between tyranny under the state and freedom "under God." If moviegoers still missed the connection to present-day politics, the official program distributed at screenings spelled it out plainly. On its final page, the noted painter Arnold Friberg depicted Moses, his arms outstretched, with the Liberty Bell ringing behind him. Across the top of the page ran the same passage from Leviticus used earlier by Spiritual Mobilization: "Proclaim Liberty Throughout All the Land, unto All the Inhabitants Thereof." "These," the program explained, "are the last words spoken by Moses in the motion picture as a mandate of liberty to the people."[31]

When the film premiered in November 1956, audiences were awestruck. DeMille had spared no expense, with his budget ultimately ballooning to an astronomical $15 million. The cast of twenty-five thousand included everyone from Hollywood stars to Bedouin tribesmen, with all their actions captured in a stunning new widescreen format known as VistaVision. Appropriately for a film of such scale, *The Ten Commandments* opened at the celebrated Criterion Theatre on Broadway. As stars left their cars, they posed for photos as crowds of screaming New Yorkers pressed against police barricades on the sidewalks. Only the Camel cigarettes billboard seemed unimpressed by the spectacle, coolly blowing smoke rings a block away. The film played to sellout crowds at the Criterion for the next year. The three-hour-and-thirty-nine-minute running time meant that the theater could show it only twice a day, except on Saturdays and holidays, when it ran three times. Yet the film was still seen at that single theater by more than 1.3 million patrons, for a box office gross of $2.5 million. Across

America, it sold nearly twenty-two million tickets in its first year of release. Even today, it still ranks as the fifth-highest-grossing film of all time, with receipts measured in constant dollars.[32]

Yet the most lasting legacy of *The Ten Commandments* was its marketing campaign. As he prepared for the debut, DeMille worked with the Fraternal Order of Eagles on an ambitious plan to establish monuments of the Ten Commandments on public property across the nation. The organization had been distributing copies of the Ten Commandments for years, inspired by an incident in which Judge E. J. Ruegemer of St. Cloud, Minnesota, learned that a juvenile defendant in his courtroom had never heard of the laws and "sentenced" the boy to learn and obey them. Ruegemer, the head of the Eagles' Youth Guidance Commission, persuaded the fraternal order to take up the cause. Members and their families volunteered to make reproductions of the Ten Commandments, initially manufacturing them as paper scrolls in St. Paul and framing them with hand-cut wood and glass. The nearly nine hundred thousand members of the organization popularized the venture, distributing scrolls far and wide. Recipients included city halls in small towns from Washington State to Pennsylvania, judges in Idaho and Massachusetts, and a police detective in Atlantic City, New Jersey.[33]

When he learned of the Eagles' campaign, DeMille immediately wanted to join in. A consummate showman, the director urged the Eagles to work on a grander scale. Instead of modest scrolls, he suggested the organization craft larger stone monuments that more closely resembled the tablets described in Exodus. In the interests of accuracy, DeMille even sent Ruegemer a sample of the granite he had carved from Mount Sinai during his personal pilgrimage to the holy site. Sharing the filmmaker's eye for detail, the judge reported back that the Eagles had decided to build their monoliths "from Wisconsin red granite, believing it to more closely resemble the Mount Sinai granite than our Minnesota reds." In the spring and summer of 1955, the fraternal organization began dedicating these new stone monuments at sites such as the lawn of the county courthouse in Evansville, Indiana. Soon after, DeMille and the Eagles joined forces. The Eagles wanted "to offer to Paramount Pictures our cooperation in publicizing and urging membership and families to see the forthcoming

Ten Commandment film." In return, DeMille promised to use the full influence of his publicity department, including personal appearances by stars of the film, to promote the Eagles' work.[34]

Together, DeMille and the Eagles established Ten Commandments monuments across America. In 1955, for instance, the organization dedicated one as the cornerstone for an addition to Milwaukee's City Hall. "It is unique," Judge Ruegemer announced, for "this is the first time in the history of our country that the Ten Commandments in the form of a monolith will appear as part of a public building." He credited the idea to DeMille, who wanted "to see the Eagles present plaques of the Ten Commandments on state capitol grounds, on courthouse lawns, public parks and other strategic places so that as many people as possible might view the laws of God." To underscore the director's importance in the process, both Donald Hayne, DeMille's executive assistant, and Yul Brynner, who played Rameses II in the film, also addressed the Milwaukee crowd. "The need for the Ten Commandments is even greater today that it was 3,000 years ago in Moses' time," Brynner insisted. "They are the cornerstone on which our freedom rests."[35]

Charlton Heston, who starred as Moses, appeared at another monument's dedication in June 1956. Under a broiling sun, a crowd of five thousand gathered to witness the installation of a monolith at the International Peace Garden located on the American-Canadian border in North Dakota. The stone symbolized, in the words of DeMille's public relations men, "the principle of freedom under God on which the governments of the two countries are based." Following performances by the North Dakota Governor's Band and a Scottish bagpipe group from Manitoba, Heston and Ruegemer unveiled the Eagles' gift. Carved from red granite, the monument bore not only the words of the Decalogue but also images of the American and Canadian flags. "The Commandments monolith," a studio release claimed, "not only serves as a reminder to visitors of God's law and their need to live by it, but of the concepts on which the laws of these nations are based—Freedom, democracy, justice, honor under God." (The concept of "freedom under God" was familiar to Heston. As a "devoted member" of Fifield's First Congregational Church, the actor had delivered some of Moses's dialogue from the film to worshipers in its sanctuary.) After the Peace Garden ceremonies, Heston

To help promote his 1956 blockbuster film *The Ten Commandments,* director Cecil B. DeMille worked with the Fraternal Order of Eagles to construct thousands of granite monuments of the commandments. The actor Charlton Heston, who portrayed Moses in the film, joined Judge E. J. Ruegemer of the Eagles, Fargo mayor Herschel Lashkowitz, and Lt. Gov. Clarence P. Dahl to dedicate one such monument in North Dakota. *Institute for Regional Studies, NDSU Fargo, (2107.30.1).*

signed autographs, took part in a family-style chicken dinner, and warmly accepted a lifetime membership in the local Eagles chapter. The biggest news of the day nearly happened on the flight home, when technical problems on his chartered plane forced Heston to help the pilot make a dramatic emergency landing.[36]

Although generally welcomed, the Eagles' campaign was not without its critics. Originally the organization prided itself on the support its activities received from Protestant, Catholic, and Jewish clergy alike. But as the campaign began to focus on placing monuments in prominent public locations, cracks appeared in this coalition. In July 1957, a Minneapolis rabbi who had long supported the Eagles' efforts wrote Ruegemer to say that his support had its limits. He praised the "highest motives" of the organization and said he still supported the placement of monuments on "private premises." But the rabbi believed "efforts to place these plaques in institutions and places, state sponsored, represents a serious threat to and departure from the classic American principle of separation of church and state." The American Jewish Congress felt the same way, he noted pointedly. Individual chapters of the American Civil Liberties Union, meanwhile, raised similar objections. In June 1957, its Ohio branch sent a polite letter of protest to the mayor of Youngstown about a proposed monument there. "The Eagles' gesture is generous and public-spirited," the letter read, but placement of such a religious icon on public land would "conflict with the healthy American tradition of separation of church and state." While such complaints would, decades later, place these Ten Commandments monuments at the center of landmark legal struggles, at the time they were easily dismissed. The Eagles proceeded with their work, ultimately establishing nearly four thousand monuments across America.[37]

A BALDING, BESPECTACLED AUSTRALIAN PHYSICIAN with jug ears and a jutting jaw, Dr. Fred Schwarz seemed unlikely to become a conservative celebrity on par with the great Cecil B. DeMille. Yet by the early 1960s, less than a decade after his arrival in America, Schwarz was unmistakably a star, considered an authority on the communist menace. *Time* called him a "keen, spell-binding" speaker who was quickly becoming "the hottest thing around," while the publisher of *Life* praised him effusively in a personal appearance at one of the massive anticommunist rallies Schwarz regularly conducted for thousands of paying participants. In 1962, a *CBS Reports* special on the state of American conservatism identified Schwarz as "a new breed of Right Winger—the salesman for the Right." Indeed, his legion of admirers soon included conservative icons such as William F. Buckley Jr., Barry Goldwater, and Ronald Reagan.[38]

With no professional training in politics and no personal experience with the Communist Party, Schwarz instead found his new profession through his faith. "I was an evangelical Christian," he later explained. "The Communists are evangelical in another sense and I know they intended to destroy what I stand for." Believing America would be the main battleground in the struggle between religious freedom and godless statism, he abandoned his medical practice in Australia and emigrated in 1952. He soon began making public appearances and radio addresses across the country, denouncing communism as a dangerous, godless ideology and urging Americans to embrace religion as their defense. "I stressed the role that atheism played in the formation of Communist doctrines, and the logical consequences," he later remembered. "I challenged Christians to be as dedicated to Christian regeneration as the Communists were to creating a godless utopia." His speaking fees helped him build a larger network for his work, though not much was really needed. In 1953, a modest $50 honorarium, given by the International Church of the Foursquare Gospel in Los Angeles, served as all the seed money he needed to create his new organization, the Christian Anti-Communism Crusade (CACC).[39]

Although the Australian doctor was more focused on international communism than domestic issues such as the New Deal state, Christian libertarians welcomed him as one of their own. In late 1952, Schwarz gave a lecture to fifteen hundred participants in the Freedom Club at First Congregational Church, earning thanks for his work in "the preservation of Freedom under God in this distracted world." Likewise, in 1953, Schwarz attended Billy Graham's crusade in Detroit and chatted with him afterward. Graham had heard his anticommunist lectures on the radio and, duly impressed, arranged for the doctor to address a luncheon of congressmen and cabinet officials in the House of Representatives Dining Room. (An Alabama congressman reported back to Graham that the "terrific" lecture had impressed leaders from both parties: "He knocked them cold.") Abraham Vereide also opened doors for Schwarz. In June 1956, select congressmen were invited to attend an ICCL meeting in the Vandenberg Room of the Senate to meet with "Dr. Fred C. Schwarz, noted surgeon, psychiatrist, and authority on the Communistic philosophy of Dialectical Materialism."[40]

Schwarz capitalized on his new influence in Congress to present himself as a leading authority on the problem of communism and the solution of Christianity. In 1957, he addressed a breakfast meeting of the Republican Club, where he so inspired attendees that they "immediately," as one told Schwarz, took steps "to refer you to the House Un-American Activities Committee and to arrange a personal interview between you and an Assistant to the President of the United States." He was soon summoned to testify before the committee's staff on the topic "The Communist Mind." In an interview that ran for an hour and twenty minutes, the doctor—who liked to compare himself to a pathologist in his new line of work—patiently led congressional aides through his diagnosis of the communist menace. Ultimately, he urged greater awareness of "the basic foundations of American civilization" as the only cure. "We must give it priority in our thinking and in our actions," he said. "We must build a strong base of freedom-loving people articulate in their faith, in their love of country, in their love of God, in their love of home, and in their love of law, and we must rally the spiritual forces in the heart of man."[41]

Improbably, Schwarz's congressional testimony quickly became a cause célèbre. The first transcripts were rapidly distributed, forcing Congress to print another fifty thousand copies the following year. Executives at the Allen-Bradley Company, an electronics corporation in Milwaukee, published large portions of the interview as a special double-page advertisement in the largest metropolitan newspapers. "WILL YOU BE FREE TO CELEBRATE CHRISTMAS IN THE FUTURE?" the headline blared. "NOT UN-LESS: You and other free Americans begin to understand and appreciate the benefits provided by God under the American free enterprise system." The ad urged Americans to read Schwarz's words and share them with friends. Much like the other corporations who sponsored like-minded messages, the Allen-Bradley Company insisted it had nothing to gain. "With this advertisement," the sponsor noted, "this company is trying to sell you nothing except the importance of holding fast to your American freedoms including the freedom to live, the freedom to worship your God, and the freedom to work as you choose." Republican senator Barry Goldwater, meanwhile, wrote an opinion piece for the *Los Angeles Times* praising both Schwarz for his insights and Allen-Bradley for its "most useful service to this republic" in reprinting his message. Thrilled by the reception, Schwarz soon repackaged his testimony as a best-selling book, *You Can Trust the Communists (. . . To Do Exactly as They Say)*. Released in 1960, it quickly sold a million copies.[42]

While Schwarz successfully spread his message in print, his energies were more devoted to a whirlwind tour of personal appearances. In 1958, the CACC launched its first School of Anti-Communism. For $5 a day— or $20 for the week—participants were treated to a slate of anticommunist films, lectures, and discussions in a packed schedule that ran from 8:30 a.m. to 9:45 p.m. Schwarz was the main attraction, but the weeklong schools provided a broader "faculty" featuring leading names from the

Fred Schwarz, founder
of the Christian Anti-
Communism Crusade,
promoted a conservative
vision of religious nationalism
in his wildly popular Schools
of Anti-Communism. CBS
identified him as "a new breed
of Right Winger—the salesman for the Right." *Courtesy
of the Ohio History Connection,
Joe Munroe Photographer,
Photograph of Fred Schwarz.*

anticommunist lecture circuit, such as Herbert Philbrick, who infiltrated the Communist Party to write the best-selling book *I Led Three Lives,* and W. Cleon Skousen, a far-right former FBI administrator who authored *The Naked Communist.* Other conservative figures lectured as well, including Frank S. Meyer, editor of *National Review,* and Kenneth Wells, president of the Freedoms Foundation. The first School of Anti-Communism was held in St. Louis, but they soon spread to cities around the nation including Los Angeles, New York, Chicago, Houston, Dallas, Miami, San Diego, San Francisco, Seattle, and Portland.[43]

Though popular across the country, the Christian Anti-Communism Crusade had its greatest successes in its Southern California home. In November 1960, Schwarz held his first anticommunism school in Los

Angeles. Registration cards stressed the dangerous advances socialism had made in America. One side of the form was filled with a bold-print reproduction of a quotation falsely attributed to Soviet leader Nikita Khrushchev: "We cannot expect the Americans to jump from Capitalism to Communism, but we can assist their elected leaders in giving Americans small doses of Socialism, until they suddenly awake to find they have Communism." Having read those words, applicants could simply turn the card over, fill in their information, and reserve a spot.[44] The appeal worked. More than three thousand came to the Biltmore Hotel to hear lectures from Schwarz, Skousen, Philbrick, and others. Delighted by the outpouring of public support, Schwarz organized another school for suburban Anaheim in March 1961. This Orange County School of Anti-Communism broke earlier records for attendance, with crowds topping a thousand a day at Disneyland hotel sessions and even selling out the seventy-five-hundred-seat La Palma Stadium for a "Student Day" event.[45]

Schwarz capitalized on these successes with two major events later that year. First, in August 1961, he opened the Southern California School of Anti-Communism. Patrick Frawley, a Bel Air millionaire who had created the leakproof Paper Mate pen and owned the Schick Safety Razor Company, led the sponsoring committee. Though once apolitical, Frawley had become deeply involved in politics after Cuban revolutionaries seized control of a Schick factory. By the end of the 1960s, he was funneling nearly $1 million a year to conservative causes, leading a progressive watchdog organization to name him the "Number One Man on the Right." Schwarz had been one of the earliest beneficiaries of his funding, beginning with an unsolicited check for $10,500. Frawley devoted himself to the Southern California school. In a sign of his grand ambitions for the event, he reserved the Los Angeles Sports Arena, a massive sixteen-thousand-seat auditorium that served as home for the Los Angeles Lakers, the Sunkist Invitational track meet, UCLA and USC men's basketball, and even the 1960 Democratic National Convention. To help pay for it all, Frawley tapped his contacts at the Los Angeles Chamber of Commerce. It held a luncheon for 641 local businessmen, complete with a speech from Fred Schwarz on "the nature and potential consequences of the threat that Communism presented to the free enterprise system," and thereby won over several new supporters. Meanwhile, Frawley purchased three prime-time television spots during which Schwarz gave viewers half-hour previews. The Richfield Oil Company came on board to broadcast all the two-and-a-half-hour evening sessions of the school. The massive outpouring of corporate support led to high expectations. Agents at the local FBI office reported that it would likely be "the largest meeting of this nature ever to be held in the world."[46]

Throughout the planning stages, organizers of the Southern California School of Anti-Communism advanced the ideology of piety and patriotism in numerous ways. Before the school, they convinced forty-one mayors from the area to declare "Anti-Communism Week in Los Angeles." In his own proclamation, Los Angeles mayor Sam Yorty asserted that all American freedom had resulted from "fundamental belief in God." The program, likewise, carried a bold-print motto: "Under God a new birth of Freedom, a new and deeper understanding of it; a new and deeper dedication to it." The program wrongly attributed these words to Abraham Lincoln; in truth, they came from a rather different Republican, Representative Walter Judd of Minnesota. A staunch conservative and a prominent member of Vereide's organization, the congressman had delivered the line as the climax of his keynote speech to the 1960 Republican National Convention. Organizers arranged for Judd to address the Southern California school through a closed-circuit connection, while other prominent figures, such as physicist Edward Teller and Democratic senator Thomas J. Dodd of Connecticut, appeared in person.[47]

While these figures gave the program gravitas, their popularity paled next to the all-star slate on Wednesday's "Youth Night." The evening began with the patriotic rituals that now routinely brought the nation's public religion to life. First, the capacity crowd of sixteen thousand teens watched a performance of "The Star-Spangled Banner," with a Marine color guard on hand; they then took part in the mass recitation of the Pledge of Allegiance. (Thousands more, turned away by anxious fire marshals, listened outside.) Then a series of celebrities took the stage. Marion Miller, a suburban housewife who had infiltrated leftist groups for the FBI, offered tales from her popular autobiography, *I Was a Spy*. Ronald Reagan warned the crowd that socialism at home was every bit as dangerous as communist attacks from abroad. "Advocates of the welfare state," the actor-turned-activist said, "fail to realize that our loss is just as great if it happens on the installment plan." Roy Rogers, Dale Evans, and John Wayne followed with similar warnings. Pat Boone closed the show, singing a few songs before offering some impromptu comments that electrified the crowd. "I don't want to live in a Communist United States," he told them. "I would rather see my four girls shot and die as little girls who have faith in God than leave them to die some years later as godless, faithless, soulless Communists." As his eyes filled with tears, the audience erupted in applause.[48]

The Southern California School of Anti-Communism proved to be a major accomplishment. The conservative columnist George Todt deemed it "eminently successful in more ways than one. From the standpoint of attendance, speakers, interest, publicity, educational programming, organization, banquet, master of ceremonies [and] accomplishments, this was one of the best performances of its kind in recent years." Others agreed. "As far as I'm concerned," columnist Vincent Flaherty wrote in the *Los Angeles Examiner,* "the most refreshing movement to be launched here in many a day is the Southern California School of Anti-Communism." While the school made an impression on the public, it also impacted the finances of the Christian Anti-Communism Crusade. The accounting firm of Ernst & Ernst reported that the organization raked in $311,253 for the week, an impressive sum in light of the low admission fees. Even after expenses, the CACC still turned nearly $250,000 in profits. Schwarz promised the proceeds would be used to operate similar schools across the country. But in the short term, he decided to capitalize on the overwhelming local popularity of the Southern California school of by staging a sequel two months later, billed as "Hollywood's Answer to Communism."[49]

Organizers worked diligently to surpass the success of the first event. Frawley again led the way, this time securing the landmark Hollywood Bowl for the rally. As master of ceremonies, he enlisted the former song-and-dance man and future US senator George Murphy. (Recruitment here was likely easy. In one of his many corporate duties, Frawley served as CEO of the Technicolor Corporation, where Murphy was then employed as a vice president.) A number of the "faculty members" who had lectured at the Southern California school made a return appearance, including Judd, Dodd, Skousen, and of course Schwarz. The actors made a curtain call as well, with Reagan, Wayne, Boone, Rogers, and Evans all on hand again. This time, though, they were joined by a cast of all-stars that included Jimmy Stewart, Rock Hudson, Robert Stack, Donna Reed, Ozzie and Harriet Nelson, Nat "King" Cole, Jane Russell, Edgar Bergen, Andy Devine, Walter Brennan, Tex Ritter, Irene Dunne, Vincent Price, Cesar Romero, and a host of others then starring on television and in film. Notable directors such as John Ford and studio executives such as Walt Disney and Jack Warner offered their support too.[50]

The program was a powerful combination of patriotic display and showmanship that, in the words of one reviewer, evoked "the same star glitter that enwraps a Hollywood premier." More than two hundred American Legionnaires worked as ushers, while 350 Boy Scouts served as a massive color guard. John Wayne led the capacity crowd of more than fifteen thousand in the Pledge of Allegiance, after which Connie Haines, a singer who had gained fame as Frank Sinatra's partner in the Tommy Dorsey Orchestra, offered her rendition of "The Star-Spangled Banner." Opening the program, George Murphy introduced the stars as "some of the crowd in Hollywood that for years have been opposing Communism." Producer Jack Warner of Warner Bros. echoed that theme in the first address of the evening, noting how communists had sought to infiltrate Hollywood "twenty-five years ago" but their industry "had the guts to fight them in the open" and drive them out. The celebrities then turned the event over to the more substantive lecturers. "When I finally spoke," Schwarz remembered, "only ten minutes remained, so I delivered an uncharacteristically brief message. It was sufficiently forceful to earn me a comparison to Adol[f] Hitler in the student newspaper of Stanford University."[51]

The highlight of the Hollywood Bowl event, however, was a special appearance by C. D. Jackson, the publisher of *Life* magazine. After the Southern California school, his publication ran a two-paragraph item that dismissed the event as a gathering of wild-eyed extremists no different from the John Birch Society. Privately, Schwarz knew well that the two far-right groups often shared a common constituency. In a nine-page, single-spaced letter, Birch Society founder Robert Welch informed him in the fall of 1960 that "we have told our members to encourage, support, and work for your 'schools' wherever they were put on, so far as they had

In 1961, Fred Schwarz introduced "Hollywood's Answer to Communism," a star-studded conservative rally at the Hollywood Bowl filled with denunciations of the communist influence at home and abroad. *Ralph Crane, The LIFE Picture Collection, Getty Images.*

the opportunity and ability to do so; and to encourage the attendance of friends and acquaintances (as well as attending themselves)." In some instances, Birchers had taken an even more prominent role in the CACC schools. "I know," Welch wrote, "that at your recent school in San Diego, some of the people who worked hardest to bring it off successfully were our members, for I saw right on the listing of committees and workers the names of some of our members who had specifically written to ask us whether or not they should participate, and whom we encouraged to do so." Likewise, "quite a number of the leaders and hardest workers" in the Milwaukee and Chicago schools had been Birchers too.[52]

Publicly, however, Schwarz bristled at any suggestion that his organization had anything in common with the increasingly marginalized Birchers. In retaliation for the hit piece in *Life*, CACC's sponsors lashed out. An FBI report noted that Frawley "at once cancelled $80,000 'Life' advertising accounts [for] Schick Razor and Technicolor." At the same time, "Richfield and other large national advertisers also withdrew substantial contracts calculated to total half million dollars." (The sponsors went after less prominent critics with equal zeal. In September 1961, an executive with Richfield Oil sent the head of the Los Angeles FBI office the names and addresses of a dozen private citizens who had written the corporation to complain about its sponsorship of the school, suggesting that they needed to be formally investigated.) Meanwhile, conservative activists organized a grassroots campaign calling for individuals to cancel their subscriptions.[53]

In panicked damage-control mode, the publisher flew from New York to attend the Hollywood rally and offer his personal apology. Before taking over *Life*, Jackson had worked first as an expert on psychological warfare in the Office of Strategic Services, the forerunner of the CIA created during the Second World War, and then as a special assistant to President Eisenhower. He was, in short, someone who could handle a crisis. Confronting an angry crowd at the Hollywood Bowl, the publisher begged for their forgiveness. He noted that Schwarz had dedicated his life to enlightening the nation, but as was the case with "all dedicated men," his selfless work was subject to slanderous attacks from others. "Regretfully, my own magazine recently published an oversimplified misinterpretation" of his work, Jackson confessed. "I believe we were wrong, and I am profoundly sorry." Seeking to atone, the publisher publicly embraced the individuals his magazine had wrongfully maligned. "It's a great privilege to be here tonight to align *Life* magazine with Senator Dodd, Representative Judd, Dr. Schwarz and the rest of these implacable fighters," Jackson announced. To demonstrate the sincerity of his remarks and the strength of his commitment to their cause, he quoted from Schwarz's *You Can Trust the Communists*, which he characterized as "one of the best books analyzing the Communist menace I have read." Dutifully reciting a lengthy section from its closing chapter, Jackson seized on Schwarz's characterization of the Cold War as a religious struggle. "Fundamentally," he read, "the problem is a moral and spiritual one."[54]

By all appearances, the publisher's public apology was accepted. "I don't believe I have witnessed a more thrilling reaction from a large crowd of people than was apparent Monday night through your appearance at the Hollywood Bowl," Murphy wrote. "It was very definitely the highlight in the entire procedure and I would like to add my voice to the literally hundreds which have called us on the phone to say it was one of the most gracious and courageous public statements that I have ever seen or heard."[55] Schwarz was also encouraged by the publisher's public apology and struck up a friendly correspondence with Jackson over the coming months, during which they shared their thoughts about the state of anti-communism in America.[56] Meanwhile, Jackson found himself overwhelmed by the support from those who had witnessed his humbling at the Hollywood Bowl. "I am still being deluged with mail," he marveled at the end of October, "more mail than I have ever received on any occasion during my thirty years with Time Incorporated, 95% enthusiastically favorable."[57]

As the publisher's mail suggested, the general reaction to "Hollywood's Answer to Communism" was overwhelmingly positive. All told, an estimated audience of four million people watched the live broadcast. KTTV, which had dominated local ratings with nightly coverage of the Southern California School of Anti-Communism, aired the Hollywood rally locally as well. Several bid to sponsor the popular program, but Frawley won the rights for Schick. As a consolation prize, Richfield Oil secured the rights to a regional broadcast on thirty-three stations across California, Oregon, Washington, Idaho, Nevada, and Arizona. Taking stock of the overnight ratings, Murphy reported that "in San Diego where we were on a CBS station we led the field by five points, in Seattle on an NBC station we lead the field by eight points, and in San Francisco on a rather poor independent station we came within two points of the leader." The broadcast was such a hit across the West that organizers edited together a three-hour film made up of highlights from the Southern California School and the Hollywood Bowl rally to be aired elsewhere. The program ran in November 1961 on WPIX in New York City, for instance, presented as a public service by Schick and Technicolor.[58]

While these corporations had long been involved in advancing the Christian Anti-Communism Crusade, other business interests came to back the Hollywood program in particular. In December 1961, for instance, Roger Milliken sponsored a broadcast of the three-hour film version of "Hollywood's Answer to Communism" through a chain of twelve stations across North Carolina, South Carolina, and Georgia. As the head of Deering-Milliken, one of the world's largest textile corporations, Milliken was at the time embroiled in an incredibly bitter struggle with local unions, one that soon led to a record fine from the National Labor Relations Board, followed by an unsuccessful appeal all the way to the Supreme Court. By sponsoring the broadcast, with its condemnations of creeping socialism and big government, the textile magnate hoped to sway opinion in the region. He was delighted with the result. "The response was unbelievable," Milliken told Schwarz excitedly. "All of the stations involved have advised us that never in their history have they had such a tremendous and overwhelming support for any program they have ever run."[59]

Some of the stations broadcasting the event did voice reservations. Before agreeing to broadcast the special on the three stations they operated in the Northwest—KING in Seattle, KGW in Portland, and KREM in Spokane—executives at Crown Stations sought assurances that the program would not contain "highly undesirable attributes of what might be called 'the Birch Society approach' to combating communism." Reassured by Richfield Oil that it would be free of "'witch hunting' or character assassination in any form," the broadcasters agreed to air it. In a rare effort to offer a counterpoint, however, they produced their own companion special to offer a more dispassionate approach to the topic. "It could bring us widespread praise," a Crown executive mused, "but more importantly, widespread viewer attention to the fact that there is more to outstripping communism than just being wildly and emotionally agin it." With support from the State Department, Crown quickly put together a ninety-minute special titled *The Threat*. It began with an introduction by Attorney General Robert Kennedy, followed by a roundtable discussion with Arthur S. Fleming, Eisenhower's secretary of health, education, and welfare; Richard Rovere, staff writer for the *New Yorker*; Gilbert Seldes, dean of the Annenberg School of Communication at the University of Pennsylvania; and Dr. Edward Teller, the famed physicist who had lectured at the Southern California School of Anti-Communism. Viewers seemed unimpressed. "I consider the remarks of Teller worth hearing," wrote one woman; "the others became so muddled in their already fuzzy thoughts that they were not worth much."[60]

The widespread replay of the Hollywood rally gave Schwarz and the Christian Anti-Communism Crusade a prominent profile in national politics. Critical appraisals of their work now appeared in mainstream magazines such as *Time* and *Newsweek* as well as prominent religious publications such as *Christian Century* and *Christianity Today*. Most of these pieces took a cautious tone, but on occasion they veered toward mockery. In his "T.R.B." column for the *New Republic,* Richard Strout passed along a tongue-in-cheek report from an informant he called "West Coast Operative X-9" who had attended a CACC organizational meeting at a private home. "Heard phrase several times, 'If Communists come . . . ,'" his informant reported. "Seemed to feel it real and imminent, a Bataan death march with children carried off." More substantively, liberal politicians and labor officials aggressively challenged the CACC. For instance, California's attorney general, Stanley Mosk, appeared on television after the successful San Francisco Bay Regional School of Anti-Communism in early 1962 to denounce it as "Patriotism for Profit." In the same vein, Walter Reuther of the United Auto Workers lambasted the CACC as an extremist organization funded entirely by corporate interests. Such attacks on Schwarz only led the right to clutch him closer. *National Review* ran three separate articles supporting the CACC in June and July 1962 alone, with titles such as "The Impending Smear of Fred Schwarz" and "The Mad Attempt to Get Schwarz."[61]

As the media firestorm began, Schwarz continued to travel the country, holding Schools of Anti-Communism wherever he could, bringing out high-profile supporters at every stop. To promote another Los Angeles School of Anti-Communism, for instance, South Carolina senator Strom Thurmond barnstormed Southern California in late 1961, making ten appearances alongside fellow conservative congressmen and celebrities such as John Wayne. Schwarz held additional schools the following year in cities as diverse as Seattle, Honolulu, and Omaha, but he focused his energies on the major school he planned for New York City. That location had been chosen, he explained, because Manhattan was home to the media that distorted and defamed his work. "We decided to meet this challenge," he noted, "and go to the source." Schwarz ventured into the city several times that year. In May, he faced Michael Harrington in a debate moderated by perennial socialist presidential candidate Norman Thomas; in June, he spoke to a cheering crowd of more than eight thousand at a rally in Madison Square Garden. In August 1962, he opened the Greater New York School of Anti-Communism at Carnegie Hall. Conservative luminaries including William F. Buckley Jr., James Burnham, and Frank Meyer served on the sponsoring committee. The highlight of his trip, Schwarz believed, was his appearance on NBC's *Meet the Press,* during which he had the chance to face his critics. Watching the show, the gossip columnist Walter Winchell was impressed with Schwarz's quick handling of the panel. "He made them all look like jerks," he noted. "He was articulate, knowledgeable and backed up everything he politely said in reply to their needling. . . . It was a delight to witness."[62]

Through his work in the Christian Anti-Communism Crusade, Schwarz emerged as one of the most energetic and effective voices advancing the cause of religious nationalism in the late 1950s and early 1960s. Taking advantage of Cold War tensions during an era of seemingly incessant turmoil, Schwarz insisted that religion would be the key to America's survival and salvation. Much like the advertising executives behind the "Religion in American Life" campaign or entertainers like Disney and DeMille, the physician-turned-preacher was at heart a promoter, one who put his considerable talents to good use convincing Americans that they needed to do more than simply pay lip service to the supposed religious roots of their nation. They needed, as DeMille had urged them, to put those words into deeds in their own lives.

PART III

CONFLICT

CHAPTER 6

"*Whose* Religious Tradition?"

For the evangelical businessmen who belonged to the Gideons International, Inc., selling God was a second calling, if not their first. Founded by a trio of traveling salesmen at the end of the nineteenth century, the Gideons made a name for themselves in the early twentieth by putting millions of copies of the Holy Bible in hotel and hospital rooms across the nation. During the Second World War, the organization distributed, with the military's blessing, a specially prepared edition of the King James Version of the New Testament and Book of Psalms to every member of the armed forces. After the conflict, the group created a new paperback version of this "Gideon Bible" (now with the Book of Proverbs as well) for distribution at public and private schools for all students between the fifth and twelfth grades. In the words of W. L. Hardin, an Atlanta contractor and past president of the Gideons, their new ministry would help them meet their long-standing goal "to win men and women for the Lord Jesus Christ" by reaching them earlier in life. "In the days of their youth, before the evil days come," Hardin said in 1946, "the boys and girls of our public schools may by means of the precious Word of God, come to know Him."[1]

In practical terms, the Gideons' program reflected their roots as salesmen. Their founders originally considered calling the new organization the Christian Traveling Men of the United States of America but abandoned the idea because, as one later noted, "traveling men don't have time to use such long names." So they settled for the simpler calling card, a name inspired by an Old Testament judge who led a small band of faithful Israelites to victory over a vastly larger force. But their identity as on-the-road representatives of business never changed. Indeed, in its first four decades, *only* traveling salesmen could join the Gideons. Even after expanding their ranks to admit a broader range of businessmen in 1937, this spirit of door-to-door salesmanship still prevailed. The postwar program to distribute their abridged Bibles to schoolchildren is perhaps the prime example. In what quickly became a standard script, a Gideon first contacted a local school board or principal to win permission. He then spoke to the entire school at a special assembly, offering an address that an observer characterized as "evangelical in tone and content, on the advantages of Bible reading." After the sales pitch, the Gideons announced that every student—or, in some cases, every student who provided written permission from a parent—was welcome to a free paperback version of the New Testament. Moving from school to school, the Gideons distributed 4.2 million of their Bibles in the first three years, with ambitious plans to distribute 25 million in all.[2]

For the Gideons, their drive to distribute Bibles at public schools seemed a natural extension of the larger effort to encourage public religion in the postwar era. While other religious innovations had been relatively uncontroversial at the time of their creation, the Gideons' ministry to schoolchildren sparked a contentious debate. Religion in the public schools had long been considered a local concern. Communities dominated by one faith traditionally instituted sectarian prayers or Bible reading in classrooms with little complaint. More diverse locales often tried to avoid the issue of religion entirely, but the Gideons brought long-simmering tensions to the forefront. Jewish leaders protested any effort to place the New Testament in public schools, while Catholic officials objected because canon law forbade members of their faith from using the King James Version. "Most children will accept anything free," noted a priest in upstate New York, and thus they would inadvertently sin in taking the gift. In Boston, it became such a widespread problem that the archdiocese instructed priests to order all Catholic children who had accepted Gideon Bibles to return them immediately. Even some liberal Protestants disapproved of the Gideons' campaign. The editors of the *Christian Century* insisted that public schools were simply "not the place" to evangelize, arguing that Christians had "a duty to respect separation of church and state in relation to the schools."[3]

The objections were strongest in religiously diverse cities and suburbs, especially in the Northeast. In the fall of 1951, the school board in suburban Rutherford, New Jersey, inadvertently caused a controversy when it accepted an offer from the Gideons of Passaic and Bergen Counties to distribute their version of the Bible to all students in grades five through twelve in the district. The board printed up permission slips for children to take home, but when scores of parents protested, it found itself on the defensive. At its next meeting, the superintendent of schools, Guy Hilleboe, insisted that "the Gideon Society was not presenting their own version of the Bible but were merely offering a New Testament with Psalms and Proverbs of the King James Version" for families who wanted it. He pointed out that the Gideons had not, in this instance, been allowed to make a special address at school assemblies, and principals had been instructed to send the permission slips home "without comment." Furthermore, Hilleboe added, the state's lawyers assured him that the practice was wholly constitutional.[4]

Despite these assurances, religious leaders and parents continued to object. A local priest asserted that, although he believed Rutherford was a "God fearing town" and he supported the general effort to get "God into the schools," the board had made a mistake. The separation of church and state had to be maintained in schools because the sectarian nature of the Gideons' work would assuredly "create tensions." Likewise, Rabbi Herman Schwartz argued that even if principals offered no comment on the program, several teachers had become "salesmen" for the proposal. The permission slips had also been prepared by school officials, he noted, and therefore the entire endeavor bore the formal approval of the district. Parents echoed these concerns. Mrs. E. K. Ingalls, for instance, reminded the board there had been a similar controversy in their high school over the state-mandated practice of Bible reading during morning assemblies. Catholic students there had refused to read from the King James Version and were castigated by the principal. Was it "good teaching," she asked, for a school to say "you will read the St. James [sic] version or else"? The superintendent recognized "the right of each child in the Public Schools to use the religion of his choice" but maintained that the board had done nothing wrong. The district's legal counsel double-checked the law and re-assured school officials that they were in the right. The Gideons, the board decided, could proceed with their evangelism in Rutherford's schools.[5]

But before they could begin, a pair of parents filed for an injunc-tion. Bernard Tudor and Ralph Lecoque, Jewish and Catholic, respec-tively, asserted that the Gideon Bible was a "sectarian work of peculiar religious value and significance to the Protestant faith." Its embrace by the schools therefore amounted to an establishment of sectarian religion. Their complaints quickly drew national attention. The Catholic diocese and the American Jewish Committee rallied behind them. Notably, civil liberties organizations did as well. While they still held that religious invocations at the national level were relatively harmless, in such local manifestations civil libertarians identified individuals who felt personally wronged by new religious policies and, more important, who would serve as plaintiffs in lawsuits against them. In March 1953, a trial judge in Hackensack heard arguments in *Tudor v. Board of Education of Ruther-ford and the Gideons International*. Leo Pfeffer, a prominent advocate for the separation of church and state, represented the plaintiffs. Bringing forth an array of witnesses with expertise in religion, law, and even child psychology, Pfeffer argued that the school board displayed an "unconsti-tutional preference" for Protestantism by embracing the Gideons and, as a result, infringed on the religious liberties of Catholic and Jewish children. The trial judge disagreed, but the New Jersey Supreme Court reversed his opinion in December, issuing a unanimous decision condemning the school board's actions as clear "favoritism" of one faith.[6]

For the Gideons, it was a stunning blow. Bewildered by the objections to what they saw as a selfless act of kindness, they were doubly shocked that the New Jersey Supreme Court had sided against them. (Search-ing for an explanation forty years later, the head of the Gideons could only surmise that "Satan has been and still is vigorously opposed to this particular program.") The organization's leaders instructed local Gideon camps to hold prayer meetings to determine if they should appeal to the US Supreme Court. The Gideons' leaders ultimately decided God wanted them to do so, but the justices refused to revisit the case in the fall of 1954. Though disheartened, the Gideons later realized the development had been a "blessing in disguise" because it meant the lower court's ruling would be limited to New Jersey. And so they continued to distribute their edition of the New Testament in public schools across the country, discovering that legal and educational responses to their work varied considerably. In Pennsylvania, the attorney general ruled that the Gideons' work was clearly unconstitutional; in Minnesota, his counterpart found nothing wrong. A suburban school board in Connecticut reported it had "successfully resisted" the Gideons' efforts; in Dade County, Florida, officials believed there was nothing to resist.[7]

By the late 1950s, the Gideons' campaign provided vivid evidence of the varied legal landscape on issues of church and state. A survey of school systems across the forty-eight states showed that roughly 43 percent of districts allowed the distribution of Gideon Bibles. Small towns were most likely to accept the Gideons' gifts, with 50 percent of communities with populations under twenty-five hundred doing so. In contrast, larger cities tended to reject the offer, with only 32 percent of districts in areas of twenty-five thousand people or more allowing it. There were regional differences as well. The more rural South and Midwest proved most amenable to the program, with 55 percent and 50 percent of school systems, respectively, allowing it. In the West, 40 percent of districts sanctioned the practice, while in the more urbanized Northeast, only 26 percent did so. Regardless of location, there was always some degree of protest. In districts in the Northeast, West, and Midwest that allowed the Gideons to distribute their literature at schools, 33 percent, 32 percent, and 25 percent, respectively, still reported some form of organized objection. Even in the overwhelmingly Protestant South, 8 percent of school districts with Gideons' programs faced protests of some kind.[8]

As the controversies made clear, public schools became a contentious site in the postwar rise of religious nationalism. In the eyes of those seeking to link piety and patriotism, schools were the obvious place to begin. Many already employed some type of traditional daily prayers or organized Bible readings, and often both. In the postwar era, new practices—such as the addition of "under God" to the Pledge of Allegiance recited by millions of schoolchildren each morning—had been adopted with little objection. But as the religious revival moved from the national level, where vaguely defined ceremonial deism held sway, to individual schools and districts, it necessarily took forms that were at once more concrete and more complicated. Educators at the state and local level required religious programs to be as detailed as the rest of their curricula, and as a result, they soon found themselves involved in controversies that national leaders had managed to avoid. While prominent voices in political and popular culture had encouraged a return to prayer in general, state-level administrators felt the need to choose or compose specific prayers for all schoolchildren to recite as one. Likewise, while religious leaders had urged Americans to turn to the Bible of their choosing, local educators had to pick a particular version, invariably offending one sect or another. And so, as they attempted to channel the "very vague religion" of the Eisenhower era into specific programs, school officials across the country sparked local controversies that, in turn, had national ramifications. The concept of "one nation under God" had seemed a simple, elegant way to bring together the citizens of a broadly religious country, but at the local level, as the Gideons had discovered, Americans were anything but united.

IN NOVEMBER 1951, THE NEW YORK Board of Regents, a thirteen-member body that oversaw all public education in the state, issued a statement on "Moral and Spiritual Training in the Schools." The formal proclamation, passed unanimously, began with a claim that had become increasingly common as the postwar revival swept across the country: "Belief in and dependence upon Almighty God was the very cornerstone upon which our Founding Fathers buil[t]." The regents reasoned that New York public schools were obligated to teach students how faith had informed American history and culture in the past and how it still influenced US politics and civics in the present. Studying America's "moral and spiritual heritage" would ensure that schoolchildren were "constantly confronted with the basic truth of their existence." To underscore the idea that all things in America originated with religion, the regents recommended that each school day likewise begin with prayer. But rather than leave religion in the realm of generalities, as most national leaders did, the board composed a new prayer they hoped would be said during the daily flag ceremonies in New York schools: "Almighty God, we acknowledge our dependence upon Thee, and we beg Thy blessings upon us, our parents, our teachers, and our Country."[9]

The board members believed this prayer—commonly known as the "Regents' Prayer"—was merely the beginning. "These troubled times," the board announced in 1954, "call for the teaching of 'Piety and Virtue' in the schools, and of that dependence upon Almighty God so clearly recognized in the Declaration of Independence, the Constitution of the United States, and the Constitution of the State of New York, and in the pronouncements of the great leaders of our country." ("Just where the Federal Constitution so clearly recognizes dependence on Almighty God, the Regents did not say," noted the theologian William Lee Miller, "but in these troubled times that may not be the kind of question one should ask.") In March 1955, the regents urged the state's schools to make students study documents that emphasized American traditions of freedom, individual rights, and "liberty under God" in general. As examples, they suggested the Declaration of Independence, several speeches made by President Eisenhower, and the new dollar bill with the motto "In God We Trust."[10]

The regents' recommendations were simply that. They had no power to impose the prayer or their other proposals but hoped that local authorities would adopt them. To their delight, many did. In June 1955, for instance, the New York City superintendents drafted a "guiding statement" meant to detail both how and why its teachers should foster "moral and spiritual values" in their classrooms and thereby help "identify God as the ultimate source of natural and moral law." These administrators offered specific suggestions for spreading religion into every corner of the curriculum. Science and math teachers were told that "consideration of the vastness and the splendor of the heavens, the marvels of the human body and mind, the beauty of nature, the mystery of photosynthesis, the mathematical structure of the universe . . . cannot do other than lead to humbleness before God's handiwork." Even in mechanical shop classes, the administrators argued, "the composition of metals, the grain and the beauty of wood, the ways of electricity and the characteristic properties of the materials used, invariably give rise to speculation about the planning and the orderliness of the natural world and the marvelous working of a Supreme Power."[11]

The reactions to the proposals of the New York City superintendents demonstrated how seemingly benign efforts at "strengthening belief in God" could instead foment religious tensions. The Catholic archdiocese of

New York offered enthusiastic support for the superintendents' statement. The Protestant Council, meanwhile, found itself divided on the matter and ultimately issued mixed comments that, on balance, were fairly critical. The New York Board of Rabbis was solidly opposed. Some teachers, it warned, would doubtlessly be "missionaries for their own religious convictions," while others, perhaps worse, would "become advocates of a watered-down, meaningless 'public school religion,' glossing over differences among religious groups that stem from vitally important convictions." Civil libertarians echoed these arguments. The New York ACLU complained that the superintendents' statement "substitutes for the belief in God a vague theism to which, it implies, we all subscribe. The fact is, we do not. Adherence to denominational beliefs is not casual or incidental. It is fundamental—including markedly different beliefs as to the nature of the godhead. To obscure this fact is to intrude secular misinterpretation of a matter that lies at the very heart of religious faith." Stung by the criticism, the superintendents withdrew their original statement and substituted what reporters called a heavily "diluted" version the following year.[12]

Elsewhere in the state, local school officials showed less ambition than the New York City superintendents. Rather than offer schools their own guidelines for religious instruction, they simply adopted the Regents' Prayer. Within a year of the regents' call to action, more than three hundred school districts had already implemented the prayer in their schools. Most of these districts were fairly small, containing just one or two schools, but large metropolitan systems in Syracuse, Rochester, and Utica also took part. In a state with three thousand districts in all, however, the number employing the prayer represented a distinct minority. Most local officials, according to one reporter, saw it as a "hot potato" that invited trouble. In the suburbs of Long Island, for instance, the Board of Education for Great Neck found that that the regents' statement on "moral and spiritual training" had stirred up such "strong differences of opinion" that the board felt compelled to produce a six-page, single-spaced report detailing at great length all the rationales presented both for and against the proposal. The arguments in favor tended to be little more than sweeping generalizations about America's religious heritage and reliance on majority rule. The arguments against, meanwhile, showed a more lawyerly attention to specific details in the state constitution and recent rulings of the Supreme Court. The pro-prayer camp in Great Neck dismissed such objections. "The board should act in accordance with the dictates of its moral, rather than legal, conscience, and decide the question upon its merits," they insisted. "The courts, if called upon, can be trusted to pass upon the legal question."[13]

In neighboring Herrick Union Free School District, parents and educators found themselves similarly torn, but in a struggle that ultimately wound up changing the nation. The boundaries of their district, like most on Long Island, had been set almost arbitrarily, well before the postwar surge in development. Rather than representing a cohesive community, the district encompassed disparate parts of Albertson, New Hyde Park, Roslyn, Roslyn Heights, and Manhasset. It contained only two elementary schools and a single junior high at the start of the 1950s, though a senior high was soon added. As the student population soared, board member Mary Harte became worried about the lack of prayer in the district's curriculum. A devout Catholic, Harte was a longtime resident of the area whose children had attended Herrick public schools. She believed religious instruction was essential to education and repeatedly urged her colleagues to adopt the Regents' Prayer. In 1956, the proposal failed in a 3–2 vote; in 1957, her motion couldn't even win a second. When new members joined the board in 1958, Harte brought the matter to a vote again. It passed by a margin of 4–1.[14]

As had happened in nearby New York City, the Regents' Prayer, intended to unify members of different faiths, only served to drive them apart. The board's vote broke along sectarian lines, with three of the four votes in favor coming from Catholics, and the fourth from a Christian Scientist married to a Catholic. The vote against, meanwhile, came from the only Jewish member of the board. These divisions repeated in the general population, as Catholic families who had lived there for generations voiced resentment about recent Jewish arrivals, grumbling about "these people who are coming out here and trying to run our schools." As the Regents' Prayer widened rifts in the district at large, it caused problems in personal relationships as well. Harte had won her first election to the school board thanks largely to the hard work of campaign manager Dan Lichtenstein and publicity director Lenore Lyons. But when Harte used her position to put prayer in the public schools four years later, she found both of her former allies lined up on the other side, as two of the five plaintiffs in a lawsuit against the board.[15]

Complaints against the board's actions had arisen immediately. When the district newsletter reported its decision, Ruth Lichtenstein and her husband, Dan, were "horrified." Prayer was a private matter for them. "It was a reversal of everything I had ever thought," Ruth remembered. "We never had prayers in my school." Another Jewish mother, Frances Roth, recalled that the news sparked a "spontaneous reaction" across the district. Several parents objected at the school board's next meeting but found officials "resistant, even obstinate." The issue was settled, declared board president William J. Vitale Jr., and would not be subject to any public referendum. In response, Larry Roth decided to act. The vice president of a small plastics manufacturer and a man with "a passion for left-wing causes," he placed an ad in the local paper announcing a lawsuit against the school board and inviting other parents to join. Fifty expressed interest, but when it came time to file, only five remained—Lenore Lyons, a Unitarian; Monroe Lerner, an Ethical Culturist; and Larry Roth, Dan Lichtenstein, and Steven Engel, all Jews. Because his name came first alphabetically, the case was called *Engel v. Vitale*.[16]

Some of the plaintiffs and their supporters worried the lawsuit would prompt an anti-Semitic backlash. "There were some who thought we shouldn't do it," Roth remembered. A rabbi from a nearby town cautioned Lichtenstein against taking part, but Lichtenstein dismissed his warning with an old joke. (Two Jews were brought before a Nazi firing squad. As the soldiers took aim, one started screaming, "Down with Hitler!" The other turned and whispered: "Morris, listen. Why make trouble?") But when the parents sought legal counsel from the ACLU, they discovered the lawyers were equally concerned about appearances. "I was a board member of the NYCLU," attorney William Butler remembered. "When the case came up, they decided that the lawyer could not be a Jew. He must be Catholic, that is, someone taking the attitude that he is *defending* prayer and religious freedom, not attacking it. And they looked down at the end of the table and saw a nice Irish-Catholic boy—William Butler." Though he was a self-described "conservative corporate lawyer" who had little experience with civil liberties cases, Butler felt compelled to take the case. "I knew," he later recalled, "that this was the first time in the history of the United States that a state had actually composed a prayer and then inserted this prayer into one of its compulsory institutions."[17]

As *Engel v. Vitale* made its way through the state courts, the parents' complaints were repeatedly brushed aside. In August 1959, Judge Bernard Meyer at the Nassau County Courthouse sided with the school board. He held that the Regents' Prayer did not violate the First Amendment's establishment clause and, at the same time, was protected by its free-exercise clause. Public prayer, Meyer asserted, was "an integral part of our national heritage." (Evidence of that alleged heritage was found on the wall of his own courtroom, which was adorned with a plaque inscribed "In God We Trust." Only months earlier, the legislative body that oversaw New York's state judicial system had urged the display of the new national motto in all its courts.) Still, the judge ruled that the board had to honor the requests of all students who asked to be excused during the prayer. Though it was hailed as a "compromise decision" by the ACLU, the parents behind the suit were not content. "It seemed strange to me," Larry Roth recalled, "that a judge would render a decision saying 'this prayer is legal, but if you do so and so it's going to be even *more* legal.'" The plaintiffs pressed on to the appellate court in Brooklyn, where they found the phrase "In God We Trust" recently inscribed over the doors. They were rebuffed there as well. Four of the five justices considered the lower court's ruling so obvious that they affirmed it without a word of explanation in October 1960. The fifth justice offered a concurring opinion that deemed the Regents' Prayer a harmless practice within the bounds of the "universally accepted tradition that ours is a nation founded and nurtured by belief in God."[18]

The plaintiffs fared no better before the Court of Appeals, the highest in the state. In 1961, the court affirmed the lower courts' rulings in a 5–2 decision. As before, the majority seemed incredulous at the plaintiffs' claims. "Not only is this prayer not a violation of the First Amendment," insisted Chief Judge Charles S. Desmond, "but holding that it is such a violation would be in defiance of all of American history." Like their colleagues on lower courts, the majority justified its decision by pointing to the many religious references in national politics. There were "literally countless illustrations" that proved "belief and trust in a Supreme Being was from the beginning and has been continuously part of the very essence of the American plan of government and society." Specifically, they pointed to the references to the Deity in the Declaration of Independence; the words of our National Anthem: "In God is our trust"; the motto on our coins; the daily prayers in Congress; the universal practice in official oaths of calling upon God to witness the truth; the official thanksgiving proclamations beginning with those of the Continental Congress and the First Congress of the United States and continuing till the present; the provisions for chaplaincies in the armed forces; the directions by Congress in modern times for a National Day of Prayer and for the insertion of the words "under God" in the Pledge of Allegiance to the Flag; [and] innumerable utterances by our presidents and other leaders.

Most of these were recent innovations not yet reviewed by the courts, but no matter. In a sign of how swiftly and thoroughly the religious revival of the 1950s had taken root, these judges cited changes that had occurred in their own recent memory as proof that the country's religious roots stretched back to time immemorial.[19]

From there, the case moved quickly to the United States Supreme Court, where the constitutionality of what Eugene Rostow would soon classify as "ceremonial deism" became the central issue.[20] When oral arguments began on April 3, 1962, the call to order reminded both sides of the pervasive presence of religion in the everyday workings of government: "Oyez! Oyez! Oyez! God save the United States and this honorable Court!" Ten years earlier, Justice William O. Douglas had cited such traditions in concluding that "we are a religious people whose institutions presuppose a Supreme Being." This judgment had come naturally to Douglas. The son of a Presbyterian minister, he had attended religious services three times a week in his younger days. As he grew older, however, he began to have doubts about the role of organized religion in America, doubts that colored his questioning in *Engel v. Vitale*. "This courtroom, where we have an announcement every time we come—'God save the United States and this honorable Court,' we haven't decided whether that's constitutional or not, have we?" he asked William Butler. "We have not decided whether compulsory prayer in the halls of Congress is constitutional. Is that case on its way here?" As nervous laughter filled the chamber, the attorney could only joke back, "If it is, Your Honor, I'm glad I'm not bringing it."[21]

But the rest of the oral arguments showed that the case Butler brought that day did, in fact, involve the constitutionality of religious expressions in public life. In his questions, Justice Potter Stewart pressed the plaintiffs' attorney about the newly amended Pledge of Allegiance. "It now includes in its language the expression 'one nation under God,'" he pointed out. "Now, what's the difference between that and this affirmation of a belief in God?" Butler dodged the issue by noting that the flag salute led children to swear loyalty to their country, not a deity. "Under God," Stewart interrupted. "Under God, yes," Butler replied, "but it's a political—" The justice broke in again: "*Under* God. *Under* God." "It is a political affirmation," the lawyer insisted. "The whole tenor of the utterance is not religious, whereas the utterance in this case is solely religious." Stewart disagreed: "The preposition 'under' presupposes and implies a dependence on a Supreme Being by this entire nation, does it not?" The otherwise composed Butler stumbled until another justice intervened, asking directly if his clients were challenging the constitutionality of the flag salute. Assured that they were not, the Court moved on.[22]

Public religious expressions likewise emerged as a central theme in arguments from the defense. Bertram Daiker, counsel for the school board, began by asserting that the Regents' Prayer was constitutional because of America's religious tradition. "Since the earliest days of this country, going back to the Mayflower Compact," he said, "the men who put the country together have publicly and repeatedly recognized the existence of a Supreme Being, a God." Pointing specifically to the references to a Creator in both the Declaration of Independence and forty-nine of the fifty states' constitutions, he claimed the prayer was "fully in accord with the tradition and heritage that has been handed down to us." When Chief Justice Warren inquired if the prayer was a religious practice, Daiker insisted it was nothing of the kind. "Whenever people gather together in a group and utter a prayer, a recognition of the Almighty, as has been consistently done since the founding of the country hundreds of years ago, we don't find constitutional objections," he said. "How, then, can we say that prayer is all right on any public occasion in a state-paid-for building, with state employees, except for the schools?" If the Regents' Prayer were unconstitutional, in other words, all the rest had to be as well.[23]

Appearing as an "intervenor" on behalf of district parents who supported the Regents' Prayer, Porter Chandler made a similar appeal about the prevalence and power of religious references in public life. He argued that banning the prayer would deprive their children of the right to take part in the nation's religious heritage. While the plaintiffs portrayed the regents' action as a dangerous new development, he asserted that it was the plaintiffs who wanted to break with tradition. Prayer had long been part of public schools, Chandler maintained, and state officials had merely built upon a century of past practice. Moreover, the Regents' Prayer was simply one of many recent manifestations of that long-standing religious tradition, such as the adding of "under God" to the flag salute. "The question was asked whether that had a religious connotation or was a religious exercise," he said. "And I say unequivocally, *yes*." Reading into the record the House of Representatives report for the pledge proposal, the lawyer left no doubt that the change had been made with religious motives in mind. In closing, Chandler sarcastically invited the opposing counsel to familiarize himself with the religious traditions of the nation. "I would ask Mr. Butler," he said, "to recite the words of the Declaration of Independence, or to say that all men are created equal and that they're endowed by their Creator with inalienable rights."[24]

That afternoon, the justices assembled in their conference room to determine their vote in *Engel v. Vitale*. Only eight justices were present, not the usual nine. Justice Charles Evans Whittaker, an Eisenhower appointee who had been overwhelmed by the rigors of the job, had suffered a nervous breakdown earlier in the spring. After spending most of March 1962 in recovery at Walter Reed Hospital, Whittaker abruptly announced his retirement, effective immediately, at the end of the month. (None of the justices knew it at the time, but their ranks would soon be thinned again. Justice Felix Frankfurter—whose constant badgering was cited by Whittaker's son as a "major factor" in his father's collapse—would suffer a debilitating stroke only two days after their discussion of *Engel*.) In keeping with tradition, no witnesses were allowed to join the judges in the conference room, but Douglas's handwritten notes offer rare insight into their discussion. As always, the chief justice spoke first, then the rest in order of seniority. Setting the tone, Warren announced he would vote to reverse the lower courts' rulings and side with the plaintiffs. The Regents' Prayer was clearly "religious instruction" that violated the First Amendment. He sidestepped the larger issue of religion in political life, noting that "the fact that we speak of God with reverence does not mean we can take the prayer into the school," where it would be "difficult" for children who objected to be excused. Hugo Black, a self-described "absolutist" on First Amendment issues, wholeheartedly agreed and voted to reverse. Frankfurter, in the final deliberation of his twenty-three years of service, did likewise. So did Douglas. Tom Clark, whose appointment had been "sacralized" by Abraham Vereide, also favored reversal because there had been clear "compulsion" by the state. Although more conservative than his colleagues, the Eisenhower appointee John Marshall Harlan II noted he too would "reluctantly" vote to reverse the earlier rulings. "This is a prayer," he said flatly, "not a celebration of a patriotic ritual." As the others agreed to reverse, Stewart remained alone on the fence. ("Not at rest," Douglas observed in clipped notes; "still in doubt.") But with seven votes for the plaintiffs, the outcome was not in doubt. After their colleagues filed out, Black asked the chief if he could have the honor of writing the opinion. Warren gladly obliged.[25]

For Black, the *Engel* case was the culmination of a complicated lifelong relationship with religion. A native of rural Alabama, he had grown up deep within the Baptist tradition. In 1907, after arriving in Birmingham to practice law, Black became an active member of its First Baptist Church. His pastor Alfred Dickinson, who had trained at Harvard and the University of Chicago, two bastions of modernist religious thought, was notoriously liberal in his theology. He stood for separation of church and state, welcomed evolutionary biology and textual criticism of the Bible, and contemptuously dismissed "noisy conversions and ecclesiastical whoopee." Black, who served as a deacon at First Baptist and taught its adult Sunday school for nearly a quarter century, came to share his pastor's perspective. "For Black," the historian Wayne Flynt wrote, "the ethics of Jesus—treating all people fairly, promoting social justice, defending the vulnerable and the powerless—were more important than personal divinity." For much of his life, Black professed to be an agnostic. "Understand," he once told his son, "I cannot believe. But I can't *not* believe either."[26]

Though he harbored doubts about standard Baptist theology, Black adhered to its political traditions, especially its centuries-old call for complete separation of church and state. Indeed, he did much to cement that doctrine in American law. In his landmark opinion in *Everson v. Board of Education,* a 1947 case involving a New Jersey statute requiring school boards to reimburse transportation costs for parents of parochial schoolchildren, Black argued that neither the states nor the federal government could "enact laws aiding one religion over another, force or influence a person toward or away from a church, belief, or disbelief, punish a person for profession or nonprofession, levy a tax to support religious activities or institutions, or participate in the affairs of any religious organization." The justice reached back to borrow a metaphor coined in a letter to his fellow Baptists in Danbury, Connecticut, two and a half centuries before. "In the words of Jefferson," Black wrote, "the clause against establishment of religion by laws was intended to erect 'a wall of separation between church and state.'"[27]

As he sat down to write the *Engel* decision fifteen years later, Black was determined to defend that wall of separation. Religious liberty was essential, he told his wife, because "when one religion gets predominance, they immediately try to suppress the others." History was littered with evidence of the dangers that inevitably followed when church and state merged. "People had been tortured, their ears lopped off, and sometimes their tongues cut or their eyes gouged out," Black continued, "all in the name of religion." To illustrate that point, the justice crafted a rigorously researched opinion. He began with the Book of Common Prayer and then reread John Bunyan's *Pilgrim's Progress,* a classic Christian allegory written by a Baptist author who had been imprisoned for defying the Church of England. That was merely the beginning. "The Judge had religious references on his fingertips," marveled one of his clerks, who ran back and forth to the library to collect them. As he wrote and rewrote the opinion, Black piled on more history each time. Lower courts had repeatedly made unsubstantiated claims about the nation's "religious heritage" to support the defendants in *Engel,* but Black was determined to expose their errors with a meticulously researched rebuttal. By the sixth draft, the bulk of his opinion had become a lengthy narrative about the tangled history of church-state relations in the entire Anglo-American world from the sixteenth to eighteenth centuries. "It is a matter of history," he insisted, "that this very practice of establishing governmentally composed prayers for religious services was one of the reasons which caused many of our early colonists to leave England and seek religious freedom in America." Based on their "bitter personal experience," Black wrote, the founders crafted the First Amendment to keep the state out of religion and religion out of the state.[28]

On June 25, 1962, the Supreme Court announced its decision in *Engel v. Vitale.* Inside the courtroom, Black arched forward in his high-backed chair, rested his arms on the bench, and began reading the opinion with unconcealed emotion. In the audience, his wife thought his delivery "sounded almost like a sermon." After explaining the details of the case, Black paused to collect himself and clutched his papers tightly. There could be "no doubt," he went on, that "the daily invocation of God's blessings [was] a religious activity" and, as a result, no doubt that New York "adopted a practice wholly inconsistent with the Establishment clause." Black asserted that the First Amendment embodied the founders' belief that faith was "too personal, too sacred, too holy to permit its 'unhallowed perversion' by a civil magistrate." (Here, an observer noted, "his voice trembled with emotion as he paused over 'too personal, too sacred, too holy.'") In Black's view, religion certainly deserved a place of prominence in American life, but the state could not dictate it. "It is no part of the business of government," he read, "to compose official prayers for any group of the American people to recite as a part of a religious program carried on by the government." Departing from his written text, Black added an impromptu plea. "The prayer of each man from his soul must be his and his alone," he said. "If there is anything clear in the First Amendment, it is that the right of the people to pray in their own way is not to be controlled by the election returns."[29]

Despite his apparently uncompromising stand on the matter, Black signaled in an important footnote that there were limits to his opinion. In response to a dissent drafted by Stewart, Black tried to reconcile the wall of separation between church and state with the many religious invocations that had been introduced to national political culture, especially in recent years. "There is of course nothing in this decision reached here," Black wrote in footnote 21, "that is inconsistent with the fact that school children and others are officially encouraged to express love for our country by reciting historical documents such as the Declaration of Independence which contain references to the Deity or by singing offi- cially espoused anthems which include the composer's faith in a Supreme Being, or with the fact that there are many manifestations in our public life of belief in God." Black concluded that "such patriotic or ceremonial occasions bear no true resemblance to the unquestioned religious exercise that the State of New York has sponsored in this instance." With the majority of the Supreme Court supporting him, Black thus affirmed the essential constitutionality of what scholars would later term ceremonial deism.[30]

One of his colleagues, however, disagreed. Douglas, who had argued only a decade earlier that the government's embrace of religion raised no constitutional problems, had begun to express doubts during the deliber- ations over *Engel*. He worried about being hypocritical. "I am inclined to reverse if we are prepared to disallow public property and public funds to be used to finance a religious exercise," Douglas explained. "If however we would strike down a New York requirement that public school teachers open each day with prayer, I think we could not consistently open each of our own sessions with prayer. That's the kernel of my problem." When the majority went out of its way to affirm the constitutionality of such practices, Douglas pushed back with a concurring opinion. He agreed that the Regents' Prayer violated the establishment clause, but then went further to challenge a broader range of religious policies. "The point for decision is whether the Government can constitutionally finance a re- ligious exercise," Douglas argued. "Our system at the federal and state levels is presently honeycombed with such financing." (Here he added an important footnote of his own, denouncing a wide array of "government 'aids' to religion," including religious proclamations by presidents, the use of "In God We Trust" on currency, and the addition of "under God" to the Pledge of Allegiance.) "Nevertheless," he continued, "I think it is an unconstitutional undertaking whatever form it takes."[31]

At the other end of the spectrum, Stewart offered the lone dissent. Though he typically took a liberal position on First Amendment issues, he argued that the majority had "misapplied a great constitutional princi- ple." "I cannot see how an 'official religion' is established by letting those who want to say a prayer say it," Stewart wrote. "On the contrary, I think that to deny the wish of these school children to join in reciting this prayer is to deny them the opportunity of sharing in the spiritual heritage of our Nation." Like Douglas, he believed the Regents' Prayer was inseparable from other manifestations of public faith. But in citing the same examples as his colleague, Stewart came to the opposite conclusion, asserting that these ceremonies should be upheld, rather than struck down, as Douglas believed. Still, he shared Douglas's puzzlement at the majority's willingness to strike down the Regents' Prayer but sanction the rest: "Is the Court suggesting that the Constitution permits judges and Congressmen and Presidents to join in prayer, but prohibits school children from doing so?" Ultimately, Stewart believed, neither the state nor the federal government, in the regular religious ceremonies of either Congress or their own court, established anything approximating an "official religion." Although alone in his dissent, Stewart soon found much of the country in agreement with him.[32]

The outraged reaction to the *Engel* decision was, in large part, driven by alarmist coverage in the press. The court's majority had gone to great lengths to note that their ruling merely struck down the Regents' Prayer and, moreover, did so only because of the unique role that New York State officials played in its composition and implementation, but newspapers lost the nuances. "God Banned from the State," ran a typically hyperbolic headline. Hostile editorials only compounded the problem. The New York *Daily News,* for instance, lambasted the "atheistic, agnostic, or what-have-you Supreme Court majority," while the *Los Angeles Times* complained they made "a burlesque show" of the First Amendment. Publisher William Randolph Hearst Jr. went so far as to call for a complete rewriting of the First Amendment in a signed editorial that ran in all his papers. The media's misrepresentations were so widespread that the *Columbia Journalism Review* devoted its fall issue to figuring out just how and why it had all gone so spectacularly wrong.[33]

The overwrought reactions in the press fueled, and were in turn fueled by, equally hyperbolic comments from politicians. As the *Columbia Journalism Review* report found, "The wire services, in their efforts to follow up an obviously 'hot' story, worked on a first-come, first-served basis in selecting persons for comment." As a result, early coverage was "heavily loaded" with negative comments from politicians, especially "Southerners already hostile to the court for its desegregation decisions." The Associated Press, for instance, updated its noon bulletin on the decision throughout the afternoon with comments from outraged southern congressmen. Representative George Grant of Alabama remarked, "They can't keep us from praying for the Supreme Court." Another Alabamian, Representative George Andrews, offered a more dramatic line. "They put the Negroes in the schools," he marveled, "and now they've driven God out of them." Less than an hour later, the AP added a comment from Representative Howard W. Smith of Virginia. "The next thing you know," he said, "they'll be telling us we can't open our daily House sessions with prayer."[34]

As the Capitol became consumed with the school prayer decision, attention turned naturally to the White House. The issue of religion in public life was especially tricky for President John F. Kennedy, the nation's first Catholic president. On the 1960 campaign trail, he had been hounded by so many accusations that he would impose his personal faith on the nation that he confronted the issue directly in an address to Protestant ministers in Houston. "I believe in an America where the separation of church and state is absolute," he had claimed, "where no Catholic prelate would tell the president (should he be Catholic) how to act, and no Protestant minister would tell his parishioners for whom to vote." Once in office, Kennedy tried to walk that line by closely following the path forged by Eisenhower. He dutifully presided over the new, uncontroversial interfaith events, such as the National Prayer Breakfast. But when it came to more personal expressions of faith he usually demurred. Where Eisenhower had delivered his "little prayer" at his inauguration, for instance, Kennedy instead invited poet Robert Frost to provide a more secular sensibility to the proceedings. For a year and a half, Kennedy managed to avoid issues of church and state. But now the Warren Court had forced his hand.[35]

In a press conference two days after the decision, Kennedy finally addressed it. In measured remarks, he cautioned Americans to approach the issue calmly. Noting that it was important to "support the Supreme Court's decisions even when we may not agree with them," the president reminded Americans that "we have in this case a very easy remedy, and that is to pray ourselves, and I would think that it would be a welcome reminder to every American family that we can pray a good deal more at home, we can attend our churches with a good deal more fidelity, and we can make the true meaning of prayer much more important in the lives of all our children." As Kennedy called for calm, however, a few of his predecessors fueled the fires. Herbert Hoover denounced *Engel* as a "disintegration of a sacred American heritage," while Eisenhower asserted that he "always thought this nation was an essentially religious one." Truman pointed out that it was actually the Court's duty to interpret the Constitution, but he was largely ignored.[36]

Congressional leaders only ramped up their rhetoric. The ruling, Senator Herman Talmadge of Georgia thundered, was "an outrageous edict" and "a blow to all believers in a Supreme Being." His colleagues in the Senate largely agreed. Barry Goldwater of Arizona denounced the decision as a "blow to our spiritual strength," while James Eastland of Mississippi likewise called it as a major step toward "the destruction of the religious and spiritual life of this country." While the Senate fretted about the country's spiritual foundations, the House decided to act. Representative Fred Marshall of Minnesota proposed placing "In God We Trust" prominently above the Speaker's dais in the chamber. He had come up with the idea years before in conversation with his recently departed colleague Louis Rabaut, but the Court's decision finally prompted action. Democratic Speaker John W. McCormack of Massachusetts soon gave his endorsement: "The words 'In God We Trust' symbolize the path that our country has always taken since its origin and, pray God, will always take." The proposal sped through the House, passing unanimously in September 1962. In case anyone missed the significance, Representative William Randolph of Missouri noted for the record that the House had given "in a not so subtle way our answer to the recent decision of the U.S. Supreme Court order banning the Regents' Prayer from the New York State schools." Indeed, he added, after passing the proposal, "some Members were heard to say that we had just reversed the decision." The Capitol architect began working on a golden engraving of "In God We Trust" to be placed above the speaker's chair. In the meantime, he painted the motto there in gilt letters as a temporary fix.[37]

Congress was far from alone in its opposition to *Engel*. As soon as the opinion went out over the wire services, Hugo Black found himself inundated with telephone calls and, soon, more than a thousand letters. The vast majority of his correspondents were outraged by what the decision said (or, rather, what they misunderstood it to say). Notably, their letters repeatedly invoked the various manifestations of religion in public life to argue that the Supreme Court had erred. "Our country was founded on faith in God," read a typical letter from a Pasadena woman. "Our Senate amended the Pledge of Allegiance to incorporate the words 'under God' to establish and confirm that fact. An invocation and a benediction are a part of the inauguration of our President. Our Congress opens its sessions with a prayer. The Supreme Court acknowledges it by use of a crier at each convening of this venerable body. In recent years, it has become a practice to hold an annual prayer breakfast, attended by the President and his Cabinet." The litany varied from letter to letter, but the sentiment remained the same. "Our nation has been greatly blessed 'under God,'" read a petition from four dozen Charlotte residents, "and our motto 'IN GOD WE TRUST' should be emphasized in every phase of our national life." An angry mother from Phoenix wrote, "As for me and my family, we believe in the *Free* America, which was brought forth by our Founding Fathers—*under God!*"[38]

Ignoring—or perhaps ignorant of—the opinion's limits, several of Black's critics warned of a slippery slope ahead. "In a country whose forefathers used the word 'God' in virtually every document written," worried a woman from San Diego, "suddenly our children might be outraged or contaminated by the very use of His name in a simple petition! Will the next step be forbidding the reading of these same documents in our American history classes? Where will this end?" "What's next?" wondered a rural Alabamian. "Will God's name be omitted from the 'Flag Salute' and 'Star Spangled Banner' to appease the atheists?" "When do you plan to require our Government to take 'IN GOD WE TRUST' off our money?" asked a Virginian. For some, dire consequences were limitless. A California man fired off his fears in rapid order: "Next God will be taken out of the oath of the President; out of the courts; out of the National Anthem, the salute to the flag; off of the coin of the U.S.; out of the Battle Hymn of the Republic; prayer will be taken out of the House and Senate; the national observance of a Day of Thanksgiving to God abandoned," and finally "Christmas and the Christian Sabb[a]th" will be objected and vetoed by our Supreme Court as embarrassing to somebody." Some imaginations

The Supreme Court's decisions striking down state-mandated programs of prayer and Bible reading in public schools generated a wide range of reactions. Here, Charles Schulz captured the popular panic that the decisions would drive religion out of public life. *PEANUTS © 1963 Peanuts Worldwide LLC. Dist. By UNIVERSAL UCLICK. Reprinted with permission. All rights reserved.*

In this image, political cartoonist Herb Block dismissed such concerns, suggesting that religion might be best encouraged in the private sphere. *A 1963 Herblock Cartoon, © The Herb Block Foundation.*

ran even wilder. "How about next time around lets abolish all references to God in official documents," wrote a woman from Fort Lauderdale. "Then the third time around lets imprison anyone mentioning God or attending a religious service, & fourth time around—set up the firing squad, & fifth—get your silver platter out & hand us over to you know who."[39]

For Black, the deluge of criticism was stunning. Reading the angry letters, he said, was a "real education." He replied to the calmer complaints, often suggesting that his correspondents had been misled about the decision and urging them to read it themselves. He largely ignored the angrier ones but occasionally felt compelled to respond. "One woman condemned Hugo to Hell," his wife recalled, "and he wrote an answer telling her a bit sarcastically, I thought, that if she would go to the library (as he was sure she would not have it in her own house) and ask for a book called the Bible, she should turn to the chapter and read where it said 'Pray in your own closet.'" Black, the former Sunday school teacher, referred other critics to that same passage, though usually in gentler tones. "To those who think prayer must be recited parrot-like in public places in order to be effective," he explained to a niece, "the sixth chapter of Matthew, 1 to 19, might be reflected upon, particularly verses 5 through 8."[40]

Black was not the only one who took solace in the Gospel of Matthew. Reverend Edward O. Miller, the liberal rector of St. George's Episcopal Church in Manhattan, applauded the *Engel* ruling in the *Christian Century*, citing the same passage as his rationale. Dean Kelley, a United Methodist minister who led the National Council of Churches' Department of Religious Liberty, parodied the same piece of Scripture to mock the Court's critics. "Practice your piety before men to be seen by them," he chided. "Require the little children to bow their heads and pray, or at least keep silent while others do, using the pious words that your rulers give you. Then everyone will remark how religious you are. Then religion will be greatly helped and faith in Faith will become very popular."[41]

Initially, these religious supporters of the decision were few in number. Reacting to the early, exaggerated reports of the ruling, most churchmen were aghast. Billy Graham was "shocked and disappointed" by the decision, which he warned was "another step toward secularism in the United States." "Followed to its logical conclusion," he said, "prayers cannot be said in Congress, chaplains will be taken from the armed forces, and the President will not place his hand on the Bible when he takes the oath of office." Francis Cardinal Spellman, Catholic archbishop of New York, likewise said he was "shocked and frightened" because "the decision strikes at the very heart of the Godly tradition in which America's children have for so long been raised." Such reactions from conservative religious figures might have been expected, but some liberal clergymen voiced the same complaints. The theologian Reinhold Niebuhr, for instance, defended the Regents' Prayer as "a symbol of the religious life and tradition of the nation" and criticized the Court for "using a meat-ax" against it. Bishop James A. Pike of the Episcopal Church likewise worried that "the decision *deconsecrates* not merely the schools, but the *nation*. It is, as someone has said, 'a new Declaration of Independence—independence from God.'"[42]

In time, however, most religious leaders made peace with the ruling. To Black's delight, Baptist bodies including the Southern Baptist Convention supported it, believing it fit well with their faith's traditional stance on separation of church and state. Jewish leaders welcomed the ruling as a defense of religious minorities' right to worship as they saw fit, an opinion echoed by smaller Christian denominations such as the Quakers. A number of prominent Protestant publications, from the liberal *Christian Century* to the conservative *Christianity Today*, offered support as well. Some Catholic periodicals did too, with one deeming the initial reactions by the church's hierarchy a "hysterical kind of nonsense" that did no good. Upon further review, even some early critics softened their stance. A few weeks after the ruling was handed down, Billy Graham told newsmen he now believed "the particular decision was all right." When confused Christians wrote for an explanation, his aide had a ready answer. "The Supreme Court has not said that to pray in public schools is unconstitutional," he explained repeatedly. "The only thing they did was to say that the New York State Board of Regents or any other government agency was not authorized to compose prayers to be said in public institutions. I am sure you do not want the New York State Board of Regents to make up your prayers for you."[43]

In fact, as they examined the details of the case, many religious leaders decided the Regents' Prayer was not much of a prayer after all. Seeking to offend no faith, the New York school officials had actually offended many. "The prayer sounds like a Boy Scout oath," scoffed Rabbi Philip Hiat of the Synagogue Council of America. "It's a downgrading prayer." Dr. Franklin Clark Fry, president of the Lutheran Church in America, agreed. "When the positive content of faith has been bleached out of a prayer," he said, "I am not too concerned about retaining what is left." The evangelical editors of *Christianity Today* refused to mourn the demise of a "corporate prayer" that represented little more than a "least-common-denominator type of religion." The *Christian Beacon,* voice of the far-right fundamentalist American Council of Christian Churches, echoed this argument. "Prayer without the name of Jesus Christ was not a non-denominational prayer—it was simply a pagan prayer," the editors announced. Reciting it was an empty gesture that would "not get higher than the ceiling anyhow."[44]

These religious leaders—and the millions who took their cues from them—came to believe that the Supreme Court had not sided against true prayer. They took solace in the opinion's assurances that all the other religious references in public life would remain undisturbed. But more important, they took to heart the idea that the *Engel* ruling had targeted a prayer that came from bureaucrats instead of the Bible. This uneasy truce between the court and the churches, however, would be short-lived.

AS RELIGIOUS AND POLITICAL LEADERS tried to make sense of the Supreme Court's decision on school prayer in 1962, many warily awaited another ruling on the related matter of Bible reading in the public schools. Devotional readings, generally drawn from the King James Version, had been part of public school curricula in much of the country since the early nineteenth century. By the middle of the twentieth century, the forty-eight states fell neatly into four categories. In twelve states and the District of Columbia, daily readings from the Bible were legally mandated in all public schools. In twelve others, legislation or legal decisions specifically permitted the practice but did not require it. Another thirteen states had never addressed the issue but seemed to permit it. In the last eleven, Bible reading had been explicitly banned from public schools either by state constitutions or by acts of the legislature.[45] Regionally, the bulk of Bible reading took place in the South and Northeast, in 77 percent and

68 percent of school systems, respectively. In the Midwest and West, by contrast, the practice was far less common, with only 18 percent and 11 percent of school districts either mandating or permitting Bible readings.[46]

In states that required the practice, public officials oversaw it with precision. In Idaho, for instance, teachers were required each morning to "read, without comment or interpretation, from twelve to twenty verses from the Standard American Version of the Bible, to be selected from a list of passages designated from time to time by the State Board of Education." School districts were legally obligated to furnish each classroom with a regulation copy of the Bible. The state board, meanwhile, fulfilled its legal duty by providing teachers a carefully prepared list of 452 sets of readings, ranging from seemingly nondenominational topics such as "Prose and Poetry" and "Great Songs and Lyrics" to explicitly Christian topics such as "Life of Jesus" and "Letters" from Paul, James, Peter, and John. Elsewhere, local boards determined the details. In Little Rock, the board of education composed a handbook on "Character and Spiritual Education" in 1954 "with the hope that it will be of help to teachers in conforming to the statutory requirements in the State of Arkansas." (Among other instructions, the guide reminded administrators that "the motto 'In God We Trust' [had] to be appropriately placed in every classroom.") On Bible reading, the school board assigned broad themes for each month of the school year and then designated specific passages for each day, with various grade ranges assigned different lessons. For instance, on the first Monday morning in the sixth month of the school calendar, students were taught "Jesus Loves Children (Mark 10:13–14, 16)" in grades 1–3, "The Kingdom of God Is the Message of Jesus (Mark 1:9–15)" in grades 4–6, "Check Yourself First (Matt. 7:1–12)" in junior high, and "The Beatitudes (Matt. 5:1–12)" in senior high.[47]

As states and cities such as these mandated Bible reading in public schools, they invited court cases that again testified to a wide range of opinion. By the mid-twentieth century, courts in fourteen states had determined that Bible reading was not a "sectarian practice" and therefore could continue.[48] In Georgia, for instance, a state court asserted in 1921 that "it would require a strained and unreasonable construction to find anything in the ordinance which interferes with the natural and inalienable right to worship God according to the dictates of one's own conscience." Courts in five other states, however, came to the opposite conclusion.[49] "It is true this is a Christian state," an Illinois court noted in 1910. "The great majority of its people adhere to the Christian religion. But the law knows no distinction between the Christian and the Pagan, the Protestant and the Catholic. All are citizens. Their civil rights are precisely equal. The school, like the government, is simply a civil institution. It is secular not religious in its purposes. The truths of the Bible," it held, "are the truths of religion, which do not come within the province of the public school."[50] Despite the differing opinions in the states, the Supreme Court never directly addressed the constitutionality of such school programs until the early 1960s.

Abington School District v. Schempp stemmed from a 1949 statute requiring teachers in Pennsylvania's public schools to read "at least ten verses from the Holy Bible" to their classes each morning without comment. Instructors who failed to do so would be fired. Civil libertarians immediately objected but resolved to wait until the policy was implemented and a plaintiff came forward to challenge it. In November 1956, the Philadelphia ACLU received a letter from Ellory Schempp, a sixteen-year-old Unitarian enrolled in Abington Senior High School, in the suburbs north of Philadelphia. Schempp had protested the mandatory Bible reading in his school that fall, refusing to stand for the ceremony and instead sitting at his desk, reading a copy of the Koran. His homeroom teacher sent him to the principal's office; the principal sent him to the guidance counselor. (As he later joked, "I was clearly in need of psychological help.") For the remainder of the school year, he was required to report to the guidance office during morning prayers. Schempp wrote his local ACLU "for any help you might offer in freeing American youth in Pennsylvania from this gross violation of their religious rights." After six months of deliberation, the organization agreed to take his case.[51]

The lawsuit was filed in the spring of 1958 by Schempp's parents, on his behalf and on behalf of his younger siblings, Roger and Donna, who objected to the Bible reading requirements in the local junior high school. Faithful members of the Germantown Unitarian Church, the Schempps complained that the state statute interfered with their right to instill in their children only the religious values of their own choosing. "We hope this action will not be interpreted as an attack on religion or the Bible,"

Edward Schempp said. "We believe that random Bible reading and state control degrades religion. To us, religion is too precious, too important, and too personal to permit the state to meddle in it." At the initial hearing, the electronics engineer asserted that the daily Bible readings were essentially a religious ceremony, an opinion backed by numerous witnesses who related that teachers and students alike called them the "morning devotions." In terms of content, Schempp objected to Old Testament selections that detailed gruesome acts such as blood sacrifices and portrayed a "god of vengeance" that, his lawyers noted, was "contrary to the concept of the deity which he had endeavored to instill in his children." His son argued that the Bible passages read in class advanced a number of beliefs—including the divinity of Christ, the immaculate conception, the Trinity, and the existence of an anthropomorphic God—that he did not hold as a Unitarian.[52]

In September 1959, a three-judge panel of the US District Court in Philadelphia ruled unanimously in favor of the Schempps. Brushing aside arguments that the Bible was somehow a "non-sectarian" work of literary or historical significance, the judges stated it was clearly "a religious document." "The daily reading of the Bible," they ruled, "buttressed with the authority of the State and, more importantly to children, backed with the authority of their teachers, can hardly do less than inculcate or promote the inculcation of various religious doctrines in childish minds." State officials immediately appealed the ruling to the US Supreme Court but also swiftly amended the Bible reading requirements, allowing students and teachers to be excused if they wished. Because the statute had been changed, the Supreme Court returned the case to the district court for reargument. Edward Schempp testified that the exemptions did not satisfy him, because his children would be "labeled as oddballs" by classmates who, his lawyers explained, "were liable to lump all particular religious differences or religious objections together as atheism and that today the word atheism is often connected with atheistic communism" and thus "un-American." In February 1962, the three judges again sided with the Schempps, ruling that the Bible reading requirements still violated the First Amendment. "There is religious establishment in this case," they held, "whether the pupils are or are not excused from attendance at morning exercises." In response, the state appealed again.[53]

As the *Schempp* case made its way to the Supreme Court, the ACLU attorneys worried it might have unwanted company. In Maryland, four-teen-year-old Bill Murray and his mother, Madalyn, filed suit against the Baltimore public schools' requirement that each day begin with "the read-ing, without comment, of a chapter of the Holy Bible and/or the use of the Lord's Prayer." Unlike the Schempp family, who the ACLU believed were "good litigants" because they were sincerely religious and "attractive, well-balanced people," the Murrays were outspoken atheists. In a court of law, the distinction was meaningless; in the court of public opinion, it mattered immensely. While her atheism worried lawyers, Madalyn Mur-ray's reputation as a loose cannon gave them even greater pause. ACLU lawyers had originally represented her, along with some other parents, in a suit against her school board, but they soon parted ways. "We would not promise her that her name would be the first in the list of plaintiffs," one lawyer recalled; "we were going to list them alphabetically. She refused, then, to work with us further." Murray found a new attorney, but when he echoed the ACLU's conclusion that they should wait until the courts ruled on already pending cases such as *Engel* and *Schempp,* she demanded he proceed. "My position is this," she wrote: *"The ACLU can go to hell, and take their opinions with them."* Her lawyer promptly resigned. "I take *orders from no client,"* he wrote back. With a third lawyer at the helm, Murray finally proceeded with her suit. On the way, she asked the ACLU to pay for publishing her briefs, but the organization refused.[54]

Unlike the Schempps' suit, Murray's did not fare well early on. In April 1961, the Supreme Court of Baltimore City dismissed the complaints and sided with the school board. Judge J. Gilbert Pendergrast held that the Murrays, as avowed atheists, had no right to religious liberty. "One cannot practice his religion if he has no religion to practice," the judge asserted. "If petitioners were granted the relief sought, then they, as non-believers, would acquire a preference over the vast majority of believers. Our gov-ernment is founded on the proposition that people should respect the re-ligious view of others, not destroy it." Undeterred, Murray pressed ahead, securing a hearing before the highest judicial body in the state that fall. On April 6, 1962, just three days after the Supreme Court heard oral ar-guments in the *Engel* case, Maryland's Court of Appeals rendered a split decision in *Murray v. Board of School Commissioners of Baltimore City.* By a narrow margin of 4–3, the majority sided with the school board. In a now familiar justification, they pointed to the prevalence of public religious rites in the state and nation.[55]

The Supreme Court heard oral arguments in *Schempp* and *Murray* on February 27 and 28, 1963. In the former case, the state's lawyer, Philip Ward, argued that reading the Bible was not a religious exercise. "We're teaching morality without religion, cut adrift from theology," he insisted. "The people of Pennsylvania have wanted to do this, they have since the beginning wanted to bring these lessons in morality to the children." They simply employed "a common source of morality, the Bible," to reach that end. In this way, the Bible was part of the "tradition of this country." Henry Sawyer, the Schempps' attorney, pressed back. "The New Testament is a teaching message," he said. "It was highly controversial teaching then and, I submit to Your Honors, it's highly controversial teaching now. Men do not agree about these things." Neither did they agree about the nation's religious tradition. "I think tradition is not to be scoffed at," Sawyer said. "But let me say this very candidly. I think it is the final arrogance to talk constantly about 'our religious tradition' in this country and equate it with the Bible. Sure, religious tradition. *Whose* religious tradition?" There were real differences among the various faiths, Sawyer pointed out, and insisting there was a single religious tradition that united them "suggests that the public schools, at least of Pennsylvania, are a kind of Protestant institution to which others are cordially invited."[56]

The debate in *Murray* circled the same issues. Baltimore's city solicitor, Francis B. Burch, denied that there was anything religious in the recitation of Bible verses or the Lord's Prayer. Such practices merely had "certain salutary effects" in teaching morality and instilling discipline in students. Hugo Black, who, an observer recorded, was "obviously not impressed," interjected: "Are you disavowing that the purpose of these exercises is to increase religious knowledge in the student?" Burch stumbled a bit, admitting that was certainly *a* purpose, but only one of many. A local school board, he insisted, had the right to determine the opening exercises in the schools it ran. Asked if he would object to the Book of Mormon being used where that faith predominated, he said if a local board so desired, that would be fine. "What you are arguing for, as I see it," Black interrupted again, "is religious local option." This line of questioning

continued when Burch's cocounsel, George W. Baker, took over. Earl
Warren asked what would happen in a hypothetical school district in the
new state of Hawaii that was 51 percent Buddhist and 49 percent Christian. If Buddhists dominated the board, the attorney replied, then they
had the right to impose their religious views on the Christian minority.
"Wouldn't it then be a contest," William O. Douglas interrupted, "to see
which church could get control of the school board?" The Court then
turned to Leonard Kerpelman, the latest attorney for the Murrays, who
ridiculed the suggestion that recitations of the Bible were not entirely
religious. "The law recognizes no 'somewhat,'" he said. "There is no such
thing as a law which restricts religious liberty only 'somewhat.'"[57]

When the justices gathered to deliberate the two cases on March 1,
1963, they found themselves revisiting a familiar issue, but with two new
colleagues. Byron White, a former pro football player who had gone on
to Yale Law School and then the Department of Justice, had replaced the
broken-down Whittaker only two weeks after the oral arguments in *Engel*.
Arthur Goldberg, a prominent labor lawyer and then secretary of labor,
had been appointed to fill the vacancy created by Frankfurter's retirement.
Though neither had taken part in the *Engel* deliberations, they soon understood that the case still had a firm hold on their colleagues. Warren
announced he would affirm the lower courts' rulings striking down the
state-ordered Bible reading as a violation of the First Amendment's establishment clause. Black, Douglas, and Clark quickly agreed. Harlan had
doubts but signaled he too would affirm, as did Brennan. Stewart noted
he would dissent once again, arguing that they should send the cases back
to the states so they could "give every sect a chance to have religious exercises in schools including atheists." But he found himself alone again, as
both White and Goldberg voted to affirm. Goldberg acknowledged that
the issues in the case were "much more religious" than the previous one,
but that meant the need to avoid religious establishment was even more
important. "Schools can't be opened to every sect," he observed, according
to Douglas's shorthand notes: "How about Black Muslims? How about
screwball groups? You can't draw a line between viable ones—it would
mean drawing a line that would interfere with Free Exercise. No better
way to respect religion than to follow Vitale."[58]

After the conference, Warren had to decide which of the eight justices in the majority would draft the opinion. "At best a nominal Baptist," as one of his biographers has written, "Warren was nonetheless profoundly religious." He held the Bible in high esteem, sending his children to Sunday school to ensure they were well versed in its wisdom and keeping a copy of his own beside his bed. Recognizing that a ruling against Bible reading could spark an even angrier reaction than *Engel,* he decided that Tom Clark's well-earned reputation as a "man of faith" made him the best spokesman. Raised Episcopalian, the Texan had converted to Presbyterianism upon his marriage. When he and his wife moved to Washington, they became active members in the National Presbyterian Church, with Reverend Edward Elson their new pastor. Clark took to heart his new denomination's traditional support for separation of church and state, believing that secular appropriations of prayer demeaned true religion. Equally important in Warren's eyes was the fact that during the public outrage over *Engel,* Clark had broken with tradition and publicly defended the decision. In a remarkable address to the American Bar Association in August 1962, Clark had reminded the lawyers—and, through the reporters in the room, the general public as well—that the Constitution demanded "that both state and federal governments shall take no part respecting the establishment of religion or prohibiting the free exercise thereof. 'No' means 'no,'" he told them, borrowing one of Hugo Black's favorite lines. "That was all the Court decided."[59]

As he crafted his opinion, Clark did all he could to preempt criticism. First and foremost, he worked to push Madalyn Murray out of the spotlight. According to standard practice, Murray should have been the captioned plaintiff, as her case had been placed on the docket first. But Clark knew that having an outspoken atheist as the face of the decision would be toxic, and so he moved the Unitarian Edward Schempp to the lead position instead. Clark likewise downplayed Murray's role in the decision itself. His first handwritten draft, in fact, made no mention of the Murrays' atheism at all, focusing instead on the Schempps' religious objections. The trial record showed how "Edward Schempp and the children testified as to specific religious doctrines purveyed by a literal reading of the Bible 'which were contrary to the religious beliefs which they held and to their familial teaching.'"Their objections stemmed not from any disrespect for religion but from a desire to worship respectfully in their own way.[60]

Clark emphasized this theme of religious liberty when he delivered the decisions in *Schempp* and *Murray* on June 17, 1963. With a delivery that one observer called "patient and persuasive," Clark spoke slowly, hoping to make clear that the court was not ruling against religion. "The place of religion in our society is an exalted one, achieved through a long tradition of reliance on the home, the church and the inviolable citadel of the individual heart and mind," he said. "We have come to recognize through bitter experience that it is not within the power of government to invade that citadel, whether its purpose or effect be to aid or oppose, to advance or retard. In the relationship between man and religion," Clark stressed, "the State is firmly committed to a position of neutrality." Without this "wholesome neutrality," there was a real danger "that powerful sects or groups might bring about a fusion of governmental or religious functions or a concert or dependency of one upon the other to the end that official support of the State or Federal Government would be placed behind the tenets of one or of all orthodoxies. This the Establishment Clause prohibits." At the same time, the First Amendment's free-exercise clause guaranteed the "right of every person to freely choose his own course" in terms of religious faith "free of any compulsion from the state." Compulsory Bible reading, he concluded, violated both halves of the First Amendment.[61]

Clark went to great lengths to assure Americans that the decision did not threaten all forms of public religion. While Black had buried his comments on religion and politics in a footnote of the *Engel* ruling, Clark addressed its constitutionality directly. "The fact that the Founding Fathers believed devoutly that there was a God and that the unalienable rights of man were rooted in Him is clearly evidenced in their writings, from the Mayflower Compact to the Constitution itself," he stated. "This background is evidenced today in our public life through the continuance in our oaths of office from the Presidency to the Alderman of the final supplication, 'So help me God.' Likewise, each House of the Congress provides through its Chaplain an opening prayer, and the sessions of this Court are declared open by the crier in a short ceremony, the final phrase of which invokes the grace of God." Clark even cited the US Census's finding that "64% of our people have church membership." He concluded that "today, as in the beginning, our national life reflects a religious people." But that tradition emphasized the right of individuals to worship on their own, without direction or demands from secular authorities. "This freedom to worship was indispensable in a country whose people came from the four quarters of the earth and brought with them a diversity of religious opinion," he noted. "Today authorities list eighty-three separate religious bodies, each with membership exceeding fifty thousand, existing among our people, as well as innumerable smaller groups."[62]

Clark had hoped his opinion would let the eight-man majority on the court speak with one voice, but the justices offered four different opinions in total. Only Warren, Black, and White joined Clark's. In one concurrence, Douglas suggested that the court should have gone further and struck down all state support of religion; in a second, Goldberg and Harlan supported the majority's decision but cautioned that "an untutored devotion to the concept of neutrality" might lead to hostility against religion. These concurrences were just slight nudges to the majority ruling, each expressed in two pages. In contrast, Brennan's elaborate concurrence ran for seventy-four pages. Rather than address what was prohibited in the realm of government and religion, he tried to detail everything that was permitted. Point by point, he listed numerous forms of religious references that he deemed constitutional. "In God We Trust," for instance, was "simply interwoven . . . so deeply into the fabric of our civil polity," he said, that it "ceased to have religious meaning." "The reference to divinity in the revised pledge of allegiance," he reasoned, "may merely recognize the historical fact that our Nation was believed to have been founded 'under God.' Thus, reciting the pledge may be no more of a religious exercise than the reading aloud of Lincoln's Gettysburg Address, which contains an allusion to the same historical fact."[63]

The initial response to *Schempp* and *Murray* was surprisingly calm. Embarrassed by their overreaction to *Engel*, most major religious denominations had anticipated a new ruling against Bible reading and already made peace with it. Indeed, before the court even issued its opinion, the United Presbyterian Office of Information had already released a three-page comment supporting it, sight unseen. When the ruling in *Schempp* and *Murray* was released, the National Council of Churches and individual

Protestant denominations promptly announced their support. The presiding bishop of the Episcopal Church insisted the ruling was "not hostile to religion" in any way, while the president of the Lutheran Church claimed that the real threats to faith were the "common-denominator religious exercises" struck down by the court. Jewish organizations universally praised the decision. The president of the Synagogue Council of America even predicted that the court's ruling would result in "a more lasting union of America under God."[64]

The Roman Catholic hierarchy and some key fundamentalist and evangelical leaders lined up on the other side of the debate. Richard Cardinal Cushing, archbishop of Boston, sent word of his disapproval from Rome, where he had traveled to elect a successor to Pope John XXIII. "To me, it is a great tragedy that the greatest book ever published and a constant best seller cannot be read in the public school system," the prelate said. James Francis Cardinal McIntyre of Los Angeles, also in Rome, attacked the ruling as having rejected "our American heritage of philosophy, of religion and of freedom." They suggested a constitutional amendment might be the only answer.[65] These Catholic prelates found an unlikely ally in Protestant evangelical and fundamentalist organizations. For decades, the two faiths had been at odds on a variety of political, not to mention spiritual, issues, but here they made common cause. Dr. Robert A. Cook, president of the National Association of Evangelicals, denounced the decision as "sad departure from this nation's heritage under God" and called for a constitutional amendment to restore Bible reading and prayers to the public schools. Fundamentalist leaders agreed. "We understand that a greater issue is at stake than simply Bible reading in the schools," Carl McIntire noted. "At stake is whether or not America may continue to honor and recognize God in the life of the nation." He too called for a constitutional amendment to reverse the ruling.[66]

While the religious critics of the court's decisions remained in the minority, the rulings revealed a growing gap between the leaders of major denominations and the laypeople to whom they ministered. "Some observers predicted that practical effects of the latest ruling might be disillusioning for the laity and divisive for the church in general," noted an astute editorial in *Christianity Today* in the summer of 1963. "Do rank and file laymen really understand why many ecclesiastical leaders countenance

and even support the suppression of prayer and Bible reading in public schools?" By all appearances, they did not. "Millions of U.S. Christians emotionally reject the Supreme Court's successive decisions against
prayer in schools," *Time* magazine reported. In spite of the assurances of
their denominational leaders, "laymen have not been convinced of the
court's wisdom to the degree that clergymen are." As Reverend Shrum
Burton, president of the Kansas City Council of Churches, said, "some
laymen have a vague feeling that we are losing all religion in public life
and that something ought to be done, but they don't know what." One
thing, though, seemed clear. If their religious representatives would not
lead the way, laypeople would find new champions who would.[67]

CHAPTER 7

"Our So-Called Religious Leaders"

O N OCTOBER 1, 1963, A grassroots organization called the Citizens Congressional Committee hand-delivered four "good and heavy" drums of paper to clerks at the House of Representatives. Once unrolled, they formed a massive petition that organizers said contained nearly a million signatures and stretched for over a mile in length. (Additional rolls, still on their way to Washington, would stretch it to three miles, they promised.) The petition called on Congress to do whatever was necessary to secure a constitutional amendment permitting "devotional exercises" in public schools. "Whereas the Supreme Court of the United States by its decisions has virtually outlawed the right to pray or read Scripture in public schools and other institutions," the petition read, "we, the undersigned citizens, respectfully petition you to take the initial steps necessary to bring about an amendment to the Constitution which will forever guarantee the protection of our Christian traditions and the right of our people to pray and honor Holy Scripture in their institutions."[1]

The executive secretary of the Citizens Congressional Committee was Charles W. Winegarner. A former advertising executive from Fort Wayne, Indiana, he now worked full-time promoting the cause. For five months, he told reporters, his colleagues had been gathering signatures from every state. At the same time, the group had been lobbying members of Congress, seeking not tacit support but active involvement. "Our Committee represents zealous, enthusiastic, and uncompromising individuals in every state and in every Congressional district in the Nation,"

Winegarner stated in January 1964. "We can no longer be satisfied with passive expressions favorable to the idea of a Constitutional amendment. We are now in a campaign to challenge every member of Congress to take a fighting stand in defense of the right of Christian devotions in our public institutions." He closed with an unsubtle threat: "As the election day approaches, I could easily imagine citizens in Congressional districts where candidates for Congress would have to answer this question: 'Has your attitude and activities in Congress been pro-prayer or anti-prayer, or have you been indifferent?'"[2]

The political stakes surrounding the prayer amendment were certainly high, but Winegarner's role in the debate was short-lived. In May 1964, columnists Rowland Evans and Robert Novak revealed that the Citizens Congressional Committee was "operated, financed, and directed by Gerald L. K. Smith, notorious promoter of right-wing causes," and that Winegarner was Smith's nephew. A onetime ally of Senator Huey Long and an outspoken anti-Semite, Smith had made no secret of his involvement, bragging that the committee was "an auxiliary, financed and directed by *The Cross and the Flag*," the far-right publication of his Christian Nationalist Crusade. In its pages, Smith attacked the "cabal of international Jews" in the Kennedy administration and the "nine-man oligarchy" they manipulated on the Supreme Court, before telling readers there was hope. With its "mammoth petition," the Citizens Congressional Committee had demanded the restoration of "the right of Christian devotions in public schools" and sparked "a revolutionary spirit among members of Congress." Following Evans and Novak's revelations, the *Washington Post* detailed the other extremist causes the Citizens Congressional Committee had supported, including abolition of the United Nations, invasion of Cuba, impeachment of Earl Warren, an end to the nuclear test ban "treason treaty," and staunch opposition to voting rights for Washington, D.C., because it was a "community three-fourths Negro."[3]

While exposure of the committee's extremist roots was embarrassing to the larger cause, it was not surprising. Indeed, the campaign for a constitutional amendment to restore prayer to public schools had quickly attracted activists on the far right. Billy James Hargis of the archconservative Christian Crusade devoted himself to circulating petitions across the West, while Carl McIntire, a fundamentalist broadcaster with an affinity for far-right politics, lobbied for it over his own network of 582 radio stations. The John Birch Society supported the amendment idea as part of its long-standing drive to impeach Earl Warren and generally discredit the Supreme Court. Similarly, segregationists who criticized the Court's rulings on civil rights latched on to the school prayer issue as a more popular and palatable way to condemn it again. Alabama governor George Wallace, generally remembered for his defiance of the Court's desegregation decisions, was equally opposed to its rulings on school prayer. Immediately before his infamous "Segregation forever!" inaugural address in 1963, for instance, Wallace was sworn in at a podium draped with a five-foot-long banner inspired by the *Engel* ruling: "IN GOD WE TRUST." "I want the Supreme Court to know we are not going to conform to any such decision," he announced after *Schempp*. Echoing his earlier promise to "stand in the schoolhouse door" to block integration, Wallace warned that if federal courts ordered "that we cannot read the Bible in some school, I'm going to that school and read it myself."[4]

The visibility of such supporters led some to dismiss the constitutional prayer amendment as a cause championed only by the far right or the Deep South, but in truth it had much broader backing. At the 1962 Governors' Conference, the leaders of forty-nine states called for a prayer amendment that "will make clear and beyond challenge the acknowledgment of our nation and people of their faith in God"; a year later, they renewed their call unanimously. The governors weren't alone. The Supreme Court's rulings against school prayer and Bible reading were deeply unpopular across the nation, and a solid majority of Americans seized on the amendment idea as a solution. In August 1963, shortly after the *Schempp* decision, Gallup asked Americans if they wanted prayer and Bible reading in public schools; 70 percent said yes. They flooded their political representatives with mail, with one study estimating that 50 percent of all correspondence to Congress in the 1963–1964 term focused on the proposal for a school prayer amendment. These letters, postcards, and petitions overwhelmingly supported the idea, with officials citing a margin of nearly twenty to one in favor. Congress leapt into action. Between the summer of 1962 and spring of 1964, 113 representatives and 27 senators introduced 146 different amendments to restore prayer and Bible reading to public schools.[5]

With such overwhelming popular and political support, the "prayer amendment" seemed sure to sail through Congress and be ratified by the states with equal speed. But the congressional hearings, which many assumed would simply be a formality, turned into a prolonged moment of national reflection. Unlike the snapshots of public opinion upon which historians often rely—the quick shutter of an overnight poll, the slower frame of the decennial census—these congressional hearings provide an in-depth picture of American attitudes about the role of religion in politics. Ostensibly about the narrow topic of prayer in public schools, the hearings took on much larger proportions in the political world and the public eye. They became, in effect, the center of a national debate about the proper relationships between piety and patriotism, religion and politics, church and state. For four years, from 1962 to 1966, Americans in Congress and countless local communities addressed the role of religion in their political life directly, some of them for the first time in their lives.

Though the two camps in this battle were far from homogeneous, each clustered around a set of convictions. To put it in broad strokes, proponents of the prayer amendment believed America was a Christian nation—or, in their more generous moments, a Judeo-Christian nation. They were deeply invested in promoting a prominent role for religion in public life, believing that formal recognition of God was not simply an affirmation of the nation's religious roots but an essential measure for preserving the country's character. In their eyes, liberty came directly from God. If Americans ever came to believe that their rights stemmed from the state instead, then those rights could just as easily be taken away by the state. Thus, the debate for the pro-amendment side was about much more than school prayer; it was about the survival of the nation.

For opponents of the amendment, the stakes were just as high. Legal and religious authorities who opposed the idea warned that a school prayer amendment would radically reshape the status quo, effectively weakening the First Amendment's guarantee of religious freedom. Under a new "tyranny of the majority," they believed, local religious minorities would be persecuted. But more than that, *all* faiths would be endangered. If the state intruded on churches' and synagogues' roles as religious educators, it would usurp not just their activities but also their authority. In their place, the state would foster a broader but blander public religion, one drained of the vital details that animated individual faiths. The prayer amendment, the heads of major denominations concluded, would ultimately hurt religion rather than help it.

As these two sides took shape in the struggle over the school prayer amendments, Americans slowly came to a sobering realization. The mingling of religion and politics, which had only recently promised to unite disparate groups in a shared heritage and a common destiny, now seemed more likely to drive them apart. Notably, this was not a case of religious conflict in which different denominations lined up against one another, but rather an unusual instance in which the leaders of various denominations largely lined up on one side of the debate and prominent numbers of their lay populations moved to the other. As they debated the prayer amendments, both sides came to agree on at least one basic fact: beyond the broad generalities of public religion, their country was not, in any meaningful sense, "one nation under God."

FOR REPRESENTATIVE FRANK BECKER, THE fight for the prayer amendment represented the culmination of his life's work. Born in Brooklyn, Becker served overseas during the First World War before coming home to start a real estate and insurance company. After the Second World War, he launched a political career as a Republican, first winning a seat in the state assembly from suburban Nassau County. He then rode Eisenhower's coattails to Congress in 1952, where he represented eastern Long Island for more than a decade. An active member of the Knights of Columbus and the American Legion, Becker was well versed in their efforts to promote public religion during the decade. He saw *Engel* as a threat to all he held dear. Though a devout Catholic, Becker had attended public schools and sent his children there too, believing the schools did a fine job inculcating religious and patriotic sentiment. And because *Engel* had come from his own congressional district, he took the ruling personally. To him, it was "the most tragic [decision] in the history of the United States" and needed to be answered immediately. To that end, he offered one of the first proposals for a constitutional amendment to ensure that "prayers may be offered in the course of any program in any public school or other public place in the United States."[6]

While other congressmen soon introduced amendments of their own, none ever matched Becker's commitment to the cause. He had already decided the 1963–1964 term would be his last and thus resolved to devote his final days in office to the prayer issue. He worked tirelessly to build public support for the idea, while he began to coordinate the drive to secure passage of a prayer amendment in Congress. In a shrewd tactical decision, Becker urged all the congressmen who had introduced amendments of their own to abandon them and instead unite around a single proposal, which he and five colleagues introduced in August 1963. Formally House Joint Resolution 693, it was commonly called the Becker Amendment. It had three main parts. The first stated that nothing in the Constitution could be construed to "prohibit the offering, reading from, or listening to prayers or Biblical scriptures, if participation therein is on a voluntary basis, in any governmental school, institution, or place." In the same spirit, the second section asserted that neither could the Constitution be read to "prohibit making reference to, belief in, reliance upon, or invoking the aid of God or a Supreme Being" in any activity or document issued by the government, including currency. The third section flatly asserted that the amendment did not "constitute an establishment of religion."[7]

As scores of congressmen rallied around the Becker Amendment, they saw Representative Emanuel Celler standing almost alone in opposition. In truth, he needed little help. Except for a brief window in which Republicans controlled the House, Celler had served as the powerful chairman of the House Judiciary Committee since 1949, a role that effectively made him the gatekeeper for all constitutional amendments proposed in that chamber. While his district in Brooklyn and Queens was physically near Becker's, politically the two men were miles apart. A staunch liberal and devout Jew, Celler devoted much of his career to defending the rights of racial and ethnic minorities. In the 1920s, he made an impression as a freshman legislator by strongly opposing popular new immigration restrictions. He worked tirelessly for decades to repeal these measures, ultimately succeeding with the passage of the Immigration and Nationality Act of 1965, landmark legislation commonly known as the Hart-Celler Act. Not surprisingly, he dismissed the idea of a constitutional prayer amendment out of hand. "No matter how narrow such a proposal may

be," he told reporters, "it is, nevertheless, an opening wedge toward elimination of one of our basic tenets, the separation of church and state." In
districts with a majority of Protestants, Catholics, or Jews, he predicted,
members of minority faiths would find their religious liberties curtailed.
Celler confidently announced that the proposed amendments stood "no
chance" of passage as long as he controlled the committee.[8]

To circumvent Celler, Becker and his allies placed their hopes in a
rarely used procedure known as the discharge petition. If they could secure signatures from a majority of their colleagues—218 in all—then they
could force the amendment out of Celler's committee and bring it to the
floor for a vote. This was, as Becker himself admitted, an unusual maneu-
ver. "For 19 years, as a member of the New York State Legislature and as
a Member of Congress, I have pursued the policy of never voting for a
motion to discharge," he announced to the House. But he would do so
for "the first time" to give the American people "the right to determine
whether the Constitution shall be amended to permit prayer in public
schools and all public places." Though the odds were long, Becker could
count on the other 113 congressmen who had offered their own amendments to sign his petition, meaning he was more than halfway there at
the start. To get the remainder, he resolved to use every means available
to him. He was now, in the words of one observer, "a zealot" on the issue.[9]

Though he had little reputation as a legislator, Becker began to demonstrate impressive powers of persuasion. He regularly took to the House
floor to cajole colleagues into signing the discharge petition, finding in-
ventive ways to apply pressure. In August 1963, he produced a report
from the American Association for the Advancement of Atheism and
read its ominous goals into the record. The seventh aim of the group—
after banning "religious proclamations by chief executives" and removing
"the superstitious inscription 'In God We Trust' from our coins"—was,
Becker noted pointedly, "exclusion of the Bible as a sacred book from the
public schools." This atheist agenda was "astounding," Becker marveled,
but there was a cure. "Each Member of this House can help to block this
spiritual catastrophe," he said. "Signing Discharge Petition No. 3 now
on the desk of the clerk will bring this issue to the floor." A few days
later, Becker spoke about an Episcopal priest in Baltimore who bemoaned
the rulings against religion in schools and wondered, "Where will this

journey end?" "My colleagues," Becker proposed, "we can end this journey by bringing a constitutional amendment to the floor of the House." A few weeks later, he shared a news report about students in Newport, Kentucky, who started a campaign to protest the ban on Bible reading and prayer because the "adults haven't put up a fight." "Have we, Mr. Speaker, put up a fight?" Becker asked. "The means to do so is provided in Discharge Petition No. 3." Over and over again, the congressman made his message clear: his colleagues could stand with children in need and men of the cloth, or they could aid the atheists. In case these statements weren't enough, Becker threatened to go to the district of every representative who failed to support his amendment during the coming election year and actively campaign against him or her.[10]

As he badgered his colleagues, Becker busied himself with meetings, addresses, and rallies to enlist the public in his fight. On September 22, 1963, for instance, he played a prominent role in a massive "School Prayer Amendment Rally" at a Long Island high school. Sponsored by a local chapter of the American Legion, the rally began with a rendition of the national anthem that, according to the program, included the stanza with the line "in God is our trust." It was followed by the mass recitation of the Pledge of Allegiance. Several speakers addressed the crowd, including Reverend George T. Cook, rector of St. George's Episcopal Church in nearby Oceanside. The "allegedly learned justices" of the Supreme Court had erred grievously, he said, even if the decisions had been "hailed by a small but loud-mouthed group of confused clergy" who "have supported the National Council of Churches in its head-long rush towards socialism." Becker was so impressed with Cook's remarks that he inserted them into the *Congressional Record*.[11]

As their involvement at the rally made clear, the American Legion emerged as a strong ally of the Becker campaign. After its convention endorsed a constitutional prayer amendment in September 1963, national commander James E. Powers explained why in an *American Legion Magazine* editorial titled "The Roots of Americanism Are Spiritual." "Under other forms of government, whatever liberty the citizen may enjoy is believed to be granted by the State—and what the State gives, it can take back. But no government can take it from us," he noted. "It is the gift of God." Accordingly, the commander urged "every Legionnaire to profess anew the faith of our fathers in 'one nation, under God.'" In December, the organization announced it would throw its weight behind the Becker Amendment. "The American Legion has supported discharge petitions but once or twice in its history, and does so now, only because of the unusual circumstances surrounding the prayer and Bible-reading issue, and related possibilities," its legislative commission noted. "There are those who now would remove the words 'under God' from the Pledge of Allegiance, and do away with 'In God We Trust' on our coinage." The head of its National Americanism Commission likewise urged Legionnaires to write their representatives and demand they sign the discharge petition. The Legion didn't act alone, as other national associations and fraternal clubs, including the Lions, Kiwanis, Civitan International, Catholic War Veterans, and Junior Chamber of Commerce, all rallied behind the amendment as well.[12]

While these established organizations dedicated themselves to the amendment, new ones formed specifically for the fight. In Baltimore, for instance, city solicitor Francis Burch, whose office had defended the school system against Madalyn Murray's lawsuit, gathered staffers in his office the night the Court ruled against them in June 1963. "The implications seemed distressing," he recalled. "We coldly examined the probable scope of this far-reaching decision," believing the court would next strike down "other traditional practices in our public life whose roots are derived from our religious background." To prevent that outcome, Burch and his allies created Constitutional Prayer Amendment, Inc. "We are dedicated to the building of loyalty to America, its ideals and its institutions," the organization announced. "One of the cornerstones of America's heritage has been a deep abiding faith in a Supreme Being. To deprive the young and the old of this recognition in public events will not only weaken this cornerstone, but, indeed, may well destroy it."[13]

Constitutional Prayer Amendment, Inc., soon became Becker's staunchest ally. Eisenhower, though retired from public service, gave the organization his strong endorsement. "I am opposed to any effort to eliminate mention of God in governmental practices," he wrote. "Your basic purpose of keeping before the public the clear fact that our form of government rests upon a religious faith is one of which I heartily approve." Active politicians offered support as well. By early 1964, the organization's letterhead included thirteen sitting governors, as well as notables such as Conrad Hilton, Jackie Robinson, Francis Cardinal Spellman, Bishop James A. Pike, and William Randolph Hearst Jr. Now known as the Constitutional Prayer Foundation, the group convened pro-amendment organizations to coordinate strategies in February. "The only battle we need to fight is to get the bill out of Congress," said Father Robert Howes of Massachusetts Citizens for Public Prayer. "After that is achieved, I am sure the public will approve it." The way to do that, argued Dr. Charles Leaming of Florida's Committee for the Preservation of Prayer and Bible Reading in Public Schools, was to "get the citizens of each and every state to deluge their congressmen with letters."[14]

The deluge soon came. "Congressional mail on this issue has grown to flood proportions," the *New York Times* reported, "exceeding the mail of the civil rights controversy." Representative Lionel Van Deerlin, a Democrat from California, noted that congressmen were "being inundated with constituent mail, the great bulk of which favors an amendment." Minnesota representative Alec Olsen claimed mail ran "at least 200 to 1 in favor of such an amendment," while Representative R. G. Stephens of Georgia was so overwhelmed by the volume—more than a thousand letters in all—that he began sending correspondents a form letter response. "For the first time since I came to Congress," a midwestern Democrat admitted off the record, "I've given up trying to answer the mail." As the pressure from constituents continued, more and more congressmen relented. In February, the Republican Policy Committee formally endorsed the Becker Amendment and urged the Judiciary Committee to discharge it. Celler refused, insisting that a "staff study" of the proposed amendments was still under way. But this transparent tactic only led more congressmen to sign the discharge petition. As the spring wore on, unofficial reports estimated it had nearly 170 signatures. "It's no secret," the *Wall Street Journal* reported, "that many more members, including some hostile to the proposal and others adverse to the irregular procedure, have warned Mr. Celler that pressure from home would force them to sign unless he made some move."[15]

Facing imminent defeat, Celler announced in mid-March that the House Judiciary Committee would finally hold hearings in April. Still, the chairman made it clear that he was, in the words of columnist

Anthony Lewis, "not in a hurry to rush an amendment out." "The nature and importance of the subject," Celler claimed, "require that the committee have all the benefit of all the best thinking of all schools of thought" during deliberations. When Celler scheduled the first day for April 22, Becker said he was "amazed" at the late date. The chairman not only delayed the hearings by weeks, Becker charged, but deliberately scheduled them to coincide with the opening of the New York World's Fair to bury the proceedings in the press. (The old Brooklyn politician protested: "I never dreamed of the World's Fair!") Moreover, Becker fumed, the chairman had "set no date or time-limit" for the end of the hearings, which meant they could drag on until it was too late to pass the amendment. These "devices for delay and derision," he charged, were yet more signs of Celler's "total and unalterable opposition" to the proposals. Defiant, Becker promised to maintain "insurmountable pressure" until this "one-man roadblock" was "smashed."[16]

While Celler's delaying tactics enraged supporters of the Becker Amendment, they proved crucial in giving opponents time to mobilize. Most civil libertarians and religious organizations had assumed the campaign for a constitutional amendment would go nowhere, but as momentum shifted in Becker's direction they realized, almost too late, what was happening. In March, ACLU headquarters sent its affiliates warnings that the discharge petition drive was "becoming alarming." They scrambled to find allies. The Baptist Joint Committee on Public Affairs, the political voice of the eight largest Baptist bodies in the nation, soon announced its opposition, claiming the Becker Amendment threatened their religious liberty. A week later, the American Jewish Committee denounced it as "the most serious challenge to the integrity of the Bill of Rights in American history." On St. Patrick's Day, representatives of Protestant and Jewish organizations and civil liberties groups gathered at a hastily arranged meeting in New York. Sizing up the situation, they realized the Becker Amendment had "an excellent chance" of winning a majority of votes from the Judiciary Committee. If that happened, the full House and Senate would invariably vote for it, and, in short order, it would be swiftly ratified by the states.[17]

At the New York meeting, an ad hoc committee was formed, led by Reverend Dean Kelley of the National Council of Churches (NCC).[18] A

Methodist minister and an absolutist when it came to the separation of church and state, Kelley became the NCC's executive for religious liberty in 1960, a post he would hold for three decades. Preventing passage of the school prayer amendment would prove to be one of the most daunting tasks of his long career. "We're up against the saints of the American Legion and the Junior Chamber of Commerce," he told a reporter, "and they're pretty formidable." As he surveyed the political landscape, Kelley saw that the opposition was not simply outnumbered but also largely hidden. "For the most part," the *Wall Street Journal* reported, "even lawmakers adamant in their opposition have kept silent in public." As a result, congressmen who opposed the amendment were often unaware of colleagues who felt the same. Kelley's committee connected them to one another and, more important, gave them political cover. Because congressional opponents of the amendment had been stigmatized as being "anti-God," they were desperate for supportive statements from religious leaders. Representative Charles Wilson of California, for instance, begged the Anti-Defamation League to find rabbis who would speak out against the amendment. "Any help you can give in this regard," he wrote, "will be much appreciated."[19]

At regular sessions at the NCC offices in Washington, Kelley's committee worked to bring the House back from the brink. Its members enlisted the Lutheran Church, the Episcopal Church, the Methodist Church, and the United Church of Christ in a massive letter-writing campaign against the amendment and convinced church publications to denounce it as well. Its members visited congressmen, especially swing members of the Judiciary Committee, "to indicate strong religious opposition to the amendment, and to make clear that Congressmen may expect help from pastors in their district if they oppose the amendment." To make the ministerial presence perfectly clear, the committee suggested, members should be sure to wear their clerical collars during their visits. "The essential point to get across to the Congressmen (by mail and other means, as well as formal testimony) is that *religious groups oppose changing the First Amendment.*" By all accounts, the message got through. Members reported "very favorable interviews" with six "swing members" on the House Judiciary Committee, "pleasant but inconclusive conversations" with three more, and "strong disagreement" from only two. "Probably no opinions were changed as a result of this activity," they concluded, but it seemed likely that a few opponents were now "encouraged to take a more active part in the hearings."[20]

As the hearings drew near, these opponents of the prayer amendment sized up the House Judiciary Committee, like trial lawyers trying to read a jury. Celler, they knew, would be a powerful ally, but the majority of the committee members would likely side against them. Nine had introduced prayer amendments of their own, and many more had made statements supporting the idea. The anti-amendment forces knew they could not win a vote at that moment. According to their estimates, nearly half of the committee would support sending an amendment to the full House for a vote, with another quarter leaning that way. An ACLU official reasoned that their best hope "would be either to lengthen the period of time for the hearings, and thus delay matters, or obtain a division within the Committee that would help to fashion opposition when the issue is reported to the House." They had to slow things down.[21]

THE HEARINGS ON THE PRAYER amendments proved to be a major endeavor. Celler convened the full Judiciary Committee for sessions that ultimately stretched to six weeks, from April 22 to June 3, 1964. From the first day, the large committee room was packed to capacity, with a long line of would-be spectators waiting outside. Reporters crowded the press tables, while television crews clogged the hallways with lights and equipment for spot interviews. Nearly two hundred people appeared in person as witnesses, with countless others offering opinions in speeches, sermons, letters, petitions, scholarly articles, and government data entered into the official record. When finally printed, the report on the hearings sprawled to fill three large volumes of single-spaced, almost illegibly small text, 2,774 pages in all. Celler insisted that a full airing of all views was essential. There were 147 resolutions pending before the committee and, even allowing for similarities between bills, they still fell into thirty-five distinct categories. "Their number and variety attest to the widespread interest and the many schools of thought on this important subject," the chairman announced. "It will be our privilege to consider the testimony of distinguished church leaders, of experts in the field of Constitutional law, theology and education, and of exponents of all points of view." Critics charged that the leisurely pace was a deliberate tactic intended to run out the clock. The Senate was at the time tangled in a filibuster over the Civil Rights Act, and Congress as a whole would adjourn in June to make way for the Republican National Convention the following month. Celler's critics repeatedly pressed him to curtail the hearings, but he refused.[22]

The first week was devoted to testimony from congressmen. Most had been sponsors of their own prayer amendments, but almost all of them now supported Becker's version. While representatives were traditionally afforded great deference at House hearings, these proceedings turned combative quickly. "The most significant fact about the first week of hearings," Dean Kelley reported, "was that the reception afforded most of the witnesses was *hostile* rather than *hospitable*." The minister had expected such "persistent probing" from Celler, but he was delighted to see another eight members take the same approach. "The persistent interrogation is broken occasionally by heated exchanges between the members of the Committee," Kelley marveled. Tensions there had been building for quite some time. For most of the summer and fall of the previous year, the Judiciary Committee had been the epicenter of a series of sharp-edged debates over the pending Civil Rights Act. Southern Democrats had been badly beaten in that struggle and now were looking for revenge. "One detects in their intensity a lingering animus from the civil rights hearings," Kelley noted. "Perhaps they feel that *this* time they will get back at the Committee, the Supreme Court and the rest of the national 'establishment,' if they have to use God to do it."[23]

The first witness, naturally, was Becker. He had barely begun condemning the "fraternity of secularists" who struck prayer from the schools before he was repeatedly interrupted by the committee. He struggled to make it through his written remarks and then found his claims challenged by the committee's counsel. Becker read a rabbi's sermon supporting religion in schools, for instance, but counsel produced a letter from the rabbi arguing against the amendment. Becker likewise cited James Cardinal Gibbons, but the attorney demonstrated that the prelate had been misquoted. Becker did not back down. He dismissed the committee's report, which detailed the potential problems in the amendment, as full of "figments of the imagination." When a committee member pointed out that religious bodies were lining up against the amendment, Becker simply dismissed them. "I think the opposition comes from the leadership of these groups but not from the mass of people," he said. For over two hours Becker and his opponents engaged in a heated back-and-forth, until the committee had to break for lunch. He seemed eager to continue, but the morning exchange apparently took a toll. When they reconvened, Celler announced that "Mr. Becker has been taken ill and will not be able to appear" for his scheduled afternoon session.[24]

Becker's colleagues carried on without him. Much like their constituents who had flooded Congress and the Supreme Court with angry letters, these congressmen invoked the many religious expressions in public life to make their case. New Jersey Republican James Auchincloss drew inspiration from the revised Pledge of Allegiance and the new national motto, for instance, while Nevada Democrat Walter Baring pointed to the use of the Bible at swearing-in ceremonies for federal officials. Changing the Constitution, they argued, would merely confirm these established traditions. "The effect of this amendment," insisted Eugene Siler, a Republican from rural Kentucky, "would be to put in writing and upon our constitutional document itself what we have already put on our pieces of money and upon the marble piece above the Speaker's chair in the House of Representatives: 'In God We Trust.'"[25]

Again, like their constituents, these congressmen argued that without the amendment, these same manifestations of public religion would be swept away. Carleton King, a New York Republican, claimed that prayers would be purged from congressional sessions, while Pennsylvania Republican Willard Curtin worried that presidential inaugurations would have to be purely secular as well. President Lyndon Johnson had recently closed an address in the Rose Garden with the words "God bless you," noted Republican John B. Anderson of Illinois. "I wonder how long it will be before someone will seek to enjoin the President of the United States from indulging in such expressions of official piety," he asked, "or perhaps from gracing the annual Presidential prayer breakfast with his presence and thereby implying the official sanction of the U.S. Government for an exercise which exalts the ministry of prayer?"[26]

Because these congressmen assumed those who opposed the amendment were atheists or secularists, they were baffled when religious leaders began to align against them. "It seems that to many of the proponents 'prayer is prayer,'" marveled Reverend Kelley. "They seem unable to realize that some devoutly religious citizens, at least, care what the content of prayer is, and do not wish to engage in a prayer whose content is so vague or innocuous as to be 'non-sectarian.'" Florida congressman Billy Matthews, who had once studied for the ministry, claimed to be "somewhat puzzled at the opposition that many of our churchmen have against the Becker Amendment." Del Latta, an active member in the Churches of Christ and a conservative Republican from Ohio, dismissed such worries. "They are fearful of the establishment of a state religion," he surmised. "I have no such fears." While these congressmen saw their differences with the clergy as an honest difference of opinion, others took a darker tone. George Goodling, a Pennsylvania Republican, added to the record an angry letter he had sent to "our so-called religious leaders" at the National Council of Churches. "Let me suggest you come from your exalted position and mingle with the 40 million rank and file [members of the NCC's constituent churches] as I do constantly," the Methodist congressman testified. "You will discover beyond any shadow of a doubt the chiefs and indians are in violent disagreement." At times, even members of the committee sparred over how well religious leaders represented their denomination's laypeople. As California's James Corman rattled off a list of organizations that had issued statements against a prayer amendment, for instance, Basil Whitener interrupted to object. "The gentleman has undertaken to put into the record that the Methodists took a position," he protested. "The Methodists have not taken that position. At least, this Methodist didn't." Statements from individual religious leaders, Whitener insisted, simply did not reflect the feelings of all members of a faith. "I don't think anybody speaks for all Methodists, or all Baptists, or all Jews."[27]

But the leaders of these religious organizations soon had a chance to testify, if only for themselves. The first testimony came from Dr. Edwin H. Tuller, head of the American Baptist Convention (ABC), who also appeared on behalf of the National Council of Churches. Tuller was an impressive witness, and his testimony took up most of the day. He noted that after the Supreme Court rulings, both the ABC and NCC had voted overwhelmingly to reaffirm traditional support for separation of church and state. "The First Amendment has served the nation well for nearly 200 years," Tuller read from his prepared notes. "It would be tragic if in a moment of emotional turmoil the Nation weakened the amendment and woke too late to the realization that a fundamental American freedom had been damaged, perhaps destroyed." He derided the government-made Regents' Prayer as "a rote thing" devoid of spirituality. "If children are taught this prayer, then my teaching that prayer is a vital relationship between the individual and his Creator through Jesus Christ is contrary to that teaching." At this, Representative Arch Moore Jr., a Methodist from West Virginia, challenged him. "I do not know why a group of children, State or teacher dictated, freely deciding that they want to recite the scriptures, would be an [invasion] of your professional responsibility," he said. "I think they are adding a little bit to you." Tuller bristled at the congressman's suggestion "that the public school should do the work the church is supposed to do. This is precisely what I reject."[28]

The church leaders who followed Tuller emphasized their widespread opposition to the proposed amendments, offering sharp rebukes to the state's meddling in religious instruction. Reverend Eugene Carson Blake of the United Presbyterian Church worried that "school prayer and Bible reading either become a ritual that is meaningless and has no effect on the children, or it is some kind of indoctrination." Either way, it amounted to "state religion," he warned. "If you get the idea that religion and Americanism are the same thing, all of us are scared to death, because we think religion transcends the State." Reverend William A. Morrison, head of the Presbyterian Board of Christian Education, was even blunter, asserting that state-ordered prayer amounted to "a theological caricature at best or a theological monstrosity at worst." In a pointed response to the Methodist members of the committee, who had been the strongest defenders of the prayer proposal, Bishop John Wesley Lord of the Methodist Church argued that in his experience school prayer accomplished little. "Despite the reading of the Bible and the offering of prayer in the past in the public school, we have produced a generation of Biblical illiterates," he charged. "The entire practice was profaned by the secularized atmosphere in which so-called worship was conducted." There had been repeated claims that some sort of meaningful religion had been struck from the schools, Lord said, but "the loss is more imagined than real."[29]

These churchmen worried that the prayer amendment would do great harm. Frederik Schiotz, president of the Lutheran Church, feared it would destroy the protections that churches enjoyed under the First Amendment. "An American ideal would be shattered," added Theodore Carcich of the Seventh-day Adventists. Rabbi Irwin Blank of the Synagogue Council warned that constitutional changes would "open the way to religious tension, a misuse of public institutions, and irreverence." Speaking for the main Baptist bodies, Dr. Emanuel Carlson argued that the amendments were unwarranted. "To those who fear that God is somehow being pushed around, locked out, and robbed of his power, our people will reply that God does not need our defense, but that we need the humility to serve him," Carlson testified. "The politician who says he believes in reducing the scope of Government and then asks for a Government role in nurturing and guiding the inner man can expect scrutinizing conversations as these issues are pursued by our people in future debate."[30]

Meanwhile, a number of major religious publications came out against the Becker Amendment, defending the rationale of church leaders who testified against it. "It is so easy to think that one is voting for prayer and the Bible," cautioned the *Christian Science Monitor*. "It comes as a shock that this is not the issue. The issue is that agencies of government cannot avoid favoring one denomination and hurting another by the practical decisions that have to be made by government authority on what version of the Bible shall be imposed and what prayer. The churches know this and that is why they are against the Becker Amendment." Some religious publications went beyond merely defending clerical opponents of the prayer amendment to attacking its secular sponsors. "Whipping the Supreme Court, even when it faithfully interprets the Constitution, is a popular pastime, and a political candidate who runs on a platform that 'defends God' expects from Providence a reciprocal courtesy," the *Christian Century* chided. "God does not need our defense, but we need to defend ourselves against religion-intoxicated fanatics, sincere but bungling religionists, and opportunistic politicians who offer us their kind of religion and their brand of God in exchange for God-given religious freedom." Throughout the hearings, Celler steadily inserted into the record such editorials from national, state, and local religious publications as an additional sign of religious resistance.[31]

As the weight of the churches bore down against the Becker Amendment, its supporters searched for clergymen who would back them. Bishop Fulton Sheen, one of the most prominent Catholics in the country, was perhaps their best hope, but even he proved halfhearted. He hesitated to support an amendment allowing Bible reading in the schools, agreeing with opponents that the "problem of pluralism" would lead different faiths to lobby for use of their own version of Scripture. But he favored restoration of a shared prayer that would avoid divisiveness. He suggested "that the prayer to be said in all of the schools in this country be the prayer that every Member of Congress is already carrying in his pocket: 'In God We Trust.'" Dr. Robert Cook of the National Association of Evangelicals went further, announcing his organization's full support for a prayer amendment. Celler pressed him on theological details that were only vaguely addressed in the amendment: "Would a Protestant child be taught papal infallibility? Would a Catholic boy or girl be required to listen to divine instruction from the Torah? Might Mohammedan parents insist their child be taught the scriptures of the Koran?" In an unusual statement for an evangelical leader, Cook dismissed those concerns, claiming that there was really "not that much difference" among the texts used in the Protestant, Catholic, Jewish, and Muslim traditions. The important issue was that religion not be overwhelmed by atheism or secularism. "We are in danger of being religiously governed by a minority," Cook claimed. "It is religious freedom that is at stake, not necessarily some of these other things."[32]

With only slight support from religious leaders, the Becker Amendment's backers had to rely on the grassroots organizations of laymen who had, through their petitions and letter-writing campaigns, prompted the hearings in the first place. Dr. Charles Leaming, the Florida evangelical who led the Committee for the Preservation of Prayer and Bible Reading in Public Schools, said there had previously been a "spirit of apathy" in the country, but the Supreme Court rulings against school devotions sparked "an awakening." Father Robert Howes, the head of Massachusetts Citizens for Public Prayer, claimed that the national religious leaders heard by the committee were "generals without armies." "We say quite frankly that isolated leaders and isolated editorials against the backdrop of the expressed will of the massive majority of Americans simply cannot be interpreted as speaking for neither the Nation nor, at least in some cases," Howes said, "for the organization itself, in terms of the people who make it up at the grassroots level." Susan Seaforth, a television actress, made these same charges in an appearance for the Hollywood-led Project Prayer. Mocking the National Council of Churches, she said her organization would never have "60 or 70 delegates out of hundreds vote on this issue and then, in even the vaguest way, infer that we are speaking for those 40 million Americans when it just plain isn't so."[33]

Despite such protestations, the leaders of pro-amendment groups nevertheless claimed to represent the majority's will themselves. Charles Winegarner, whose Citizens Congressional Committee had unrolled their mile-long petition on the Capitol steps a year before, claimed that the impact of their grassroots campaign was already evident in Congress. Many of his congressional allies had assured him the Becker Amendment would win passage "by a handsome majority" if the Judiciary Committee would only end its obstruction. If it did not, there would be a political price to pay. "A rather meticulous survey on my part leads me to believe that opposition candidates for Congress are likely to spring up all over America in campaigns inclined to identify not only those who have opposed this legislation" but also those "who even neglected to give aggressive support to this thing. . . . An indignant populace," Winegarner warned, "might identify them with a campaign to remove the tradition of faith from the bloodstream of American life." At this, Celler interrupted: "Is that a threat?" "No," Winegarner protested, "it is not." "Members of Congress would resent threats, would they not?" The witness sheepishly said he hoped it did not come to that. Celler asked him to leave his written statement with the clerk and abruptly excused him from the witness chair. (It was likely no coincidence that, only days later, the well-connected Washington columnists Evans and Novak wrote their exposé on Winegarner's roots in the radical right.)[34]

Other lobbying organizations tried to distance themselves from Winegarner's extremism but fared little better. On behalf of the Constitutional Prayer Foundation, Francis Burch insisted his intentions were pure. "I am no alarmist," the Baltimore city solicitor stated. "I belong to no extremist group, but I say to you with all my heart that America is in danger if the very foundations upon which this Nation was built continue to be chipped away." Celler nevertheless treated Burch with suspicion, interrupting his testimony and challenging his claims. When Burch warned the committee members that "ignoring the amendments before you" was the same thing as "favoring the goals that had been established by the atheists," Celler stopped him cold. "I am opposed to these amendments and I don't subscribe to any of the tenets of the atheist association," he huffed. And when Burch went on at length about his worries that the Court would turn against other expressions of religion in public life, Celler noted that the Court had explicitly sanctioned such measures in "plain English." When Burch persisted, the chairman finally threw up his hands: "You are seeing ghosts under the bed."[35]

Popular opinion shifted dramatically as the hearings wore on. By the third week, reporters around the Capitol noted that congressional mail, once "as high as 100 to 1, and in no case less than 10 to 1" in favor of the amendment, had swung the other way. The reasons were clear. "Mail opposing an amendment picked up noticeably after a series of eminent church leaders urged the committee not to tamper with the First Amendment," the Associated Press related. Churches had not simply inspired their members but organized them. Initially, the AP noted, "opposition mail was almost entirely handwritten and on an individual basis," in sharp contrast to the mass of preprinted postcards and petitions that supporters had used. "Now cards and form letters are appearing in large numbers" in opposition "as some churches belatedly organize drives to offset the pro-amendment efforts."[36]

As the hearings entered their sixth and final week, Celler told reporters what they already understood. "The Becker Amendment will fail," he told them. "The tide originally in favor of it has turned. The hearings have caused the public to have second thoughts. They do not now wish to tinker with the Bill of Rights." The Judiciary Committee had second thoughts as well. While observers estimated in April that a large majority of committee members would vote for the Becker Amendment, an informal poll in June showed that at least twenty of the thirty-five would vote against it now. The mobilization of religious leaders seemed key. "The effect of the churches has been to reverse the tide," Celler reflected, especially with members of the committee, who had received a hundred thousand letters between them. With his colleagues now behind him, Celler concluded the hearings on June 3. Without any action or announcement, the Becker Amendment quietly died. "The only reason its obituary notice hasn't gone out already," a committee member said a few weeks later, "is that we still don't know how to write it without risking another furor." In mid-July, Dean Kelley noted that six weeks had gone by since the end of the hearings and the full committee had yet to meet. "When it does," he predicted, "the prayer amendment issue will be superseded by other Committee business, and there will be no general urgency to get to it."[37]

Becker refused to accept defeat. "I challenge Mr. Celler to bring an amendment to the floor of the House," he said from the floor of the chamber. "I know he is afraid to do this, and it is a tragedy that one man in Congress can so block the will of the American people." As it became clear that Celler would not release the amendment, Becker revived his plan to use a discharge petition. He announced he could easily secure the 218 signatures he needed. The discharge petition already had 167, Becker bragged, and the remainder would be easy to secure now that Celler's stalling tactics had ruled out regular action. Becker's opponents, however, were no longer worried. One of the anti-amendment members of the Judiciary Committee joked to a reporter off the record that "unleashing Frank Becker at this point is like unleashing Chiang Kai-Shek"—a belli-cose threat that realists knew would never materialize. Indeed, to Becker's embarrassment, not only was he unable to secure more signatures for the discharge petition, but several of the signers withdrew their names. The Becker Amendment, columnist Drew Pearson wrote that summer, had proved to be the "biggest flop Congress has seen in years." As a consola-tion prize, the Republican National Convention adopted a watered-down proposal for a prayer amendment in its party platform. But that measure died a quiet death too, going down to defeat with Barry Goldwater that fall. A few months later, Becker left office.[38]

THE DEFEAT OF THE BECKER Amendment led some observers to surmise that the issue had finally been laid to rest. In reality, the pro-longed fight over the amendment marked not the end of a struggle but the beginning. The House hearings revealed how fault lines across the country were shifting on the issue of separation of church and state.

Clerical leaders had taken stands that were largely in line with their denominations' traditional perspectives on the matter, but conservative laymen recoiled from their arguments. They felt bewildered—and, in many instances, betrayed—by their leaders' objections to seemingly wholesome traditions such as school prayer and Bible reading. Their faiths' traditional stances on issues of church-state separation had always seemed academic. In the wake of Becker's failure, conservative laymen began to doubt the authority of their religious representatives and look for new leaders to replace them.

In select cases, the conflict over the Becker Amendment brought into the open ongoing struggles between ministers and laymen. The National Council of Churches, which played a prominent role in coordinating religious opposition to the school prayer amendments, had spent much of the previous decade embroiled in a bitter struggle between liberal clergymen and more conservative laymen. In the early 1950s, a group of businessmen took charge of a new National Lay Committee in an overt effort to curtail the NCC's involvement in political, social, and economic issues. Notably, the Lay Committee was led by many of the same businessmen—including DuPont's Jasper Crane, Chrysler's B. E. Hutchinson, and Sun Oil's J. Howard Pew Jr., who served as its chairman—who had helped promote Spiritual Mobilization and other Christian libertarian groups in the 1940s. "Our premise was that, instead of appealing to government, the church should devote its energies to the work of promoting the attributes of Christianity . . . in the hearts and minds of men," Pew recalled. "We attempted to emphasize that Christ stressed not the expanded state but the dignity and responsibility of the individual." Under his leadership, the Lay Committee regularly denounced the NCC for making broad proclamations on "secular affairs" that were at odds with the opinions of laymen. In response to the constant criticism, the NCC disbanded the committee in 1955. "Clergy and laity active in organized Protestantism seemed to have lost the capacity to understand each other," Pew lamented. By the dawn of the 1960s, some conservatives in the NCC believed that clerical leaders were actively undermining their interests. "In sober truth," said Reverend Edmund A. Opitz, a conservative Unitarian, "many of our most articulate religious leaders are part of the problem, not part of the remedy."[39]

The battle over the Becker Amendment created many new rifts in religious bodies as well. Baptists, who had been committed to the complete separation of church and state for centuries, now had second thoughts about their stance. Next to the NCC's Dean Kelley, no religious figure had been more important in opposing Becker than Emanuel Carlson, director of the Baptist Joint Committee on Public Affairs (BJC). At the House hearings, he had presented himself as the spokesmen for twenty million Baptists, "insofar as anyone can speak for them." But his well-publicized opposition to the amendment there came as a shock to many rank-and-file Baptists, weakening his standing and that of the BJC. Though it represented eight different bodies, the BJC had its roots in the Southern Baptist Convention (SBC). Even there, Carlson's outspoken resistance to the prayer amendment sparked a major backlash. "I am being besieged with a flood of letters and phone calls from Southern Baptists who are protesting the recently released statement of the Joint Committee," convention president K. Owen White wrote Carlson in March 1964. "Having had opportunity during the past months to visit in many areas of our convention coast to coast, I am in a position to tell you that there is a wide difference of opinion among our people and at the grass roots level the overwhelming majority of our pastors and people are out of sympathy with the decision of the Supreme Court." White counted himself among them. The *Engel* and *Schempp* rulings, he believed, would inevitably lead to the removal of all recognition of God from public life and government. In a letter to an old friend, the Houston minister confided that he had been asked to testify against the prayer amendment in the House hearings but had refused, "since I am in favor of such an amendment or something similar to it."[40]

As the annual meeting of the Southern Baptist Convention approached that summer, White braced for an open revolt. To avoid "a very heated controversy" over Carlson's opposition to the amendment, White penned an article for the Baptist press that distanced Carlson from the convention. "It seems very difficult for many people to realize that there is no such thing as '*The Southern Baptist Church*,'" he wrote. "No one speaks for Southern Baptists other than Southern Baptists themselves." Yet White used the rest of the article, titled "Southern Baptists at the Crossroads," to reckon with the political controversies that were dividing the convention's ten million members, with "the question on Bible reading and prayer in the public schools" at the forefront. He made his dissatisfaction with the Court's rulings clear but warned like-minded conservatives that "it would be neither wise nor possible" to address the matter in length at the annual meeting in Atlantic City. But not every reader heeded him. At the convention, a Virginia delegate—a "messenger" in the SBC's language—proposed amending a traditional, broad statement on the First Amendment to affirm "the historic right of our schools to engage voluntarily, on a non-sectarian basis, in prayer, Bible reading, and other devotional exercises." Without giving opponents a chance to speak, White pushed the matter to a vote, where it passed narrowly. At this, opponents called for reconsideration as supporters chanted, "No, no, no!" The tension was broken only a half hour later, when the same Virginia delegate changed the language of his motion to one that supported "the historic right of our schools for full academic freedom in pursuit of all knowledge, religious or otherwise." The new language did not mention the Becker Amendment and instead affirmed SBC support for the First Amendment, opposing "any further amendment" in the realm of religion. Thus reworded, the measure passed nearly unanimously. Few reporters noted the short window during which the SBC formally stood in favor of school prayer. Most offered accounts as straightforward as their headlines: "Baptists Vote 'No' on Prayer Amendments."[41]

Yet across Christian denominations, the rising discontent of the laity was perhaps most evident in the lay organizations that continued to press for a prayer amendment on their own. Within months of the Becker Amendment's death in the House, the Constitutional Prayer Foundation began aggressively lobbying the Senate in hopes that the proposal might fare better there. Through late 1964 and early 1965, Francis Burch blanketed the upper chamber with letters urging senators to pass an amendment that would "restore the traditional meaning of the First Amendment and eliminate once and for all the chance of further judicial erosion of voluntary, non-denominational reverence from our national life." The responses to his entreaties revealed a wide range of senatorial opinion on the subject, with large numbers expressing unqualified support.[42]

Senators who supported a prayer amendment believed, as Burch did, that the idea still had broad popular support. "Both this office and the

Senate Judiciary Committee have received so much mail on the 'prayer' issue that with our present staffs it is physically impossible to answer all of it," noted Democratic senator James Eastland of Mississippi. The Becker Amendment, in their view, had fallen short only because of the obstructionist tactics of its opponents. "The leisurely pace of those hearings," complained Pennsylvania Republican Hugh Scott, "indicated the considerable opposition by the Democratic Chairman." Though the senators believed the House had thwarted the will of the people, they worried that the testimony of religious leaders at the Becker hearings might be impossible to overcome, even if the Senate proved a more favorable setting.[43]

That said, there was no clear indication that the Senate would be more amenable to the prayer amendment cause. The Senate Judiciary Committee was in the hands of an ally, Jim Eastland, rather than an opponent like Celler, but the chamber as a whole seemed cooler to the idea of an amendment than the House had two years before. While representatives with reservations about the prayer amendment had answered inquiries like Burch's with broad statements of studious concern, the senators who opposed the idea were blunt. "I am afraid that I can't be of much help to you," replied Robert F. Kennedy of New York, "as I support the Supreme Court's decision on school prayer." "The Supreme Court has spoken," Oregon's Wayne Morse replied. "Its decision is final." For these opponents, the opposition of clergymen offered political cover. Vance Hartke of Indiana framed his opposition this way, saying he agreed "with most religious leaders of all faiths that the Court has strengthened, not weakened, religion in America." Daniel Inouye of Hawaii, meanwhile, explained his opposition by quoting Carlson's Baptist Joint Committee: "Religion on a government platter has never provided much spiritual nurture for the people, nor has it given strength to the nation."[44]

The Senate moved slowly on Burch's proposal. For much of 1965, the chamber was consumed by the ambitious legislative agenda of President Johnson's Great Society programs, devoting its energies to drafting, debating, and passing major pieces of legislation such as the Voting Rights Act, Medicare, and Medicaid. In 1966, however, the drive for a prayer amendment picked up with renewed energy, as it found the champion it needed: Senate minority leader Everett Dirksen of Illinois. Recognizable for his shock of white hair and thick black glasses, the seventy-two-year-old Dirksen was a political powerhouse. Despite an overwrought speech-making style that earned him the nickname "the Wizard of Ooze," the gravel-voiced Republican was an effective legislator who had rallied liberals and moderates in his caucus to cross the aisle and support the Civil Rights Act. Still, on school prayer his leadership came as a surprise. In 1964, Dirksen had publicly dismissed the Becker Amendment's chances soon after its introduction in the House. A year later, he showed little interest in Burch's pleas to revive the idea, offering only bland assurances that he would give "my very careful attention" if someone else ever brought the matter before the Senate. Privately, though, Dirksen was a great believer in prayer. "Church was a large part of our early lives," he stressed in his memoirs, recounting that his mother had helped construct the house of worship of his childhood Reformed Church congregation. As an adult, Dirksen believed that prayer had saved his career. He had served eight terms as a congressman before his badly deteriorating eyesight forced him to resign in 1949. When doctors recommended removal of one eye, Dirksen turned to prayer, dropping to his knees on the train home to Illinois to ask God if he should have the procedure. "He said, 'No,'" Dirksen recalled. "Just as emphatic as it could be." Refusing treatment, he relied on the power of prayer. Dirksen's eyesight soon recovered and, after a successful Senate run in 1950, so did his career. From then on, the Republican remained convinced that prayer was nothing less than "a pipeline to God Almighty."[45]

In March 1966, Dirksen proposed yet another constitutional amendment to restore prayer to the public schools. The Dirksen Amendment refined previous versions into a short, sixty-five-word proposal:

Nothing contained in this Constitution shall prohibit the authority administering any school, school system, educational institution or other public building supported in whole or in part through the expenditure of public funds from providing for or permitting the voluntary participation by students or others in prayer. Nothing contained in this article shall authorize any such authority to prescribe the form or content of any prayer.

Dirksen warned colleagues that a "storm of protest" over the Supreme Court rulings against school prayer was "gathering again in all parts of the nation." "I expect nation-wide support," he announced with confidence. "Since these court decisions struck prayer from the schools, polls have been taken and more than 81 percent of the people appear to disagree with the courts. Prayer groups are organizing. One man dumped 52,000 letters of protest on my desk two weeks ago."[46]

The Dirksen Amendment relit the political firestorm from two years earlier and set the Senate on edge. A reporter for the *Los Angeles Times* noted that liberal members were "uniformly resentful of Dirksen's fanning the flames of what they view as one of the ugliest controversies to sweep over the American political landscape in recent years." Opponents quietly complained but were wary about making public statements in an election year. "It would be like denouncing motherhood," one said. But they took comfort in the knowledge that hearings had effectively killed the Becker Amendment. "People calmed down," a liberal senator noted, "when they saw the parade of horrible possibilities that had been forecast—such as deleting 'In God We Trust' from our currency—never materialized." They hoped a similar cooling off might happen now. Dirksen worried about the same thing, however, and sought to avoid hearings altogether, arguing that his proposal was similar enough to the Becker Amendment to make the matter moot. "Every shade of opinion and viewpoint was presented to the [House Judiciary] Committee," Dirksen noted. "It involved Jews, Catholics, Protestants of all denominations, ministers, laymen, lawyers, professors and others. I can think of nothing that was left unsaid." Repeated efforts to force his proposal to the floor failed, however, and Dirksen resigned himself to a longer path to passage that would begin with hearings before the Senate Subcommittee on Constitutional Amendments.[47]

Dirksen strove to build support inside and outside Congress. First he lobbied his colleagues, to great success. Within a week of its introduction, twenty-five senators had signed on as cosponsors of the Dirksen Amendment; by midsummer, the number had nearly doubled to forty-seven. He kept at it even after he broke a thigh bone in May and wound up on crutches for the rest of the summer. Mail continued to pour in, with Dirksen's staff claiming more than seventy thousand letters of support by

June. Meanwhile, organizers circulated petitions at both the national and local levels demanding passage of a prayer amendment. A housewife from Kenosha, Wisconsin, for instance, stopped by Dirksen's office in Washington, D.C., to present roughly three thousand signatures gathered by her Mothers Crusade to Establish Prayers in Public Schools. Dirksen also counted on conservative stars such as Pat Boone, who revived his lobbying through the Project Prayer program.[48]

The Senate hearings on the Dirksen Amendment were ultimately a faint echo of the House hearings on the Becker Amendment. While the earlier amendment had brought together the full House Judiciary Committee for six weeks of well-publicized testimony from hundreds of witnesses, the Senate hearings took just six days before the much smaller Subcommittee on Constitutional Amendments with only a few dozen testifying. The lack of interest was made clear by members themselves. On the first day, just four senators from the nine-man subcommittee were present. By the middle of the week, only the chairman was there: Birch Bayh, a thirty-eight-year-old Democratic freshman from Indiana. Dirksen himself only showed up for the first day, even though he was the ranking Republican on the subcommittee. All sides, it seemed, believed the sessions were simply a procedural step before the real action of a full Senate debate.[49]

The low stakes aside, the Dirksen hearings took the pulse of the nation on the school prayer issue. Key witnesses from the House hearings reprised their roles for the new round, but the Senate hearings did not simply rehash the earlier ones. They brought into focus much more directly the question of just who truly spoke for ordinary Americans in determining the proper place of faith in the nation—their religious representatives, who largely opposed the amendment drive, or their political representatives, who more often supported it. This tension was evident in the testimony of the very first witness, Father Robert Drinan, dean of Boston College Law School. The Jesuit priest, who would win election to the House four years later, bluntly condemned the opportunistic pandering of politicians on the issue. He produced one of the three thick volumes of testimony from the House hearings, noting that the "overwhelming majority of leaders" in the Protestant, Catholic, and Jewish faiths were "strongly opposed to any constitutional change."

Why is it then, I ask, that 40 Members of the U.S. Senate introduced in March 1966 a resolution seeking to do that which is directly opposed to the best judgment of virtually all of the religious leaders and denominational groups in the Nation? Why have these 40 Senators subscribed to a resolution seeking to accomplish an objective which the leading churches and synagogues of America have vehemently repudiated as unwise and unconstitutional? For what reasons do 40 Senators seek to appear more pious than the churches and more righteous than the Supreme Court?

In Drinan's view, Congress was tempting "a profound mistake" solely because its members were interested in political games.[50]

Dirksen, present in the room that day, rose to the challenge. He had the whole set of House testimony before him too, the minority leader mused, and he had been flipping through its pages taking note of the kind of witnesses heard there: priests, ministers, and rabbis; divinity school deans, professors, and theologians; leaders of church foundations and interfaith councils; and so on. "Somehow we had every sophisticated argument except an argument from the common man of this country, who was defined as one who works and prays and pays his bills and goes to church, rears a family in decency as law-abiding children," Dirksen observed. "We are beginning to hear from him by the millions, and he is going to have his say." Senator Roman Hruska of Nebraska, one of the forty-eight cosponsors of the amendment, seconded the claim that "sophisticated arguments" from experts were overrated. Drinan was taken aback. "Are you suggesting," he asked, "that the National Council of Churches, which represents virtually all Protestant bodies, is not actually speaking for its constituency?" "They are speaking as well as they know," Hruska allowed, but they could never truly speak for the people.[51]

The leaders of the NCC had a chance to speak later that same day. Dr. David Hunter, an Episcopal priest who served as NCC deputy general secretary, acknowledged that a few religious organizations favored the prayer amendment: the Greek Orthodox Archdiocese of North and South America, the National Association of Evangelicals, and the fundamentalist American Council of Christian Churches. "Without imputing these views to any but the leaders who expressed them," Hunter continued,

"I find it significant to note that the three official national leaders cited above as favoring a prayer amendment direct a total constituency of not more than 3,700,000, whereas those opposing such an amendment are looked to for spiritual guidance by 56,794,674 Americans, or a ratio of 15 to 1." There was some truth, Hunter admitted, in the charges that the churchmen who opposed the Becker Amendment had originally been "generals without armies," but in the years since "they have been joined by the 'armies' which caught up to them." As proof, he cited resolutions against the prayer amendment passed at annual meetings of a half-dozen major denominations.[52]

As other witnesses made clear, however, the issue was still controversial at the grassroots. At the end of the first day, Bayh added to the official record a letter from a scattering of laymen's committees and congregations who were furious at the NCC leadership and wanted to "categorically repudiate" its statements on the matter. "The National Council of Churches has never been authorized by the millions of members it purports to 'speak for' to appear before any Congressional, State, or local committees," it read. In the same spirit, a Protestant minister testified that many clergymen had disagreed with NCC leaders. "We began to suspect that a false impression that ministers opposed prayers had been created artificially," Reverend Gary Cohen said. "Many of us discussed the disturbing problem and felt that it was time to demonstrate that clergymen, at least a high percentage if not the overwhelming percentage, do in fact favor voluntary prayer and Bible reading in the schools." As proof, he offered the names of thirty-nine hundred Protestant ministers from eighty-three denominations.[53]

The senators on the subcommittee were not impressed. Bayh pointed out that the number offered represented only about 5 percent of all clergymen in the country, hardly the "overwhelming percentage" Cohen claimed. Joe Tydings of Maryland went even further, doubting that the individuals listed were even ministers. He noted that the petition contained eighteen names from his hometown of Baltimore and, in a bit of courtroom drama, proceeded to pull out phone books to double-check the listings. "Five are not listed either under the list of ministers in the yellow pages or as ministers by name," he concluded, "so I question the validity of the list." At this, Carl McIntire Jr., the son of the American Council of Christian

Churches' leader and himself the head of International Christian Youth, seemed taken aback: "You are not questioning our honesty?" "All I want to have," Tydings replied, "are the facts." "To the best of our sincere intentions," McIntire replied, "we have done what we feel is right."[54]

While the NCC had its authority publicly challenged, other religious organizations found themselves facing criticism in private. Emanuel Carlson, for instance, again presented himself as the spokesman for roughly twenty-two million Baptists. Bayh probed him on that point, asking if there had been any effort to "assess the way the lay members feel" about the issue at hand. It was complicated, Carlson admitted, in that individual congregations sent messengers to the various conventions and they, in turn, passed resolutions that were sent on to the BJC for coordinated action. But Carlson believed that his testimony still reflected the general will of Baptists. Once again, however, the Southern Baptist Convention found itself besieged by laymen who refused to believe that a Baptist spokesman had testified against the school prayer amendment. H. Franklin Paschall, the new SBC president, distanced the convention from Carlson even more than his predecessor had. "Dr. Carlson," he wrote to critics, "certainly was not speaking for all Southern Baptists any more than I can speak for all Southern Baptists." Still, Paschall volunteered an opinion all the same, one that contradicted not just the BJC lobbyists but his own convention's formal resolutions. "I am sure," he stated, "that Southern Baptists in general favor voluntary prayer and Bible reading in the public schools."[55]

After the hearings, the debate over who could speak for ordinary Americans on the prayer issue spilled over into the press. "It may seem an anomaly that the most concerted and vocal opposition to Sen. Dirksen's proposed constitutional amendment to permit voluntary prayer in the public schools should come from spokesmen for leading American churches," observed the *Chicago Tribune*. Groups such as the NCC, its conservative editors noted, were not to be trusted. "These organizations, professing to speak for millions of communicants, indicate by their doctrinal positions that they are more concerned with social engineering, world politics, and the governmental panaceas of the moment than they are with their traditional province. It is little wonder," the editors noted, "that we are presented with the spectacle of churchmen who journey to Washington to speak against prayer." A syndicated column by Roscoe Drummond of the *Christian Science Monitor* began with the same premise—"one of the most striking facts" of the hearings was that "most religious denominations in the United States are against any such amendment"—but reached a different conclusion. Drummond accepted without question the idea that Protestant and Jewish spokesmen who opposed the amendment were doing so on behalf of their communicants, but when it came to Catholic spokesmen who supported the proposal, he had his doubts. "Important Catholic churchmen strongly favor the Dirksen amendment," he acknowledged, "but Catholic support of it is not monolithic." But neither, of course, was the Protestant or Jewish opposition.[56]

As Dirksen worked to bring his amendment to a vote, he advanced some of the same arguments. The religious leaders who opposed his efforts, he claimed at a news conference in mid-September, were disconnected from the laymen. Their testimony had bothered him "not one bit," Dirksen insisted. "I'm not interested in social engineers, but in soul-savers who live close to their flocks—that means the little preachers." He would press on, he announced, because of "the ministers and the millions who have written me in support of school prayers." A few days later, Dirksen pointedly dismissed the authority of religious leaders in a speech on the Senate floor. The chamber was virtually empty, except for a few tourists sleeping in the galleries, but Dirksen nevertheless made an impassioned final plea for his proposed amendment. (He became so animated that a colleague compared him to the overzealous Professor Henry Hill from *The Music Man*. Dirksen disagreed: "Hell, I sound like Billy Graham. I'm positively evangelical about this.") Citing recent polls showing that roughly 80 percent of people supported the amendment, Dirksen lashed into the NCC. "They come down here and make it appear they speak for 40 million people," he said. "They do nothing of the kind! They are out of touch with their people." As an added insult, Dirksen placed a pair of hit pieces in the official record—an article from the conservative magazine *Human Events* that criticized the NCC for its "invariably liberal" politics and a right-wing piece from Louisiana charging that the NCC, "although not Communistic, has been an aid to the Communist conspiracy." Outraged leaders of a dozen denominations demanded an apology from Dirksen. None came.[57]

In late September 1966, Dirksen succeeded in finally bringing his amendment to the floor for a vote. In a bit of legislative sleight of hand, he took a pending resolution about the United Nations Children's Fund (UNICEF), removed the original text, and replaced it with the Dirksen Amendment. Before the Senate could vote, however, Bayh offered an alternative proposal of his own. "I don't want the Senate to play God," he explained, "and we're close to it." The real problem, he insisted, was popular confusion over the real meaning of the Supreme Court's rulings. And if they amended the Constitution to clarify every decision of the Court, it would soon be "five feet high." Instead, Bayh called for a resolution that simply expressed the "sense of Congress" that the Court's rulings still allowed for periods of silent meditation in schools. Dirksen dismissed the compromise, claiming that a nonbinding resolution was "a frivolous thing" and "not worth a damn." The schools needed religion. "They teach the little children sex in the schools," Dirksen argued in a full-throated appeal. "They teach them about Communism. They even teach them ballet! Why not God Almighty?"[58]

Dirksen ultimately failed to convince his colleagues that the prayer amendment would not do more harm than good. His opponents offered rationales taken directly from the arguments made by religious leaders in the House and Senate hearings. "One's religious practice," majority leader Mike Mansfield of Montana said, is "too personal, too sacred, too private to be influenced by pressures for change each time a new school board is elected." Even conservative members who had been assumed to be supporters of the Dirksen Amendment seemed to have taken the words of religious leaders to heart. Sam Ervin of North Carolina, a former state supreme court judge and a member of the Judiciary Committee, drew on their language in an impassioned speech that a reporter noted "fairly shook" the chamber. "If you're going to amend the Constitution," he shouted at Dirksen, "for God's sake, draw an amendment that will give religious equality to everyone in the United States regardless of what his religion might be!" In the end, the Dirksen Amendment failed. With a final tally of 49 to 37, it fell nine votes short of the necessary two-thirds majority. Bayh's resolution went down to an even larger defeat. Needing only a simple majority, it was beaten back by a margin of 33 to 51.[59]

Undaunted, Dirksen refused to accept defeat. "This crusade will continue," he announced. "The next time, we will be better organized throughout the country." In a telephone call the night before the vote, he had been assured by Dr. Daniel Poling, the eighty-one-year-old fundamentalist and former editor of the *Christian Herald*, that a new grassroots organization would rise up to champion the cause of school prayer. Its leaders would be Poling, Billy Graham, and a "Catholic prelate" to be named later. That specific organization never came to pass, but the proposal was prescient. For too long, religious conservatives believed that their voice in political matters—especially when it came to the role of religion in public life—had been drowned out by the more liberal leaders of their denominations. If conservative Christians at the grassroots would simply organize themselves according to their *politics* rather than their particular denominations, they could end the reign of the religious establishment. If effective leaders could bridge the long-standing gaps between different faiths—and bring together, as Poling proposed, conservative Catholics with fundamentalist and evangelical Protestants—then laypeople would finally have their say.[60]

CHAPTER 8

"Which Side Are You On?"

I N CARLSTADT, NEW JERSEY, A tiny borough just outside East
Rutherford, a middle-aged longshoreman named Walter Lantry had
watched the struggle over school prayer with growing alarm. A devout
Catholic and active member of the Knights of Columbus, he worried that
the religious foundation of the nation was being eroded, first by the actions of the Supreme Court and then by the inaction of Congress. In the
fall of 1964, Lantry found a way to fight back: he created large banners
bearing the words "One Nation Under God" to be flown as a show of
patriotic faith. "My idea came after I read a small article by Madalyn Murray on removing prayer from the public schools," he told reporters. "The
purpose of the pennant was only to alert the American public to what was
taking place. We lost prayer in the schools while we were sleeping. The
Supreme Court is more or less governed by the will of the people, and a
lot of noisy minority groups have been taking advantage of it. I wanted to
make the majority noisy too, to create a fervor."[1]

In October 1964, the "One Nation Under God" banners began spreading across the New Jersey suburbs, appearing on flagpoles at borough halls,
municipal offices, city parks, and public schools in some sixty towns. Officials explained their support in specific terms. As Sayreville borough
council president Joseph A. Rzigalinski said, "It is a good way of combating the Supreme Court decision barring prayer in the public schools."
Sayreville's mayor agreed that there was nothing untoward in it. "After
all, we have the words 'In God We Trust' on our money," he pointed out,

"and we say 'One Nation Under God' when we salute the flag." (The only question was how best to express the sentiment. According to an official with Protestants and Other Americans United for the Separation of Church and State, "Sayreville, NJ, citizens for hours argued over whether 'One Nation Under God' banners should be placed on city garbage trucks. Some claimed this would please atheists. No one wanted to do this. Others argued that 'Garbage men believe in God, too.'") The pennants proved incredibly popular. Small ones cost $1.45, large ones $3.25. Sales soon took off in New York and Connecticut, and by early 1965, Lantry was filling orders in twenty-seven different states, mostly in the Midwest and West. Three of his local suppliers soon ran out of stock, but not before turning a $60,000 profit. National organizations such as the American Legion and the John Birch Society stepped in to meet the demand.[2]

As the "One Nation Under God" banners spread, so did the sense of defiance for those who flew them. In November 1964, the New Jersey Knights of Columbus pledged that an "all-out war and the full resources of the state council" would be brought against anyone who dared mount a legal challenge against the pennants. When the state ACLU sent letters to boroughs flying the banner, expressing concern that government officials were supporting a measure "motivated largely to demonstrate defiance and contempt for a ruling of the United States Supreme Court," the civil liberties group found itself roundly vilified. "If they want to make an issue of it," said Midland Park's mayor, "let them take it to court." "I'll fight this thing to the hilt," vowed the deputy mayor of South Hackensack. Even the ads for the pennants took on a confrontational tone: "Which Side Are You On?" Conservative organizations, from the mainstream American Legion to the extremist John Birch Society, quickly rallied to the cause, giving "one nation under God" an ever more partisan tone in the late 1960s. Soon enough, the phrase was being used to promote not just the original cause of school prayer but a host of other issues dear to conservatives.[3]

Most notably, as American involvement in Vietnam escalated, prowar hawks increasingly employed the phrase both to show support for the war and to silence its critics. In May 1965, as the first regular US Army troops were sent into combat there, Walter Lantry told a correspondent that a brand-new set of "One Nation Under God" postcards had been "distributed in the thousands by religious, civic and patriotic groups in backing our President in his stand in Viet Nam." For Lantry, supporting the troops was not an abstract idea; his son, a Coast Guard lieutenant, was stationed in Vietnam. While they worried about his safety overseas, Lantry and his wife focused on shoring up support for the war at home. When they heard that Rutgers University professor Eugene Genovese said at an antiwar "teach-in" that he was rooting for a communist victory, they traveled downstate to take part in a similar event in October 1965. They convinced the moderator to begin the program with the Pledge of Allegiance and national anthem, but such shows of patriotic unity were soon swept away by the conflict over the war. A few hours into it, Mrs. Lantry slapped a sneering male student, who then slapped her back before the crowd could separate them. As the war expanded, such confrontations became increasingly commonplace. By 1967, there were nearly half a million American troops in Vietnam, prompting more protests from the men who would be drafted next and more counterprotests from the parents of those who already had been. In April, after hundreds of thousands of protesters came together for the largest antiwar demonstration in New York City's history, the head of the American Legion's "One Nation Under God committee" urged supporters to rally around the phrase as a show of their support. "In these days when many young Americans (while only a minority) are protesting against our President's Policy on Viet Nam," he said, "we of the American Legion should lead the way to remind all Patriotic Americans that our country truly is 'ONE NATION UNDER GOD.'"[4]

By the late 1960s, "one nation under God"—and the broader fusion of patriotism and piety that it had come to represent—had become an important touchstone in an aggressive new conservatism. Frustrated by a "noisy minority" on the left, Lantry had hoped the rallying cries of religious nationalism might "make the majority noisy, too." And, indeed, it soon found its voice. Political observers began to speak about an emerging "Silent Majority" of ordinary Americans who rejected the liberal movements of the era, especially the protests against the Vietnam War, but who had not yet made their opposition known. In the 1968 presidential election, the signs of this Silent Majority's emergence were everywhere. When the conservative populist George Wallace launched his independent presidential campaign that year, reporters were struck by a common theme on cars across the South. "The largest number of bumper stickers by far advertise Wallace for President," one journalist noted. "Coming in second are those which read: 'One Nation—Under God' or 'God is not dead: I talked with Him this morning!'" (Democratic candidate Hubert Humphrey tried to pry the phrase away from Wallace, telling a crowd of Connecticut factory workers that America should be "one nation under God, not under a demagogue." For such sacrilege, he was loudly booed.) Wallace was a capable champion of this ascendant conservatism, but he could never match the two men who had been present at the creation of that politics: Richard Nixon and Billy Graham.[5]

When the Cold War era's religious nationalism took root during Dwight Eisenhower's administration, his vice president and his favorite preacher had been key agents in the change. Nixon and Graham had front-row seats, often literally, for major developments in that transformational moment in American political culture, from the first inaugural prayer and first presidential prayer breakfast, through the adoption of the mottos "one nation under God" and "In God We Trust," and on to the era's wider embrace of religion in industry, advertising, and entertainment. They understood the political power of public displays of faith and, more important, the price of its absence. When he tried to explain his razor-thin loss in the 1960 presidential race, Nixon often singled out a last-minute decision by *Life* publisher Henry Luce to scrap an article in which Graham had given him a strong endorsement. Both Nixon and Graham believed the article would have made the difference.[6]

Eight years later, they were determined not to repeat that mistake. Echoing his earlier service to Eisenhower, Graham proved pivotal both in Nixon's decision to run and in his performance on the campaign trail. "You are the best prepared man in the United States to be president," Graham reportedly told him in January 1968. "I think it is your destiny to be president." Unlike his coy approach in 1952, this time he made no secret of his support. At a Billy Graham crusade in Portland, Oregon, he introduced Nixon's daughters to the crowd and announced that "there is no American I admire more than Richard Nixon." At the Republican National Convention in Miami in August, Graham provided a prayer after Nixon's acceptance speech and then participated in top-level discussions about potential running mates. In September, Nixon took a place of honor next to Graham on stage at another crusade in Pittsburgh, where the preacher told the worshipers and those watching at home that his long friendship with Nixon had been "one of the most moving religious experiences of my life." Shortly before the election, Graham informed the press that he had already cast an absentee ballot for Nixon, a fact that was repeated in Republican television ads right up to election day. That night, after Nixon's victory had been confirmed, the president-elect welcomed the minister to his suite in a New York City hotel where his family, friends, and advisors had gathered. "Billy, I want you to lead us in prayer," Nixon said. "We want to rededicate our lives." As Graham recalled, they all joined hands as he offered a short blessing. "And then [Nixon] went straight off to meet the press."[7]

When Nixon entered the White House, he brought Graham with him. A constant presence and trusted advisor, the minister became, in the words of biographer Marshall Frady, "something like an extra officer of Nixon's Cabinet, the administration's own Pastor-without-Portfolio." Others were more critical. Will Campbell, a liberal southern preacher, denounced Graham as "a false court prophet who tells Nixon and the Pentagon what they want to hear" while journalist I. F. Stone dismissed him as a "smoother Rasputin." Whatever the critics said, Graham's influence in the Nixon White House was profound. His words and deeds helped make piety and patriotism seem the sole property of the right. By the mid-1970s, the transformation was so complete that novelist Walker Percy asserted that a southern conservative was just "Billy Graham on Sunday and Richard Nixon the rest of the week." In truth, the words of the two men were practically interchangeable. "I have faith in [America] not because we are the strongest nation in the world, which we are, and not because we are the richest nation in the world, which we are," Nixon announced at ceremonies for Billy Graham Day in 1971; "but because there is still, in the heartland of this country, a strong religious faith, a morality, a spiritual quality which makes the American people not just a rich people or a strong people, but . . . a people with that faith which enables them to meet the challenge of greatness." After the president's address, a reporter asked Graham if he thought Nixon might be sounding more like a preacher these days. Perhaps, he mused. "Maybe I'm sounding more like him."[8]

With Graham's involvement, the Nixon White House gave new life to old public rituals and, more important, created religious ceremonies of its own. These new manifestations of public religion—most notably, regular church services held inside the White House and a pair of giant rallies for God and country outside it—proved far more overtly partisan than their predecessors. "Every president in American history had invoked the name and blessings of God during his inauguration address, and many . . . had made some notable public display of their putative piety," religious scholar William Martin observed, "but none ever made such a conscious, calculating use of religion as a political instrument as did Richard Nixon." Not even Eisenhower came close. While his purposely bland public religion had helped unite Americans around a seemingly nonpartisan cause, the starkly conservative brand of faith and politics advanced by Nixon and Graham only drove them apart.[9]

THE INAUGURATION OF RICHARD MILHOUS Nixon involved an unprecedented display of public prayer and formal worship. The organizers, led by the Mormon hotel magnate J. Willard Marriott, worked diligently to evoke the spirit of Eisenhower's first inauguration sixteen years before. The retired president issued a press release asserting that Nixon's inauguration should be a day of rejoicing "because it is a clear promise that our faith in him will be vindicated, our prayers for America." Reporters noted that Eisenhower was convalescing at the Walter Reed Medical Center but otherwise would have gladly taken part in the day. Though he was absent, his influence was everywhere.[10]

For months, a special Religious Observance Committee had been working feverishly to establish a spiritual tone for the inauguration. Led by Judge Boyd Leedom, a North Dakotan who had headed both Eisenhower's National Labor Relations Board and Abraham Vereide's International Council for Christian Leadership, the committee called for religious observances to be held in all churches and synagogues in the weeks before the inauguration. This period of prayer, Leedom explained, would culminate in a national moment of worship on Inauguration Day, when Americans would pause at exactly 11:00 a.m. for three minutes of prayer "to commemorate with joyful reverence this peaceful transfer of authority and to proclaim to all the world our faith in God and our spiritual rededication." As the inauguration neared, the committee distributed a special collection of prayers, Bible readings, and quotations to encourage the revival. While selections were purportedly chosen to illuminate links between faith and freedom, several advanced a decidedly conservative vision. A passage from 1 Peter, for instance, called to mind law-and-order themes of Nixon's campaign: "Be subject for the Lord's sake to every human institution, whether it be to the emperor as supreme, or to governors as sent by him to punish those who do wrong and to praise those who do right." Another prayer, attributed to George Washington, evoked conservative complaints about antiwar protesters, asking God to inspire in the citizenry "a spirit of subordination and obedience of government." Elsewhere, the Religious Observance Committee was even less subtle. Ten thousand cards depicting a pair of hands clasped in prayer, for instance, were distributed for display in the windows of homes and businesses across Washington. Upon the cards ran the words "THANKSGIVING. BLESSING. REDEDICATION. GUIDANCE." And then Nixon's campaign slogan: "FORWARD TOGETHER."[11]

The committee's greatest achievement was its creation of a religious service as an official part of the Inauguration Day festivities. "It was one of the few times, possibly the first since George Washington," the *New York Times* noted, "that a full-scale worship service had been part of an inaugural program." While past presidents had prayed privately at churches around the capital, Nixon's rites were held in the West Auditorium of the State Department, a huge room three stories high. At 9:00 a.m., a capacity crowd of 750 supporters joined the Nixons in prayers led by figures from five different faiths. The clergymen included prominent leaders, such as the head of the Synagogue Council of America and the Catholic archbishop of Washington, as well as lesser-known individuals such as the former pastor of Nixon's childhood Quaker congregation. The highlight of the service, though, was Reverend Norman Vincent Peale's "Call for Spiritual Renewal," an address that was reprinted widely and even disseminated to military chaplains for the benefit of armed services personnel.[12]

Following the five clergymen in the morning, another five offered blessings during the swearing-in ceremonies at noon. "Never before," marveled a Presbyterian minister, "had so much prayer been invoked to place this nation's Chief of State in office." As with the morning services, one clergyman stood out from the crowd. Following a rendition of "This Is My Country" by the Mormon Tabernacle Choir, Billy Graham strode to the podium, bundled up against a windy thirty-degree day. Graham had been invited by Nixon to deliver the invocation, but his comments ranged much more broadly than that. *Time* called it "Billy Graham's mini-inaugural address," while the editors of the *Christian Century* were harsher, denouncing his "raucous harangue." The preacher reasserted the old religious nationalism of the Eisenhower years and applied it to the new political ends of the Nixon era. "Our Father and our God," he began, "we recognize on this historic occasion that we are 'a nation under God.' We thank Thee for this torch of faith handed to us by our forefathers. May we never let it be extinguished. Thou alone hast given us our prosperity, our freedom and our power. This faith in God is our heritage and our foundation!" Graham warned that the religious "pillars of our society" had "eroded in an increasingly materialistic and permissive society," and the nation was "now reaping a whirlwind of crime, division, and rebellion." The departing president Lyndon Johnson winced visibly at these words, but Graham assured the crowd that all was not lost. "We recognize, O Lord, that in Thy sovereignty Thou has permitted Richard Nixon to lead us at this momentous hour of our history." He asked God's blessing in helping the new president lead a "moral and spiritual restoration" across the nation. Eschewing the ecumenical tones of past invocations, Graham specified that Americans needed to be "born again" though a renewed faith in Jesus Christ. "We pray this humbly in the Name of the Prince of Peace who shed His blood on the Cross that men might have eternal life. Amen."[13]

After Graham's invocation came the oath of office, delivered by Chief Justice Earl Warren. Warren and Nixon had a long and complicated relationship, stretching back to their early days as California Republicans jockeying for position on the national stage. Warren had been the party's vice presidential nominee in the near-miss 1948 campaign, and after the GOP won the White House in 1952 with Nixon as the vice presidential nominee, Warren was placed on the Court. Initially he seemed an ally of Nixon and Graham, but they drifted apart over the next decade. In his

1968 presidential campaign, Nixon turned his old ally into a punching bag, making repeated criticisms about the "permissive" rulings of the Warren Court. Many expected the swearing-in to be a tense moment—there would only be "a Bible between them," as a *Washington Post* piece worried—but it went smoothly. In truth, there were two Bibles between them, as Nixon again mimicked Eisenhower by resting his left hand on a pair of open Bibles as he recited the oath.[14]

In his first address as president, Nixon delivered a sermon. His text, one clergyman later said, was "replete with references to God and the Bible, the American spirit, the spirit of Christmas, our virtues and vices—even the angels." These grace notes were gathered together in a message that echoed Graham's prayer. "We have found ourselves rich in goods, but ragged in spirit; reaching with magnificent precision for the moon, but falling into raucous discord on Earth," the president claimed. "We are caught in war, wanting peace. We are torn by division, wanting unity. We see around us empty lives, wanting fulfillment. We see tasks that need doing, waiting for hands to do them." Much like Graham, the president professed to see a nation—"one nation, not two," he insisted—in dire need of religious revival. "To a crisis of the spirit," Nixon observed, "we need an answer of the spirit." He urged his fellow Americans to join together with him to "build a great cathedral of the spirit—each of us raising it one stone at a time, as he reaches out to his neighbor, helping, caring, doing." After the president's address, the Mormon Tabernacle Choir offered a stirring rendition of "The Star-Spangled Banner." At the end of the performance, the solemnity of the moment was ruined when a joker in the press stands yelled: "Okay, play ball!"[15]

All in all, the day seemed a deliberate throwback to the Eisenhower era. "With the prevalence of clergy, including Dr. Norman Vincent Peale and Billy Graham, with the sturdy Mormon entrepreneur, J. Willard Marriott, as the inaugural committee chairman, with George Romney and Guy Lombardo the principal attractions at one of the balls, and with all the nicely groomed Junior League type women handling the chores," a *Newsday* columnist concluded, "the inauguration comes off as square, earnest and right." "It was almost as if the sixties had never happened and there had been no riots or assassinations or demonstrations or marches on the Pentagon or draft trials," marveled Tom Wicker of the *New York*

Times. But perhaps that was fine. "It may well be that the old values, re-examined and ably preached, are what the country really needs; there was something reassuring today in the determination with which religious faith and patriotism and brotherhood were cited again and again by earnest men."[16]

The themes of the inauguration were repeated a week later when Nixon presided over the annual National Prayer Breakfast. "He has been one of the most regular and faithful supporters of the movement since its inception in 1953," a Presbyterian minister wrote at the time. "In fact, he has attended these functions more consistently than the services of any denomination, including [his own childhood tradition of] the Friends." With a deep appreciation of the event's importance, Nixon had strategized with Graham beforehand. The preacher recommended that the president's remarks "should be very low-key and appear to be impromptu," with general discussion of "the impact of religious people on his life." Nixon followed his advice to the letter. On the morning of January 30, 1969, after first taking part in another prayer breakfast with six hundred worshipers, the president joined two thousand others in the grand ballroom of the Sheraton Park Hotel. Flanked by perennial prayer breakfast participants such as Graham and former senator Frank Carlson, as well as First Lady Pat Nixon and Vice President Spiro Agnew, the president told the crowd that letters he received from ordinary citizens demonstrated there was still a "deep religious faith" in the United States. "Even in this period when religion is not supposed to be fashionable, when agnosticism and skepticism seem to be on the upturn," he reflected, "most of the people seem to be saying 'We are praying for you, Mr. President, and for the country.'" He appeared sincere, but later, when an aide praised his performance, Nixon laughed it off. He'd simply fed the crowd some "church stuff" to keep them happy.[17]

If Nixon had been more focused on performance than penance, Graham was not that different. In his formal remarks, he called on Americans to recognize the good things about the nation. There was "a crisis of the spirit," he said, echoing the president's inaugural address, but perhaps Americans were guilty of "too much introspection." They needed to move away from "the over-self-criticism" of the era and remember "we have a great government and a great way of life." The preacher followed his own advice, exuding a confidence and complacency that some friends found disturbing. North Carolina's Governor Bob Scott, for instance, recalled his unease at all the pomp and pageantry and, more so, Graham's delight in it all. "They had all those guards around in those silly little uniforms Nixon had designed for them, played 'Ruffles and Flourishes' when Nixon came in, all those trumpet fanfares they used back then," Scott remembered. "And then Billy came through the door with his own entourage, and you'd have thought he was some high office-holder himself—running around greeting everybody with his great grin and shaking everybody's hand just like Nixon. It just seemed he'd gotten caught up in that aura of power—just completely caught up in it."[18]

NIXON AND GRAHAM WERE SO enamored with the National Prayer Breakfast that they resolved to replicate the annual tradition with a more regular one: Sunday services at the White House. Despite the public religiosity of past presidents, this was something altogether new. "I've never heard of anything like it happening here before," White House curator James Ketcham told *Time*. (In fact, religious rites had previously taken place at the presidential mansion, but only in unusual circumstances. The Sunday after John F. Kennedy's funeral, for example, Lyndon Johnson invited the cabinet, senior staffers, and a few personal friends to join him for a service there.) The new White House church services took place in the East Room, a showcase space noted for its sparkling chandeliers and gold silk tapestries. Instead of pews, oak dining room chairs with seats of yellow brocade were arranged in rows of twenty. A piano and an electric organ, donated to the White House by a friendly merchant, were positioned at the north end of the room, with space to the side for a rotating cast of choirs to perform. Between them stood a mahogany lectern where the president and the "pastor of the day" would make remarks.[19]

Naturally, Graham presided over the initial White House church service, held the first Sunday after the inauguration. As worshipers entered the East Room, they picked up liturgical programs adorned with the official presidential seal and found their way inside while a Marine master sergeant played soothing hymns on the organ. Soon every one of the 224 seats in the room was taken, with two-thirds of the Cabinet and several senior staffers on hand; still more stood at the rear. As large portraits of George and Martha Washington looked on, Nixon strode to the podium, welcomed the assembled to "this first worship at the White House" and invited up his "long-time personal friend." Graham graciously returned the compliment, using the president's inaugural address as the basis for his remarks. He urged the country to heed Nixon's warnings about the "crisis of the spirit" that was sweeping across college campuses and asked God to guide the administration as it dealt with that problem and others. When the service concluded, White House waiters ushered guests into the State Dining Room for coffee, juice, and sweet rolls. As they went, they passed through a receiving line made up of Nixon, Agnew, Graham, and their wives. Shortly after, Graham and the Nixons posed for photographers on the north portico. The delighted chief of staff, Bob Haldeman, raved about the day in his diary: "Very, very impressive."[20]

Some outside the White House were less impressed, denouncing the church services as crassly political. One minister, for instance, complained to the *New York Times* that "the president is trying to have God on his own terms." The administration and its allies replied indignantly to allegations that Nixon was politicizing religion. "The President would be appalled at the thought," insisted Norman Vincent Peale. "The White House, after all, is Mr. Nixon's residence. And if there's anything improper about a man worshiping God in his own way in his own home, I'm at a loss to know what it is." Graham agreed that the White House services were simply a private means of sincere worship. "I know the President well enough to be entirely sure that the idea of having God on his own terms would never have occurred to him," he protested. White House communications director Herb Klein likewise maintained the services were "never political" but merely "a social thing" that allowed Nixon's family and friends to pray in solitude.[21]

Behind the scenes, however, the ulterior motives were clear. "Sure, we used the prayer breakfasts and church services and all that for political ends," Nixon aide Charles Colson later admitted. "One of my jobs in the White House was to romance religious leaders. We would bring them into the White House and they would be dazzled by the aura of the Oval Office, and I found them to be about the most pliable of any of the special interest groups that we worked with." The East Room church services were crucial to his work. "We turned those events into wonderful quasi-social, quasi-spiritual, quasi-political events, and brought in a whole host of religious leaders to [hold] worship services for the president and his family—and three hundred guests carefully selected by me for political purposes." Notably, Haldeman was deeply involved in the planning. Before joining the administration, he had been an advertising executive at the J. Walter Thompson Company, back when it handled promotions for events such as Spiritual Mobilization's "Freedom Under God" ceremonies and the Ad Council's "Religion in American Life" campaign. Well versed in the public relations value of public piety, Haldeman exploited the services to their full potential. At his suggestion, for instance, the supposedly private programs were broadcast over the radio, with print reporters, photographers, and TV cameramen on hand to record the spectacle for wider distribution.[22]

Ultimately, though, all this activity originated with Nixon. "The President is very much personally involved in these services, and the impressions they create among the people and in the press," Haldeman lectured the White House staff. "He gives a great deal of time and attention to this." Nixon sent Haldeman a steady stream of memos about the services. Typically, he focused on the choice of clergymen or congregants for a coming church service, but often the president micromanaged mundane details such as the proper protocols for the receiving line. Even with his oversight, mistakes were still made. One weekend, Nixon became so concerned about an error in the program for the Sunday service that Haldeman noted that "the phone calls from the President started at 9:00 o'clock Saturday evening, and continued until 1:30 Sunday morning."[23]

Nixon's aides relied on Graham in planning the services. Despite assumptions that the preacher served as a regular officiant in the East Room, Graham led only four services there over the next five years, though he appeared at others in a supporting role. Behind the scenes, however, he gave more practical support. He advised the planners on the format and frequency of the services, musical groups that might be used, and, most important, potential speakers, selected with an eye to both denominational diversity and political loyalties. On the last point, Graham's intervention was vital, as he provided the White House staff with the names of conservative Protestant ministers who would readily answer the president's call.[24]

The pastors who followed Graham to the White House's pulpit were largely cut from the same cloth as the conservative preacher. The second service in the East Room, for instance, featured Reverend Richard Halverson from the prestigious Fourth Presbyterian Church in Bethesda, Maryland. Halverson was, not coincidentally, vice president of Vereide's International Council for Christian Leadership and a vocal supporter of the Presbyterian Lay Committee that J. Howard Pew and other businessmen had created in the 1950s to criticize clergymen involved in liberal causes. As a fellow minister noted, "Presbyterians of Halverson vintage have resented the pro–civil rights, antiwar stance which their denomination has taken in recent years." Halverson's sermon in the East Room, "The Loneliness of a Man in Leadership," urged Nixon and other administration officials to understand that the Lord stood by them, even if earthly critics did not. Other officiants were even more direct in blessing the president. In June 1969, Rabbi Louis Finkelstein, chancellor of the Jewish Theological Seminary of America, concluded his sermon with a bold prophecy. "I hope it is not too presumptuous of me, in the presence of the President," he noted, "to say that future historians, looking back at our generation, may say that in a period of great trials and tribulations the finger of God pointed to Richard Milhous Nixon, giving him the vision and the wisdom to save the world and civilization."[25]

Such comments were no accident. The White House staff went to great lengths to ensure that clergymen invited to the East Room were conservatives connected to a major political constituency. In recommending Archbishop Joseph Bernardin of Cincinnati as officiant for a service before St. Patrick's Day, a cover memo noted bluntly that "Bernardin was selected because he is the most prominent Catholic of Irish extraction and *a strong supporter of the President. We have verified this.*" Harry Dent, a former aide to Strom Thurmond who directed the administration's "southern strategy," likewise forwarded a list of "some good conservative Protestant Southern Baptists" who could be trusted to preach a message that pleased the president. Graham helped as well. When Nixon sent an emissary to the Vatican and unwittingly upset Baptists, Graham suggested that inviting Carl Bates, president of the Southern Baptist Convention, to preach in the East Room "might negate some of the criticism." Likewise, in 1971, Graham encouraged the White House to invite Fred Rhodes, a lay preacher who seemed sure to run for the SBC presidency that year. An internal memo enthusiastically noted that Rhodes was a "staunch Nixon loyalist." "A White House invitation to speak would aid greatly in his campaign for this office," the memo continued, "and if elected, Colson feels that Rhodes would be quite helpful to the President in 1972."[26]

Political considerations dictated the selection of speakers in more obvious ways. In September 1969, for instance, Reverend Allan Watson of Calvary Baptist Church in Tuscaloosa, Alabama, served as the East Room officiant. After the services, Watson posed with the president for the now customary photograph on the North Portico. They were joined by his twin brother, Albert Watson. A congressman who had abandoned the Democratic Party over its support of civil rights, he was at the time running for governor of South Carolina as a Republican, at Agnew's urging. To the delight of Harry Dent, who had made arrangements for the visit, the photograph circulated widely in the campaign. Likewise, in February 1970, Reverend Henry Edward Russell of Second Presbyterian Church of Memphis was given the honor of leading the East Room services. Many of his family members attended, but reporters paid particular attention to his brother, Senator Richard Russell of Georgia, who happened to chair the committee that would soon pass judgment on Nixon's prized plan for an anti-ballistic-missile treaty. Even choirs were selected with political affairs in mind. During the 1970 midterm election campaign, Nixon aide Bill Timmons "strongly recommended" inviting a particular Presbyterian boys' choir from Memphis, as it would "be *very* helpful to Bill Brock in his attempt to unseat Albert Gore in the Senate race."[27]

Political concerns also dictated who attended each service. Low-level members of the White House staff, such as switchboard operators or limousine drivers, were occasionally invited, to support the illusion that these were private affairs for the larger White House "family," but internal policies instructed that no more than a quarter of the attendees should be "non-VIPs." Instead, the congregation was composed of prominent members of the White House and its supporters, so much so that the *New York Times* joked: "The administration that prays together, stays together." Invitations usually went to the administration's allies in Congress, but occasionally they were used to lobby more independent members about particular bills. In July 1969, as the Senate deliberated the anti-ballistic-missile treaty and the House considered an anti-inflationary surtax proposal, Nixon instructed his aides to invite legislators who would cast crucial votes on both. "The President would like to have a heavy 'sprinkling' of the Senators who endorsed the ABM program and 'four or five other Senators'" who were "marginal," explained Dwight Chapin, special assistant to the president. "In regard to House Members, he would like to have conservative Republicans—he said 'some who have not been here previously and supported the surtax.'" Notes to the president explained how to finesse each member in the receiving line after the services.[28]

With the bulk of the seats reserved for administration officials and congressmen they might sway, the remaining few were precious political commodities. Potential campaign donors were always given preference. An early "action memo" to Colson ordered him to follow up on the "President's request that you develop a list of rich people with strong religious interest to be invited to the White House church services." At this, Colson had quick success. The guests for an ensuing East Room service, for instance, included the heads of AT&T, Bechtel, Chrysler, Continental Can, General Electric, General Motors, Goodyear, PepsiCo, Republic Steel, and other leading corporations.[29]

Occasionally, the presence of a particular guest at the East Room services had special political importance. In March 1969, for instance, the White House welcomed Dr. S. I. Hayakawa, the president of San Francisco State College, who had recently made headlines for his ruthless handling of student protesters. ("There are no more innocent bystanders," he had announced, before ordering police to clear the entire campus.) Seeking to make good on the tough law-and-order rhetoric of the presidential campaign, Nixon had been preparing a major statement on campus disorders to be given later that week. He made sure the controversial college president was available to reporters for comments after the church services. "My principle for dealing with disturbances is 'Have plenty of police,'" Hayakawa explained. "Many say that it destroys the academic atmosphere, but it does not destroy it as much as the goon squads roaming campus." The publicity helped make Hayakawa a conservative celebrity. In 1976, he won a US Senate seat in California, beating an incumbent Democrat.[30]

Nearly a year after Hayakawa's visit, the White House used another East Room service to score political points. Graham served as the pastor of the day, but the *Chicago Tribune* noted that "two controversial persons took the spotlight" away from him—Judge Clement Haynesworth, whose nomination to the Supreme Court as Nixon's "law-and-order" candidate had failed the previous November, and Judge Julius Hoffman, who had presided over the notorious Chicago Seven trial that had concluded the month before. Both had become heroes for conservatives who complained about lenient treatment of criminal defendants in the courts. Nixon welcomed them warmly, signaling his sympathies. As Haynesworth neared the president in the receiving line, Nixon grabbed the judge's hand, threw his other arm around Graham's shoulder, and announced loudly enough for reporters to hear: "This is one of your supporters!" Hoffman was likewise lavished with attention and given a chance to make self-deprecating comments before reporters. "Well, you had quite a performance in your court," noted Federal Reserve chairman Arthur Burns. "I wouldn't choose it for a summer vacation," Hoffman replied.[31]

As the political purpose of the White House church services became obvious, criticism from the press increased. Originally, Nixon thought it would be "very useful" to win the media's approval for the new tradition and decided to invite several prominent reporters, pundits, newspaper publishers, and network presidents to a service early in his administration. Guests included CBS anchorman Walter Cronkite and newspaper publisher Samuel I. Newhouse, as well as prominent reporters from major dailies. For his sermon to the press, Reverend Louis H. Evans Jr. dwelled on the dangers of passing judgment without having the full facts at hand. "Can we be accepted for what we truly are, can we accept others for what they are," Evans asked, "or will they cling to stereotypes, to distorted *priori* portraits?" Such blunt entreaties did not, of course, keep the press from passing judgment. In July 1969, the *Washington Post* challenged the sincerity of this "White House Religion." "Unfortunately, the way religion is being conducted these days—amid hand-picked politicians, reporters, cameras, guest-lists, staff spokesmen—has not only stirred needless controversy, but invited, rightly or not, the suspicion that religion has somehow become entangled (again needlessly) with politics," the editors chided. "Kings, monarchs, and anyone else brash enough to try this have always sought to cajole, seduce or invite the clergy to support official policy—not necessarily by having them personally bless that policy, but by having the clergy on hand in a smiling and prominent way." In the end, the *Post* gently suggested it might be best "to avoid using the White House as a church."[32]

Religious leaders began to denounce the East Room church services as well. Reinhold Niebuhr, once an outspoken critic of Spiritual Mobilization, now targeted its apparent heirs. For an August 1969 issue of *Christianity and Crisis,* the seventy-seven-year-old theologian penned a scathing critique titled "The King's Chapel and the King's Court." The founding fathers had expressly prohibited establishment of a national religion, he wrote, because they knew from experience that "a combination of religious sanctity and political power represents a heady mixture for status quo conservatism." In creating a "kind of sanctuary" in the East Room, Nixon committed the very sin the founders had sought to avoid. "By a curious combination of innocence and guile, he has circumvented the Bill of Rights' first article," Niebuhr charged. "Thus he has established a conforming religion by semi-officially inviting representatives of all the disestablished religions, of whose moral criticism we were [once] naturally so proud." The "Nixon-Graham doctrine of the relation of religion to public morality and policy" neutered the critical functions of independent religion, he warned. "It is wonderful what a simple White House invitation will do to dull the critical faculties, thereby confirming the fears of the Founding Fathers."[33]

Other theologians echoed Niebuhr's concerns. "The President is talking about a religion of social control where Christian worship is explicitly linked to national values," Reverend Harvey Cox wrote. Even if his motives were pure, the Harvard theologian continued, the divisive president might not be the best person to lead a revival. "Frankly," Cox noted, "we have enough problems persuading young people to become interested in religion without having Nixon support it." The Catholic lay theologian Daniel Callahan, meanwhile, criticized the Nixon White House for digging up the "corpse of civic religion" in a clear effort to push back against the radicalism of that same younger generation. He believed both sides were equally deluded. "What the underclasses—students, blacks, jaded intellectuals—seek in sexual revolution, drugs, revolution, the overclasses seek in a return to the old sources," he wrote in the *National Catholic Reporter.* "The former want to create new gods, labeled

freedom, self-fulfillment, liberation, while the latter are willing to propi-
tiate and invoke the old ones: law, order, discipline."[34]

In spite of criticism from liberal critics and the press—or perhaps because of it—the East Room church services continued for the remainder of
Nixon's term in office. According to social secretary Lucy Winchester, they
were "the most popular thing we do in the White House." "People don't
identify very well with state dinners, but they are familiar with prayer,"
she noted on another occasion. "The honor of being able to pray with the
President is something that they regard as special." And, by all accounts,
the East Room church services were immensely popular. "Congressmen
have flooded the White House with the names of clergymen constituents
wanting a turn in the Presidential pulpit," the *Wall Street Journal* reported.
"Hundreds of ministers have written directly, some enclosing photographs
and programs of services they have conducted." Critics continued to scoff.
"It gives the White House an unpleasant touch of Mission Inn," Garry
Wills wrote with disdain. But for many Americans—especially the ones
whose support Nixon so avidly desired—there was nothing unpleasant
about it, or the Mission Inn hotel and spa, for that matter. "And so they
come," a *New York Times* reporter noted in 1971, "not the poor and op-
pressed or the minorities that make for discomforting headlines, but the
powerful in Washington and a healthy sprinkling of the people who put
Mr. Nixon in office, and they sit around him, in worship of the Almighty."[35]

IF THE EAST ROOM RELIGIOUS services provided the president
a "kind of sanctuary" from his critics beyond the walls of the White
House, they couldn't shield him entirely. This became abundantly clear
in the spring of 1970, when antiwar protests exploded after revelations
that Nixon had widened the Vietnam War into Cambodia and the subsequent shootings of student demonstrators by National Guardsmen at
Kent State and Jackson State. Protests spread across 350 campuses that
May, with estimates suggesting that a quarter of all college students in
America were taking part. Some turned ugly, with thirty ROTC buildings
burned or bombed. National Guard units were deployed to restore order
in sixteen states, but not even they could end the revolt. Ultimately, more
than seventy-five colleges and universities decided to shut down entirely

for the rest of the academic year. Rather than end the unrest, however, the closures only channeled demonstrators to Washington, where they sought congressional support for the antiwar cause. In some cases, entire college populations migrated to the capital. Virtually everyone at Haverford College came down to Washington: 575 of 640 undergraduates, 40 of 70 faculty members, and 10 of 12 administrators.[36]

On May 9, 1970, roughly seventy-five thousand antiwar protesters gathered on the Ellipse, the fifty-two-acre park located just south of the White House, for a massive rally with Jane Fonda, Dr. Benjamin Spock, and Coretta Scott King, among others, giving speeches. With his fiercest critics camped at his doorstep, Nixon became unnerved. In the early morning hours before the rally, the president snuck out of the executive mansion with his personal valet and some "petrified" Secret Service agents in tow, to engage the activists face-to-face. The results were surreal. "After a nearly sleepless night in an empty and barricaded White House, President Nixon emerged early yesterday morning to talk to student demonstrators about 'the war thing' and other topics," the *Washington Post* reported. The embattled leader told students it was "all right" that they had come "to demonstrate and shout your slogans on the Ellipse," as long as they kept it peaceful. He awkwardly tried to relate, asking campus radicals from Syracuse about their football team and making small talk about surfing with a California activist. Realizing that no common ground could be found, Nixon beat a hasty retreat. As the presidential limousine pulled away, a bold student ran alongside, flashing a middle finger to the glass. "Right in the same window, right in the bearded young face, Nixon put up his own fist and extended his middle finger, too," Tom Wicker later recalled. "*They* understood each other."[37]

The next morning, the president sought solace at the White House church service. Nixon had ordered his staff to schedule the service in late April, as he prepared his speech announcing the Cambodian invasion, apparently hoping to blunt criticism of his decision. Tellingly, ambassadors from a dozen nations were invited to attend the service. Following Nixon's order to get "a good conservative Protestant minister" to serve as the "pastor of the day," his aides selected Reverend Stephen T. Szilagyi of the Philippus United Church of Christ in Cincinnati. "He was an active member of the Ohio Clergy for Nixon-Agnew, and delivered the invocation at the rally held in Cincinnati during the fall of 1968," an internal memo noted. "He is a recipient of the DAR Americanism Award and is now Chaplain of the Ohio American Legion. He is described as very patriotic and very articulate." Predictably, Szilagyi urged the attendees to stay the course, "to give not away your God, give not away your country, to those who would toss it aside and give it to others." Even the visiting choir from Calvin College, whose arrival had been prefaced with a formal statement from the school's faculty and students that their appearance should not be construed as "either an endorsement or a repudiation of any policies of our national administration," ultimately offered kind words for their host. "When asked by the press for their opinion of the President's stand on Cambodia," an aide reported excitedly, "they said he was our President and we stand behind him."[38]

Whatever comfort Nixon found in the sanctuary of the White House services, he soon realized that outside support for his administration was growing alongside the burgeoning antiwar movement. The day before the Ellipse rally, construction workers had disrupted another antiwar demonstration in New York's financial district. Wading into the protesters and striking them with their hard hats and heavy work tools, they managed to disperse the crowd and reraise the American flags that had been lowered by Mayor John Lindsay in honor of the students slain at Kent State and Jackson State. ("Wow," an insurance underwriter said from the sidewalk. "Just like John Wayne taking Iwo Jima!") For those involved, the "hard hat riot" represented the nation at its best. "The whole group started singing 'God Bless America' and it damn near put a lump in your throat," a construction worker recalled. "If I live to be a hundred, I don't think I'll ever live to see anything like that again." A week later, Peter Brennan of the city's Building Trades Council built on the momentum, bringing more than a hundred thousand construction workers together for a huge pro-administration rally, complete with signs reading "God Bless the Establishment" and "We Support Nixon and Agnew." On May 26, an appreciative Nixon brought Brennan to the White House, where the union head presented him with a custom-made construction hat, labeled "Commander in Chief." Visibly moved, Nixon announced that the hard hat would long "stand as a symbol along with our great flag, for freedom and patriotism and our beloved country."[39]

The White House, as always, complained that the media was against it. In a conversation with the president, Graham commented that "CBS in its coverage of the construction workers march gave approximately a minute of time to the 150,000 who demonstrated in New York and two to three minutes to the 1,000 left-wing lawyers who came to Washington." Nixon devoted himself and his staff to finding ways to counteract such "unbalanced coverage." Throughout May, Bob Haldeman chronicled in his diary the president's obsession with the issue. "Wants to try to implement Billy Graham's idea about a big pro-America rally, maybe on 4th of July," he noted after the Ellipse rally. "Thinks we're still too timid on mobilizing the Silent Majority," he added a week later. "Feels he should probably go out into country and draw crowds and show popular enthusiasm." Plans for the Fourth were forming, but Nixon wanted to take action sooner. Once again, his spiritual advisor rode to the rescue, inviting the president to address an upcoming Billy Graham Crusade at the University of Tennessee in Knoxville at the end of May.[40]

Nixon accepted, sensing the chance for a political masterstroke. College campuses contained the administration's harshest critics and, as a result, the president largely avoided them. Over his first year and a half in office, he had spoken at only two colleges—a tranquil state school in South Dakota and the United States Air Force Academy in Colorado Springs. A speech at the largest public university in the South would, Graham suggested, allow Nixon to "show the younger generation that the President is listening to them," but in the safest setting imaginable. Both the campus and the city were "Big Orange Country," an especially conservative corner of a conservative state. "Town, gown, bank, church and Crusade were of one mind," Garry Wills wrote in *Esquire*. "If this was not Nixon Country, then what is?" If protests were unlikely in such a setting, the protective bubble of the Billy Graham Crusade made them even less so, as a Tennessee statute made "disrupting a religious service" a criminal offense.[41]

And so on May 28, 1970—just two days after he welcomed the hard hats to the White House—Nixon traveled to the University of Tennessee to address the crusade. Graham publicly promised that there "will not be anything political, I hope, in his visit," but the signs of partisanship were perfectly clear. As the presidential motorcade roared down the four-lane highway from an Air National Guard airport, thousands of supporters lined the route, holding aloft posters with the words "Cambodia Was Right," "Win in Vietnam—Right On," and "Happiness is a Republican President." The guest list showed similar politicization. "All the state's Republicans seemed to have got religion at the same time," Wills wrote. An array of GOP candidates had been invited to join Nixon on stage, the most prominent being Congressman Bill Brock, whom the president had personally recruited to run against Senator Albert Gore in the upcoming midterms. (Gore was actually in Knoxville that day, but like the state's other Democrats, he had been excluded from the nominally nonpartisan event.) Sitting alongside Graham and Nixon onstage, according to White House aides, would provide "just the right touch" for Brock's campaign. Indeed, he capitalized on the crusade publicity in his race that fall, contrasting it repeatedly with Gore's vote against the Dirksen prayer amendment. Not surprisingly, the Republican won.[42]

The crusade proved to be the largest public gathering in the history of the state. Roughly a hundred thousand spectators crammed into Neyland Stadium, filling every seat and packing the ramps and roads around it as well. Thousands stood on a sloping hill at the open end of the horseshoe-shaped stands; police estimated that thousands more were stuck outside in the middle of another record: the worst traffic jam in Knoxville's history. The crowd represented an impressive showing of the Silent Majority, a vast sea of clean-cut white southerners, with thousands of men in white shirts and neckties. Trim members of the Fellowship of Christian Athletes guarded the stage at the twenty-yard line, as plainclothes detectives and uniformed policemen worked the stands. The few protesters who braved the stadium found themselves challenged at every turn. (One activist saw a crusade participant with a crucifix pin and offered him an antiwar pamphlet. "Stick it up your ass," he spat back.) When Nixon and Graham strode onto the synthetic turf together, a two-minute ovation completely drowned out the chants of the outnumbered activists.[43]

The official theme was "Youth Night," but most of the speakers directed their comments to the fifty-seven-year-old Nixon. The minister who gave the invocation asked for God's blessings for "our beloved president," while elderly gospel singer Ethel Waters likened Nixon himself to a blessing from the Lord. "He belongs to everyone who wants to

President Richard Nixon regularly used the rites of public religion for his own political ends, often with the assistance of Reverend Billy Graham. In May 1970, when he was under fire for his expansion of the Vietnam War into Cambodia, Nixon made an appearance at a Billy Graham Crusade at the University of Tennessee in Knoxville to reach out to supporters. *Courtesy of the Office of the University Historian Collection, University of Tennessee, Knoxville–Libraries.*

receive and accept him," she told the believers. Graham sounded the same themes. "I'm for change," he told the students, "but the Bible teaches us to obey authority. . . . In this day of student unrest on the campus, here on one of the largest universities in America tens of thousands have been demonstrating their faith in the God of our fathers!" At this, protesters began chanting, "Politics! Politics! Politics! Politics!" Graham continued: "All Americans may not agree with the decisions a president makes, but he is our president."[44]

When Nixon took the pulpit, he basked in the moment. Graham had warned him there would be "different points of view" on display at the Crusade, he said, before adding with a grin: "I'm just glad that there seems to be a rather solid majority on one side rather than the other side tonight." The stadium thundered again. Nixon then began reading what was, in essence, a presidential sermon on the need for faith in God and country. "America would not be what it is today, the greatest nation in the world, if this were not a nation which had made progress under God," he intoned. "If we are going to bring people together as we must bring them together, if we are going to have peace in the world, if our young people are going to have a fulfillment beyond simply those material things," Nixon said, "they must turn to those great spiritual forces that have made America the great country that it is." The protesters began chanting, "Bullshit! Bullshit! Bullshit!" But once again, they were drowned out by an increasingly loud majority.[45]

The crusade worked wonders for the president. The Billy Graham Evangelical Association produced a triumphant film of the festivities, editing out all signs of dissent. The movie, distributed widely, showed the president basking before an enthusiastic crowd on a major campus. (Watching the film a month or so later, not even Graham could believe it. "Boy," he muttered in awe, "they really gave him an ovation.") The press praised Nixon effusively as well. *Time* called his address "one of the most effective speeches he has yet delivered." *Newsweek* characterized it as "a suitably evangelistic ending for a Presidential week that started out seemingly beyond redemption."[46]

NOT A WEEK LATER, GRAHAM once again demonstrated his value to the administration. At a press conference on June 4, 1970, he unveiled plans for the "pro-America rally" he had earlier proposed for the Fourth of July. With comedian Bob Hope at his side, the minister told reporters that "Honor America Day" would be "the biggest celebration in America's history." The daylong event would take place at the capital's major monuments, with Graham leading a religious service at the Lincoln Memorial in the morning and Hope emceeing an all-star program of music and comedy from the Washington Monument in the evening. The entire extravaganza, Hope said, would show the world that "Americans can put aside their honest differences and rally around the flag to show national unity."[47]

Though organizers insisted the event was for all Americans, the program had been carefully designed to appeal to the Silent Majority. Dwight Chapin, who had followed Haldeman from J. Walter Thompson to the White House, explained the early plans in a memo to his boss. "All this is excellent!" an enthusiastic Haldeman wrote in the margins, but "we need a solid *cornball* program developer." Accordingly, they enlisted J. Willard Marriott to bring the same sort of old-fashioned entertainment that he had provided for the inauguration a year before. He soon announced commitments from mainstream performers including comedians Jack Benny and Red Skelton and musicians Glen Campbell, Connie Stevens, and Dinah Shore. Kate Smith would perform her rendition of "God Bless America," which she had been singing for nearly a quarter century, while a recent runner-up in the Miss Teen America pageant would recite an original composition titled "I Am an American." (When radicals mocked the lineup as "a program for fossils and dinosaurs," Marriott made a show of searching for hipper acts, such as the comedian Dick Gregory and the folk trio Peter, Paul and Mary. But all of them, he reported, had prior commitments.)[48]

Funding for Honor America Day followed the same general pattern. Publicly, organizers remained coy. Asked by reporters how it would be financed, Hope asked, "Do you have any ideas? So far we're using a pay phone." Out of sight, though, Marriott had it well in hand. A seasoned Republican fund-raiser, he quickly secured over $285,000 in donations, largely from corporate leaders. Some were philanthropists who had supported similar celebrations in the past, most notably J. Howard Pew, who had bankrolled Spiritual Mobilization's Fourth of July celebrations in the early 1950s, and Patrick Frawley, who had funded Fred Schwarz's Christian Anti-Communism Crusade programs in the early 1960s. They were joined by corporations that had often donated to those same earlier endeavors: General Motors, Caterpillar Tractor, Marshall Field, Standard Oil, Union Carbide, US Steel, and more. But the most significant funding came from corporate leaders who had been singled out that same month by Nixon's aides as "financial angels" of the administration. Elmer Bobst, a pharmaceutical executive who had donated generously to the Nixon campaign, promised $5,000. Bob Abplanalp, head of the Precision Valve Corporation and a close ally of the president, donated another $15,000. From the headquarters of *Reader's Digest,* Nixon loyalists Hobart Lewis and DeWitt Wallace sent along $17,000 more.[49]

The Nixon administration took an even more direct hand in recruiting rank-and-file supporters from the Silent Majority. As he reviewed the early plans, Haldeman worried that the event needed more "professional press/publicity work" and "some real, tough, nitty gritty crowd building." To that end, Chapin brought in Ronald Walker, who handled those same duties for official presidential visits as Nixon's chief advance man. "Dwight [Chapin] said, 'Look, Ron's got these thirty-some-odd guys, they're sensational, they're our advance men, they know how to build crowds and stuff,'" Walker recalled. "'The President wants that Honor America Day to be the biggest happening on a Fourth of July ever in Washington, D.C. Let's let them have it.'" The order, he remembered, "was just like a gift from heaven" because it let his team start mobilizing members of the Silent Majority two years before the coming re-election campaign. "I turned those guys loose," Walker recounted with pride. "Crowd raising, handbills, leaflets, telephone, boiler room operations." White House advance teams established offices in Washington, across Maryland and Virginia, and in Chicago, Philadelphia, and New York City in order to ensure that the administration's supporters turned out for Honor America Day. Peter Brennan organized "a whole train of hardhats," seventeen cars long, to come down from New York, Walker recalled. Likewise, H. Ross Perot, another "financial angel" of the administration, rented two planes to fly more supporters in from Texas. "Honor America Day was a real plus," the advance man remembered. It "took what I'd been building for a year" and "just highlighted it."[50]

Though much of the Nixon administration's role in planning the event took place behind the scenes, the conservative leanings of the celebration were clear to all. Organizers Graham and Marriott, of course, were longtime friends of the Nixons; the president's brother even worked for Marriott as a hotel executive. And the involvement of Bob Hope, another well-known ally of the administration, only fueled the suspicions of cynics. "They have some cause to wonder just how 'nonpolitical' Mr. Hope really is," the *Wall Street Journal* acknowledged, rattling off recent instances of the comedian "popping up in situations that are unquestionably political, partisan, and Republican." Hope had been busy on the campaign trail that year, stumping for GOP candidates across the country. Meanwhile, he vocally supported Spiro Agnew's attacks on administration critics. "I travel a lot," he told an Ohio audience, "and most people I have found think that he is saying the right things." Hope was aligned with the administration but, more important, he was also associated with the increasingly polarizing war in Vietnam. He had long toiled on USO tours to entertain troops overseas and had recently turned to drumming up support for the war stateside. Just a week before the Kent State shootings, Hope headlined a "Wake Up, America!" rally in Boston that saw an estimated sixty-five thousand clean-cut supporters of "the Constitution, God and Country" march from Boston Common to City Hall Plaza.[51]

The prominent involvement of the administration and its allies led many to dismiss the event as little more than a rally for the right. "While the 'Honor America Day' celebration in Washington has been advertised as nonpartisan," the columnist Art Buchwald noted, "any professional politician knows that when the public sees Billy Graham, Bob Hope and Lawrence Welk on the platform, the Nixon Administration will be the only ones enjoying the fireworks." But, of course, the target audience for the event was much larger than that. Members of the Silent Majority, upset by the turmoil of the 1960s, increasingly looked back to the stability of the 1950s with nostalgia. The religious rhetoric and rituals of the Eisenhower years had been key markers of that era's seeming Cold War consensus with its conservative social values, and the Silent Majority readily seized on them in hopes that they might help them turn back the clock.[52]

Organizers continued to insist that Honor America Day was for everyone, though qualifications increasingly colored their claims. Two days before the event, Graham and Marriott held a press conference at the Mayflower Hotel, site of the first National Prayer Breakfast, to note that the day was for all Americans—or at least all who loved God and country. "We've tried to get every shade of philosophy into the program," Marriott said. "But we're not after people who shine their shoes with the flag. I don't think those people want to honor America." Religious belief, of course, was a key part of that patriotism. "Only atheists and agnostics were not invited to participate," Graham explained, "because they don't believe in God." Nevertheless, the minister extended an olive branch to the other side. Antiwar protesters surely loved their country, he said at the press conference, so they "would come out and wave the flag too." In a sign of his sincerity, the night before the rally Graham ventured out to the Washington Monument to chat briefly with hundreds of radicals who had camped out for a "marijuana smoke-in" the next day. They offered the preacher some pot, but he declined. As he walked away, several flashed him a peace sign. In an echo of the president's own impromptu meeting with students at the Lincoln Memorial, a single finger shot up in response. With Graham, however, it was an *index* finger, his friendly insistence that Jesus Christ was the one true way.[53]

As the Fourth of July dawned, with a forecast calling for high heat and humidity, crowds began converging on the capital. Special trains and nearly five hundred chartered buses brought thousands from across the Northeast, while a five-hundred-car caravan made its way from Richmond, Virginia. Despite organizers' insistence that the attendees would be diverse, they turned out to be overwhelmingly white, middle-class, and middle-aged. "The styles were straight," a reporter for the *Baltimore Sun* wrote. "There were fewer black faces than one might have expected in Alaska." This was the Silent Majority in the flesh. "They gathered in front of the Lincoln Memorial, where so many others have assembled in protest," *Time* reported, "to bear witness that it was their country too, a country more right than wrong." A woman in the crowd expressed the same sentiment, but in more confrontational terms. "The hippies have had their demonstration," she said. "Now it's our turn."[54]

Honor America Day began, as planned, with the morning religious service at the Lincoln Memorial. Roughly fifteen thousand spectators attended, but the television networks broadcast the service, allowing thousands more to follow along at home. "It was like a small-town Fourth of July on a super scale," the *Washington Post* noted, "with the favorite ordained men thoroughly fusing God and country." Dressed in a blue-and-white striped suit with a red pocket handkerchief, Pat Boone led the crowd in the national anthem. The Centurymen Choir of Fort Worth and the US Army Band joined together to perform "America the Beautiful," but Kate Smith stole the show with her rendition of "God Bless America." For the scripture reading, Rabbi Marc Tanenbaum selected a passage from Chapter 25 of the Book of Leviticus, the same passage the Committee to Proclaim Liberty had used in its Fourth of July festivities nineteen years earlier.[55]

Graham, of course, was the main attraction. Standing in the same spot where Martin Luther King Jr. had delivered his address to the March on Washington seven years before, the evangelist cast himself as an heir to the slain civil rights leader with a sermon unsubtly titled "The Unfinished Dream." "We have listened and watched while a relatively small extremist element, both to the left and to the right in our society, have knocked our courts, desecrated our flag, disrupted our educational system, laughed at our religious heritage, and threatened to burn down our cities," the preacher said. "The overwhelming majority of concerned Americans— white and black, hawks and doves, parents and students, Republicans and Democrats—who hate violence have stood by and viewed all this with mounting alarm and concern." At long last, these once silent Americans were starting to speak out, "to say with loud voices that in spite of their faults and failures, we believe in these institutions! Let the world know that the vast majority of us still proudly sing: 'My country 'tis of thee / Sweet land of liberty!'" The crowd roared in approval.[56]

Graham insisted that the secular institutions of American life were worth defending because they were rooted in spiritual truths. "Why should I, as a citizen of Heaven and a Christian minister, join in honoring any secular state?" he asked. "The Bible says, 'Honor the nation.' As a Christian, or as a Jew, or as an atheist, we have a responsibility to an America that has always stood for liberty, protection, and opportunity." In Graham's view, those national values were no accident but were instead rooted in the founding fathers' explicit embrace of the Judeo-Christian tradition. "The men who signed the Declaration of Independence were moved by a magnificent dream," Graham claimed. "This dream was rooted in a Book called the Bible. It proclaimed freedoms which most of the world thought impossible of fulfillment." The vision he attributed to the founders had not been fully realized, he acknowledged, but it was within reach. "I call upon Americans to bend low before God and go to their knees as Washington and Lincoln called us to our knees many years ago," he implored. "I submit that we can best honor America by rededicating ourselves to God and the American dream." A return to religion, Graham argued, would bind the wounds of the nation and "stop this polarization before it is too late."[57]

As Graham looked out from the Lincoln Memorial, though, it seemed it might already be too late. The crowd before him welcomed his message, but they had become increasingly distracted by a smaller contingent of radicals arrayed behind them. Roughly a thousand sprawled in the shadows

For the Fourth of July in 1970, the Nixon administration and its allies promoted "Honor America Day," which was highlighted by a morning religious service led by Billy Graham at the Lincoln Memorial and an evening entertainment program emceed by Bob Hope at the Washington Monument. Nominally a celebration for all Americans, the event proved in practice to be a rally for the conservative Silent Majority. *AP Images.*

of the Washington Monument, smoking red-white-and-blue joints and waving Vietcong flags. Though Graham had hoped to win them over, they still viewed him and his supporters with suspicion. (Speaking with a reporter, a young man with long brown hair and a drooping mustache referred to Graham's clean-cut crowd as "the Americans.") As the service went on, a few hundred radicals, some completely nude, waded waist deep into the reflecting pool and launched into antiwar chants. At the near end of the pool, Graham's audience watched with rising anger. Allen Brassill, a Kraft Foods salesman and chairman of the Americanism Committee of Maumee, Ohio, had driven to Washington with his wife the day before. "The speeches were inspiring," he said, his eyes shaded by a straw hat with a small American flag tucked into the band. "But we haven't enjoyed some of what we've seen here. Those filthy hippies in the pool, they should be locked up." For others, confronting radicals was the entire point of the event. Jim Reilly, a fireman from Maryland, said it was "the main reason

I'm here. I want to show those characters who are yelling obscenities that we don't have to take anything from a small minority." When mounted policemen finally intervened to keep the hecklers at bay, the conservative crowd cheered them on. "Push 'em back," yelled a man in yellow Bermuda shorts. "They can use a bath!" "They ought to be clubbed," said a bald man in a striped shirt. An angry housewife upped the ante: "I hope they break a few necks, that's what I hope."[58]

The disruption aside, Honor America Day continued as planned. Bishop Fulton Sheen brought the morning religious service to a close with his benediction. In a rebuke to the radicals in the reflecting pool, he proposed a West Coast counterpart to the Statue of Liberty, a "Statue of Responsibility" to "remind Americans that we have no rights without corresponding duties." Fireworks soon screeched from behind the Lincoln Memorial, exploding in a colorful display that ended with tiny American flags, attached to parachutes, floating gently down to the crowd. As the speakers descended the steps, they joined the crowd in a procession down Constitution Avenue. US servicemen and Boy Scouts led the way with the American flag and the flags of states and territories. Hippies stood on the sidelines chanting "One, two, three, four! We don't want your fucking war!" but the color guard focused on reaching the Ellipse. "There," *Newsday* noted, "on the very spot where students staged their bitter protest" two months before, Honor America Day participants raised a giant American flag. They then planted their small flags "into the letters U.S.A. which have been carved 42 by 24 feet into the green sod." Relay racers who had set out the day before from Independence Hall, Colonial Williamsburg, and Valley Forge soon arrived, planting their flags as well. As military bands performed throughout the afternoon, more and more members of the Silent Majority filed past, adding their individual flags to a growing "sea of red, white and blue" and reclaiming the Ellipse from the radicals.[59]

That evening, Honor America Day moved to the Washington Monument. Despite a late afternoon thunderstorm that soaked the lawn and drove the humidity even higher, the crowd only continued to swell. American Legionnaires, unmistakable in their caps displaying their names and post numbers, turned up in clusters across the crowd. A group of short-haired high school kids in hard hats loudly sang patriotic songs; empty beer cans piled up beside them. Teams of Boy Scouts rushed around providing first aid to those suffering in the heat, while roughly five hundred members of the conservative Young Americans for Freedom sported armbands that identified them as official "information aides" for the event. By nightfall, park police estimated that more than 350,000 had gathered for the evening's entertainment, forming a thick carpet of people, picnic baskets, and blankets that stretched out from the spotlighted monument a half mile in all directions.[60]

The few thousand antiwar protesters, now badly outnumbered, had been pushed to the fringes. Nevertheless, they had grown bolder over the afternoon, "liberating" a concession stand, raiding two Pepsi trucks, and, most improbably, flipping a giant spotlight into the reflecting pool. "The police are under orders to play it cool, to lean over backwards to avoid violence," a *Time* reporter explained in a wire to his office. Policemen tried to preserve the "DMZ" between the Honor America Day crowd and the radicals taunting them, but when a small group started throwing rocks, bottles, and cherry bombs, they moved in. As the US Navy Band began "The Star-Spangled Banner," park police launched tear gas into the thicket of protesters. They misjudged the wind, however, and the smoke swept over the celebration's attendees. "To the final strains of the anthem," a reporter wrote, "there was a mad stampede of weeping hippies and Middle Americans away from the fumes."[61]

When the evening's entertainment began, the crowd tuned out the protesters at the perimeter. As promised, master of ceremonies Bob Hope kept the program largely apolitical, though partisanship occasionally crept in. A prerecorded message from Nixon drew applause and a scattering of boos from the back, and when Hope set up a joke about a possible monument to Agnew, the crowd interrupted him, cheering the premise more than the punch line. On a few occasions, however, the political emphasis was quite overt. Country singer Jeannie C. Riley, best known for her hit "Harper Valley PTA," a send-up of small-town hypocrisy, performed Merle Haggard's Silent Majority anthem "The Fightin' Side of Me" instead. "If you don't love it, leave it: Let this song that I'm singin' be a warnin'," she sang to sustained cheers. "If you're runnin' down my country, man, you're walkin' on the fightin' side of me." Later, comedian Red Skelton recited the Pledge of Allegiance, defining each word at length as he went. "Since I was a small boy," Skelton observed at the very end, "two words have been added to the Pledge of Allegiance: 'Under God.' Wouldn't it be a pity if someone said *that* is a prayer and *that* be eliminated from our schools, too?" At this, the crowd came alive, whistling and hooting.[62]

For the most part, though, the performers stuck to traditional patriotic routines. Dinah Shore, who had been picked up from the Washington airport and whisked to the vice president's mansion the day before, played it straight with a standard rendition of "America the Beautiful." The Centurymen Choir, participants in the morning program, returned with the sentimental "We'll Find America." Occasionally these anthems served as an ironic score for the chaos unfolding in front of the performers. While the earnest New Christy Minstrels performed a sanitized version of "This Land Is Your Land," the crowd watched park police handcuff a black teen and usher him into a paddy wagon. In the end, only the magnificent final fireworks display brought all the crowd together, however briefly, in a shared moment of awe. As soon as it was over, the two sides went their separate ways.[63]

The next day, the men behind Honor America Day were quick to pronounce it a major success. "It was a great Fourth of July celebration," Nixon claimed, "the kind of patriotic thing we need." Organizers were thrilled that the size of the crowd had lived up to their highest hopes, despite the brutal weather. The television audience at home was even more encouraging; three-quarters of TVs in Washington had tuned in, and countless more across the country. Marriott had no doubts that the event had resonated with its target audience. "The people who attended were nice looking," he reflected the next day. "They were Middle Americans, the backbone of the country. That's what thrilled me." (As for the antiwar protesters, he had a different take: "It's too bad we have to have people like that trying to destroy the country.") To spread the message more broadly, organizers made arrangements for the production of a special two-disc collector's album of the event titled *Proudly They Came . . . To Honor America*. The recording was narrated by actor Jimmy Stewart, in echoes of his earlier service as emcee of the "Freedom Under God" festivities decades earlier. The Capitol Record Club soon made the double album its selection of the month and had to send out "reservation certificates" for copies when demand far surpassed the original supply.

Meanwhile, *Nation's Business,* a publication of the United States Chamber of Commerce, started selling copies of the record as well. All things considered, Marriott reflected, the event had been "very successful."[64]

Those outside the administration's orbit disagreed. "Successful at doing what?" the editors of *Newsday* asked. "Bringing America together? Perhaps. But which America? Certainly not those who would not or could not go. Not those whose attempts to disrupt the affair with their obscenities and harassment and hurling of fireworks so aggrieved the participants that some returned to their homes muttering things like: 'Now we know who the enemy is.'" Some critics believed the event had succeeded, at least in terms of its unacknowledged political agenda. "The 'Honor America Day' rally brought them together, all right," columnist Mary McGrory noted, "and sent them away farther apart than ever." Reporters for the *Washington Post* agreed, concluding that the Fourth of July festivities had simply "illustrated, perhaps better than any study or commission could, the polarization of American society."[65]

The critics were right, though they little realized of how deep the roots of Honor America Day ran. The event, and the larger efforts of the Nixon administration to use religious nationalism for its own ends, stemmed not just from the readily apparent polarization of the early 1970s but from the forgotten polarization of the 1930s as well. In their struggle against the New Deal, the business lobbies of the Depression era had allied themselves with conservative religious and cultural leaders and, in so doing, set in motion a new dynamic in American politics. The activism of Christian libertarians such as James Fifield and Abraham Vereide had sought to provide the right with its own brand of public religion that could challenge the Social Gospel of the left. But the rhetoric and rituals they created to topple the New Deal lived on long after their heyday, becoming a constant in American political life in the Eisenhower era and beyond.

By Honor America Day in 1970, the fundamental dynamics of this new public religion had significantly changed. At the dawn of the Cold War, the Eisenhower administration had united Americans under the broad rubric of "one nation under God," largely by shedding the more confrontational libertarianism that Fifield, Vereide, and Graham had espoused in their fight against the New Deal state. Instead, Eisenhower had reframed that phrase in such a way that it welcomed in large swaths of

Americans, whatever their religion or politics. But as the country became more polarized over the course of the ensuing decades, the slogans of the Eisenhower era could no longer hold them together. More than that, the religious rhetoric itself often became a source of division, especially at the local level, as seen in the struggles over school prayer. The Nixon White House had hoped to repeat the earlier work of the Eisenhower years, in many cases tapping the same political and religious figures for leadership positions, the same conservative philanthropists and corporations for funding, the same patriotic and fraternal organizations for grassroots support, and even some of the same sympathetic entertainers as its public face. But the political climate had been thoroughly transformed. The rhetoric of "one nation under God" no longer brought Americans together; it only reminded them how divided they had become.

Epilogue

ALMOST EXACTLY A DECADE AFTER the Honor America Rally, Ronald Reagan accepted the presidential nomination of the Republican Party. Though the setting of the Joe Louis Arena in Detroit was far removed from the National Mall in both location and allure, the crowd arrayed before Reagan nevertheless looked a lot like the one at the earlier rally: largely white, middle-aged, middle-class, and conservatively dressed, with many waving signs that professed love of God and country. Billy Graham had once again given the invocation, but that night Reagan showed the crowd, and the millions more watching at home, that he was just as proficient in Graham's idiom. At the end of his speech, Reagan dramatically departed from the text that had been distributed to reporters. "I have thought of something that is not part of my speech and I'm worried over whether I should do it," he began cautiously. He scanned the crowd and his eyes began to water, but he plunged ahead, asserting that "only a divine Providence" could have created the United States. He asked the Republican delegates gathered before him that "we begin our crusade joined together in a moment of silent prayer." The cheers and clapping stopped as heads bowed in reverence across the arena. After fifteen seconds, the candidate, with a slight catch in his voice, broke the silence with a closing benediction: "God bless America."[1]

Speechwriters had been carefully crafting his acceptance address for six weeks, but for Reagan it had been a lifetime in the making. Raised in a Democratic family that credited the New Deal with helping them survive the Depression, he had long considered Franklin D. Roosevelt his political hero; even as he accepted the Republican nomination, he praised the Democratic president not once but twice. But in 1952, Reagan became captivated by the candidacy of Dwight D. Eisenhower and cast his first-ever ballot for a Republican. When he ran for the office himself, he kept the lessons of his predecessor close to his heart. Like Eisenhower, Reagan routinely called his presidential campaign a "crusade" and encouraged supporters to believe his election would lead to a "spiritual renewal" across the nation. Most notably, Reagan often invoked the religious rhetoric that had been crafted in the Eisenhower era. "There are people who want to take 'In God We Trust' off our money," he warned in one speech. "I don't know of a time when we needed it more." The defining issue in the coming election, he claimed, was "whether this nation can continue, this nation under God."[2]

At the Republican National Convention, Reagan's stress on "old-fashioned values" found a receptive audience. His running mate, George H. W. Bush, likened the nominee to Eisenhower, while the delegates embraced a deeply conservative party platform that called for a constitutional amendment to restore prayer in public schools. "The political commandments endorsed by the Republican Party here this week may not be chiseled in stone," the *Washington Post* noted, "but, as one preppy-looking California Christian put it, 'they ought to be. It's right down the line an evangelical platform.'" The rest of the convention had similar overtones, delighting those inside the arena but alienating some outside it. Media critic Tom Shales remarked that it all reminded him of "the new breed of evangelical talk shows carried on TV stations throughout the country, where the vacant grins of ceaselessly smiling hosts and guests are usually dead giveaways that up above the eyebrows, nobody's home."[3]

Rather than simply reaffirm the old faith of the Eisenhower era, Reagan created new political rites and rituals suited to his own time. The silent prayer at the end of his speech was one innovation; the sign-off of "God bless America" was another. While the phrase had a long history in American culture, it had actually been used only once before in a major address by a president or presidential candidate. (And according to the thorough study by communications scholars David Domke and Kevin Coe, that occasion was an inauspicious one: a speech Nixon made when he was seeking a way out of the Watergate scandal in 1973.) Earlier presidents and presidential candidates had used other forms of divine invocation, of course, but only sparingly. By Domke and Coe's count, the eight presidents from FDR through Carter called for God's blessing in less than half of their speeches; indeed, most of them did so in only a quarter. But from Reagan on, presidents have asked for God's blessing in roughly nine out of every ten speeches they made. Reagan's campaign represented a turning point, a moment when this "God strategy" became the new norm.[4]

As Reagan's strategists understood in 1980, the electorate was primed for such shows of public piety. In the previous presidential election, self-described "born-again Christian" Jimmy Carter had drawn the media's attention to previously overlooked religious voters, prompting *Newsweek* to anoint 1976 as "The Year of the Evangelical." But few appreciated the importance of this development until those same supporters started to turn on Carter late in his term. In the lead-up to the 1980 election, a Gallup poll revealed an electorate in the midst of a religious revival. More than 80 percent of Americans accepted the divinity of Jesus Christ, almost half professed confidence in the inerrancy of the Holy Bible, and, most surprising, nearly a third identified themselves as having had a "born-again" experience of their own. Underscoring the strength of religious conservatism, breathless reporters described for the uninitiated the expansive reach of an "electric church," a network of influential religious broadcasters who spread their message across thirteen hundred radio and television stations—one out of every seven stations in the country—and claimed an audience of nearly 130 million and profits in the neighborhood of $1 billion. "We have enough votes to run the country," boasted religious broadcaster Pat Robertson. "And when the people say, 'We've had enough,' we're going to take over the country."[5]

Reagan resolved to win the votes of this newly discovered "religious right" at all costs. On paper, a divorced former Hollywood actor who rarely attended church seemed unlikely to attract the deeply devout, but his past experience with the politics of piety and patriotism—in stints promoting the Committee to Proclaim Liberty and speaking at Christian Anti-Communism Crusade events, for instance—had prepared him well. Reagan quickly made common cause with leaders of the religious right such as Jerry Falwell, head of the new Moral Majority organization, and worked to convert rank-and-file religious conservatives to his campaign. The climax came in August 1980, when he accepted an invitation to address the National Affairs Briefing of the Religious Roundtable in Dallas. Some fifteen thousand evangelical and fundamentalist ministers, including Falwell, Robertson, and the head of the Southern Baptist Convention, were on hand, hoping they might finally find a champion in Reagan. He did not disappoint. In his speech, he complained that "over the last two or three decades the Federal Government seems to have forgotten both 'that old-time religion' and that old time Constitution." In a line that had been scripted by his hosts, Reagan declared his loyalty to the audience. "I know you can't endorse me," he told them. "But I want you to know I endorse you and what you are doing." Duly impressed, religious conservatives rallied around him, and when Reagan swept to victory that November, they were happy to claim the credit. As Falwell put it, the conservative landslide was "my finest hour."[6]

Once in office, Reagan helped deepen the sacralization of the state. "I am told that tens of thousands of prayer meetings are being held on this day; for that I am deeply grateful," he said in his first inaugural address. "We are a nation under God, and I believe God intended for us to be free. It would be fitting and good, I think, if on each inaugural day in the future years it should be declared a day of prayer." Though Reagan rarely went to church—he averaged just three trips annually in his first three years in office, according to press estimates—he faithfully attended rituals of public religiosity such as the National Prayer Breakfast. Most of his predecessors had studiously avoided politicizing that event and similar ones, but when Reagan attended he pressed hard for partisan issues that were important to the religious right, such as school prayer, Bible reading, and abortion restrictions. "God, the source of our knowledge, has been expelled from the classroom," he said at the 1982 prayer breakfast. "He gives us his greatest blessing, life, and yet many would condone the taking of an innocent life."[7]

The school prayer amendment in particular was a recurring theme for Reagan, as he repeatedly called on Congress to pass the measure in his first term. Its prospects in the Senate looked stronger than they had since the Dirksen era, as a new class of conservative evangelicals swelled the ranks of the religious right there. The Senate's prayer breakfast meetings, which had dwindled to a handful of participants in the prior decade, now saw a full fourth of the chamber participate each and every week. The senators' spouses, meanwhile, met for a weekly Bible study meeting, while eight hundred staffers took part in monthly prayer breakfasts of their own. Those who attended the official Senate prayer breakfast meetings insisted politics played no role in the proceedings, but their staffers' sessions were another matter. At a December 1981 gathering, an aide to Republican senator Roger Jepsen of Iowa played a video produced by Pat Robertson's Christian Broadcasting Network about court rulings on the separation of church and state. "At each decision, the Supreme Court building grows slightly more red," a *Washington Post* reporter noted, "until by 1980 it glows with a vicious crimson. The viewers bend forward on their chairs, and there are frequent sighs of 'Ohhh!' or 'Can you *believe* it?'" Ultimately, though, moderates in both parties prevented Reagan's prayer amendment from passing the Senate. The House, under Democratic control, was seen as a lost cause.[8]

BUT FAILURE HAD ITS OWN rewards. As Reagan planned his re-election campaign, he knew that emphasizing social issues might keep the religious right on board, since it had hopes of finishing the crusade it began four years before. Notably, the seventy-three-year-old Reagan announced his plan to run for a second term late on a Sunday night in January 1984, just minutes before giving a televised address to the National Association of Religious Broadcasters (NARB). The president invoked God two dozen times in the speech and proclaimed to cheers that he wore the ACLU's criticism of his proclamation making 1983 the "Year of the Bible" as "a badge of honor." The purpose of it all, a GOP strategist explained at the time, was to "energize our base with the religious right." By all accounts, it worked. According to Lou Cannon, a veteran reporter who had covered Reagan for over a decade, the NARB speech resulted in "one of the most enthusiastic receptions of his presidency." For Cal Thomas, spokesman for the Moral Majority, it proved that Reagan was committed to their cause, regardless of his lapse in church-going. Carter had faithfully attended worship services, he pointed out, but he "appointed people who were pro-abortion."[9]

As the campaign began, conservative publishing houses rushed to print new books about Reagan's faith. Many suggested that the president had been divinely ordained. *Reagan Inside Out*, a book by Christian Broadcasting Network University president Bob Slosser, began with the tale of a "prophecy" made at a 1970 prayer meeting that Reagan attended along with Pat Boone. "If you will walk uprightly before Me," a California businessman intoned, channeling God's word to Reagan, "you will reside at 1600 Pennsylvania Avenue." David R. Shepherd, who compiled a number of Reagan's religious statements and speeches as a paperback titled *Ronald Reagan: In God I Trust*, shared this sentiment. "The King's heart is in the hand of the Lord; he directs it like a watercourse wherever he pleases," Shepherd noted, citing Proverbs. "How pleased the Lord must be," he added, "with a leader who does not resist that turning." Books like these soon filled entire shelves at Christian bookstores across the country, alongside tracts such as *Abortion and the Conscience of the Nation*, whose authorship was attributed to Reagan even though it only included one article by him, and even that had been ghostwritten. In all, hundreds of thousands of copies of these books were sold. Meanwhile, Nickelodeon Records repackaged old recordings the former actor had made the 1950s as brand-new albums titled *President Reagan Reads Stories from the Bible*.[10]

But no one was more effective at promoting Reagan than Reagan himself. On the day he accepted his party's renomination as president, he first made a triumphant return to Reunion Arena in Dallas, the site of the National Affairs Briefing four years before. With a choir of two thousand at his back, the president addressed a capacity crowd of seventeen thousand religious leaders and Republican delegates. "The truth is, politics and morality are inseparable," he insisted. "And as morality's foundation is religion, religion and politics are necessarily related." Speaking at length about the Supreme Court's rulings against state-mandated school prayer and programs of Bible reading, he claimed they had represented an important turning point in the nation's history. They set a dangerous precedent, inspiring more lawsuits to remove the words "under God" from the pledge or "In God We Trust" from U.S. currency and promoting secularism. Liberals said they challenged such religious mottos in the spirit of tolerance of all faiths, but the president scoffed at their claims. "Isn't the real truth that they are intolerant of religion?" he asked. "They refuse to tolerate its importance in our lives." At the close of his speech, Reagan delivered a line that would be cited repeatedly by conservatives in the days and, indeed, decades to come: "If we ever forget that we're one nation under God, then we'll be a nation gone under."[11]

The blending of religion and politics was, of course, a two-way street. That same night, after Reagan and Bush were formally renominated, Jerry Falwell asserted in his closing prayer that the two men were "God's instruments in rebuilding America." In the same vein, Reverend E. V. Hill, a Baptist minister and longtime ally of Billy Graham, concluded his own address by declaring, "I'm glad I'm a member of the Prayer Party." Leaders of the religious right once again lined up with the Republicans. Falwell claimed his Moral Majority had registered more than five million conservative Christians since its founding in 1979 and promised to add another million to the rolls before election day. Christian Voice likewise led massive voter registration drives at houses of worship, while broadcasting by satellite seminars explaining the details of party politics to more than two thousand fundamentalist churches across the nation. "1984 is the harvest year," claimed Ray Allen, chairman of Concerned Christians for Reagan. "We're reaping the rewards of ten years of work." The president also reaped the rewards that fall, taking in 66 percent of the evangelical vote as well as solid majorities of the Catholic and mainline Protestant vote in another landslide victory.[12]

THOSE WHO SOUGHT TO SUCCEED Reagan watched closely and tried to follow his example. Vice President George H. W. Bush, an old-school Episcopalian, lacked Reagan's ease with the evangelical base but had something the president did not: a longtime personal friendship with Billy Graham. In April 1986, the preacher opened a crusade in Washington, D.C., for the first time since the Eisenhower era, and granted his old friend the honor of addressing the crowd of twenty-one thousand worshipers. "The strength of our nation is our faith," Bush assured them. "We do believe that when all is said and done that we are indeed a nation under God." Meanwhile, other contenders for the nomination endeavored to show that they too could serve as Reagan's successor. "Freedom is a gift from God, not government," asserted Kansas senator Bob Dole. Representative Jack Kemp of New York insisted that "one of the reasons I'm running for president is because I believe I have an obligation as a

Christian to be involved in politics." Sincere though they may have been, these claims paled next to the public piety of Pat Robertson. The religious broadcaster made a surprisingly strong showing in early primaries and, in the process, shifted the field further right. Bush secured the nomination, but in so doing he inherited a party that was wedded even more closely to the religious right than ever before.[13]

At the 1988 Republican National Convention in New Orleans, the new nominee sought to show Americans that he would be an able heir to Reagan. The Democrats had already begun mocking him for his lack of eloquence—the aristocratic Bush, according to Texas governor Ann Richards, had been "born with a silver foot in his mouth"—but the vice president bent the jibes to his benefit. "I may sometimes be a little awkward," he said in his speech, "but there's nothing self-conscious in my love of country." While he could never match the oratorical skills of the "Great Communicator," Bush shrewdly mimicked his predecessor's handling of the important acceptance speech. As he neared the end of his prepared remarks, Bush abruptly departed from the text, just as Reagan had eight years before. Where Reagan had inserted a dramatic call for a silent prayer for the nation, Bush made an even simpler appeal. "It is customary to end an address with a pledge, or saying, that holds special meaning," he told the delegates. "I've chosen one that we all know by heart, one that we all learned in school. And I ask everyone in this great hall to stand and join me." At this, the Superdome crowd rose to its feet, waving a sea of American flags, and joined their nominee in reciting the Pledge of Allegiance. At the end, the candidate added a quick "God bless you" before the delegates erupted in applause.[14]

Much as Reagan used school prayer as a partisan issue, Bush used the pledge. His opponent in the general election, Massachusetts governor Michael Dukakis, had vetoed a bill in 1977 that would have fined public school teachers who refused to lead classes in the pledge, after the state's highest court suggested that the bill was unconstitutional. Republican strategists unearthed the story and made it central to the 1988 campaign. "Should public school teachers be required to lead our children in the Pledge of Allegiance?" Bush asked in his acceptance speech. "My opponent says no—but I say yes." Out on the campaign trail, the Republican nominee repeatedly led crowds in mass recitations of the pledge, sometimes asking surrogates such as actor Charlton Heston to stand in for him. (The ritual became so central to the Republican campaign that one history of the election was simply titled *Pledging Allegiance*.) Meanwhile, Republicans in the House joined in, introducing a measure to mandate daily recitation of the pledge in the chamber. They admitted off the record that they had done so mainly to drive a wedge between southern Democrats and Dukakis. Democratic Speaker Jim Wright originally objected to the transparent ploy, asserting that "the Pledge of Allegiance to the flag is something meant to unite us, not intended to divide us." But when House Democrats realized that any opposition would be seen as another sign that their party could not match the GOP's love of God and country, they quickly relented.[15]

Dukakis was slower to recognize the political power of the pledge. He protested that he had nothing against it and resented the attacks on his patriotism, but his advisors refused to go any further. "If they think they're going to get anywhere with the Pledge issue, they're wrong," campaign manager Susan Estrich insisted. "We've got the Supreme Court answer." Convinced their position would hold up in a court of law, Dukakis's staff neglected the court of public opinion. And according to an analyst with the Gallup organization, voters were siding with the Republicans by a three-to-one margin on the matter. John Chubb, a scholar at the Brookings Institution, noted that whatever the legal facts were, the political realities were something else entirely: "Bush is saying, 'I'm willing to say that the courts are wrong. Public teachers should lead the pledge.' Dukakis is saying, 'I bow before the courts.'" While legal experts and editorials overwhelmingly agreed that the Democrat's position was wholly correct, the public was not persuaded. "Dukakis made a major mistake," noted former Democratic Party chairman Bob Strauss. "He captured the hearts of 17 lawyers and lost 3 million voters." Belatedly comprehending the problem, the Democrat caved and staged a photo op at the Statue of Liberty, dutifully reciting the Pledge of Allegiance for the cameras, in front of a sea of American flags. But the damage was done. Once far behind in the polls, Bush used the pledge and other wedge issues to surge ahead after the conventions. He never looked back.[16]

Having wrapped himself in the flag during the campaign, Bush continued to make good use of it as president. In June 1989, the Supreme Court struck down the "flag desecration" statutes that had been passed in forty-eight of the fifty states during the Vietnam War. The case at hand, *Texas v. Johnson,* stemmed from a flag-burning incident that took place in Dallas the day before Reagan and Bush were renominated at the 1984 Republican National Convention. Now, as president, Bush denounced flag burning as "dead wrong" and promised to do something about it. A few days after the court ruling, a *Newsweek* poll showed that 71 percent of Americans favored a constitutional amendment to outlaw flag burning. The president soon announced his own support for such a measure. Standing before the Iwo Jima monument, with its famous sculpture of Marines raising the American flag on Mount Suribachi, Bush declared that "patriotism is not a partisan issue, it is not a political issue." But only Republican officials had been invited to join him on the platform that day; some, such as Senator Bob Dole, practically dared opponents to make a stand against the amendment. "Democrats," an op-ed columnist advised, "get that message: Vote against the flag amendment and consider the TV ad your next opponent will put together against you."[17]

The call for a constitutional amendment forced the nation to reassess the flag's meaning. Over the preceding decades the flag had become, in the words of anthropologist David Kertzer, "the holy icon of American civil religion." But as the president moved to end its "desecration," even some prominent conservatives chafed at his framing of the issue. "'Desecration' is a word rooted in sacredness," scolded former Nixon speechwriter William Safire. "Americans do not consecrate—make holy—our political signs and documents, nor can anyone 'desecrate' them." For others, the real sin was an emptiness of ideas. Edward Crane, head of the libertarian Cato Institute, mocked Republicans for abandoning their substantive small-government principles and instead "flailing about and breast-beating over opinion-poll-driven issues like burning the flag [and] the Pledge of Allegiance." But as the initial furor died down, so did the campaign for the amendment. When the vote was taken in October, the measure fell fifteen votes short of the two-thirds majority it needed. A *Chicago Tribune* columnist noted the parallels with a previous controversy that had likewise fired up religious conservatives but then flamed out in Congress: the prayer amendments of the 1960s.[18]

During the remainder of the Bush era, the Republican Party became increasingly Christianized. Though he had failed to win its presidential nomination, Pat Robertson worked diligently to take control of the party itself. Speaking to supporters in the Christian Coalition in September 1991, the religious broadcaster set a goal of having "a working majority of the Republican Party in the hands of pro-family Christians by 1996." This was not idle talk. By the next summer, Christian Coalition members and their allies held more than a third of the seats on the Republican National Committee and a majority in ten state party organizations. Their influence was abundantly clear at the 1992 Republican National Convention, where they succeeded in adding to the party platform references to "our country's Judeo-Christian heritage" and a call for the required recitation of the Pledge of Allegiance in public schools "as a reminder of the principles that sustain us as one Nation under God." The convention itself kicked off with a raucous "God and Country" rally, hosted by Robertson, with appearances by Pat Boone and Vice President Dan Quayle, a favorite of the religious right. They all recited the Pledge of Allegiance together, with the crowd practically shouting when they came to the phrase "one nation under God." The defining moment of the convention, though, came with the famous "culture war" speech of Pat Buchanan, who had made a strong primary challenge to the president from the right. The election was nothing less than a "religious war," he warned. "In that struggle for the soul of America, Clinton and Clinton are on one side," Buchanan charged, "and George Bush is on our side." His attacks electrified delegates in the Houston Astrodome but played poorly outside it. Liberal columnist Molly Ivins joked that Buchanan's speech "probably sounded better in the original German."[19]

THAT YEAR, THOUGH, THE DEMOCRATS refused to cede religion to the Republicans. Unlike Dukakis, whom historian Garry Wills called "the first truly secular candidate we ever had for the presidency," Arkansas governor Bill Clinton was proudly religious. A Southern Baptist who attended church regularly and even sang in the choir, Clinton recalled that his grandmother had told him he "could be a preacher if I were just a better little boy. So I ended up in politics." Not surprisingly, the Democratic nominee made liberal use of religious references in his acceptance speech at the convention, citing Scripture, referring to God, even reciting that key passage of the Pledge of Allegiance. Most tellingly, Clinton framed his grand plan for the country in explicitly religious terms, calling for the creation of a "New Covenant, a solemn agreement between the people and their government based not simply on what each of us can take but what all of us must give to our Nation." Locking hands with running mate Senator Al Gore Jr.—a fellow Southern Baptist—Clinton made it clear that the politics of piety and patriotism would no longer be confined to the Republican Party.[20]

Bush denounced his opponents for a lack of faith all the same. In a speech to evangelical Christians in Dallas, he said he had been "struck by the fact that the other party took [thousands of] words to put together their platform and left out three simple letters: G-O-D." Clinton quickly hit back, denouncing Bush's attacks outside a Methodist church where he and his running mate had just attended services. "He has basically said that unless you believe in the Republican platform, you don't believe in God and you're not an American," Clinton claimed. "The implication that he has made that the Democrats are somehow Godless is deeply offensive." Liberal religious figures agreed that Bush had crossed a line. Dozens of church leaders, including the heads of the National Council of Churches and the president's own Episcopal Church, wrote an open letter that claimed it was "blasphemy" for anyone "to invoke the infinite and holy God to assert the moral superiority of one people over another or one political party over another." Another fifty clergymen issued a warning of their own: "Faith in God should unite us, not divide us." Bush overreached with a strident brand of religious politics, and Clinton's softer touch won out.[21]

As president, Clinton applied the same soft religiosity to national political life. He faithfully participated in the National Prayer Breakfasts, as his Republican predecessors had, but unlike them, he used the events not to advance a legislative agenda but rather to shield himself from criticism. "Sometimes I think the commandment we most like to overlook in this city is 'thou shall not bear false witness,'" he said at the 1994 breakfast. At the next year's event, he condemned the rise in negative political attacks and encouraged the worshipers to heed Paul's advice to the Romans: "Repay no one evil for evil." He used the 1997 breakfast to urge attendees to "rid ourselves of this toxic atmosphere"; a year later, as the Monica

Lewinsky scandal threatened to end his presidency, he asked his audience for their prayers so he could survive the crisis and "take our country to higher ground." At these events and others, Clinton emphasized an inward-looking salvation. While his Republican predecessors had aligned themselves with leading social conservatives of the religious right, Clinton's "spiritual soul mate" was instead Reverend Robert Schuller, the apparently apolitical pastor of the extravagant Crystal Cathedral and noted practitioner of a spirituality of self-esteem and enrichment. "This is the ideal theological accompaniment to the presidency of Bill Clinton, which operates on smoke and mirrors rather than hard labor," observed the *Washington Post*'s Jonathan Yardley. "A match made in Heaven."[22]

WHEN HE RAN FOR THE White House, Texas governor George W. Bush took a similarly soft approach, though one that came from the right. A born-again Christian, he shared Clinton's ability to discuss his faith openly. When Republican primary candidates were asked to name their favorite philosopher in a 1999 debate, for instance, Bush immediately named Christ, "because He changed my heart." Despite the centrality of faith in his own life, Bush assured voters that he would not implement the rigid agenda of the religious right. Borrowing a phrase from author Marvin Olasky, Bush called himself a "compassionate conservative" and said he would take a lighter approach to social issues including abortion and gay rights than culture warriors such as Buchanan. But many on the right took issue with the phrase. For some, the "compassionate" qualifier implicitly condemned mainstream conservatism as heartless; for others, the phrase seemed an empty marketing gimmick. (As Republican speechwriter David Frum put it, "Love conservatism but hate arguing about abortion? Try our new *compassionate conservatism*—great ideological taste, now with less controversy.") But the candidate backed his words with deeds, distancing himself from the ideologues in his party. In a single week in October 1999, for instance, Bush criticized House Republicans for "balancing the budget on the backs of the poor" and lamented that all too often "my party has painted an image of America slouching toward Gomorrah."[23]

In concrete terms, Bush's "compassionate conservatism" constituted a promise to empower private religious and community organizations and thereby expand their role in the provision of social services. This "faith-based initiative" became the centerpiece of his campaign. In his address to the 2000 Republican National Convention, Bush heralded the work of Christian charities and called upon the nation to do what it could to support them. After his inauguration, Bush moved swiftly to make the proposal a reality. Indeed, the longest section of his 2001 inaugural address was an expansive reflection on the idea. "America, at its best, is compassionate," he observed. "Church and charity, synagogue and mosque lend our communities their humanity, and they will have an honored place in our plans and in our laws." Bush promoted the initiative at his first National Prayer Breakfast as well. But it was ill-fated. Hamstrung by a lack of clear direction during the administration's first months, it was quickly overshadowed by a new emphasis on national security after the terrorist attacks of 9/11.[24]

Bush continued to advance his vision of a godly nation. Soon after 9/11, he made a special trip to the Islamic Center of Washington, the very same mosque that had opened its doors to celebrate the Eisenhower inauguration a half century earlier. No sitting president had ever visited an Islamic house of worship, but Bush made clear by his words and deeds there that he considered Muslims part of the nation's diverse religious community. He denounced recent acts of violence against Muslims and Arab Americans in no uncertain terms. "Those who feel like they can intimidate our fellow citizens to take out their anger don't represent the best of America," he said; "they represent the worst of humankind and they should be ashamed." Referring to Islam as a "religion of peace" and citing the Koran, he closed his address with the same words of inclusion he would have used before any audience, religious or otherwise: "God bless us all." The president was not alone in enlisting religious patriotism to demonstrate national unity after the attacks. On September 12, 2001, congressional representatives from both parties joined together on the Capitol steps to sing "God Bless America." Meanwhile, several states that did not already require recitations of the Pledge of Allegiance in their schools introduced bills to do just that.[25]

But the efforts to use the pledge as a source of unity were soon thrown into disarray. In June 2002, a federal court ruled that the phrase "one nation under God" violated the First Amendment prohibition against the establishment of a state religion. The case *Newdow v. Elk Grove Unified School District* had been filed in 2000 by Michael Newdow, an emergency room doctor who complained that his daughter's rights were infringed because she was forced to "watch and listen as her state-employed teacher in her state-run school leads her classmates in a ritual proclaiming that there is a God, and that ours is 'one nation under God.'" In a 2-to-1 decision, the court agreed. It held that the phrase was just as objectionable as a statement that "we are a nation 'under Jesus,' a nation 'under Vishnu,' a nation 'under Zeus,' or a nation 'under no god,' because none of these professions can be neutral with respect to religion." The reaction from political leaders was as swift as it was predictable. The Senate suspended debate on a pending military spending bill to draft a resolution condemning the ruling, while dozens of House members took to the Capitol steps to recite the pledge and sing "God Bless America" one more time. White House spokesman Ari Fleischer announced that the president thought the decision was "ridiculous"; Democratic senator Tom Daschle called it "nuts." The reaction was so pronounced, in fact, that the appeals court delayed implementation of its ruling until an appeal could be heard.[26]

As the case made its way through the courts, the nation had to reckon anew with the meaning of "one nation under God." According to Newdow, an atheist, the language of the amended pledge clearly took "one side in the quintessential religious question 'Does God exist?'" The Bush administration, defending the pledge, asserted that reciting it was no more a religious act than using a coin with "In God We Trust" inscribed on it; both merely acknowledged the nation's heritage. A separate brief filed by conservative religious organizations, however, argued that the pledge was "both theological *and* political." Reviving claims of the Christian libertarians, it asserted that the words "under God" were added to underscore the concept of limited government. They were meant as a reminder that "government is not the highest authority in human affairs" because, as the Declaration of Independence claimed, "inalienable rights come from God." In June 2004, the Supreme Court ruled that Newdow technically lacked standing to bring the suit and thus dismissed the lower court's ruling, dodging the issue for the time being.[27]

Having survived that challenge in the courts, the concept of "one nation under God" thrived on the campaign trail. Seeking to rally religious voters for the 2004 election, Republican strategist Karl Rove advocated a "play-to-the-base" plan to exploit the concerns of the religious right for electoral gain. The president passed two major pieces of pro-life legislation and then joined the campaign for a Federal Marriage Amendment to ban homosexual unions. Many on the right saw the coming campaign as the kind of "religious war" that Pat Buchanan heralded a decade before. The Bush campaign worked to capitalize on "the God gap" in the electorate, mobilizing religious conservatives in record numbers. In Allentown, Pennsylvania, one backer erected a billboard that summed up the unofficial strategy of the Republicans: "Bush Cheney '04—One Nation Under God." The Democrats, meanwhile, gave the politics of religion comparatively little attention. John Kerry's presidential campaign relegated much of its national religious outreach to a twenty-eight-year-old newcomer who had virtually no institutional support, not even an old database of contacts. "The matchup between the two parties in pursuit of religious voters wasn't just David versus Goliath," the journalist Amy Sullivan wrote. "It was David versus Goliath and the Philistines and the Assyrians and the Egyptians, with a few plagues thrown in for good measure."[28]

THE NOTABLE EXCEPTION TO THE Democrats' avoidance of religious rhetoric came at the party's national convention. Then a largely unknown state senator from Illinois, Barack Obama introduced himself to the country with a stirring speech that emphasized religious values as a source of national unity. Obama dismissed those who would "use faith as a wedge to divide us," proclaiming to loud applause that "we worship an 'awesome God' in the blue states." "We are one people," Obama insisted, "all of us pledging allegiance to the Stars and Stripes, all of us defending the United States of America." Citing the Declaration of Independence, he rooted his fellow citizens' rights in their Creator but insisted that their responsibilities stemmed from God as well. What "makes this country work," Obama observed, was a belief based on lessons in the Bible: "I am my brother's keeper; I am my sister's keeper." He ended his address with an optimistic invocation of piety and patriotism reminiscent of the speeches of Ronald Reagan. "The audacity of hope!" he proclaimed. "In the end, that is God's greatest gift to us, the bedrock of this nation." As the crowd roared, he completed his speech with a now-familiar ritual: "God bless you."[29]

The keynote address made Obama a contender in the presidential contest just four years later, but it did not protect him from doubts about his commitment to his God and his country. In early 2008, inflammatory comments made by Reverend Jeremiah Wright, his longtime pastor at Trinity United Church of Christ in Chicago, came to light, threatening to cripple his campaign. In an excerpt from a 2003 sermon replayed endlessly on cable news networks, the fiery preacher told his congregation that African Americans should condemn the United States. "God damn America for treating our citizens as less than human!" Wright shouted. "God damn America for as long as she acts like she is God and she is supreme." Obama stated that he thought his pastor's "rants" were "appalling," and in March 2008, he confronted the controversy in a major speech in Philadelphia. Though race, rather than religion, emerged as the central theme, Obama employed the language of faith to explain his pastor's statements and, at the same time, distance himself from them. "I have asserted a firm conviction—a conviction rooted in my faith in God and my faith in the American people," Obama insisted, "that working together we can move beyond some of our old racial wounds, and that in fact we have no choice if we are to continue on the path of a more perfect union."[30]

Religion played an even more prominent role in the race for the Republican nomination. In a November 2007 debate, CNN showed a videotaped question from a voter who held up a Christian version of the Bible and said, "How you answer this question will tell us everything we need to know about you: Do you believe every word of this book?" The conservative columnist Charles Krauthammer insisted that the candidates should have answered that it was "none of your damn business," but instead all of them "bent a knee and tried appeasement with various interpretations of scriptural literalism." Indeed, the Republican field seemed especially eager to outdo one another's professions of piety. Arizona senator John McCain, who had boldly denounced Jerry Falwell and Pat Robertson as "agents of intolerance" in his losing bid in the 2000 primaries, spent much of his second run mending fences with them. He made a major address at Falwell's Liberty University, where he asserted, despite all evidence to the contrary, that "the Constitution established the United States of America as a Christian nation." New York City mayor Rudy Giuliani, meanwhile, proudly won Robertson's endorsement. Not to be outdone, Arkansas governor Mike Huckabee, a former Baptist minister, attributed his strong showing in the polls to "the same power that helped a little boy with two fish and five loaves feed a crowd of 5,000 people."[31]

No Republican candidate, however, was challenged more by questions of faith than Massachusetts governor Mitt Romney. The first Mormon to make a significant run for the presidency, he found his campaign struggling to overcome distrust by evangelical voters at the party's base. Romney staged a major speech on "Faith in America" at the presidential library of George H. W. Bush. Though he stood by his faith and made clear that he shared common ground with more traditional Christians, Romney only used the word "Mormon" once. Instead, the bulk of his address focused on the proper place of faith in American politics. "Freedom requires religion," he argued, "just as religion requires freedom." He promised never to force his own values on the nation as a whole, but also said he believed that religious principles in general were essential to the continued health of the nation. The Constitution rested on a "foundation of faith," Romney said, and its framers "did not countenance the elimination of religion from the public square. We are a nation 'under God,' and in God we do indeed trust."[32]

THESE INVOCATIONS REVEAL THAT THE rhetoric and rituals of public religion detailed in this book have lived on to the present day. Indeed, if anything, such touchstones of religious nationalism have only become more deeply lodged in American political culture over time, as the innovations of one generation became familiar traditions for the next. But as these religious notes have been drummed into the national consciousness, almost by rote, we have forgotten their origins. More than that, we have forgotten they have origins at all.

And their origins, it turns out, are rather surprising. The rites of our public religion originated not in a spiritual crisis, but rather in the political and economic turmoil of the Great Depression. The story of business leaders enlisting clergymen in their war against the New Deal is one that has been largely obscured by the very ideology that resulted from it.

Previous accounts of the tangled relationship between Christianity and capitalism have noted the "uneasy alliance" between businessmen and the religious right which helped elect Ronald Reagan and end the New Deal order, but the careers of the Christian libertarians in the 1930s and 1940s show that their alliance was present at the creation of the New Deal. Their ideology of "freedom under God" did not topple the regulatory state as they hoped, but thanks to the evangelism of conservative clergymen such as James Fifield, Abraham Vereide, and Billy Graham, it ultimately accomplished more than its corporate creators ever dreamed possible. It convinced a wide range of Americans that their country had been, and should always be, a Christian nation.

In the early 1950s, the long crusade of the Christian libertarians apparently reached its triumphant climax with the election of Dwight Eisenhower. But the new president proved to be transformative in a sense his corporate backers had not anticipated. Although he was certainly sympathetic to the secular ends they sought, Eisenhower proved to be much more interested in the spiritual language they had invented as a means of achieving those ends. Uncoupling their religious rhetoric from its roots in the fight against the New Deal, he considerably broadened its appeal, expanding its reach well beyond the initial circle of conservative Protestants to welcome Americans across the political and religious spectrum. In doing so, Eisenhower ushered in an unprecedented religious revival, one that temporarily filled the nation's churches and synagogues but permanently altered its political culture. From then on, the federal government, which the Christian libertarians had long denounced as godless, was increasingly seen as quite godly instead. Congress cemented these changes, adding "under God" to the Pledge of Allegiance and adopting "In God We Trust" as the nation's first official motto. Hollywood and Madison Avenue, meanwhile, helped promote this understanding of America as a religious nation and Americans as an inherently religious people.

The new rituals of public religion crafted in the Eisenhower era were seen at the time as symbolic flourishes with little substance to them. But the rites and rhetoric that Eugene Rostow dismissed as mere "ceremonial deism" in 1962 were soon revealed to have incredible political power. National controversies over school prayer—which unfolded first in the Supreme Court and then in Congress—demonstrated that the symbols and slogans of the Eisenhower era, instituted less than a decade earlier, had quickly been embraced by many Americans as ironclad evidence of the nation's religious roots. As conservatives fought to restore school prayer and to roll back other social changes in the turbulent 1960s, they rallied around phrases like "one nation under God." As a result, the religious rhetoric that had recently been used to unite Americans began to drive them further apart. At the decade's end, Richard Nixon helped complete this polarization of the nation's public religion, using it to advance divisive policies both at home and abroad.

This history reminds us that our public religion is, in large measure, an invention of the modern era. The ceremonies and symbols that breathe life into the belief that we are "one nation under God" were not, as many Americans believe, created alongside the nation itself. Their parentage stems not from the founding fathers but from an era much closer to our own, the era of our own fathers and mothers, our grandfathers and grand-mothers. This fact need not diminish their importance; fresh traditions can be more powerful than older ones adhered to out of habit. Neverthe-less, we do violence to our past if we treat certain phrases—"one nation under God," "In God We Trust"—as sacred texts handed down to us from the nation's founding. Instead, we are better served if we understand these utterances for what they are: political slogans that speak not to the origins of our nation but to a specific point in its not-so-distant past. If they are to mean anything to us now, we should understand what they meant then.

ACKNOWLEDGMENTS

This book would not have been possible without the inspiration and support of countless colleagues, friends, and family. There are not enough pages here to thank them properly or enough time to express the depths of my debt to them all.

First, I must thank the academic community I've been lucky to call home for a decade and a half now. As a member of the faculty at Princeton University, I have been fortunate to have so many colleagues who are both rich with insight and generous with their time. This project has benefited immensely from several workshops in the Department of Religion and the Shelby Cullom Davis Center for Historical Studies and informal chats with many of my colleagues at the Center for the Study of Religion. Special thanks to Wallace Best, Jessica Delgado, Judith Weisenfeld, and Bob Wuthnow. In one form or another, the entire Department of History—faculty, staff, graduate and undergraduate students—has helped make me a better historian and this a better book. But for their collegiality and contributions to this project, I owe a special debt to Margot Canaday, Alec Dun, Yaacob Dweck, Shel Garon, Michael Gordin, Molly Greene, Josh Guild, Dirk Hartog, Alison Isenberg, Rob Karl, Mike Laffan, Jon Levy, Erika Milam, Rebecca Rix, Dan Rodgers, Keith Wailoo, Wendy Warren, Sean Wilentz, and Julian Zelizer. I owe my department chair, Bill Jordan, my deepest appreciation for his unflagging support. Our staff, of course, is the backbone of our department, and I thank them for the invaluable help they provide us all every day: Elizabeth Bennett, Brooke Fitzgerald, Judy Hanson, Barb Leavey, Pamela Long, Debbie Macy, Kristy Novak, Etta Recke, Max Siles, Jackie Wasneski, and Carla Zimowsk. My graduate students, past and present, all deserve credit for inspiring me to work as diligently as they do. In particular, conversations with Leah Wright Rigueur and Sarah Milov have helped me fine-tune my thinking on the issues in this book, while Dov Grohsgal has doggedly secured the prints and permissions for the images in it. Olivier Burtin graciously offered to look for material related to the project when he made his own early research trips to the American Legion archives and returned with more than I'd even imagined possible.

Beyond Princeton, countless other scholars have helped this project as well. Sections of the book were presented early on as papers at annual meetings of the American Historical Association and the Organization of American Historians, as well as at smaller conferences, workshops, and invited lectures at Binghamton University, Boston University, Cornell University, Emory University, King's College London, Southern Methodist University, the University of California at Santa Barbara, and the University of Sussex. Many thanks to the receptive audiences at these events and the scholars who participated: Uta Balbier, Anja-Maria Bassimir, Eileen Boris, Heike Bungert, Jim Cobb, Joe Crespino, Jonathan Ebel, Wayne Flynt, Healon Gaston, Lily Geismer, Sally Gordon, Andy Graybill, Stephen Green, Alison Colis Greene, Darren Grem, Ray Haberski, Matt Hedstrom, Heather Hendershot, John Lee, Nelson Lichtenstein, Emma Long, Jonathan Lurie, John McGreevey, Bethany Moreton, Alice O'Connor, Kathy Olmsted, Steve Ortiz, Andrew Preston, Mark Rose, Bruce Schulman, Elizabeth Shermer, Matt Sutton, Stephen Tuck, Wendy Wall, Clive Webb, Jana Weiss, and Diane Winston. Later on, Brian Balogh did me the great honor of inviting me to present a draft of the manuscript at the 2013 Miller Center Fellowship Spring Conference at the University of Virginia, where three phenomenal scholars—Doug Blackmon, Mike Lienesch, and Darren Dochuk—provided thorough feedback and enthusiastic support. Darren, in particular, has to be singled out for praise, as he not only provided me with several rounds of feedback over the course of this project but also put up with me as we presented our work together in a half-dozen panels and presentations over a year's span.

I owe Ari Kelman and Eric Rauchway a tremendous debt, as they read through an early draft of the manuscript, providing terrific suggestions at a crucial stage, and then helped me think through countless new issues as I revised the manuscript over the next few years. Several other scholars deserve my sincere thanks for taking the time to read the entire manuscript in later stages of its evolution, offering insight and much-needed encouragement to press on: Paul Harvey, Andrew Preston, Larry Moore, Matt Sutton, Bob Wuthnow, and Neil J. Young. Gill Frank and Kim Phillips-Fein, meanwhile, offered invaluable feedback on individual chapters. For additional conversations and insights that shaped the book in important ways, I must also thank Tony Badger, Tim Borstelmann, Jon Butler, Nathan Connolly, Jeff Cowie, Mary Dudziak, Sally Gordon, Mary Beth Norton, Matt Lassiter, Dick Polenberg, Nick Salvatore, Andrew Sandoval Strausz, Bryant Simon, and Tom Sugrue. And I owe special thanks to three complete strangers who generously offered to help me track down key materials for this project: Rich Kimball and Kara Hansen, who helped me secure photocopies from the Cecil B. DeMille archives, and

Sam Brenner, who graciously loaned me FBI files on the Christian Anti-Communism Crusade that he had unearthed in his own research.

Many institutions and individuals made the research for this book possible. Financial support from the Princeton University Committee on Research and the Department of History subsidized several research trips to various archives, while the excellent staff at our Firestone Library worked tirelessly to dig up countless copies of obscure books, magazines, and periodicals on short notice. Most important, this book owes a great deal to the resourcefulness and helpfulness of a good number of archivists, librarians, and staff members around the nation. As any historian can attest, the insight and assistance of archivists can make or break a project, and there are several who deserve special mention for their kind help: Jim Armistead at the Truman Presidential Library, Brian Keough at the University of Albany, Dan Linke at the Mudd Manuscript Library at Princeton, Ron McDowell of the Fraternal Order of Eagles, Simone Munson at the Wisconsin Historical Society, John Nemmers at the University of Florida, Bruce Tabb at the University of Oregon, Howard Trace at the American Legion, Randy Vance at Texas Tech University, and Stacey Wright at Valdosta State University. Three archives, in particular, were vitally important for this project, and luckily for me, they were all run by exceptional archivists: Bob Shuster at the Billy Graham Center Archives, Bill Sumners at the Southern Baptist Historical Library and Archives, and the late Herb Pankratz at the Eisenhower Presidential Museum and Library. Without the generous assistance (and general kindness) that they and their outstanding staffs provided, this book would not have been possible. To anyone whose name should be here but is not, I ask that you please forgive me for the oversight.

Geri Thoma has been an incredible advisor and advocate, and I cannot imagine navigating the unfamiliar terrain of trade publishing without her. The entire staff at Basic Books has been simply wonderful. Dan Gerstle did amazing work in the final line edits. My editor Lara Heimert is likewise simply phenomenal, and I can't thank her enough for her passion for this project and her commitment to it. Her assistant, Leah Stecher, helped me handle countless last-second crises as the book went to press. Likewise, Rachel King and her staff ensured the final work looked terrific.

On a more personal note, I have many friends to thank for making sure I didn't disappear into the archives altogether: Martha D'Avila and Jim Burton, Eric and Pam Greenhut, Dan and Melanie Goldey, Dave and Jen Haslam, John and Ali Lee, Clea Karlstrom and Steve Selwood, Ben and Caddie Kopke, David and Christina Krol, Shirley Paddock, John Pijanowski, Steve Raizes, Pranay and Erin Reddy, Greg and Megan Robinson, Liz and Kayvan Sadeghi, Nathan and Chris Seay,

David and Sara Schivell, Kurt and Kat Schliemann, Colleen Schwartz, Jon and Oriyan Schwartz, Sheraz and Sarah Shere, Dan and Maria Smith, Pete Smith, Tim and Christina Sobon, David and Wilma Solomon, and Sandro and Jen Vitaglione.

As always, my incredible family managed to keep me going throughout this project. My in-laws, Lorne and Marg Hamilton, have always made me feel like a son instead of a son-in-law, while Marlo, Chris, and Mason Gaddis have welcomed me warmly into their family as well. My sisters, Amy and Lisa, and my brother, Eric, have always been there to lift my spirits when I needed it and to put me in my place when I needed that. Their spouses, Jim Hubbuch, Eric Link, and Shala Kruse, have given me a great deal of encouragement, while Emily Hubbuch, Megan Hubbuch, Kelsie Hubbuch, Caitlin Carter, Reece Kruse, and Bailey Kruse have given me nothing but joy. My mother, Mary Jean Kruse, has been my greatest cheerleader and source of support for as long as I can remember. Sadly, my father, Mike Kruse, passed away in 2012. I have missed him every day since.

I owe my greatest debt to my wife and my best friend, Lindsay. I am constantly amazed at everything she does, and does so well. Accomplished in her own career, she is every bit a committed partner and a devoted mother. She has tolerated my absence when the writing was going well and, worse, my presence when it was not. Most of all, she has given me the two greatest gifts I will ever receive: our daughter, Maggie, and our son, Sam. I began researching this project just before Maggie was born, and then started writing soon before Sam completed our family. This book has been in the background their entire lives; it seems the least I can do is not just dedicate it to them but dedicate myself to them for the rest of my life too. I love the three of you more than words can say.

NOTES

ABBREVIATIONS

Periodicals

BG	*Boston Globe*
BS	*Baltimore Sun*
CR	*Congressional Record*
CSM	*Christian Science Monitor*
CT	*Chicago Tribune*
LAT	*Los Angeles Times*
NYHT	*New York Herald Tribune*
NYT	*New York Times*
ST	*Seattle Times*
WP	*Washington Post*
WSJ	*Wall Street Journal*

Archival Collections

AES   Adlai E. Stevenson Papers, Seeley G. Mudd Manuscript Library, Princeton University, Princeton, New Jersey

ACHF   Ad Council Historical Files, University Archives, University of Illinois, Champaign, Illinois

ACLU   American Civil Liberties Union Records, Seeley G. Mudd Manuscript Library, Princeton University, Princeton, New Jersey

AL   Records of the American Legion, Video Collection, Library and Museum, American Legion National Headquarters, Indianapolis, Indiana

ALM   Papers of the Americanism Division, Records of the American Legion (Microfilm), Library and Museum, American Legion National Headquarters, Indianapolis, Indiana

AS-DDE   Administration Series, Ann Whitman Files, Dwight D. Eisenhower Papers, Dwight D. Eisenhower Presidential Museum and Library, Abilene, Kansas

AUSCS	Americans United for Separation of Church and State Records, Seeley G. Mudd Manuscript Library, Princeton University, Princeton, New Jersey
AW	Arthur White Collection, Archives and Special Collections, Odum Library, Valdosta State University, Valdosta, Georgia
AWR	A. Willis Robertson Papers, Special Collections, Earl Gregg Swem Library, College of William and Mary, Williamsburg, Virginia
BB	Bruce Barton Papers, Wisconsin Historical Society Archives, Madison, Wisconsin
BGCA	Billy Graham Evangelical Association, Crusade Activities Collection, Billy Graham Center Archives, Wheaton, Illinois
BGTO	Billy Graham Evangelical Association Team Office, Executive Assistant Team Activities Records, Billy Graham Center Archives, Wheaton, Illinois
CBD	Cecil B. DeMille Papers, L. Tom Perry Special Collections Library, Harold B. Lee Library, Brigham Young University, Provo, Utah
CDJ	C. D. Jackson Papers, Dwight D. Eisenhower Presidential Library and Museum, Abilene, Kansas
CEB	Charles E. Bennett Papers, Special and Area Studies Collections, George A. Smathers Libraries, University of Florida, Gainesville, Florida
CF-DDE	Central Files, Dwight D. Eisenhower Papers, Dwight D. Eisenhower Presidential Museum and Library, Abilene, Kansas
CS-DDE	Cabinet Series, Ann Whitman Files, Dwight D. Eisenhower Papers, Dwight D. Eisenhower Presidential Museum and Library, Abilene, Kansas
CUAEL	Collection of Underground, Alternative, and Extremist Literature, Department of Special Collections, University of California, Los Angeles, California
DB	Don Belding Papers, Southwest Collection, Special Collections Library, Texas Tech University, Lubbock, Texas
DSB	Dorothy Stimson Bullitt Papers, Special Collections, University of Washington Libraries, Seattle, Washington
EH	Earl Hankamer Papers, Billy Graham Center Archives, Wheaton, Illinois
EMD	Everett M. Dirksen Papers, The Dirksen Congressional Center, Pekin, Illinois
FAS	Fred A. Seaton Papers, Dwight D. Eisenhower Presidential Library and Museum, Abilene, Kansas
FBI-CACC	Federal Bureau of Investigation Files, "Christian Anti-Communism Crusade," Los Angeles File # 62–4580
FEF	Frederic E. Fox Papers, Dwight D. Eisenhower Presidential Library and Museum, Abilene, Kansas
FF	Fred Friendly Papers, Rare Book and Manuscript Library, Butler Library, Columbia University, New York, New York
FJB	Frank John Becker Papers, M. E. Grenander Department of Special Collections and Archives, State University of New York, Albany, New York
FOE	Fraternal Order of Eagles Museum, Grove City, Ohio

GF-DDE	General Files, Dwight D. Eisenhower Presidential Papers, Dwight D. Eisenhower Presidential Library and Museum, Abilene, Kansas
HD	Harold Dudley Papers, Special Collections, University of Maryland Libraries, College Park, Maryland
HFP	H. Franklin Paschall Papers, Southern Baptist Historical Library and Archives, Nashville, Tennessee
HH	Individual Correspondence Files, Post-Presidential Period, Herbert Hoover Papers, Herbert Hoover Presidential Library and Archives, West Branch, Iowa
HLB	Hugo L. Black Papers, Manuscript Division, Library of Congress, Washington, D.C.
HST	Harry S. Truman Presidential Papers, Harry S. Truman Presidential Library and Museum, Independence, Missouri
JCI	James C. Ingebretsen Papers, Special Collections & University Archives, University of Oregon Libraries, Eugene, Oregon
JFD	John Foster Dulles Papers, Seeley G. Mudd Manuscript Library, Princeton University, Princeton, New Jersey
JHP	J. Howard Pew Papers, Hagley Museum and Library, Wilmington, Delaware
JML	James M. Lambie Jr. Records, Dwight D. Eisenhower Presidential Library and Museum, Abilene, Kansas
JWM	John Willard and Alice Sheets Marriott Papers, Special Collections and Archives, J. Willard Marriott Library, University of Utah, Salt Lake City, Utah
JWT-AF	J. Walter Thompson Company, Account Files, Rare Book, Manuscript, and Special Collections Library, Duke University, Durham, North Carolina
JWT-NC	J. Walter Thompson Company, Newsletter Collection, Rare Book, Manuscript, and Special Collections Library, Duke University, Durham, North Carolina
KC	Knights of Columbus Archives, Knights of Columbus Museum, New Haven, Connecticut
KOW	K. Owen White Papers, Southern Baptist Historical Library and Archives, Nashville, Tennessee
NAE	National Association of Evangelicals Records, Special Collections and Archives, Wheaton College, Wheaton, Illinois
NAM	National Association of Manufacturers Collection, Hagley Museum and Library, Wilmington, Delaware
NS-DDE	Name Series, Dwight D. Eisenhower Papers (Ann Whitman File), Dwight D. Eisenhower Presidential Library and Museum, Abilene, Kansas
OF-DDE	Official Files, White House Central Files, Dwight D. Eisenhower Records as President, Dwight D. Eisenhower Presidential Library and Museum, Abilene, Kansas
OH-DDE	Oral History Collection, Dwight D. Eisenhower Presidential Library and Museum, Abilene, Kansas

PPF-DDE   President's Personal File, Records as President, White House Central File, Dwight D. Eisenhower Presidential Library and Museum, Abilene, Kansas

RF   Ralph Flanders Collection, Special Collections Research Center, Syracuse University, Syracuse, New York

RFF   Records of the Fellowship Foundation, Billy Graham Center Archives, Wheaton, Illinois

RM-RMN   Religious Matters Series, White House Central Files, Richard M. Nixon Presidential Library and Museum, Yorba Linda, California

ROF   Robert O. Ferm Papers, Billy Graham Evangelical Association, Billy Graham Center Archives, Wheaton, Illinois

RPPL-DDE   Reports to the President on Pending Legislation, White House Records Office, Dwight D. Eisenhower Presidential Papers, Dwight D. Eisenhower Presidential Library and Museum, Abilene, Kansas

RRF   Reading Room Files, Billy Graham Center Archives, Wheaton, Illinois

SBC-CLC   Southern Baptist Convention, Christian Life Commission Resource Files, Southern Baptist Historical Library and Archives, Nashville, Tennessee

SBC-ECR   Southern Baptist Convention, Executive Committee Records, Southern Baptist Historical Library and Archives, Nashville, Tennessee

SRB   J. Walter Thompson Company, Sidney Ralph Bernstein Company History Files, 1873–1964, Rare Book, Manuscript, and Special Collection Library, Duke University, Durham, North Carolina

SS-DDE   Speech Series, Ann Whitman Files, Dwight D. Eisenhower Papers, Dwight D. Eisenhower Presidential Museum and Library, Abilene, Kansas

SW   Sinclair Weeks Papers, Rauner Special Collections Library, Dartmouth College, Hanover, New Hampshire

TCC   Tom C. Clark Papers, Tarlton Law Library, University of Texas, Austin, Texas

USCOC   US Chamber of Commerce Records, Hagley Museum and Library, Wilmington, Delaware

WH   Willis Haymaker Collection, Billy Graham Center Archives, Wheaton, Illinois

WOD   William O. Douglas Papers, Manuscript Division, Library of Congress, Washington, D.C.

INTRODUCTION

1. *NYT,* 5 June 1952; *WP,* 6 November 1952; Billy Graham, *Just as I Am: The Autobiography of Billy Graham* (San Francisco: Harper, 1997), 199.

2. Mrs. Joseph W. Barker to Hugh Scott, 19 December 1952, Box 737, OF-DDE; *WP,* 21 January 1949, 20 January 1953; Sherman Adams, *Firsthand Report: The Story of the Eisenhower Administration* (New York: Harper and Brothers, 1961), 65.

3. Norman Grubb, *Modern Viking: The Story of Abraham Vereide, Pioneer in Christian Leadership* (Grand Rapids, MI: Zondervan, 1961), 111; Graham, *Just as I Am*, 199; *NYT*, 20 January 1953.

4. *LAT*, 21 January 1953; Dwight D. Eisenhower, inaugural address, 20 January 1953, *Public Papers of the Presidents of the United States: Dwight D. Eisenhower, 1953* (Washington, DC: US Government Printing Office, 1960), 1; Grubb, *Modern Viking*, 131; "President Eisenhower's Inaugural Prayer," pamphlet, Box 102, JFD.

5. Dwight D. Eisenhower, *Mandate for Change, 1953–1956* (Garden City, NY: Doubleday, 1963), 100; Eisenhower, inaugural address, 20 January 1953, 2–3; *CT*, 21 January 1953; *BG*, 20–21 January 1953; *NYT*, 19 January 1953.

6. Program, International Council for Christian Leadership, Annual Christian Action Conference, 5–9 February 1953, Box 504, RFF; "The Breakfast Groups" newsletter, March 1953, RRF; Dwight D. Eisenhower, "Remarks at the Dedicatory Prayer Breakfast of the International Christian Leadership," 5 February 1953, *Public Papers of the Presidents of the United States: Dwight D. Eisenhower, 1953* (Washington, DC: US Government Printing Office, 1960), 37–38; Nancy Gibbs and Michael Duffy, *The Preacher and the Presidents: Billy Graham in the White House* (New York: Hachette, 2007), 43.

7. Historians have chronicled at length the "moral establishment" of Protestant piety that informed and inflected the United States from its founding, of course, but this religious sensibility was never codified or made nearly as concrete in earlier eras as it would be in the modern one. See Isaac Kramnick and R. Laurence Moore, *The Godless Constitution: The Case Against Religious Correctness* (New York: W. W. Norton, 1997); David Sehat, *The Myth of American Religious Freedom* (New York: Oxford University Press, 2011).

8. For recent examples of the growing literature on the religious nature of the Cold War, see Andrew Preston, *Sword of the Spirit, Shield of Faith: Religion in American War and Diplomacy* (New York: Knopf, 2012); Jonathan Herzog, *The Spiritual-Industrial Complex: America's Religious Battle Against Communism in the Early Cold War* (New York: Oxford University Press, 2011); T. Jeremy Gunn, *Spiritual Weapons: The Cold War and the Forging of an American National Religion* (Westport, CT: Praeger, 2008); William Inboden, *Religion and American Foreign Policy, 1945–1960: The Soul of Containment* (New York: Cambridge University Press, 2008).

9. A. Roy Eckhardt, *The Surge of Piety in America: An Appraisal* (New York: Association Press, 1958), 22–23; Stephen J. Whitfield, *The Culture of the Cold War*, 2nd ed. (Baltimore: Johns Hopkins University Press, 1996), 83; Leo Calvin Rosten, *Religions in America* (New York: Simon and Schuster, 1963), 327.

10. Steven B. Epstein, "Rethinking the Constitutionality of Ceremonial Deism," *Columbia Law Review* (December 1996), 2091; 343 US 312–313.

CHAPTER 1: "FREEDOM UNDER GOD"

1. *NYT*, 8 December 1940; *NYHT*, 14 December 1940.

2. Wendy L. Wall, *Inventing the "American Way": The Politics of Consensus from the New Deal to the Civil Rights Movement* (New York: Oxford University Press, 2008),

53–54; Kim Phillips-Fein, *Invisible Hands: The Making of the Conservative Movement from the New Deal to Reagan* (New York: Norton, 2009), 13–14; Elizabeth A. Fones-Wolf, *Selling Free Enterprise: The Business Assault on Labor and Liberalism, 1945–1960* (Urbana: University of Illinois Press, 1994), 25–26.

3. Frederick Rudolph, "The American Liberty League, 1934–1940," *American Historical Review,* 56:1 (October 1950): 20; *NYT,* 25 August 1934; William E. Leuchtenburg, *The FDR Years: On Roosevelt and His Legacy* (New York: Columbia University Press, 1995), 124; transcript, Press Conference #137, Executive Offices of the White House, 24 August 1934, in *Complete Presidential Press Conferences of Franklin D. Roosevelt* (New York: Da Capo Press, 1972), 4:17–18.

4. For an excellent overview of Roosevelt's religious faith, see Andrew Preston, *Sword of the Spirit, Shield of Faith: Religion in American War and Diplomacy* (New York: Knopf, 2012), 315–326.

5. James MacGregor Burns, *The Lion and the Fox* (New York: Harcourt, Brace and World, 1956), 476; Samuel I. Rosenman, *Working with Roosevelt* (New York: Harper and Brothers, 1952), 23; transcript, Franklin D. Roosevelt, address accepting presidential nomination at the Democratic National Convention in Chicago, 2 July 1932, and transcript, Franklin D. Roosevelt, inaugural address, 4 March 1933, located in John T. Woolley and Gerhard Peters, American Presidency Project (http://www.presidency.ucsb.edu/ws); Alison Collis Greene, "No Depression in Heaven: Religion and Economic Crisis in Memphis and the Delta, 1929–1941," Ph.D. diss., Yale University, 2010, 138.

6. James A. Morone, *Hellfire Nation: The Politics of Sin in American History* (New Haven, CT: Yale University Press, 2003), 350–377; *NYT,* 13 July 1933; Jonathan Herzog, *The Spiritual-Industrial Complex: America's Religious Battle Against Communism in the Early Cold War* (New York: Oxford University Press, 2011), 33.

7. *CSM,* 7 December 1940; *NYT,* 8 December 1940; *WSJ,* 9 and 10 December 1940; transcript, H. W. Prentis Jr., "Our American Heritage," speech before the general session of the US Chamber of Commerce, 4 May 1939, reprinted in *Vital Speeches of the Day,* 15 June 1939.

8. Ann Fields, "Apostle to Millionaires," *Coronet,* August 1944, 84–85.

9. Ralph Lord Roy, *Apostles of Discord: A Study of Organized Bigotry and Disruption on the Fringes of Protestantism* (Boston: Beacon Press, 1953); Chadwick Hall, "America's Conservative Revolution," *Antioch Review,* Summer 1955, 207; James W. Fifield Jr., *The Single Path* (Englewood Cliffs, NJ: Prentice-Hall, 1957), 87.

10. Darren Dochuk, *From Bible Belt to Sun Belt: Plain-Folk Religion, Grassroots Politics, and the Rise of Evangelical Conservatism* (New York: Norton, 2010).

11. *LAT,* 14 December 1934, 17 September 1938; Fields, "Apostle to Millionaires," 85–87; James W. Fifield Jr. with Bill Youngs, *The Tall Preacher* (Los Angeles: Pepperdine University Press, 1977), 94–109; program, Sunday Evening Club, n.d. [1946], Box 914, CBD.

12. Fields, "Apostle to Millionaires," 87; *LAT,* 18 May 1934, 31 October 1934, 25 April 1941; *Time,* 25 April 1927; *NYT,* 22 November 1942.

13. Fifield, *The Tall Preacher,* 95, 112–113; *Time,* 3 August 1942.

14. Brooks R. Walker, *The Christian Fright Peddlers* (New York: Doubleday, 1964), 137; Fifield, *The Tall Preacher,* 141.

15. *LAT,* 23 December 1939.

16. Roy, *Apostles of Discord,* 286; Tenth Fall Bulletin, Spiritual Mobilization, n.d. [1944], 2, copy in Box 20, BB.

17. Fifield, "Religious Ideals and the Government's Program," number 9, series III, 25 July 1937, copy in Box 59, HH; Fifield, "America's Future," number 5, series IV [May 1938], Box 59, HH.

18. Herbert Hoover to Fifield, 28 April 1938, Box 59, HH; Fifield to Hoover, 31 October 1938, Box 59, HH; Fifield, "Christian Ministers and America's Future," n.d. [October 1938], Box 59, HH; Hoover to Fifield, 10 November 1938, Box 59, HH.

19. Fifield to Hoover, 14 November 1938, Box 59, HH; Fifield to Hoover, 14 May 1941, Box 59, HH; Fifield, "A Nation Being Led to War," number 5, series VII, May 1941, copy in Box 59, HH.

20. *LAT,* 15, 17 June 1940; Tenth Fall Bulletin, Spiritual Mobilization, n.d. [1944], 6, 16, copy in Box 20, BB.

21. Eckhard V. Toy Jr., "Spiritual Mobilization: The Failure of an Ultraconservative Ideal in the 1950's," *Pacific Northwest Quarterly* 61, no. 2 (April 1970): 78; Fifield to Bruce Barton, 8 September 1945, Box 20, BB.

22. Fifield to J. Howard Pew, 14 September 1944, Box 6, JHP; Tenth Fall Bulletin, Spiritual Mobilization, n.d. [1944], 2, 3, 5, 11–12, 15, copy in Box 20, BB.

23. Fifield to Pew, 17 March 1944, Box 6, JHP; Fifield to Pew, 16 January 1945, Box 8, JHP; Fifield to Pew, 15 December 1944, Box 8, JHP; Pew to H. W. Prentis Jr., 13 January 1945, Box 8, JHP; Prentis to Pew, 15 January 1945, Box 8, JHP; Prentis to John Ballantyne, 15 January 1945, Box 8, JHP.

24. *Philadelphia Inquirer,* 27 April 1992.

25. Pew would spend much of his energy in the postwar era working within the Presbyterian Church and the National Council of Churches to reverse their trend toward liberalism. See E. V. Toy Jr., "The National Lay Committee and the National Council of Churches: A Case Study of Protestants in Conflict," *American Quarterly* 21 (Summer 1969): 190–209.

26. Pew to Alfred P. Haake, 6 April 1948, Box 235, JHP; Niels Bjerre-Poulsen, *Right Face: Organizing the American Conservative Movement, 1945–1965* (Copenhagen: Narayana Press, 2002), 105; Fifield to Pew, 28 September 1944, Box 6, JHP.

27. Pew to Fifield, 10 November 1944, Box 6, JHP; flyer, "Spiritual Mobilization," n.d. [1944], Box 6, JHP; Pew to Haake, 13 July 1945, Box 235, JHP.

28. *NYHT,* 22 September 1934, 14 September 1938; *BG,* 18 March 1950; *NYT,* 3 November 1961.

29. Haake to Pew, 5 February 1945, and Pew to Haake, 8 February 1945, Box 235, JHP; Alfred P. Haake, "Outline for Spiritual Mobilization," 13 January 1945, Box 235, JHP.

30. Haake to Fifield, 13 August 1945, Box 235, JHP; *Spiritual Mobilization in Action: A Crusade for Freedom,* booklet, n.d. [September 1945], copy in Box 59, HH; Wall, *Inventing the "American Way,"* 77–87.

31. Albert W. Hawkes to Pew, 18 March 1946, Box 10, JHP; Dochuk, *From Bible Belt to Sun Belt,* 116–117; Philips-Fein, *Invisible Hands,* 53–56; Fifield, "Looking Towards a Better World," 7 May 1946, 5, copy in Box 10, JHP; Fifield to Pew, 7 January 1947, Box 15, JHP.

32. Fifield to Pew, 27 February 1947, Box 15, JHP; Fifield, "Director to Representatives," *Spiritual Mobilization,* n.d. [1946], 1, in Box 10, JHP.

33. Letter from Rev. E. Ray Burchell, Chester, Connecticut, *Spiritual Mobilization,* n.d. [1946], 4, in Box 10, JHP; "What Can I Do About It?," *Spiritual Mobilization,* 15 April 1947, 3, in Box 15, JHP.

34. *LAT,* 15 July 1947; *CT,* 16 August 1947; *Norfolk Journal and Guide,* 11 October 1947; *BG,* 11 October 1947; Table 1, *U.S. Census of Population, 1950,* part IV, volume I (Washington, DC: Government Printing Office, 1951); "About National Preaching Program," *Spiritual Mobilization,* 28 November 1947, 3, in Box 15, JHP.

35. Fifield to Pew, 4 September 1947, Box 15, JHP; Pew, Form Letter Draft, n.d. [September 1947], Box 15, JHP; Fifield to Pew, 24 September 1947, Box 15, JHP; Spiritual Mobilization Contributors List, n.d. [September 1947], Box 15, JHP; Fifield to Alfred P. Sloan Jr., 16 March 1949, Box 54, JCI; Pew to William M. Rand, 22 October 1947, Box 15, JHP; Pew to Otto D. Donnell, 22 October 1947, Box 15, JHP.

36. Carey McWilliams, "Battle for the Clergy: The Story of 'Spiritual Mobilization,' a Growing Protestant Movement," *The Nation,* 7 February 1948, 150–152.

37. Charles M. White to "Dear Friend," 31 March 1948, Box 19, JHP; Patsy Peppers to Pew, 24 May 1948, Box 19, JHP; Fifield to Pew, 2 August 1948, Box 19, JHP.

38. Fifield to Pew, 21 March 1949, Box 24, JHP; Fifield to Martin H. Hannum, 20 January 1950, Box 54, JCI; Pew to Fifield, 22 November 1950, Box 27, JHP.

39. *The Freedom Story,* pamphlet, n.d. [1949], Box 27, JHP; Ingebretsen to Fifield, 31 January 1950, Box 54, JCI.

40. See episode list and specific summaries for "The South Comes Back" (episode #39B) and "Boy Scouts of America" (episode #40B), available at Radio Gold Index (http://radiogoldindex.com/cgi-local/p2.cgi?ProgramName=The+Freedom+Story; accessed 7 March 2011).

41. Fifield to Bruce Barton, 8 November 1949, Box 20, BB; Fifield to Pew, 30 March 1949, Box 24, JHP; "Memorandum from Dr. Fifield," 2 September 1949, Box 24, JHP; *Faith and Freedom* 1 (June 1950): 14; Fifield to Hoover, 31 October 1951, Box 59, HH.

42. Eckard V. Toy, "*Faith and Freedom,* 1949–1960," in *The Conservative Press in Twentieth-Century America,* ed. Ronald Lora and William Henry Longton (Westport, CT: Greenwood Press, 1999), 154–156; Philips-Fein, *Invisible Hands,* 81–83; Donald T. Critchlow, *Phyllis Schlafly and Grassroots Conservatism: A Woman's Crusade* (Princeton, NJ: Princeton University Press, 2005), 25–26; Judith Thurman, "Wilder Women," *New Yorker,* 10 August 2009, 74–80; Rose Wilder Lane, *Give Me Liberty* (n.p.: Liberty Library, 1945), 56.

43. Haake to Pew, 5 February 1945, Box 235, JHP; "The Editor Comments," *Faith and Freedom,* December 1949, 1–3.

44. "The Director's Page," *Faith and Freedom,* September 1951, 12; "The Director's Page," *Faith and Freedom,* December 1949, 4; Roy, *Apostles of Discord,* 292; "The Director's Page," *Faith and Freedom,* September 1951, 12.

45. "The Editor Comments," *Faith and Freedom,* May 1952, 2; Irving E. Howard, "The Origins of the Social Gospel," *Faith and Freedom,* May 1952, 3–7; Henry C. Link, "A Plea for Religious Intolerance," *Faith and Freedom,* October 1950, 3–5.

46. George S. Benson, "The Conch Island Disaster," *Faith and Freedom,* June 1950, 3–4; Ludwig von Mises, "The Alleged Injustice of Capitalism," *Faith and Freedom,* June 1950, 5–8; R. J. Rushdoony, "Noncompetitive Life," *Faith and Freedom,* June 1950, 9–10; Allen W. Rucker, "Human Rights and Property Rights," *Faith and Freedom,* June 1950, 12–13; *Faith and Freedom,* June 1950, 1, 15.

47. Fifield to Alfred P. Sloan [Jr.], 29 November 1950, Box 54, JCI.

48. See, for instance, "The Director's Page," *Faith and Freedom,* March 1951, 14.

49. *Los Angeles Examiner,* 8 June 1951.

50. Committee to Proclaim Liberty, press release, 11 June 1951, Box 69, JCI.

51. Pew to Fifield, 22 May 1951, Box 28, JHP; Committee to Proclaim Liberty, press release, 11 June 1951, Box 69, JCI; *LAT,* 1 July 1951; Arthur M. Schlesinger, *The Coming of the New Deal, 1933–1935* (Cambridge, MA: Houghton Mifflin, 1958), 411; Charles K. McFarland, *Roosevelt, Lewis and the New Deal* (Fort Worth: Texas Christian University Press, 1970), 37.

52. "The Preface to the Declaration of Independence," *Faith and Freedom,* June 1951, 3.

53. Committee to Proclaim Liberty, booklet, Box 737, OF-DDE.

54. *Faith and Freedom,* September 1951, 6; "Proclaim Liberty" packet, n.d. [1951], Box 69, JCI. The worship calendars were available on short notice, but Spiritual Mobilization still claimed it answered requests for more than seventy thousand within a few days' time. See "The Story Behind the Committee to Proclaim Liberty," n.d. [1951], Box 69, JCI.

55. "The Story Behind the Committee to Proclaim Liberty"; "Proclaim Liberty Throughout All the Land," pamphlet, n.d. [1952], Box 69, JCI; *Faith and Freedom,* September 1951, 6–7.

56. Kenneth W. Sollitt, "Freedom Under God," *Faith and Freedom,* September 1951, 8–11.

57. Donald Hayne to Cecil B. DeMille, telegram, 24 May 1951, Box 945, CBD; transcript, "Mr. Ingebretsen's Telephone Conversation with Mr. Merle Jones and Mr. S. M. Nicholson of Columbia Broadcasting System," 8 June 1951, Box 69, JCI.

58. Memorandum and handwritten note, Box 945, CBD; transcript, "Telephone Conversation Between Mr. McCray and Mr. Ingebretsen," 12 June 1951, Box 69, JCI; "Proclaim Liberty" packet, n.d. [1951], Box 69, JCI; "The Story Behind the Committee to Proclaim Liberty"; transcript, General Matthew B. Ridgway, "Freedom Under God," 1 July 1951, Box 69, JCI.

59. News clippings, Box 69, JCI.

60. Similar "Freedom Under God" proclamations were issued by the governors of the states of Arkansas, Connecticut, Delaware, Georgia, Idaho, Indiana, Maine, Maryland, Minnesota, Mississippi, Nevada, New York, Ohio, Rhode Island, South Dakota, Utah, and Washington, as well as the territory of Hawaii, and also by the mayors of Birmingham, Charlotte, Cheyenne, Chicago, Indianapolis, Minneapolis, New Orleans, New York City, Norfolk, Phoenix, Providence, St. Louis, Seattle, and Wilmington. See "Proclaim Liberty" packet; "The Story Behind the Committee to Proclaim Liberty"; and transcript, "Telephone Call to Mr. Ingebretsen from Mr. Gamble," 12 June 1951, all in Box 69, JCI.

61. News clippings, Box 69, JCI; "The Story Behind the Committee to Proclaim Liberty."

62. "The Story Behind the Committee to Proclaim Liberty"; Fifield to Pew, 9 November 1951, Box 30, JHP; Fifield to Hoover, 9 November 1951, Box 59, HH.

CHAPTER 2: THE GREAT CRUSADES

1. Billy Graham, "We Need Revival," text reprinted in Billy Graham, *Revival in Our Time* (Wheaton, IL: Van Kampen Press, 1950), 69–80; *LAT,* 26 September 1949; *Los Angeles Sentinel,* 29 September 1949.

2. Graham, "We Need Revival," 72–73; *LAT,* 29 September, 31 October, 21 November 1949; Marshall Frady, *Billy Graham: A Parable of American Righteousness* (New York: Simon and Schuster, 1979), 201–204; "A Spiritual Upheaval! The 1949 History-Making Billy Graham Revival in Los Angeles," pamphlet, Box 1, WH.

3. For recent examples of the growing literature on the religious traits of the Cold War, see Preston, *Sword of the Spirit, Shield of Faith*; Herzog, *Spiritual-Industrial Complex*; Gunn, *Spiritual Weapons*; Inboden, *Religion and American Foreign Policy.*

4. Billy Graham, "God Before Gold," *Nation's Business,* September 1954, 34 (emphasis in original).

5. William Martin, *A Prophet with Honor: The Billy Graham Story* (New York: William Morrow, 1991), 140; John Corry, "God, Country, and Billy Graham," *Harper's Magazine,* February 1969, 34.

6. James L. McAllister, "Evangelical Faith and Billy Graham," *Social Action,* March 1953, 23; William C. Loughlin, *Billy Graham: Revivalist in a Secular Age* (New York: Ronald Press, 1960), 99–100.

7. Loughlin, *Billy Graham,* 99, 102–103.

8. Transcript, Franklin D. Roosevelt, inaugural address, 20 January 1937, located in Woolley and Peters, American Presidency Project (http://www.presidency.ucsb.edu/ws); Abraham Vereide to Franklin Roosevelt, 5 February 1937, President's Personal File, Container 231, Franklin D. Roosevelt Library, cited in Ronald Isetti, "The Moneychangers and the Temple: FDR, American Civil Religion, and the New Deal," *Presidential Studies Quarterly,* Summer 1996, 682.

9. *ST,* 20 October 1917, 29 May 1927, 11 September 1955; Jeff Sharlet, *The Family: The Secret Fundamentalism at the Heart of American Power* (New York: HarperCollins, 2008): 96; Grubb, *Modern Viking,* 47–49.

10. William E. Leuchtenburg, *Franklin D. Roosevelt and the New Deal* (New York: Harper, 1963), 113–114; Sharlet, *The Family,* 101–108; Kevin Starr, *Endangered Dreams: The Great Depression in California* (New York: Oxford University Press, 1997), 93–120.

11. Richard C. Berner, *Seattle 1921–1940: From Boom to Bust* (Seattle: Charles Press, 1992), 333–348; *ST,* 27 May 1934; *Seattle Post-Intelligencer,* 13 May 1934; Bruce Nelson, *Workers on the Waterfront: Seamen, Longshoremen, and Unionism in the 1930s* (Urbana: University of Illinois Press, 1990), 190.

12. Grubb, *Modern Viking,* 54–56; *ST,* 15 December 1943; "Christian Leaders: On the Way Up," *Christian Life,* August 1955, clipping in Box 456, RFF; Sharlet, *The Family,* 111.

13. Grubb, *Modern Viking*, 57; Berner, *Seattle*, 349–355, 398–401; *LAT*, 10 March 1938; *NYT*, 10 March 1938; *WSJ*, 10 March 1938; Roger Morris, *Richard Milhous Nixon: The Rise of an American Politician* (New York: Henry Holt, 1991), 726.

14. *ST*, 14 July 1935; "A National Program for City Chapel, Inc.," report, n.d. [1942], Box 496, RFF; "The Breakfast Groups, Information and Invitation," copy, n.d. [1943], Box 496, RFF; Grubb, *Modern Viking*, 66; Vereide to Walter Bailey, 26 March 1946, Box 497, RFF.

15. "The Breakfast Group," pamphlet, n.d. [1942], RRF; Grubb, *Modern Viking*, 69–70; House of Representatives Breakfast Group, program, March 1944, RRF; House of Representatives Breakfast Group, program, September 1945, RRF; United States Senate Breakfast Group, program, May 1945, RRF.

16. The presidency of the House prayer group largely rotated between Democratic and Republican members, for instance, but of the Democrats who held the leadership post in the years between 1942 and 1958, seven of the eight represented southern states. See James B. Utt to Le Roy Anderson, 15 March 1959, Box 407, RFF.

17. House of Representatives Breakfast Group, program, March 1944, RRF; Grubb, *Modern Viking*, 72.

18. Floyd M. Downs to Vereide, 23 March 1945, Box 497, RFF; Vereide to Downs, 28 March 1945, Box 497, RFF; Harold H. Burton to Downs, 29 March 1945, Box 497, RFF.

19. Grubb, *Modern Viking*, 71, 74–75, 82, 87, 89; Raymond Willis and Vereide to Joseph N. Pew Jr., 14 June 1945, and J. N. Pew Jr. to Vereide, 18 June 1945, Box 497, RFF.

20. Vereide to Frank [Carlson?], 29 June 1946, Box 497, RFF; Sharlet, *The Family*, 156–157; *The Breakfast Groups Informer*, January 1946, RRF.

21. Grubb, *Modern Viking*, 111.

22. Vereide to Alexander Wiley and A. Willis Robertson, 12 January 1950, Box 466, RFF; Drew Pearson, "A Prayer Dissolves Party Lines," *WP*, 5 February 1950.

23. Pearson, "A Prayer Dissolves Party Lines"; John Phillips to Vereide, 9 August 1948 and 10 August 1948, Box 407, RFF; Vereide to Phillips, 19 August 1948, Box 407, RFF; *Christianity Today*, 14 March 1960; "Christian Leaders: On the Way Up"; *1950 Program of the Annual Meeting of International Christian Leadership, Inc.*, Box 504, RFF; *Christian Leadership News*, August 1952, copy in Box 106, RF.

24. [Vereide] to Members of the House of Representatives Breakfast Group, 15 August 1949, Box 407, RFF.

25. Frady, *Billy Graham*, 216; Martin, *Prophet with Honor*, 123–124, 133; Gibbs and Duffy, *The Preacher and the Presidents*, 6–7; Greater Atlanta Evangelistic Crusade, pamphlet, n.d. [1950], Box 1, WH; *CSM*, 13 April 1950; *LAT*, 14 September 1950; Greater Fort Worth Evangelistic Crusade, statistical summary, n.d. [March 1951], Box 1, WH; Greater Fort Worth Evangelistic Crusade, press release, n.d. [February 1951], Box 1, WH.

26. Bryan Burrough, *The Big Rich: The Rise and Fall of the Greatest Texas Oil Fortunes* (New York: Penguin, 2009), 251; Robert A. Caro, *The Path to Power* (New York: Vintage Books, 1981), 617; John Connally with Mickey Herskowitz, *In History's Shadow: An American Odyssey* (New York: Hyperion, 1994), 139; James Reston

Jr., *The Lone Star: The Life of John Connally* (New York: Harper & Row, 1989), 159; Robert A. Caro, *Master of the Senate* (New York: Knopf, 2002), 305.

27. Reston, *Lone Star,* 159; Randall B. Woods, *LBJ: Architect of American Ambition* (New York: Free Press, 2006), 145; Alfred Steinberg, *Sam Rayburn: A Biography* (New York: Hawthorne Books, 1975), 273; Frady, *Billy Graham,* 231–232; Sam Kashner and Jennifer MacNair, *The Bad and The Beautiful: Hollywood in the Fifties* (New York: Norton, 2003), 123–124; promotional booklet for *Oiltown, U.S.A.*, n.d. [1954], Folder 3, EH.

28. Loughlin, *Billy Graham,* 97–98; McAllister, "Evangelical Faith and Billy Graham," 23; Billy Graham, "God Is My Witness," *McCall's,* June 1964, 64.

29. Frady, *Billy Graham,* 240; Martin, *A Prophet with Honor,* 131–133.

30. Merle Miller, *Plain Speaking: An Oral Biography of Harry S. Truman* (New York: Berkley, 1974), 363; Gibbs and Duffy, *The Preacher and the Presidents,* 20.

31. Martin, *A Prophet with Honor,* 144; *WP,* 15 July 1950; Loughlin, *Billy Graham,* 108–109.

32. Billy Graham to "Dear Pastor," 5 January 1952, Box 1, WH; invitation, Business Men's Luncheon Meetings, Greater Washington Evangelistic Crusade, n.d. [1951], Box 1, WH; *WP,* 5 May 1951; A. S. Herlong Jr., Clarence G. Burton, Katherine St. George, and Vereide to Members of the House Breakfast Group, 14 December 1951, Box 504, RFF; Donald Scott McAlpine, "Mr. Christian of Washington," *United Evangelical Action,* 1 July 1954, 6; Gibbs and Duffy, *The Preacher and the Presidents,* 26–27.

33. *WP,* 13, 21, 26–27 January, 16 February 1952; prayer card, n.d. [1952], Box 1, WH; Martin E. Marty, *Under God, Indivisible: Modern American Religion* (Chicago: University of Chicago Press, 1996), 3:153; "Rockin' the Capitol," *Time,* 13 March 1952; *LAT,* 24 January 1952.

34. Gibbs and Duffy, *The Preacher and the Presidents,* 27; William Martin, *With God on Our Side: The Rise of the Religious Right in America* (New York: Broadway Books, 1996), 31; *CSM,* 4 February 1952; *BG,* 4 February 1952; *LAT,* 4 February 1952; *WP,* 4 February 1952.

35. Martin, *A Prophet with Honor,* 132; Joan M. Morris to Harry S. Truman, 31 July 1950, Box 12, White House Central Files, Public Opinion Mail File, HST.

36. Diary entry, 18 February 1952, in *Off the Record: The Private Papers of Harry S. Truman,* ed. Robert H. Ferrell (New York: Harper & Row, 1980), 239. In the King James Version of the Bible, the first six verses of the sixth chapter of the Book of Matthew read: "Take heed that ye do not your alms before me, to be seen of them: otherwise ye have no reward of your Father which is in heaven. Therefore when thou doest thine alms, do not sound a trumpet before thee, as the hypocrites do in the synagogues and in the streets, that they may have glory of me. Verily I say unto you, They have their reward. But when thou doest alms, let not thy left hand know what thy right hand doeth: That thine alms may be in secret: and thy Father which seeth in secret himself shall reward thee openly. And when thou prayest, enter into thy closet, and when thou hast shut thy door, pray to thy Father which is in secret; and thy Father which seeth in secret shall reward thee openly."

37. *CR*, 5 February 1952, 771; *BG*, 5 February 1952.

38. Frederic Fox, "The National Day of Prayer," *Theology Today* 29, no. 3 (October 1972): 258–259. The quotation within the presidential proclamation cited the language of the resolution. See *CR*, 14 February 1952, 977–978.

39. Martin, *With God on Our Side*, 31.

40. Paul Hutchinson, "The President's Religious Faith," *Life*, 22 May 1954, 151–153; Jerry Bergman, "President Eisenhower and the Influence of the Jehovah's Witnesses," *Kansas History*, Autumn 1998, 149–167.

41. Martin, *A Prophet with Honor*, 147; Paul Hutchinson, "The President's Religious Faith," *Life*, 22 May 1954, 156; Carlo D'Este, *Eisenhower: A Soldier's Life* (New York: Holt, 2003), 527.

42. Dwight D. Eisenhower to Clifford Roberts, 29 July 1952, Box 27, NS-DDE; news clipping, "Dwight D. Eisenhower's Bible-Based Legacy," Box 48, FEF; *NYT*, 4 May 1948.

43. Connally, *In History's Shadow*, 143; Graham, "God Is My Witness," 64; Graham, *Just as I Am*, 188–189; Frady, *Billy Graham*, 255.

44. Graham, *Just as I Am*, 190; Martin, *A Prophet with Honor*, 147; Reston, *Lone Star*, 164.

45. *LAT*, 5 June 1952; *CSM*, 5 June 1952; *NYT*, 5 June 1952.

46. *CSM*, 12 July 1952; *BS*, 12 July 1952; Graham, *Just as I Am*, 191; Gibbs and Duffy, *The Preacher and the Presidents*, 38–39; Eisenhower to Arthur B. Langlie, 11 August 1952, Box 966, PPF-DDE.

47. M. J. Heale, *American Anticommunism: Combatting the Enemy Within, 1830–1970* (Baltimore: Johns Hopkins University Press, 1990), 161; Loughlin, *Billy Graham*, 110–112, 115; Frady, *Billy Graham*, 254.

48. John W. Turnbull to Herman Smith, 29 September 1952, Box 246, AES.

49. For his part, Niebuhr denounced Spiritual Mobilization as a front group for business, an organization that "has a political program identical with that of the National Association of Manufacturers, to which it adds merely a prayer and religious unction." Reinhold Niebuhr, "U.S. Protestantism and Free Enterprise," *The Reporter* 6, no. 4 (19 February 1952): 26. Fifield angrily denied the charges as "untrue" in his own journal; "The Director's Page," *Faith and Freedom*, April 1952, 13. See also Martin E. Marty, "Reinhold Niebuhr: Public Theology and the American Experience," *Journal of Religion* 54, no. 4 (October 1974): 332–359, especially 349.

50. John W. Turnbull to Herman Smith, 29 September 1952, Box 246, AES; Christian Action, draft of press release, 24 October 1952, Box 246, AES; Chairman to John W. Turnbull, 30 October 1952, Box 246, AES; Charles W. Phillips to Hermon D. Smith, Box 246, AES; *LAT*, 31 October 1952.

51. *Christian Leadership News*, August 1952, 5, copy in Box 106, RF; Sharlet, *The Family*, 194.

52. "The Christian's Political Responsibility," *Faith and Freedom*, September 1952, 5–8; John Temple Graves, "Eisenhower's Convictions," *Charleston News and Courier*, 10 September 1952.

53. *WP,* 6 November 1952.

54. Graham, *Just as I Am,* 199; Frady, *Billy Graham,* 257.

CHAPTER 3: "GOVERNMENT UNDER GOD"

1. *BG,* 23 December 1952; *LAT,* 23 December 1952; *NYT,* 23 December 1952.

2. For an exhaustive account of the many reactions to, and uses of, Eisenhower's comment, see Patrick Henry, "'And I Don't Care What It Is': The Tradition-History of a Civil Religion Proof-Text," *Journal of the American Academy of Religion,* March 1981, 35–49.

3. William Lee Miller, *Piety Along the Potomac: Notes on Politics and Morals in the Fifties* (Boston: Houghton Mifflin, 1964), 34; Robert N. Bellah, "Civil Religion in America," *Daedalus: Journal of the American Academy of Arts and Sciences,* Winter 1967, 1–21; Will Herberg, *Protestant-Catholic-Jew: An Essay in American Religious Sociology* (Chicago: University of Chicago Press, 1983), 84.

4. Paul Hutchinson, "The President's Religious Faith," *Life,* 22 March 1954, 162; Eckhardt, *The Surge of Piety,* 22–23; Whitfield, *Culture of the Cold War,* 83; Luther G. Baker, "Changing Religious Norms and Family Values," *Journal of Marriage and the Family* 27 (1965): 6; Rosten, *Religions in America,* 327.

5. *NYT,* 2 June 1949, 22 April 1950, 23 December 1952, 22 February 1953; *LAT,* 24 June 1949, 6 April 1951, 23 December 1952; *CT,* 22 November 1949; Freedoms Foundation Annual Report, "Four Years Work for Freedom," 31 August 1953, Box 5, DB; *WP,* 10 February 1950.

6. First Congregational Church, "Fifteenth Anniversary Program," 8 January 1950, Box 206, CBD; Don Belding to Eisenhower, 18 June 1952, Box 5, DB; National Better Business Bureau, Report on Freedoms Foundation, Inc., 11 December 1952, Papers of the Americanism Division, ALM; *LAT,* 6 April 1951; Roy, *Apostles of Discord,* 298; photograph, Freedoms Foundation Medal, "Committee to Proclaim Liberty 'Freedom Under God,'" 1951, Box 69, JCI; *CT,* 22 November 1949; Dwight D. Eisenhower, Text of Prepared Remarks, "Valley Forge, Pennsylvania, November 21, 1949," Box 5, DB.

7. Don Belding, "My First Meeting with General Eisenhower," 10 September 1948, Box 5, DB; Freedoms Foundation Annual Report, "Four Years Work for Freedom," 31 August 1953, Box 5, DB.

8. Eisenhower, Notarized Statement, Cook County, Illinois, 28 June 1952, Box 5, DB; Freedoms Foundation Annual Report, "Four Years Work for Freedom," 31 August 1953, Box 5, DB.

9. Eisenhower to Clifford Roberts, 29 July 1952, Box 27, NS-DDE; Graham, *Just as I Am,* 191–192.

10. Diary entry, 1 February 1953, in *The Eisenhower Diaries,* ed. Robert H. Ferrell (New York: W. W. Norton, 1981), 226. For greater detail on Elson's promises of privacy and the president's reaction to the unwanted publicity, see Dwight D. Eisenhower to Milton S. Eisenhower, 2 February 1953, copy in *The Papers of Dwight David Eisenhower,* volume XIV: *The Presidency: The Middle Way,* ed. Louis Galambos and Daun Van Ee (Baltimore: Johns Hopkins University Press, 1996).

11. Whitfield, *Culture of the Cold War,* 88; James Hagerty, interview by Ed Edwin, Columbia University Oral History Project, Interview 7, 17 April 1968, copy of transcript located in Oral History #91, OH-DDE. Emphasis added.

12. American Legion, Digest of Minutes, National Executive Committee Meetings, 24 and 28 August 1952, 84, Reference Room, AL; American Legion, Digest of Minutes, National Executive Committee Meetings, October 1952, 36, Reference Room, AL; American Legion, "Back to God: Grace Before Meals" table card, Papers of the Americanism Division, ALM.

13. American Legion, Reports to the 35th Annual National Convention, August 1953, 126–127, Reference Room, AL; *CSM,* 30 January 1953; *BG,* 1 February 1953; *CT,* 2 February 1953; American Legion, Digest of Minutes, National Executive Committee Meetings, October 1953, 93, Reference Room, AL; American Legion, "Back to God" television program, 1 February 1953, Video Collection, AL, DVD copy in author's possession.

14. *NYT,* 8 February 1942; *CT,* 3 May 1942; American Legion, 1953 "Back to God" program, Video Collection, AL.

15. American Legion, 1953 "Back to God" program, Video Collection, AL; Dwight D. Eisenhower, "Remarks Recorded for the American Legion 'Back to God' Program," 1 February 1953, *Public Papers of the Presidents of the United States: Dwight D. Eisenhower, 1953* (Washington, DC: US Government Printing Office, 1960), 11–12.

16. Press release, remarks of the president for "Back to God" program, 7 February 1954, Box 6, SS-DDE; Press release, remarks of the president for "Back to God" program, 20 February 1955, Box 11, SS-DDE.

17. Sharlet, *The Family,* 187; *NYT,* 22 April 1947, 22 June 1952.

18. Robert Wuthnow, *Red State Religion: Faith and Politics in America's Heartland* (Princeton, NJ: Princeton University Press, 2012), 207–210; Frank Carlson to Sherman Adams, 4 December 1952, Box 824, PPF-DDE; Carlson, "Background of the Presidential Prayer Breakfast," February 1967, Box 456, RFF; Carlson, interview by David Horrocks, 7 March 1975, transcript located in Oral History #488, OH-DDE.

19. Conrad Hilton, "America on Its Knees," in *We Believe in Prayer,* Lawrence M. Brings, ed. (Minneapolis: T. S. Denison, 1958), 40–41; *International Christian Leadership Bulletin,* June 1953, RRF; transcript, International Council for Christian Leadership, Third Annual Prayer Breakfast, 3 February 1955, copy in Box 819, PPF-DDE.

20. Program, International Council for Christian Leadership, Annual Christian Action Conference, 5–9 February 1953, Box 504, RFF; "The Breakfast Groups" newsletter, March 1953, RRF; Eisenhower, "Remarks at the Dedicatory Prayer Breakfast of the International Christian Leadership," 5 February 1953, *Public Papers of the Presidents of the United States: Dwight D. Eisenhower, 1953* (Washington, DC: US Government Printing Office, 1960), 37–38.

21. "The Breakfast Groups" newsletter, March 1953, RRF; Grubb, *Modern Viking,* 131.

22. "The Breakfast Groups" newsletter, March 1953, RRF; Vereide to Thomas E. Stephens, 25 February 1953, Box 819, PPF-DDE; *International Christian Lead-*

ership Bulletin, September 1954, RRF; news clipping, *Christian Life*, August 1955, Box 456, RFF; Doug Coe to E. Ross Adair, 10 November 1959, Box 407, RFF.

23. Vereide to Chester McFee, 7 February 1945, Box 497, RFF; *International Christian Leadership Bulletin*, January 1954, RRF. The Army and Navy Club Breakfast Group featured a steady stream of government officials as speakers. In the months after Chief Justice Warren's "dedication ceremony," that particular prayer breakfast featured speeches by Senator John Stennis, Secretary of Labor James Mitchell, Secretary of the Navy Robert Anderson, US District Court Judge Luther Youngdahl, and the heads of the Office of Defense Mobilization and the General Services Administration. See *International Christian Leadership Bulletin*, May 1954, RRF.

24. Graham, *Just as I Am*, 202; transcript, "Government Under God," International Council for Christian Leadership, Annual Christian Action Conference, 4 February 1954, Box 819, PPF-DDE; *International Christian Leadership Bulletin*, March 1954, RRF.

25. Transcript, International Council for Christian Leadership, Third Annual Prayer Breakfast, 3 February 1955, copy in Box 819, PPF-DDE; *Bulletin of International Christian Leadership*, March 1955, RRF; program, International Council for Christian Leadership, Annual Christian Action Conference, February 3–5, 1955, Box 504, RFF.

26. Remarks of the President, 2 February 1956, Box 14, SS-DDE; *Bulletin of International Christian Leadership*, March 1956, RRF; *CSM*, 2 February 1956, 21 March 1956.

27. Ezra Taft Benson, *Cross Fire: The Eight Years with Eisenhower* (Garden City, NY: Doubleday, 1962), 36–38.

28. Ibid., 49; Herbert S. Parmet, *Eisenhower and the American Crusades* (New York: Macmillan, 1972), 176; Edward L. R. Elson to Eisenhower, 14 January 1953, Box 401, CF-DDE; Eisenhower to cabinet members, 3 February 1953, Box 1, CS-DDE; minutes of cabinet meeting, 6 February 1953, Box 1, CS-DDE.

29. Parmet, *Eisenhower and the American Crusades*, 168, 186. For an overview of Dulles's religious faith and its influence on his public life, see Preston, *Sword of the Spirit, Shield of Faith*, 384–409, 450–464.

30. Committee to Proclaim Liberty, Press Release, 11 June 1951, Box 69, JCI; note, Oveta Culp Hobby [February 1953], Box 1, CS-DDE.

31. Benson, *Cross Fire*, 47–48; G. Bromley Oxnam to Dulles, 24 June 1952, Box 63, JFD; minutes of National Conference on Maintenance of United States Constitutional Separation of Church and State, 13 October 1947, Box 16, AUSCS; Fulton J. Sheen to Dulles, 2 December 1952, Box 64, JFD; *The Secretary of State on Faith of Our Fathers* (Washington, DC: US Government Printing Office, 1954), 2, 6, copy in Box 58, JFD.

32. Sidney Hatkin to William L. White, 4 February 1954, Box 6, ACLU; Hatkin to White, 18 April 1954, Box 6, ACLU; program, Pentagon Good Friday service, 16 April 1954, Box 6, ACLU; Leo Pfeffer to Herbert Monte Levy, 4 March 1954, Box 6, ACLU; minutes, Free Speech Committee, American Civil Liberties Union,

16 March 1954, Box 6, ACLU; confidential memorandum, Theodore Leskes to Nathaniel H. Goodrich, 2 March 1954, Box 6, ACLU.

33. Peter Lyon, *Eisenhower: Portrait of the Hero* (Boston: Little, Brown, 1974), 466–467; Parmet, *Eisenhower and the American Crusades,* 170–171; Ann Fears Crawford and Jack Keever, *John B. Connally: A Portrait in Power* (Austin, TX: Jenkins, 1973), 81.

34. Parmet, *Eisenhower and the American Crusades,* 171–172; Benson, *Cross Fire,* 33–34; Robert H. Ferrell, ed., *The Eisenhower Diaries* (New York: Norton, 1981), 227; T.R.B., "Washington Wire," *New Republic,* 15 December 1952; Adams, *First-hand Report,* 62.

35. "The Shape of Things," *The Nation,* 24 January 1953, 61; Claude Robinson to Sinclair Weeks, 24 March 1953, Box 48, SW; Opinion Research Corporation, "Business Leaders in Washington," report, March 1953, Box 48, SW.

36. Eisenhower to Edgar Newton Eisenhower, 8 November 1954, *The Papers of Dwight David Eisenhower,* volume XV, *The Presidency: The Middle Way.*

37. Stephen E. Ambrose, *Eisenhower: The President* (New York: Simon & Schuster, 1984), 115, 158, 249–250, 459–460; Eisenhower, *Mandate for Change,* 501–502, 547–549; Rick Perlstein, *Before the Storm: Barry Goldwater and the Unmaking of the American Consensus* (New York: Hill and Wang, 2001), 27.

38. Clyde W. Taylor to the President, 10 April 1953, Box 830, PPF-DDE.

39. Memorandum for Mr. Stephens, 19 May 1953, Box 830, PPF-DDE; memo for Betty Sisk, 12 June 1953, Box 830, PPF-DDE.

40. Rutherford L. Decker to Carl F. H. Henry, 25 May 1953, Box 66, NAE; promotional poster, March of Freedom, n.d. [1953], Box 66, NAE. After providing its inspiration, Carl Henry had not been involved in the development of the program and was horrified to see what had resulted. He had envisioned an event with real meaning to evangelical Christianity, but considered this list to be little more than a "promotional gimmick" that was "a big disappointment." See Henry to Decker, 28 May 1953, Box 66, NAE.

41. R. L. Decker, "March of Freedom," typescript, 1 June 1953, Box 66, NAE; memorandum, "A Description of the March of Freedom," Box 66, NAE.

42. Jaeger and Jessen Inc., "Advance File on March of Freedom," n.d. [1953], Box 66, NAE.

43. National Association of Evangelicals, "March of Freedom News," n.d. [1953], Box 66, NAE; *CSM,* 2 July 1953; *NYT,* 3 July 1953; *WP,* 3 July 1953; *Time,* 15 July 1953; Decker, "March of Freedom."

44. *Faith and Freedom,* June 1953, 10–12; "Proclaim Liberty Throughout the Land," pamphlet, Box 69, JCI; Earl Warren, Independence Day proclamation, 29 June 1953, copy in Box 69, JCI.

45. Frederic Fox, "The National Day of Prayer," *Theology Today,* October 1972, 260; Fulton J. Sheen to Eisenhower, 6 May 1953, and Eisenhower to Sheen, 13 May 1953; memorandum for Mr. Shanley, 3 June 1953; National Day of Prayer proclamation, June 1953, all in Box 737, OF-DDE.

46. Miller, *Piety Along the Potomac*, 42; Eisenhower to Francis Joseph Spellman, 8 July 1953, copy in *The Papers of Dwight David Eisenhower,* volume XIV, *The Presidency: The Middle Way*

CHAPTER 4: PLEDGING ALLEGIANCE

1. *CT*, 18 May 1954; *BG*, 18 May 1954; Richard Kluger, *Simple Justice: The History of Brown v. Board of Education and Black America's Struggle for Racial Equality* (New York: Vintage, 1975), 702, 708; US Congress, 83rd Cong., 1st Sess., S.J. Res. 87.

2. Morton Borden, "The Christian Amendment," *Civil War History,* June 1979, 156–167; Kramnick and Moore, *The Godless Constitution,* 144–149.

3. Ralph E. Flanders, *Senator from Vermont* (Boston: Little, Brown, 1961), 122–131, 171–178; Flanders, "Business Looks at the N.R.A.," *Atlantic Monthly,* November 1933, 625–634; Ben Pearse, "The Case of the Unexpected Senator," *Saturday Evening Post,* 31 July 1954, 65; Flanders to Julius C. Holmes, 12 May 1952, Box 106, RF; Flanders to Frank Carlson, 14 May 1952, Box 106, RF.

4. See, for instance, Testimony of Mrs. P. de Shishmareff and A. J. MacFarland, US Congress, Senate, 83rd Cong., 2nd Sess., Subcommittee on Constitutional Amendments, Judiciary Committee, "Proposing an Amendment to the Constitution of the United States Recognizing the Authority and Law of Jesus Christ," 13 and 17 May 1954 (hereafter cited as "Christian Amendment Hearings"), 3, 25.

5. Testimony of R. E. Robb, Christian Amendment Hearings, 26–31. Robb's arguments on the "twofold" nature of the Constitution of the United States appear to have been considerably drawn from the work of the nineteenth-century Transcendentalist author Orestes A. Brownson. See Brownson, *The American Republic: Constitution, Tendencies and Destiny* (New York: P. O'Shea, 1866), especially chapter X.

6. Testimony of J. Renwick Patterson, Christian Amendment Hearings, 44.

7. 343 US 312–313.

8. Epstein, "Ceremonial Deism," 2091.

9. Ibid.

10. Richard J. Ellis, *To the Flag: The Unlikely History of the Pledge of Allegiance* (Lawrence: University of Kansas Press, 2005), 24–33.

11. Ibid., 13–19.

12. Ibid., 54–71; *Time,* 17 May 1954; *NYT,* 22 April 1953.

13. Christopher J. Kauffman, *Faith and Fraternalism: The History of the Knights of Columbus, 1882–1982* (New York: Harper & Row, 1982), 137, 377, 385; "Let's Get This Clear," *Columbia,* August 1955, 3; *Knights of Columbus News,* 24 May 1954, copy in periodicals collection, KC.

14. *WP,* 14 November 1961; Ellis, *To the Flag,* 131; extension of remarks by Louis C. Rabaut, 21 April 1953, *CR*, Appendix, A2063.

15. *ADA World,* September 1953, 2A. The ADA charted legislators' liberalism by scoring their stances on eleven key issues during the 1953 term. With a perfect ADA score, Rabaut took the liberal position on every single issue.

16. *The Gallup Poll: Public Opinion, 1935–1971* (New York: Random House, 1972), 2:1140; *LAT,* 11 May 1953; Ellis, *To the Flag,* 131–132.

17. George M. Docherty, *I've Seen the Day* (Grand Rapids, MI: William C. Eerdmans, 1984), 139–149, 169–174; *WP,* 3 February 1952.

18. Program, the Seventh Washington Pilgrimage, "This Nation Under God," April 1957, Box 1, HD; *WP,* 10 January 1950, 27 September 1951, 12 January, 19 April, 5 May 1952, 6 July 2002; *NYT,* 20, 29 September 1951; *CSM,* 29 September 1951; Docherty, *I've Seen the Day,* 158–159.

19. George M. Docherty, "Under God," sermon preached at New York Avenue Presbyterian Church, Washington, DC, 7 February 1954, copy located online, www.nyapc.org/congregation/Sermon_Archives/text/1954/undergodsermon.pdf, accessed 21 January 2011; *WP,* 6 July 2002.

20. Docherty, "Under God."

21. Ibid. In later decades, Docherty would express reservations about his sermon, especially the comments toward atheists. "I still consider my reasoning to be valid," he wrote in his 1984 autobiography, "but the times should have overruled my philosophical arguments as irrelevant in light of the greater issues at hand. A false patriotism was being aroused by the bogus threat of Communist encroachment; McCarthyism darkened the airwaves; superpatriots were prone to ask not whether they were on God's side, but whether God was on theirs." Politically, Docherty drifted ever more to the left in the ensuing decades, marching with Martin Luther King Jr. in the Selma protests and supporting his criticism of the Vietnam War. See Docherty, *I've Seen the Day,* 160 (quotation), 187–266.

22. Docherty, *I've Seen the Day,* 159; *Newsweek,* 31 May 1954; Gerard Kaye and Ferenc M. Szasz, "Adding 'Under God' to the Pledge of Allegiance," *Encounter* 34 (1973): 52; *WP,* 6 July 2002; Albert J. Drake to Dwight D. Eisenhower, 10 March 1954, Box 10, GF-DDE; Sherman Adams to Edward J. Cronin, 3 June 1954, Box 10, GF-DDE; *NYT,* 23 May 1954.

23. *Christian Century,* 26 May 1954; Alan Reitman, memorandum to Washington office, 24 May 1954, Box 1, ACLU; *Church and State,* June 1954, 7.

24. Specifically, the resolutions and their main sponsors in the 83rd Congress were, in order of bill introduction, H.J. Res. 243 (Louis C. Rabaut, Michigan Democrat); H.J. Res. 334 (John R. Pillion, New York Republican); H.J. Res. 345 (William E. Miller, New York Republican); H.J. Res. 371 (Charles Oakman, Michigan Republican); H.J. Res. 383 (Oliver P. Bolton, Ohio Republican); H.J. Res. 479 (Melvin Laird, Wisconsin Republican); H.J. Res. 497 (Peter J. Rodino, New Jersey Democrat); H.J. Res. 502 (Francis E. Dorn, New York Republican); H.J. Res. 506 (Hugh J. Addonizio, New Jersey Democrat); H.J. Res. 513 (William T. Granahan, Pennsylvania Democrat); H.J. Res. 514 (Barratt O'Hara, Illinois Democrat); H.J. Res. 518 (Thomas J. Lane, Massachusetts Democrat); H.J. Res. 519 (John P. Saylor, Pennsylvania Republican); H.J. Res. 521 (John J. Rooney, New York Democrat); H.J. Res. 523 (John E. Fogarty, Rhode Island Democrat); H.J. Res. 529 (Homer T. Angell, Oregon Republican); H.J. Res. 531 (Frazier Reams, Ohio Independent). Information from Louis C. Rabaut to Dwight D. Eisenhower, 9 June 1954, Box 443, OF-DDE.

25. *ADA World,* September 1954, 2M-3M.

26. US Congress, House, 83rd Cong., 2nd Sess., *CR,* 12 February 1954–1700. Oakman's conservatism was made clear in the ADA rankings for that year's legislative

session. While Rabaut took the progressive side of an issue in eight of the nine votes used by the ADA that year, Oakman only did so in two of the nine. See *ADA World,* September 1954, 2M.

27. US Congress, House, 83rd Cong., 2nd Sess., *CR,* 12 February 1954, 1697–1700.

28. *WP,* 18 May 1954; US Congress, House, 83rd Cong., 2nd Sess., *CR,* 5 May 1954, 6077–6078; US Congress, House, Report No. 1693, "Amending the Pledge of Allegiance to the Flag of the United States," 83rd Cong., 2nd Sess., 28 May 1954; US Congress, House, 83rd Cong., 2nd Sess., *CR,* 7 June 1954, 7758–7766; Kaye and Szasz, "Adding 'Under God,'" 53.

29. Louis C. Rabaut to Dwight D. Eisenhower, 9 June 1954, Box 22, RP-PL-DDE; Homer H. Gruenther to Gerald D. Morgan, 9 June 1954, Box 22, RP-PL-DDE; Thomas E. Stephens to Gerald D. Morgan, 10 June 1954, Box 22, RP-PL-DDE; *CT,* 15 June 1954; US Congress, Senate, 83rd Cong., 2nd Sess., *CR,* 22 June 1954, 8617–8618.

30. *WP,* 12 June 1955; *Chicago Defender,* 15 January 1955; *LAT,* 17 February, 13 October 1955; program, the Seventh Washington Pilgrimage, "This Nation Under God," April 1957, Box 1, HD.

31. *NYT,* 28 July 1956.

32. Ibid.

33. *Christophers News Notes* 59 (May 1954): 2; *NYT,* 19 November 1986; US Congress, Senate, 83rd Cong., 1st Sess., *CR,* 27 March 1953, 2370–2371; *ADA World,* September 1953, 4A; *WP,* 12 April 1953; *NYT,* 12 April 1953.

34. *NYT,* 12 April 1953, 26 February, 4 April 1954; *NYHT,* 4 April 1954, cited in US Congress, House, 83rd Cong., 2nd Sess., *CR,* 8 April 1954, 4929–4930; US Congress, Senate, 83rd Cong., 2nd Sess., *CR,* 8 April 1954, 4867–4869; *CT,* 4 April 1954.

35. *WP,* 4 and 7 April 1954; US Congress, Senate, 83rd Cong., 2nd Sess., *CR,* 8 April 1954, 4867–4869; *NYT,* 9 April 1954.

36. *WP,* 21 April 1954; *Church and State,* May 1954, 1, 6.

37. US Congress, House, 83rd Cong., 2nd Sess., *CR,* 14 April 1954, 5187; US Congress, House, 84th Cong., 1st Sess., Report Authorizing Special Canceling Stamp "Pray for Peace," H.R. 692, 7 June 1955; US Congress, Senate, 84th Cong., 2nd Sess., Transcript of Proceedings Before the Committee on the Post Office and Civil Service, H.R. 692, 6 March 1956; Maurice H. Stans to Percival F. Brundage, 13 June 1956, Box 75, RPPL-DDE; Roger W. Jones to Dwight D. Eisenhower, 15 June 1956, Box 75, RPPL-DDE; Miller, *Piety on the Potomac,* 41.

38. *The Numismatist,* October 1954, 1064; memorandum, "Re: In God We Trust," 24 May 1972, Box 6, CEB; Donald K. Carroll to Charles E. Bennett, 28 December 1954, Box 83, CEB.

39. *Florida Times-Union,* 9 September 2003, 13 December 2010; *NYT,* 24 September 2010.

40. Donald K. Carroll to Charles E. Bennett, 28 December 1954, Box 83, CEB; James B. Utt to Le Roy Anderson, 15 March 1959, Box 407, RFF; *International Christian Leadership Bulletin,* February 1954, RRF.

41. *CSM,* 11 January 1955; Donald K. Carroll to Charles E. Bennett, 13 January 1955, Box 83, CEB; Philip J. Philbin to Frank Carlson, 12 January 1955, Box 407, RFF.

42. George M. Humphrey to Nelson A. Rockefeller, 25 February 1955, Box 565, OF-DDE; Nelson A. Rockefeller, memorandum for the president, 3 March 1955, Box 565, OF-DDE; Eisenhower to Rockefeller, 5 March 1955, Box 31, AS-DDE; W. Randolph Burgess to Charles Bennett, 7 April 1955, Box 83, CEB; Rockefeller, memorandum for the president, 22 April 1955, Box 31, AS-DDE; Eisenhower, memorandum for the secretary of the treasury, 26 April 1955, Box 31, AS-DDE.

43. US Congress, House, Committee on Banking and Currency, 84th Cong., 1st Sess., *Miscellaneous Hearings* (Washington, DC: US Government Printing Office, 1956); *ADA World,* September 1955, 2M–3M; Religious News Service, "House Unit Approves Motto on Currency," report, 17 May 1955, Box 83, CEB; US Congress, House, Report No. 662, "Providing That All United States Currency and Coins Shall Bear the Inscription 'In God We Trust,'" 84th Cong., 1st Sess., 26 May 1955; US Congress, House, 84th Cong., 1st Sess., *CR,* 7 June 1955, 7795–7796; *LAT,* 8 June 1955.

44. US Congress, Senate, 84th Cong., 1st Sess., Transcript of Proceedings Before the Committee on Banking and Currency, Nomination of William J. Hallahan to the Home Loan Bank Board and Other Matters, 27 June 1955; *CT,* 30 June 1955.

45. Typewritten notes for Bennett, n.d. [July 1955], Box 83, CEB; memorandum, H.R. 619, 1 July 1955, Box 565, OF-DDE; Eisenhower to Bennett, 14 July 1955, Box 565, OF-DDE; Murray Snyder to Howard Pyle, 29 March 1956, Box 565, OF-DDE.

46. Press release, Treasury Department, 25 July 1957, Box 83, CEB; *NYT,* 2 October 1957; Bennett to Robert B. Anderson, 27 July 1957, Box 83, CEB; Anderson to Bennett, 2 August 1957, Box 83, CEB; *LAT,* 20 August 1955; *CT,* 28 July 1957. After its introduction to the dollar bill in 1957, the motto was gradually applied to the new plates for other denominations, a time-consuming process that was not completed until October 1966. See H. J. Holtzclaw to Bennett, 27 October 1966, Box 6, CEB.

47. Bennett, interview by Don North, 17 December 1970, copy of transcript located in OH-DDE; Bennett to Legislative Reference Service, 28 April 1955, Box 83, CEB; Harold E. Snide, "The Officially Recognized Motto of the United States," 5 May 1955, Box 6, CEB.

48. Bennett to "Dear Colleague," 21 July 1955, Box 83, CEB; US Congress, House, 84th Cong., 1st Sess., *CR,* 21 July 1955, 11193.

49. Bennett to James B. Frazier Jr., 18 January 1956, Box 83, CEB; US Congress, House, Subcommittee No. 4, Judiciary Committee, 84th Cong., 2nd Sess., Hearings, "To Establish a National Motto of the U.S." (unpublished), 24 February 1956; Ernest S. Griffith to Bennett, 14 March 1956, Box 83, CEB; Bennett to Emanuel Celler, 19 March 1956, Box 83, CEB; *ADA World,* August 1956, 3A; US Congress, House, Report No. 1959, "National Motto," 84th Cong., 2nd Sess., 28 March 1956; *NYT,* 17 April 1956.

50. Louis Joughin, memorandum, "Re: Hennings Committee—Religion Area," 22 September 1955, Box 1, ACLU; Alan Reitman, memorandum, "Re: In God We Trust Motto," 8 May 1956, Box 6, ACLU; Reitman, memorandum, "In God We Trust Motto," 17 May 1956, Box 800, ACLU; memo from Washington office to Reitman, "Re: In God We Trust Motto," 18 May 1956, Box 800, ACLU; *WP,* 30 April 1956.

51. Letter Draft, "Dear Senator," 29 May 1956, Box 6, ACLU; Patrick Murphy Malin to Everett McKinley Dirksen, 25 June 1956, Box 800, ACLU.

52. Bennett to Spessard L. Holland, 26 April 1956, Box 83, CEB; US Congress, Senate, Report No. 2703, "National Motto," 84th Cong., 2nd Sess., 20 July 1956; US Congress, Senate, 84th Cong., 2nd Sess., *CR,* 23 July 1956, 13917; *NYT,* 24 July 1956; memorandum, "H.J. Res. 396, To Establish a National Motto of the United States," 30 July 1956, Box 85, RPPL-DDE.

CHAPTER 5: PITCHMEN FOR PIETY

1. *LAT,* 18 July 1955; ABC-TV, *Dateline Disneyland,* 17 July 1955 (http://www.youtube.com/watch?v=JuzrZET-3Ew).

2. Robert Pettit, "One Nation Under Walt: Disney Theme Parks as Shrines to American Civil Religion," paper presented at the 1986 annual conference of the Popular Culture Association, copy in author's possession; ABC-TV, *Dateline Disneyland.*

3. Steven Watts, "Walt Disney: Art and Politics in the American Century," *Journal of American History* 82 (June 1995): 100–105.

4. Robert De Roos, "The Magic Worlds of Walt Disney," in *Disney Discourse: Producing the Magic Kingdom,* ed. Eric Smoodin (New York: Routledge, 1994), 67; Steven Watts, *The Magic Kingdom: Walt Disney and the American Way of Life* (Columbia: University of Missouri Press, 2001), 417.

5. *NYT,* 17 May 1962; Neal Gabler, *Walt Disney: The Triumph of the American Imagination* (New York: Vintage, 2007), 499, 578; Watts, *Magic Kingdom,* 392–393; *LAT,* 9 July 1957; *WSJ,* 4 February 1958.

6. Robert Griffith, "The Selling of America: The Advertising Council and American Politics, 1942–1960," *Business History Review,* Autumn 1983, 389–390; *NYT,* 14 and 16 November 1941; *CSM,* 17 November 1941; C. B. Larrabee, "If You Looked for a Miracle," *Printer's Ink,* 21 November 1941, 15.

7. John Carlyle, "How Advertising Went to War," *Nation's Business,* November 1944, 72; Don Wharton, "The Story Back of the War Ads," *Reader's Digest,* July 1944, 103–105; Griffith, "The Selling of America," 391–402; Wall, *Inventing the "American Way,"* 190–197; John Vianney McGinnis, "The Advertising Council and the Cold War," Ph.D. diss., Syracuse University, 1991, 28–68.

8. *The J.W.T. News,* 30 October 1950, JWT-NC; Griffith, "The Selling of America," 395–396.

9. "Religion & Madison Avenue," *Bulletin of Religion in American Life,* January 1966, copy in Box 6, SRB; Volker R. Henning, "The Advertising Council and its 'Religion in American Life' Campaign," Ph.D. diss., University of Tennessee, 1996,

107–110; advertisement proofs, Religion in American Life campaign, n.d. [1949], File #469, ACHF.

10. *The J.W.T. News*, 30 October 1950, JWT-NC; Committee for Religion in American Life, 1956 Annual Report, n.d. [June 1957], Box 38, JML; transcripts, public service announcements, Religion in American Life campaign, 1955, File #984, ACHF; *J. Walter Thompson Company News*, 19 November 1956, 25 November 1957, JWT-NC.

11. Advertising Council, "Radio Fact Sheet," n.d. [1955], File #984, ACHF; transcripts, public service announcements, Religion in American Life Campaign, 1955, File #984, ACHF; Committee for Religion in American Life, 1956 Annual Report, n.d. [June 1957], Box 38, JML.

12. See generally Craig Allen, *Eisenhower and the Mass Media: Peace, Prosperity and Prime-Time TV* (Chapel Hill: University of North Carolina Press, 1993); John E. Hollitz, "Eisenhower and the Admen: The Television 'Spot' Campaign of 1952," *Wisconsin Magazine of History* 66 (Autumn 1982): 25–39; Stephen C. Wood, "Television's First Political Spot Ad Campaign: Eisenhower Answers America," *Presidential Studies Quarterly* 20 (Spring 1990): 265–283; Kurt Lang and Gladys Lang, *Politics and Television* (Chicago: Quadrangle, 1968), 84–91.

13. Advertising Council, "Radio Fact Sheet," n.d. [1955], File #984, ACHF; Committee for Religion in American Life, 1956 annual report, n.d. [June 1957], Box 38, JML.

14. Committee for Religion in American Life, 1956 Annual Report, n.d. [June 1957], Box 38, JML.

15. Religion in American Life, 1956–57 Promotional Kit, Fall 1956, Box 39, JWT-AF; Committee for Religion in American Life, 1956 Annual Report, n.d. [June 1957], Box 38, JML. Sample ads for the 1956–57 campaign may be found in File #753, ACHF.

16. "Seven Steps to a Successful Local Religion in American Life Program," Religion in American Life, 1956–57 Promotional Kit, Fall 1956, Box 39, JWT-AF.

17. "Suggested Proclamation by Mayors," "Sample News Release on Your RIAL Campaign" (emphasis in original), and "Suggested Editorial," Religion in American Life, 1956–57 Promotional Kit, Fall 1956, Box 39, JWT-AF.

18. Committee for Religion in American Life, 1956 Annual Report, n.d. [June 1957], Box 38, JML; Religion in American Life, "Radio Fact Sheet," October 1957, File #821, ACHF; *J. Walter Thompson Company News*, 19 November 1956, JWT-NC.

19. Fred Seaton, transcript, first draft, "RIAL Speech—3/7/57" [28 February 1957], Box 12, Speech Series, FAS.

20. Committee for Religion in American Life, 1956 Annual Report, n.d. [June 1957], Box 38, JML.

21. Douglas T. Miller, "Popular Religion of the 1950's: Norman Vincent Peale and Billy Graham," *Journal of Popular Culture* 9 (Summer 1975): 66–67; Robert S. Brustein, "The New Faith of the *Saturday Evening Post*," *Commentary* 16 (October 1953): 367–369; *Dwight D. Eisenhower's Favorite Poetry, Prose and Prayers*, copy in Box 48, FEF.

22. Luccock cited in Eugene Exman, "Reading, Writing and Religion," *Harper's Magazine*, May 1953, 84; Miller, "Popular Religion," 67; *Publishers Weekly*, 23 January 1954; Elson, *America's Spiritual Recovery*, 51.

23. Miller, "Popular Religion," 73, 67; Elson, *America's Spiritual Recovery*, 41; Whitfield, *Culture of the Cold War*, 85.

24. Scott Eyman, *Empire of Dreams: The Epic Life of Cecil B. DeMille* (New York: Simon & Schuster, 2011), 369, 382, 396.

25. *LAT*, 9 April 1949, 9 January 1950, 25 March 1950, 10 March 1951; Fifteenth Anniversary Program, First Congregational Church, Los Angeles, 8 January 1950, Box 206, CBD; Cecil B. DeMille, "Champion of Democracy," 8 January 1950, Box 206, CBD.

26. Cecil B. DeMille, "Champion of Democracy," 8 January 1950, Box 206, CBD; Committee to Proclaim Liberty, press release, 11 June 1951, Box 69, JCI; memorandum and handwritten note, Box 945, CBD; Frady, *Billy Graham*, 202, 271.

27. Eyman, *Empire of Dreams*, 372–375, 399; Fifield, Memorandum, Box 15, JHP.

28. *BG*, 3 August 1952; *CSM*, 14 August 1952; *LAT*, 12 February 1956; *WP*, 24 October 1956.

29. *NYT*, 31 July 1955.

30. Eyman, *Empire of Dreams*, 440; Henry S. Noerdlinger, *Moses and Egypt: The Documentation to the Motion Picture, The Ten Commandments* (Los Angeles: University of Southern California Press, 1956).

31. Trailer and souvenir program, *The Ten Commandments*, directed by Cecil B. DeMille, 1956, in special edition DVD (Los Angeles: Paramount Studios, 2011); Eyman, *Empire of Dreams*, 473.

32. *LAT*, 12 February, 30 December 1956; *Chicago Defender*, 11 November 1957; *NYT*, 10 November 1957; *Irish Times*, 10 July 2009.

33. E. J. Ruegemer to DeMille, 20 June 1955, Box 990, CBD; Manny Meyers, "Spreading the Commandments," *Eagle*, July 1954, 18–19, copy courtesy of FOE.

34. Cecil B. DeMille, "I Bare You on Eagles' Wings," *Eagle*, January 1955, FOE; Ruegemer to DeMille, 20 June 1955, Box 990, CBD.

35. Transcript, "Milwaukee Morning Exercises," *n.d.* [1955], Box 993, CBD; Yul Brynner, "Ten Commandment Monolith Unveiled," *Eagle*, April 1957, FOE.

36. *LAT*, 12 August 1956; DeMille to Ruegemer, 18 April 1956, Box 490, CBD; press release, Paramount Pictures News, 8 June 1956, Box 469, CBD; Manuel Meyers, "Monolith in the Peace Garden," *Eagle*, November 1956, FOE; news release, International Peace Garden Committee, 3 June 1956, Box 490, CBD; news release, Paramount Studios, n.d. [June 1956], Box 490, CBD; Ruegemer to DeMille, 21 June 1956, Box 469, CBD; Manuel Meyers, "Modern Moses," *Eagle*, February 1957, FOE.

37. Albert G. Minda to Ruegemer, 31 July 1957, Box 490, CBD; Edwin A. Bennett to Frank X. Kryzan, 21 June 1957, Box 801, ACLU; *Minneapolis Star-Tribune*, 30 August 2003.

38. *Time*, 9 February 1962; transcript, *CBS Reports: Thunder on the Right*, 22 February 1962, Box 177, FF; Frederick Schwarz, *Beating the Unbeatable Foe: One*

Man's Victory over Communism, Leviathan, and the Last Enemy (Washington, DC: Regnery, 1996), 297–300, 319–322, 326–330, 467–468.

39. Schwarz, *Beating the Unbeatable Foe*, 104–105.

40. Keith Wheeler, "Who's Who in the Tumult of the Far Right," *Life*, 9 February 1962, 117; Schwarz, *Beating the Unbeatable Foe*, 154–155, 204; Charles Raper Jonas to Frank B. Fuhr, 26 May 1956, Box 407, RFF.

41. Schwarz, *Beating the Unbeatable Foe*, 156–157; US Congress, House, Committee on Un-American Activities, 85th Cong., 1st Sess., *International Communism (The Communist Mind), Staff Consultation with Frederick Charles Schwarz* (Washington, DC: US Government Printing Office, 1957).

42. Schwarz, *Beating the Unbeatable Foe*, 157; *CT*, 30 December 1957; *WSJ*, 29 January 1958; *CSM*, 5 February 1958; Barry Goldwater, "Understanding Communism," *LAT*, 8 March 1961; Marty, *Under God, Indivisible*, 371.

43. Schwarz, *Beating the Unbeatable Foe*, 162–167; program, School of Anti-Communism, Los Angeles, 11–15 December 1961, Box 43, CUAEL; program, Puget Sound School of Anti-Communism, 12–16 February 1962, Box 22, SBC-CLC; program, Greater New York School of Anti-Communism, 27–31 August 1962, Box 22, SBC-CLC; *CACC Newsletter*, October 1960; *CT*, 13 September 1960.

44. *LAT*, 8, 12 November 1960; registration form, Los Angeles Anti-Communism School, n.d. [1960], Section 1, FBI-CACC. The "small doses" quotation attributed to Khrushchev was widely disseminated in conservative circles, but no proof of its authenticity was ever established. In 1962, Representative Morris Udall (D-Ariz.) sought to determine its provenance, enlisting a range of authorities on the Soviet Union working at the Library of Congress, the Legislative Reference Service, the State Department, and the US Information Agency. None of them could find evidence that Khrushchev had ever said it. See Morris K. Udall, "Khrushchev Could Have Said It," *New Republic*, 7 May 1962, 14–15.

45. Program, Greater Los Angeles School of Anti-Communism, 7–11 November 1960, Section 1, FBI-CACC; *LAT*, 12 November 1960, 9 March 1961.

46. *WP*, 30 August 1970; Schwarz, *Beating the Unbeatable Foe*, 192–193, 208–211, 214; *NYT*, 9 November 1998; memorandum, "SAC, Los Angeles, to Director, FBI," 29 August 1961, Section 1, FBI-CACC.

47. *Los Angeles Examiner*, 18 August 1961; *LAT*, 28 August 1961; program, Greater Los Angeles School of Anti-Communism, 7–11 November 1960, Section 1, FBI-CACC; *NYT*, 26 July 1960.

48. Program, Southern California School of Anti-Communism, 28 August–1 September 1961, Section 1, FBI-CACC; *LAT*, 23, 27, 31 August 1961; *Los Angeles Herald-Express*, 30 August, 7 September 1961; *Los Angeles Mirror*, 31 August 1961; Samuel Lawrence Brenner, "Shouting at the Rain: The Voices and Ideas of Right-Wing Anti-Communist Americanists in the Era of Modern American Conservatism, 1950–1974," Ph.D. dissertation, Brown University, 2009, 11, 236; Dochuk, *From Bible Belt to Sun Belt*, 223–224.

49. *Los Angeles Herald-Express*, 7 September 1961; *Los Angeles Examiner*, 4 September 1961; *LAT*, 29 September, 13 October 1961; *NYT*, 3 September 1961.

50. *NYT,* 16 October 1961; *LAT,* 17 October 1961; press release, KING News, 9 October 1961, Box 36, DSB; press release, KGW-TV Promotion Department, 10 October 1961, Box 36, DSB; telegram, Fred M. Jordan to Otto P. Brandt, 6 October 1961, Box 36, DSB.

51. *CSM,* 19 October 1961; *LAT,* 17 October 1961; *Los Angeles Herald-Express,* 17 October 1961; *Los Angeles Examiner,* 17 October 1961; *Los Angeles Mirror,* 17 October 1961; Schwarz, *Beating the Unbeatable Foe,* 226–229.

52. Robert Welch to Fred Schwarz, 6 September 1960, Box 94, CDJ.

53. *Los Angeles Herald-Express,* 7 September 1961; memorandum, SAC, Los Angeles, to director, FBI, "Re: California School of Anti-Communism (CSAC)," 18 October 1961, Section 1, FBI-CACC; [name redacted] to William G. Simon, 8 September 1961, Section 1, FBI-CACC.

54. *LAT,* 17 October 1961; prepared remarks, C. D. Jackson, "Hollywood's Answer to Communism," 16 October 1961, Box 94, CDJ.

55. George Murphy to C. D. Jackson, 18 October 1961, Box 94, CDJ.

56. In a frank but friendly exchange, Jackson repeated his newfound belief that the Australian was not the extremist he had originally believed him to be, but begged him "to disassociate yourself and your Crusade in a clear and cleancut way from the John Birch Society, which I frankly consider beyond the pale." In response, Schwarz insisted he did not agree with the far-right views of Robert Welch but had "been trying to avoid fighting with other organizations thus wasting time and energy." Despite their different stance on the Birchers, Schwarz concluded, the two men were clear allies in the fight to defend America. Jackson to Schwarz, 24 January 1962, Box 94, CDJ; Schwarz to Jackson, 27 January 1962, Box 94, CDJ.

57. Jackson to H. E. Christiansen, 31 October 1961, Box 94, CDJ.

58. Brenner, "Shouting at the Rain," 3–4; *LAT,* 29 September, 8, 16 October 1961; George Murphy to Jackson, 18 October 1961, Box 94, CDJ; *NYT,* 29 October, 3 November 1961.

59. Schwarz, *Beating the Unbeatable Foe,* 230; *CACC Newsletter,* February 1962; Joseph Crespino, *Strom Thurmond's America* (New York: Hill and Wang, 2012), 123–124.

60. Otto Brandt to Walter Wagstaff and Bob Temple, 28 September 1961, Box 36, DSB; Brandt to Kai Jorgensen, 2 October 1961, Box 36, DSB; memorandum from Bob Schulman to Mrs. Bullitt et al., 29 September 1961, Box 36, DSB; Memorandum from Lee Schulman to Mrs. Bullitt, Otto Brandt, and Bob Schulman, 9 October 1961, Box 36, DSB; *Saturday Review,* 27 January 1962; Patrick Murphy Malin to Fred Thrower, 3 February 1962, Box 36, DSB; *ST,* 17 October 1961; Mrs. Payne Karr to Mrs. Scott Bullitt, 25 October 1961, Box 36, DSB.

61. *Time,* 9 February 1962; "Evangelicals and the Right-Wing Renascence," *Christianity Today,* 22 December 1961, 25–26; "Contra the Schwarz Crusade," *Christian Century,* 7 February 1962, 170–171; "T.R.B. from Washington," *New Republic,* 1 January 1962, 3; Schwarz, *Beating the Unbeatable Foe,* 274–283; *National Review,* 5 and 19 June 1962, 31 July 1962.

62. Program, School of Anti-Communism, Los Angeles, 11–15 December 1961, Box 43, CUAEL; Fred Schwarz to "Dear Friend," 6 September 1962, Box

10, SBC-CLC; *CACC Newsletter,* May 1962, August 1962; Schwarz, *Beating the Unbeatable Foe,* 13–14.

CHAPTER 6: "WHOSE RELIGIOUS TRADITION?"

1. M. A. Henderson, *Sowers of the Word: A 95-Year History of the Gideons International, 1899–1994* (Nashville, TN: The Gideons International, 1995), 53, 100–105.

2. Ibid., 4–5, 37; Leo Pfeffer, "The Gideons March on the Schools," *Congress Weekly,* 5 October 1953, 7; *NYT,* 22 August 1949.

3. Pfeffer, "The Gideons March on the Schools," 7.

4. Typewritten copy of original letter, John Van Der Ems to Guy Hilleboe, 10 May 1951, Box 800, ACLU; Rutherford Public Schools, "To All Parents," memorandum, 21 November 1951, Box 800, ACLU; meeting minutes, Rutherford Board of Education, 10 December 1951, Box 800, ACLU.

5. Meeting minutes, Rutherford Board of Education, 10 December 1951, Box 800, ACLU; meeting minutes, Rutherford Board of Education, 14 January 1952, Box 800, ACLU.

6. 14 N.J. 31, 100 A. 2d 857 (1953); *NYT,* 17 March 1953, 4 and 6 October 1953; *Church and State,* November 1953, 5; Pfeffer, "The Gideons March on the Schools," 8–9; Kevin M. Schultz, *Tri-Faith America: How Catholics and Jews Held Postwar America to Its Protestant Promise* (New York: Oxford University Press, 2011), 128–134; *Church and State,* January 1954, 6.

7. Henderson, *Sowers of the Word,* 105–106; Donald G. Paterson to Dean M. Schweickhard, 29 March 1957, Box 801, ACLU; Schweickhard to Paterson, 2 April 1957, Box 801, ACLU; Robert Satter to Lewis Joughin, 16 June 1955, Box 800, ACLU; press release, "Education Board Approves Bible Distribution in Miami Schools," 3 September 1956, Box 801, ACLU.

8. Richard B. Dierenfield, *Religion in American Public Schools* (Washington, DC: Public Affairs Press, 1962), 83–87.

9. State Board of Regents, "The Regents Statement on Moral and Spiritual Training in the Schools," 30 November 1951, Box 809, ACLU.

10. William Lee Miller, "The Fight over America's Fourth 'R,'" *The Reporter,* 22 March 1956, 20; *NYT,* 29 March 1955.

11. Miller, "The Fight over America's Fourth 'R,'" 21.

12. Ibid., 21–22; *NYT,* 5 August 1956; New York Board of Rabbis, "An Analysis of the New York Board of Superintendents' Guiding Statement for Supervisors and Teachers on Moral and Spiritual Values and the Schools," Box 22, SBC-CLC; "New York ACLU Warns School's 'Moral-Spiritual' Program Invades First Amendment," press release, 9 April 1956, Box 809, ACLU.

13. *NYT,* 13 January, 12 October 1952; [Max J. Rubin and Frank E. Karelsen], "Arguments For and Against the Regent's Recommendation for Public School Prayer," 21 February 1952, Box 799, ACLU.

14. Fred W. Friendly and Martha J. H. Elliot, *The Constitution: That Delicate Balance* (New York: Random House, 1984), 110; Theodore Powell, "Caesar, God

and the Public Schools," unpublished manuscript, Chapter III, 2–4, copy in Box 807, ACLU.

15. Powell, "Caesar, God and the Public Schools," Chapter III, 3–5.

16. Ibid. Chapter III, 6–10; "The Court Decision—and the School Prayer Furor," *Newsweek,* 9 July 1962, 43; Joshua Hammer, "The Sly Dog at Fox," *Newsweek,* 25 May 1992, 62.

17. Powell, "Caesar, God and the Public Schools," Chapter III, 10; Friendly and Elliott, *The Constitution,* 118–119.

18. *NYT,* 27 January, 25 February, 31 March, 25 August 1959; DVD recording, *CBS Reports: Storm over the Supreme Court: The School Prayer Case* (Princeton, NJ: Films for the Humanities and Sciences, 2004); Theodore Leskes and Sol Rabkin, memorandum for American Jewish Committee, "*Engel v. Vitale,* New York Public School Prayer Case," Box 1365, ACLU; "New York Court Hands Down Compromise Decision," press release, 30 November 1959, Box 1365, ACLU; Friendly and Elliott, *The Constitution,* 120; 206 N.Y.S. 2d 183 (1960) 188.

19. 10 N.Y. 2d 174 (1961) 180–181.

20. Some assumed the justices would simply let the lower courts' rulings stand without review, but in January 1962 a strong majority—seven out of nine—voted to hear arguments in the case that term. Justice Charles Whittaker was the sole vote against, with no vote recorded for Justice Potter Stewart. See notes, "Engel et al. v. Vitale et al.," 23 January 1962, Box 1276, WOD.

21. *CBS Reports: Storm over the Supreme Court;* audio recording, oral arguments, *Engel v. Vitale,* 370 U.S. 420 (1962), Oyez Project, Chicago-Kent College of Law (www.oyez.org/cases/1960–1969/1961/1961_468/); Michal R. Belknap, "God and the Warren Court: The Quest for a 'Wholesome Neutrality,'" *Seton Hall Constitutional Law Journal* 9 (1999): 404; Friendly and Elliott, *The Constitution,* 121–122.

22. Oral arguments, *Engel v. Vitale,* 370 U.S. 420 (1962).

23. Ibid.

24. Ibid.

25. *Pittsburgh Post-Gazette,* 30 March 1962; Roger K. Newman, *Hugo Black: A Biography* (New York: Fordham University Press, 2006), 482, 520–521; William O. Douglas, handwritten notes, "Conference, April 3, 1962, No. 468—Engel v. Vitale," Box 1276, WOD.

26. Newman, *Black,* 521; Wayne Flynt, "Justice Hugo Black, Judge Roy Moore, the Ten Commandments, and Southern Identity: The Supreme Court and Southern Evangelicalism," paper in author's possession; Wayne Flynt, *Alabama Baptists: Southern Baptists in the Heart of Dixie* (Tuscaloosa: University of Alabama Press, 1998), 246–262; Hugo Black Jr., *My Father: A Remembrance* (New York: Random House, 1975), 172–174.

27. Newman, *Black,* 361–365.

28. Hugo L. Black and Elizabeth Black, *Mr. Justice and Mrs. Black* (New York: Random House, 1986), 95; Flynt, "Justice Hugo Black"; Newman, *Black,* 521–522.

29. Black and Black, *Mr. Justice and Mrs. Black,* 95; "While Most Believe in God . . . ," *Newsweek,* 9 July 1962, 11; Flynt, "Justice Hugo Black"; Newman, *Black,* 522–523; James E. Clayton, *The Making of Justice: The Supreme Court in Action* (New

York: E. P. Dutton, 1964), 21; Theodore Powell, "The School Prayer Battle," *Saturday Review,* 20 April 1963, 63.

30. 370 U.S. 435, n. 21.

31. William O. Douglas to Hugo [Black], n.d. [1962], Box 1276, WOD; 370 U.S. 436; 370 U.S. 436 n. 1.

32. 370 U.S. 450.

33. Friendly and Elliot, *The Constitution,* 125; Powell, "The School Prayer Battle," 62; William A. Hachten, "Journalism and The Prayer Decision," *Columbia Journalism Review,* Fall 1962, copy in Box 11, SBC-CLC.

34. Hachten, "Journalism and The Prayer Decision," copy in Box 11, SBC-CLC.

35. *Washington Post,* 13 September 1960; *CSM,* 30 January 1961.

36. "While Most Believe in God . . . ," 11; Hachten, "Journalism and The Prayer Decision," copy in Box 11, SBC-CLC; *US News and World Report,* 9 July 1962.

37. Barry Goldwater, "Blow to Our Spiritual Strength," *LAT,* n.d. [1962], Box 358, HLB; Friendly and Elliot, *The Constitution,* 125; US Congress, House, 87th Cong., 2nd Sess., *CR,* 27 September 1964, 21100–21102; *Religious Herald,* 18 October 1962; news clippings, Fred Marshall Papers, Minnesota Historical Society, St. Paul, Minnesota.

38. Mary D. Carter to Black, 19 April 1962, Box 355, HLB; Petition to Justices of the Supreme Court, n.d. [1962], Box 355, HLB; Mrs. Shadwell S. H. Bowyer to Black, 10 December 1963, Box 357, HLB.

39. Mary K. Woolpert to Black, 26 June 1962, Box 361, HLB; Mrs. A. C. McGill Sr., to Black, 4 March 1963, Box 355, HLB; Eula Phillips to Black, n.d., Box 361, HLB; R. W. Ricketts to Black, n.d. [1962], Box 362, HLB; Mary Crum to Black, 4 July 1962, Box 359, HLB.

40. Newman, *Black,* 523–524; Black and Black, *Mr. Justice and Mrs. Black,* 95.

41. Edward O. Miller, "True Piety and the Regents' Prayer," *Christian Century,* 1 August 1962, 934; *NYT,* 21 September 2000.

42. *NYT,* 26 June 1962; Reinhold Niebuhr, "A Dissenting Opinion," *New Leader,* 9 July 1962, 3; William J. Butler and James A. Pike, "Has the Supreme Court Outlawed Religious Observance in the Schools?" *Reader's Digest,* October 1962, 78–85.

43. Religious News Service, Bulletin, "The Week in Religion," 21 July 1962, Box 1365, ACLU; Executive Committee of the National Association of Evangelicals, "Statement on the Supreme Court Ruling Regarding 'Regents' Prayer,'" n.d. [1962], Box 66, NAE; Charles D. Burge to the Billy Graham Evangelistic Association, 2 August 1962, Box 4, ROF; Robert O. Ferm to Mrs. William Gunnet, 24 August 1962, Box 4, ROF.

44. "The Court Decision—and the School Prayer Furor," *Newsweek,* 9 July 1962, 45; Daniel K. Williams, *God's Own Party: The Making of the Christian Right* (New York: Oxford University Press, 2010), 63; *Christian Beacon,* 13 September 1962.

45. As of 1956, Bible reading was required by law in Alabama, Arkansas, Delaware, the District of Columbia, Florida, Georgia, Idaho, Kentucky, Maine, Massachusetts, New Jersey, Pennsylvania, and Tennessee. It was permitted by law or judicial decision in Colorado, Iowa, Indiana, Kansas, Michigan, Minnesota, Mississippi, Nebraska, North Dakota, Ohio, Oklahoma, and Texas. Bible reading was

permitted, under general terms of the law or by judicial silence, in Connecticut, Maryland, Missouri, New Hampshire, North Carolina, Oregon, South Carolina, South Dakota, Rhode Island, Vermont, Virginia, and West Virginia. The states that had banned the practice were Arizona, California, Illinois, Louisiana, Nevada, New Mexico, New York, Utah, Washington, Wisconsin, and Wyoming. See Dierenfield, *Religion in American Public Schools*, 21.

46. Dierenfield, *Religion in American Public Schools*, 51.

47. Handbook, State of Idaho, Department of Education, "List of Selections from the Standard American Version of the Bible," n.d. [1950s], Box 801, ACLU; Handbook, Board of Education, Little Rock Public Schools, "Character and Spiritual Education," September 1954, Box 800, ACLU.

48. These were Colorado, Georgia, Florida, Iowa, Kentucky, Maine, Massachusetts, Minnesota, Nebraska, New York, Ohio, Pennsylvania, Tennessee, and Texas.

49. These were Illinois, Louisiana, South Dakota, Washington, and Wisconsin.

50. The quoted opinions come from *Wilkerson v. City of Rome*, 152 Ga. 652 (1921) and *People v. Board of Education of District 24*, 92 N.E. 251 (Illinois, 1910), both cited in Dierenfield, *Religion in American Public Schools*, 34–35.

51. Joseph Lewis to Stanley C. Fellows, 3 May 1950, Box 1669, ACLU; George Soll to Joseph Lewis, 19 July 1950, Box 1669, ACLU; Spencer Coxe, draft statement, "Re: Schempp Case," 13 February 1958, Box 1669, ACLU; *CT,* 18 June 1963; DVD recording, *CBS Reports: Storm over the Supreme Court: Bible-Reading in the Public Schools* (Princeton, NJ: Films for the Humanities and Sciences, 2004); [unknown], address on Schempp case, 17 June 1962, Box 1669, ACLU.

52. Spencer Coxe, office memorandum, "Re: Bible Reading in Public Schools," 11 March 1957, Box 1669, ACLU; Spencer Coxe, draft statement, "Re: Schempp Case," 13 February 1958, Box 1669, ACLU; "Weekly Bulletin," 23 June 1958, Box 1669, ACLU; [unknown], address on Schempp case, 17 June 1962, Box 1669, ACLU.

53. Sol Rabkin and Theodore Leskers, memorandum, "Schempp v. School District of Abington Township," 2 October 1959, Box 1669, ACLU; "Weekly Bulletin," 20 February 1961, Box 1669, ACLU; [unknown], address on Schempp case, 17 June 1962, Box 1669, ACLU; "Weekly Bulletin," 7 May 1962, Box 1669, ACLU.

54. Helen H. Ludwig, "The Baltimore Lord's Prayer Court Case," *Background Reports,* copy in Box 805, ACLU; Irving Murray to Leanne Golden, 21 October 1963, Box 806, ACLU; Roland Watts to Harold Buchman, 12 January 1961, Box 805, ACLU; Madalyn E. Murray to Harold Buchman, 18 January 1961, Box 805, ACLU; Harold Buchman to Madalyn E. Murray, 23 January 1961, Box 805, ACLU; Roland Watts to Ludlow P. Mahan Jr., 17 May 1961, Box 805, ACLU.

55. Sol Rabkin and Theodore Leskes, memorandum, "Murray v. Board of School Commissioners of Baltimore City," n.d. [1962], Box 1952, ACLU; Ludwig, "The Baltimore Lord's Prayer Court Case."

56. Peter Irons and Stephanie Guitton, eds., *May It Please the Court: The Most Significant Oral Arguments Made Before the Supreme Court Since 1955* (New York: The New Press, 1993), 61–69.

57. "Supreme Court Hears Religion Cases," *Church and State*, April 1963, 6.

58. Memorandum, "No. 142," Box 1295, WOD; conference notes, "No. 142—School Dist. of Abington Township v. Schempp," 1 March 1963, Box 1295, WOD; Michal R. Belknap, "God and the Warren Court," 435.

59. Ed Cray, *Chief Justice: A Biography of Earl Warren* (New York: Simon & Schuster, 2008), 387; Mimi Clark Gronlund, *Supreme Court Justice Tom Clark: A Life of Service* (Austin: University of Texas Press, 2010), 212; Alvin Warnock, "Associate Justice Tom C. Clark: Advocate of Judicial Reform," Ph.D. diss., University of Georgia, 1972, 259; Ellis M. West, "Justice Tom Clark and American Church-State Law," *Journal of Presbyterian History* 54 (1976): 387–388, 400; Newman, *Black*, 523.

60. Belknap, "God and the Warren Court," 436; 374 U.S. 206, 208.

61. "The Meaning of the Supreme Court Decision," news clipping [1963], Box 11, SBC-CLC; Gronlund, *Supreme Court Justice Tom Clark*, 197; 374 U.S. 222.

62. 374 U.S. 212–213.

63. Memorandum, clerk ["MJF"] to Justice Tom Clark, 22 May 1963, Tom C. Clark Papers, Tarlton Law Library, University of Texas, Austin, Texas; online collection (http://tarlton.law.utexas.edu/clark/schempp.html; accessed 14 August 2012); Paul G. Kauper, "The Warren Court: Religious Liberty and Church-State Relations," *Michigan Law Review* 67 (December 1968): 282–283; 374 U.S. 306; 374 U.S. 303, 304.

64. "The Meaning of the Supreme Court Decision," news clipping, *Christianity Today* [1963], Box 11, SBC-CLC; *CT*, 18 June 1963; *CSM*, 19 June 1963; "The Supreme Court: Bible Reading and Prayer," reprint, *The Dialogue* [1963], Box 11, SBC-CLC.

65. *CSM*, 19 June 1963; "The Supreme Court: Bible Reading and Prayer."

66. "The Supreme Court: Bible Reading and Prayer"; Williams, *God's Own Party*, 65; Billy James Hargis, "America: Let's Get Back to God!" *Christian Crusade*, August 1963, 26.

67. "Impact of the Ruling," news clipping, *Christianity Today* [1963], Box 11, SBC-CLC; *Time*, 19 June 1964; William M. Beaney and Edward N. Beiser, "Prayer and Politics: The Impact of *Engel* and *Schempp* on the Political Process," *Journal of Public Law* 13 (1964): 484.

CHAPTER 7: "OUR SO-CALLED RELIGIOUS LEADERS"

1. *CT*, 2 October 1963; *LAT*, 2 October 1963; Donald H. Gill, "Will the Bible Get Back into School?," *Eternity*, May 1964, 9; petition, Citizens Congressional Committee [October 1963], Drawer 72, AWR.

2. *LAT*, 2 October 1963; Charles W. Winegarner to "Dear Congressman," 25 September 1963, Drawer 72, AWR; Winegarner to A. Willis Robertson, Drawer 72, AWR.

3. Rowland Evans and Robert Novak, "Inside Report," *NYHT*, 12 May 1964; Gerald L. K. Smith, "We Are in Trouble!!!," *The Cross and the Flag*, December 1963, 3, 21; *WP*, 17 May 1964.

4. *WP,* 17 May 1964; Group Research Report, "Prayer Amendment Draws Extremist Support," 1 May 1964, Box 808, ACLU; Beaney and Beiser, "Prayer and Politics," 486–487; *Milwaukee Journal,* 6 August 1963.

5. *NYT,* 4 July 1962, 25 July 1963; *Time,* 19 June 1964; *US News and World Report,* 4 May 1964; Beaney and Beiser, "Prayer and Politics," 492; Donald R. Reich, "The Supreme Court and Public Policy: The School Prayer Cases," *Phi Delta Kappan,* September 1966, 30; Gill, "Will the Bible Get Back into School?," 9.

6. Biographical sketch, FJB; Beaney and Beiser, "Prayer and Politics," 494; H. J. Res. 752, 87th Cong., 2d Sess.

7. Beaney and Beiser, "Prayer and Politics," 494–495.

8. *WP,* 27 June 1962; *BG,* 27 June 1962.

9. US Congress, House, 88th Cong., 1st Sess., *CR,* 19 June 1963, 10557; Belknap, "God and the Warren Court," 446.

10. US Congress, House, 88th Cong., 1st Sess., *CR,* 14 August 1963, A5156–A5157; annual report, Association for the Advancement of Atheism, n.d., Box 2, Series IV, FJB; US Congress, House, 88th Cong., 1st Sess., *CR,* 19 August 1963, 14477; news clipping and speech transcript, "Extension of Remarks," 19 September 1963, Box 2, Series IV, FJB; Beaney and Beiser, "Prayer and Politics," 496.

11. Program, School Prayer Amendment Rally, 22 September 1963, Box 2, Series IV, FJB; Rev. George T. Cook, prepared remarks, 22 September 1963, Box 2, Series IV, FJB; US Congress, House, 88th Cong., 1st Sess., *CR,* 17 October 1963, A6536–A6537.

12. US Congress, House, 88th Cong., 2nd Sess., *CR,* 20 February 1964, A799; James E. Powers, "The Roots of Americanism Are Spiritual," *American Legion Magazine,* September 1963, copy in ALM; American Legion, news release, 20 December 1963, Box 4, Series IV, FJB; American Legion, National Legislative Commission, "Voluntary Prayer in Schools," 10 January 1964, ALM; Maurice T. Webb to members, National Americanism Commission, 19 December 1963, Box 4, Series IV, FJB; memorandum to department legislative chairmen, American Legion Auxiliary, 13 January 1964, ALM; "American Legion Fact Sheet," n.d. [January 1964], ALM; *WSJ,* 22 April 1964.

13. *BG,* 1 December 1963; report, Constitutional Prayer Amendment, Inc., n.d. [1963], Box 809, ACLU.

14. Report, Constitutional Prayer Amendment, Inc., n.d. [1963], Box 809, ACLU; Robert L. Mauro to Daniel Foley, 28 March 1964, ALM; *BS,* 5 October 1963, 18 February 1964.

15. *NYT,* 23 April 1964; Beaney and Beiser, "Prayer and Politics," 495–496; *WSJ,* 22 April 1964; Belknap, "God and the Warren Court," 446.

16. *NYT,* 20 March 1964; *WP,* 21 March 1964; Beaney and Beiser, "Prayer and Politics," 497; Becker, "The Prayer Hearings: Bane or Blessing?," press release, 25 March 1964, ALM.

17. Leanne Golden to affiliates, 12 March 1964, Box 808, ACLU; *WP,* 21 March 1964; Beaney and Beiser, "Prayer and Politics," 497; "A Discussion of Efforts to Amend the First Amendment," confidential report, 17 March 1964, Box 808, ACLU.

18. Though attendance at their meetings varied, they typically included representatives of Protestant bodies such as the National Council of Churches, United Presbyterian Church, Baptist Joint Committee, Seventh-day Adventists, Friends Committee, and Unitarian Fellowship for Social Justice; Jewish organizations such as the Anti-Defamation League, American Jewish Congress, and Union of American Hebrew Congregations; and civil libertarians aligned with the ACLU. See "Meeting in Washington to Discuss Efforts to Amend the First Amendment," confidential report, 4 April 1964, Box 809, ACLU.

19. *NYT,* 14 May 1997; *WP,* 18 May 1997; *WSJ,* 22 April 1964; Beaney and Beiser, "Prayer and Politics," 495–497.

20. "Report of a Second Meeting to Consider Measures to Oppose Amendment of the First Amendment," confidential report, 1 April 1964, Box 809, ACLU; "Meeting in Washington to Discuss Efforts to Amend the First Amendment," confidential report, 4 April 1964, Box 809, ACLU; "Action Meeting on Becker Amendment," report, 20–21 April 1964, Box 809, ACLU.

21. Memorandum, "U.S. House of Representatives Committee on the Judiciary," n.d. [1964], Box 809, ACLU; "Report of a Second Meeting to Consider Measures to Oppose Amendment of the First Amendment," confidential report, 1 April 1964, Box 809, ACLU; "Meeting in Washington to Discuss Efforts to Amend the First Amendment," confidential report, 4 April 1964, Box 809, ACLU; memorandum, "Opinions on the Becker Bill," 21 April 1964, Box 808, ACLU; Alan Reitman to Mr. Speiser, 2 April 1964, Box 808, ACLU.

22. "Report on Hearings on Becker Amendment," *Report from the Capital,* April–May 1964, 4; Beaney and Beiser, "Prayer and Politics," 499; *NYT,* 23 April 1964.

23. Dean Kelley, "Analysis of Hearings on Constitutional Amendments to Permit Prayer and Bible-Readings in Public Schools" [April 1964], Box 808, ACLU; Clay Risen, *The Bill of the Century: The Epic Battle for the Civil Rights Act* (New York: Bloomsbury, 2014), 141–158.

24. US Congress, House, 88th Cong., 2nd Sess., Committee on the Judiciary, "Proposed Amendments to the Constitution Relating to Prayers and Bible Readings in the Public Schools," 22–24 and 28–30 April; 1, 6–8, 13–15, 20–21, and 27–28 May; 3 June 1964 (hereafter cited as "Becker Amendment Hearings"), Pt. I, 212, 215–216, 219–221, 230, 244, 259.

25. Becker Amendment Hearings, Pt. I, 309, 376–377, 437, 375.

26. Becker Amendment Hearings, Pt. I, 314, 427, 320–321, 306.

27. Dean Kelley, "Analysis of Hearings on Constitutional Amendments to Permit Prayer and Bible-Readings in Public Schools" [April 1964], Box 808, ACLU; Becker Amendment Hearings, Pt. I, 420, 424, 520, 594.

28. Becker Amendment Hearings, Pt. I, 660, 667, 666.

29. Becker Amendment Hearings, Pt. I, 774, 778; Pt. II, 1077, Pt. III, 2096.

30. Becker Amendment Hearings, Pt. III, 1973, Pt. II, 1192, 979, Pt. III, 2233.

31. *CSM,* 30 March 1964; *Christian Century,* 1 April 1964.

32. Becker Amendment Hearings, Pt. I, 829; Pt. II, 975–976.

33. Becker Amendment Hearings, Pt. I, 902; Pt. II, 987, 1008, 1560.

34. Becker Amendment Hearings, Pt. II, 1039, 1041–1042.

35. Becker Amendment Hearings, Pt. II, 1209–1210, 1211, 1213, 1229–1232.

36. *Louisville Journal-Courier,* 11 May 1964.

37. *NYT,* 28 May 1964; *Time,* 19 June 1964; *Louisville Journal-Courier,* 11 May 1964; *WSJ,* 16 July 1964; report, Department of Religious Liberty, National Council of Churches, 15 July 1964, Box 809, ACLU.

38. "Becker Challenges Celler," press release, 11 August 1964, Box 6, Series IV, FJB; *LAT,* 7 July 1964; *WSJ,* 16 July 1964; report, Department of Religious Liberty, National Council of Churches, 15 July 1964, Box 809, ACLU; *WP,* 9 July 1964; *BS,* 28 June 1964.

39. E. V. Toy Jr., "The National Lay Committee and the National Council of Churches: A Case Study of Protestants in Conflict," *American Quarterly* 21 (Summer 1969): 190–209.

40. C. Emanuel Carlson, executive director's report, Baptist Joint Committee on Public Affairs, 5–6 October 1965, Box 8, SBC-ECR; Becker Amendment Hearings, Pt. III, 2227; K. Owen White to C. Emanuel Carlson, 27 March 1964, Box 1, KOW; K. Owen White to C. Emanuel Carlson, 2 April 1964, Box 1, KOW; K. Owen White to Rev. Krama Fay DeSha, 8 April 1964, Box 1, KOW.

41. K. Owen White, "Southern Baptists at the Crossroads," article draft, Box 1, KOW; "Religious Liberty Resolution," 22 May 1964, Box 11, SBC-CLC; *WP,* 23 May 1964; *CT,* 23 May 1964.

42. Ray M. White to Francis B. Burch, 5 January 1965, Folder 2064, EMD; Strom Thurmond to Burch, 6 January 1965, Folder 2064, EMD; George Murphy to Burch, 8 March 1965, Folder 2065, EMD; J. Caleb Boggs to Burch, 4 January 1965, Folder 2064, EMD.

43. James O. Eastland to Burch, 13 April 1965, Folder 2066, EMD; Hugh Scott to Burch, 2 February 1965, Folder 2065, EMD.

44. Robert F. Kennedy to Burch, 25 July 1965, Folder 2066, EMD; Wayne Morse to Burch, 12 April 1965, Folder 2066, EMD; Vance Hartke to Burch, 17 February 1965, Folder 2065, EMD; Daniel K. Inyoue to Burch, 5 January 1965, Folder 2064, EMD.

45. William Barry Furlong, "The Senate's Wizard of Ooze: Dirksen of Illinois," *Harper's Magazine,* December 1959, 44–49; Dirksen to Burch, 8 March 1965, Folder 2065, EMD; Everett Dirksen, *The Education of a Senator* (Pekin, IL: Dirksen Center, 1998), 6; *WP,* 4 July 1966.

46. US Congress, Senate, 89th Cong., 2nd Sess., *CR,* 22 March 1966, 1700; 6176–6277; *LAT,* 23 March 1966; *NYT,* 23 March 1966; *CT,* 23 March 1966.

47. *LAT,* 24 March 1966; Baptist Press, "Dirksen Amendment Set for Hearings," report, 17 July 1966, Box 14, HFP; Everett Dirksen to Birch Bayh, 7 April 1966, Folder 2158, EMD.

48. Burch to Clyde Flynn, 30 March 1966, Folder 2066, EMD; *WP,* 7 April, 10 August 1966; *CT,* 19 June, 27 August 1966; *BS,* 20 April 1966; *LAT,* 22 July 1966.

49. US Congress, Senate, 89th Cong., 2nd Sess., Judiciary Committee, Subcommittee on Constitutional Amendments, "School Prayer," 1–5, 8 August 1962 (hereafter cited as "Dirksen Amendment Hearings").

50. Dirksen Amendment Hearings, 9–10, 12.

51. Ibid., 13, 19; *LAT,* 2 August 1966; *NYT,* 27 April 1999.

52. Dirksen Amendment Hearings, 36–37.

53. Ibid., 211–212, 276; *WP,* 3 August 1966.

54. Dirksen Amendment Hearings, 279, 283–285.

55. Ibid., 213–214; Thomas G. Cash to Pascall, n.d. [August 1966], Box 14, HFP; Eva A. Simmons to Paschall, 26 August 1966, Box 14, HFP; Paschall to Simmons, 10 September 1966, Box 14, HFP; Paschall to Anna Caughron, 28 September 1966, Box 14, HFP.

56. *CT,* 7 August 1966; *LAT,* 29 August 1966.

57. *LAT,* 17 September 1966; *CT,* 17 and 20 September 1966; *BS,* 21 September 1966; *WP,* 24 September 1966.

58. *NYT,* 22 September 1966; *CT,* 20–21 September 1966; *BG,* 20 September 1966.

59. *BG,* 21–22 September 1966; *CT,* 22 September 1966.

60. *NYT,* 22 September 1966; *CSM,* 26 September 1966.

CHAPTER 8: "WHICH SIDE ARE YOU ON?"

1. *Hackensack Record,* 8 February 1965.

2. *Newark Star-Ledger,* 13 November 1964; *WSJ,* 11 December 1964; "Super Silly Season in Religion Is Upon Us," press release, 18 December 1964, Box 808, ACLU; *Hackensack Record,* 8 and 9 February 1965.

3. *Coatesville* (PA) *Record,* 17 November 1964; Emil Oxfeld to the mayor and council, 28 January 1965, Box 812, ACLU; *Hackensack Record,* 8 and 10 February 1965; *CT,* 27 August 1965.

4. Walter J. Lantry to Commander Johnson, 26 May 1965, ALM; Paul F. Hart to John E. Davis, 19 April 1967, ALM; *Rutgers Daily Targum,* 18 October 1965; Marilyn B. Young, *The Vietnam Wars, 1945–1990* (New York: HarperCollins, 1991), 139, 197.

5. *Hackensack Record,* 10 February 1965; *Interplay of European-American Affairs* 2 (1968): 47; *WP,* 19 October 1968.

6. Martin, *Prophet with Honor,* 278–280; Rick Perlstein, *Nixonland: The Rise of a President and the Fracturing of America* (New York: Scribner, 2008), 59.

7. David Aikman, *Billy Graham: His Life and Influences* (Nashville: Thomas Nelson, 2007), 207; Martin, *Prophet with Honor,* 350–355.

8. Walker Percy, *Lancelot* (New York: Farrar, Straus and Giroux, 1977), 220; Gibbs and Duffy, *The Preacher and the Presidents,* 199; Frady, *Billy Graham,* 452; Martin, *Prophet with Honor,* 360–361.

9. Martin, *Prophet with Honor,* 355.

10. *LAT,* 21 January 1969.

11. Charles P. Henderson Jr., *The Nixon Theology* (New York: Harper & Row, 1972), 3–4; *Bulletin of International Christian Leadership,* March 1957, RRF; *LAT,* 19 January 1969; *NYT,* 15 January 1969.

12. *NYT,* 18 and 21 January 1969. The West Auditorium has since been renamed the Dean Acheson Auditorium.

13. Henderson, *Nixon Theology*, 5; *NYT*, 21 January 1969; Aikman, *Billy Graham*, 211; *Newsday*, 24 January 1969; Gibbs and Duffy, *The Preacher and the Presidents*, 174; text of Billy Graham's inaugural prayer, Billy Graham Evangelical Association (http://www2.wheaton.edu/bgc/archives/inaugural05.htm).

14. *CT*, 20 January 1969; *WP*, 20 January 1969.

15. Henderson, *Nixon Theology*, 5–6; *CT*, 21 January 1969; *NYT*, 21 January 1969.

16. *CT*, 20 January 1969; *Newsday*, 20 January 1969; *NYT*, 21 January 1969.

17. Henderson, *Nixon Theology*, 19; *BS*, 31 January 1969; *WP*, 31 January 1969; H. R. Haldeman, *The Haldeman Diaries: Inside the Nixon White House* (New York: Putnam, 1994), 24.

18. *WP*, 31 January 1969; Frady, *Billy Graham*, 455.

19. Gibbs and Duffy, *The Preacher and the Presidents*, 175; *WP*, 27 January 1969.

20. Martin, *Prophet with Honor*, 357; *WP*, 27 January 1969; *BS*, 27 January 1969; *CT*, 27 January 1969; *Newsday*, 27 August 1969; Haldeman, *Haldeman Diaries*, 22.

21. Gibbs and Duffy, *The Preacher and the Presidents*, 175; *NYT*, 28 April 1969.

22. Martin, *With God on Our Side*, 98–99; Gibbs and Duffy, *The Preacher and the Presidents*, 175; *WP*, 27 January 1969; Ollie Atkins to Ron Ziegler, 17 September 1969, Box 7, RM-RMN; Larry Higby to Haldeman, 30 June 1969, Box 7, RM-RMN.

23. Haldeman to Bud Wilkinson, 1 July 1969, Box 7, RM-RMN; Nixon to Haldeman, 30 June 1969, Box 7, RM-RMN; Nixon to Ehrlichman, 16 June 1969, Box 7, RM-RMN; Haldeman to Dwight Chapin, 21 May 1969, Box 7, RM-RMN.

24. Martin, *Prophet with Honor*, 356; Frady, *Billy Graham*, 452; Charles B. Wilkinson to Billy Graham, 24 January 1969, Box 6, RM-RMN; memorandum, "Check List for Sunday Services," n.d. [1969], Box 7, RM-RMN.

25. Martin, *Prophet with Honor*, 358; Henderson, *Nixon Theology*, 29–30; *WP*, 2 and 3 February 1969, 30 June 1969; Jim Atwater to Ken Cole, 26 June 1969, Box 7, RM-RMN.

26. Martin, *Prophet with Honor*, 357–358; Harry Dent to Lucy Winchester, 29 April 1970, Box 12, RM-RMN; Gibbs and Duffy, *The Preacher and the Presidents*, 176–177; Constance Stuart to George Bell, 23 July 1970, Box 12, RM-RMN.

27. *LAT*, 29 September 1969; *BS*, 29 September 1969; Charles B. Wilkinson to Haldeman, 1 July 1969, Box 7, RM-RMN; Jim Atwater to Ken Cole, 25 September 1969, Box 7, RM-RMN; *WP*, 4 February 1970; *WSJ*, 2 April 1970; *NYT*, 8 August 1971; Dwight Chapin to Lucy Winchester, 9 July 1970, Box 12, RM-RMN.

28. Dwight L. Chapin to Bryce Harlow and Rose Mary Woods, 20 July 1969, Box 7, RM-RMN; Bill Timmons to Bryce Harlow, 28 June 1969, Box 7, RM-RMN; *NYT*, 8 August 1971; White House Church Services Permanent Invitation List, n.d. [1969], Box 12, RM-RMN.

29. Bud Wilkinson to Rose Mary Woods and Lucy Winchester, 2 June 1969, Box 7, RM-RMN; Dwight Chapin to Rose Mary Woods, 7 July 1969, Box 7, RM-RMN; *CT*, 27 January 1969; *WP*, 3 February, 17 March 1969; *LAT*, 29 September 1969; Martin, *Prophet with Honor*, 356–357.

30. Perlstein, *Nixonland*, 358; *WP*, 17 March 1969; *CT*, 17 March 1969.

31. *CT*, 16 March 1970; *WP*, 16 March 1970.

32. Nixon to Herb Klein, 16 June 1969, Box 7, RM-RMN; "First Priority List for Church Services," n.d. [June 1969], Box 7, RM-RMN; *WP*, 17 March, 1 July 1969.

33. Reinhold Niebuhr, "The King's Chapel and the King's Court," *Christianity and Crisis,* 4 August 1969; *NYT,* 7 August 1969; *BS,* 7 August 1969.

34. *NYT,* 10 August 1969.

35. *Newsday,* 27 August 1969; *NYT,* 8 August 1971; *WSJ,* 2 April 1970; Garry Wills, *Nixon Agonistes: The Crisis of the Self-Made Man* (New York: Houghton Mifflin, 2002), 183.

36. James Patterson, *Grand Expectations: The United States, 1945–1974* (New York: Oxford University Press, 1996), 753–755; Young, *Vietnam Wars,* 248; Perlstein, *Nixonland,* 496.

37. *LAT,* 10 May 1970; *NYT,* 11 May 1970; *WP,* 11 May 1970; Perlstein, *Nixonland,* 497; Wicker, *One of Us,* 634.

38. Guest list, "Worship Service, Sunday, May 10, 1970," Box 12, RM-RMN; Dwight Chapin to Connie Stuart and Lucy Winchester, 28 April 1970, Box 12, RM-RMN; Haldeman to Constance Stuart, 29 April 1970, Box 12, RM-RMN; *WP,* 11 May 1970; Statement of Faculty and Students, Calvin Theological Seminary, n.d. [May 1970], copy in Box 12, RM-RMN; Martha Doss to Noble Mellencamp, 11 May 1970, Box 12, RM-RMN.

39. As another token of his appreciation, Nixon appointed Brennan as secretary of labor in his second term. Perlstein, *Nixonland,* 488–499; Jonathan Schell, *Time of Illusion* (New York: Vintage, 1975), 101–102.

40. Memorandum, Richard Nixon to Bob Haldeman, 25 May 1970, reprinted in Bruce Oudes, ed., *From the President: Richard Nixon's Secret Files* (New York: Harper and Row, 1988), 139–140; Haldeman, *Haldeman Diaries,* 165, 168.

41. Frady, *Graham,* 452; *CT,* 29 May 1970; Garry Wills, "How Nixon Used the Media, Billy Graham, and the Good Lord to Rap with Students at Tennessee U," *Esquire,* September 1969, 119; *Newsday,* 29 May 1970.

42. Perlstein, *Nixonland,* 500–501; *CT,* 29 May 1970; Wills, "How Nixon Used the Media," 122; Martin, *Prophet with Honor,* 369.

43. *Newsday,* 29 May 1970; *WP,* 29 May 1970; Perlstein, *Nixonland,* 501–502; *CT,* 29 May 1970.

44. Perlstein, *Nixonland,* 501–503; *Newsday,* 29 May 1970.

45. *BG,* 29 May 1970; Perlstein, *Nixonland,* 502; Wills, "How Nixon Used the Media," 122; Henderson, *Nixon Theology,* 42.

46. Frady, *Graham,* 453; Martin, *Prophet with Honor,* 369–370; Perlstein, *Nixonland,* 503; Gibbs and Duffy, *The Preacher and the Presidents,* 187.

47. *WP,* 5 June 1970; *BS,* 19 June 1970; *NYT,* 24 June 1970.

48. Gibbs and Duffy, *The Preacher and the Presidents,* 188; *WP,* 28 June 1970; *BS,* 28 June 1970.

49. *WP,* 5 June 1970; handwritten memorandum, "Contributing Corporations," n.d. [June 1970], JWM; memorandum, Larry Higby to H. R. Haldeman, 19 June 1970, reprinted in Oudes, ed., *From the President,* 142; memorandum, "Contributors—Corporations," n.d. [June 1970], Box 173, JWM.

50. Gibbs and Duffy, *The Preacher and the Presidents,* 188; transcript, exit interview with Ronald H. Walker, conducted by Susan Yowell, 29 December 1972, Richard M. Nixon Presidential Library (www.nixonlibrary.gov/virtuallibrary/documents /cxitinterviews/walker.php; accessed 20 November 2013); *NYT,* 4 July 1970.

51. *WSJ,* 3 July 1970; *BG,* 2, 12, 16, 26, 27, 28 April, 14 June 1970; *BS,* 27 April 1970; program, Honor America Day, 4 July 1970, Box 178, JWM.

52. *LAT,* 30 June 1970.

53. *NYT,* 3, 4 July 1970; Gibbs and Duffy, *The Preacher and the Presidents,* 188; *WP,* 3 July 1970.

54. *Newsday,* 3 July 1970; *BS,* 5 July 1970; *Time,* 13 July 1970; *WP,* 5 July 1970.

55. *WP,* 5 July 1970; program, Honor America Day, 4 July 1970, Box 178, JWM.

56. Billy Graham, "The Unfinished Dream," speech transcript, 4 July 1970, Box 222, BGCA.

57. Ibid.

58. *Newsday,* 6 July 1970; Arthur White, telex report, "Honor America Day—Take 7," 4 July 1970, Box 16, AW; *WP,* 5 July 1970.

59. Arthur White, telex report, "Honor America Day—Saturday Updating—Take V," 4 July 1970, Box 16, AW; *Newsday,* 3 July 1970; schedule, "Honor America Day," n.d. [July 1970], Box 178, JWM.

60. *Newsday,* 3 and 6 July 1970; *BS,* 5 July 1970; *BG,* 5 July 1970; Arthur White, telex report, "Honor America Day—Saturday Updating—Take Six," 4 July 1970, Box 16, AW.

61. Arthur White, telex report, "Honor America Day—Saturday Updating—Take V," 4 July 1970, Box 16, AW; *Newsday,* 6 July 1970; Arthur White, telex report, "Honor America Day—Saturday Updating—Take Six," 4 July 1970, Box 16, AW.

62. Audio recording, "Proudly They Came to Honor America," 1970, copy in author's possession; *CT,* 5 July 1970.

63. *Newsday,* 6 July 1970.

64. *WP,* 6 and 7 July 1970; *LAT,* 6 July 1970; Kenneth Shaw to "Dear Member," n.d. [1970], Box 177, JWM; Capitol Record Club, "Reservation Certificate," n.d. [1970], Box 177, JWM; "Proudly They Came . . . ," advertisement, *Nation's Business,* July 1971, copy in Box 179, JWM.

65. *Newsday,* 7 July 1970; *BG,* 6 July 1970; *WP,* 5 July 1970.

EPILOGUE

1. *LAT,* 18 July 1980; *CSM,* 16 July 1980; *WSJ,* 18 July 1980.

2. *BG,* 18 July 1980; *BS,* 18 July 1980; *NYT,* 27 May 1980.

3. *WP,* 16, 18 July 1980; "Reagan's 'Crusade' Begins," *Newsweek,* 28 July 1980.

4. David Domke and Kevin Coe, *The God Strategy: How Religion Became a Political Weapon in America* (New York: Oxford University Press, 2010), 48, 61–64.

5. *Newsweek,* 25 October 1976; Michael Lienesch, *Redeeming America: Piety and Politics in the New Christian Right* (Chapel Hill: University of North Carolina Press, 1993), 1–2; *Newsday,* 12 October 1980.

6. Williams, *God's Own Party,* 187; Martin, *With God on Our Side,* 220.

7. *CT,* 21 January 1981, 4 February 1983; *LAT,* 27 February 1982; *Newsday,* 14 February 1984; *WP,* 5 February 1982; *CSM,* 4 February 1983.

8. *WP,* 20 December 1981, 19 September 1982; *CT,* 8 February 1981.

9. *NYT,* 3 February 1984; *WP,* 5 February 1984; *Newsday,* 14 February 1984.

10. *LAT,* 21 July 1984; David R. Shepherd, ed., *Ronald Reagan: In God I Trust* (Wheaton, IL: Tyndale House, 1984); *NYT,* 28 September 1984.

11. *LAT,* 23 August 1984; *NYT,* 24 August 1984; *BS,* 9 September 1984.

12. *Newsday,* 23, 27 August 1984; *LAT,* 29 December 1984.

13. Gibbs and Duffy, *The Preacher and the Presidents,* 285–298; *NYT,* 24 April 1986; *WP,* 28 April 1986; *LAT,* 6 March 1988.

14. *CT,* 18 July 1988; *NYT,* 19 August 1988.

15. *WP,* 24 August, 10 September 1988; *NYT,* 26 August, 10 September 1988; Sidney Blumenthal, *Pledging Allegiance: The Last Campaign of the Cold War* (New York: HarperCollins, 1990); *BS,* 21 September 1988; *LAT,* 9, 13, 22 September 1988.

16. Blumenthal, *Pledging Allegiance,* 308; *CSM,* 21 September 1988; *LAT,* 11 September 1988.

17. *LAT,* 30 June 1989; *CT,* 9 July 1989.

18. *LAT,* 4 July 1989; *NYT,* 3 July 1989; *WSJ,* 5 July 1989; *CT,* 22 October 1989.

19. Williams, *God's Own Party,* 231–232; *NYT,* 18 August 1992; *WP,* 18 August 1992; *NYT,* 1 February 2007.

20. Garry Wills, *Under God: Religion and American Politics* (New York: Simon and Schuster, 1990), 60; *WP,* 29 June, 12, 17, 18 July 1992.

21. *WP,* 24 August 1992; *NYT,* 24, 30 August 1992; Domke and Coe, *God Strategy,* 133–134.

22. *WP,* 4 February 1994, 7, 12, 17 February 1997; *NYT,* 3 February 1995, 7 February 1997; 6 February 1998; *Philadelphia Tribune,* 14 February 1997.

23. *NYT,* 15 December 1999; David Frum, *The Right Man: An Inside Account of the Bush White House,* 2nd ed. (New York: Random House, 2005), 5–6; Lou Cannon and Carl M. Cannon, *Reagan's Disciple: George W. Bush's Troubled Quest for a Presidential Legacy* (New York: Public Affairs, 2008), 81.

24. *NYT,* 21 January, 4 February 2001; *Philadelphia Tribune,* 2 February 2001; Kevin M. Kruse, "Compassionate Conservatism: Religion in the Age of George W. Bush," in *The Presidency of George W. Bush: A First Historical Assessment,* ed. Julian E. Zelizer (Princeton, NJ: Princeton University Press, 2010), 227–251.

25. *NYT,* 12, 18 September 2001.

26. *NYT,* 27 June 2002.

27. *NYT,* 22 March 2004; brief for the Christian Legal Society et al., as amici curiae, *Elk Grove Unified School District v. Michael A. Newdow* (www.clsnet.org /document.doc?id=256).

28. Esther Kaplan, *With God on Their Side* (New York: New Press, 2004), 156–161; *NYT,* 31 October 2004; *LAT,* 12 August 2004; Amy Sullivan, *The Party Faithful* (New York: Scribner 2008), 116–117.

29. *WP,* 27 July 2004

30. *Jerusalem Post,* 16 March 2008; *NYT,* 15, 19 March, 1 May 2008; *Irish Times,* 25 March 2008.

31. *NYT,* 7 October, 8 November, 7 December 2007; *Jerusalem Post,* 17 December 2007.

32. *NYT,* 6, 7 December 2007.

INDEX

Abington School District v. Schempp, 192–195, 198–199
Advertising Council, 131–138
Advertising industry, 130–138
Agnew, Spiro (vice president), 248, 253, 265, 271
Alplanalp, Bob (executive), 264
Allen, Ray (Concerned Christians for Reagan), 281
Allen-Bradley Company, 150
"America on Its Knees" (painting), 77
American Civil Liberties Union (ACLU), xv–xvi, 84, 99, 107, 121–122, 148
   Madalyn Murray and, 194
   "One Nation Under God" banners, 240
   prayer amendment and, 213, 215
   Ronald Reagan and, 279
   school mandatory Bible reading and, 192, 194
   school prayer and, 172, 174–175
American Council of Christian Churches, 190, 232
American Cyanamid and Chemical Corporation, 18
"American Economic System" ad campaign, 131
American Jewish Committee, 84, 168, 213
American Jewish Congress, 83–84, 147
American Legion
   "Back to God" movement, 73–75, 110
   "In God We Trust" motto support, 116

"One Nation Under God" banners, 240–241
   Pledge of Allegiance change, 104
   prayer amendment support, 210–211
   promotion of public religion, 207
American Liberty League, 4, 7, 16
"American way of life," 105–106
Americans for Democratic Action (ADA), 103, 108, 113
Anderson, John B. (representative), 217
Anderson, Robert (secretary of the treasury), 84, 120
Andrews, George (representative), 184
Anti-ballistic-missile treaty, 253–254
Anti-Defamation League, 214
Antiwar protests, 241, 257–259, 266–271
Associated Refineries, 84
AT&T, 254
Atheists/atheism, 106–107, 149, 194, 197, 209–210, 217, 221, 223, 240, 266, 268, 289

"Back to God" movement, 73–75, 110
Baker, George (lawyer), 196
Baptist Joint Committee on Public Affairs (BJC), 213, 226, 228, 234
Barkley, Alben (vice president), 54, 102
Bates, Carl (SBC president), 252
Bayh, Birch (senator), 231, 233–234, 236
Bechtel Corporation, 254
Becker, Frank (representative), 207–211, 213, 216–217
Becker Amendment, 208, 211, 213, 218, 220–224, 226–227, 229
   See also Prayer amendment

Belding, Don (advertising executive), 69–70, 141
Bellah, Robert (sociologist), 68
Bellamy, Francis (minister), 100–102
Bennett, Charles E. (representative), 116–124
Benson, Ezra Taft (secretary of agriculture), 81–82, 83, 85
Benson, George S. (college president), 26
Bernardin, Joseph (Catholic archbishop), 252
Bible
    Gideon version, 165–169
    King James Version, 190
    Reader's Digest version, 138–139
    readings in public schools, 190–201, 205
    Revised Standard Version, 139
    Standard American Version, 191
Billy Graham Evangelical Association, 38, 263
Black, Hugo (justice), 179–182, 185–186, 188, 195–196
Blake, Eugene Carson (minister), 219
Block, Herb (political cartoonist), 187
Bobst, Elmer (executive), 264
Boone, Pat (singer), 154–155, 267, 280, 285
Bowron, Fletcher (mayor), 34, 141
Boy Scouts of America, 23, 71, 270–271
Brennan, Peter (union leader), 259, 265
Brennan, William J., Jr. (justice), 196, 199
Brock, Bill (representative), 253, 261
Brown v. Board of Education, 95
Brownell, Herbert (attorney general), 67, 85
Buchanan, Pat (politician), 285, 290
Buchwald, Art (columnist), 266
Buckley, William F., Jr. (commentator), 148, 161
Bunyan, John (author), 180
Burch, Francis B. (Baltimore city solicitor), 195, 211, 222–223, 227–229
Burnham, James (political theorist), 161
Burns, Arthur (Federal Reserve chairman), 255

Burns, James MacGregor (historian), 5
Burton, Harold (senator), 44–46, 79
Burton, Shrum (minister), 201
Bush, George H. W. (president), 275, 281–282, 284, 286
Bush, George W. (president), 287–290
Butler, William (attorney), 174–177
Byrnes, James (justice), 49

Callahan, Daniel (theologian), 256–257
Campbell, Will (minister), 243
Cannon, Lou (journalist), 279
"Capital Crusade Day," 88
Capitalism, Christianity linked to, 7–8, 10, 37, 86, 293
Carlson, Emanuel (BJC director), 220, 226, 234
Carlson, Frank (senator), 59–60, 75–76, 78, 91, 248
Carroll, Donald (Florida American Legion commander), 116–118
Carter, Jimmy (president), 277, 279
Case, Clifford (senator), 116
Caterpillar Tractor Company, 264
Celler, Emanuel (representative), 122, 208–209, 212–213, 215–217, 220–224
Ceremonial deism, 99–100, 113, 124, 169, 176, 182, 293
Chandler, Porter (lawyer), 178
Chapin, Dwight (Nixon assistant), 254, 263, 265
Chase, Salmon (secretary of the treasury), 112
Chevrolet, 46
Chicago & Southern Airline, 37
Childs, Marquis (journalist), 63–64
"Christ for Greater Los Angeles" campaign, 36
Christian Action, 62
Christian amendment proposal, 95–98, 100
Christian Anti-Communism Crusade (CACC), 149, 151, 154, 156, 158–161
Christian Coalition, 285
Christian Crusade, 204

Christian Leadership breakfast groups, 41–45, 47–48
Christian libertarianism, xiv–xv, 7–8, 31, 36–39, 72, 103, 109, 140, 149, 273
  Dwight D. Eisenhower election and, 293
  Fred Schwarz welcomed by, 149
  Freedoms Foundation and, 69
  Pledge of Allegiance, 104
  "Religion in American Life" (RIAL) campaign and, 132
Christian Nationalist Crusade, 204
Christianity, capitalism linked to, 7–8, 10, 37, 86, 293
Chrysler Corporation, 20, 28, 84, 142, 225, 270
Chubb, John (scholar), 283
Church membership/attendance, xv, 68, 132–133, 137–138, 199
Citizens Congressional Committee, 203–204, 222
City Chapel, 41–43, 46
Civil libertarians, 100, 168, 172, 213, 240
Civil Rights Act (1964), 216, 229
Clark, Tom (justice), 47, 79, 179, 196–199
Clergy
  ceremonial deism support, 99–100
  Faith and Freedom (publication), 24–27
  New Deal support by, 5–6
  at Nixon inauguration, 245–246
  opposition to prayer amendment, 206–207, 213–215, 217–221, 225–226, 231–234
  Spiritual Mobilization recruitment of, 12–14, 16–21, 24–25
  White House church services, 251–253, 255–257
Clinton, Bill (president), 285–287
Cohen, Gary (minister), 233
Coins, "In God We Trust" motto on, 112, 116, 119, 121, 176, 209
Cold War, 22, 35–36, 48, 109, 161, 242, 266
Colgate-Palmolive-Peet Company, 20

Colson, Charles (Nixon aide), 250, 253–254
Columbus Day, 101
Committee for the Preservation of Prayer and Bible Reading in Public Schools, 212, 221
Committee to Proclaim Liberty, 27–34, 69–70, 77, 83, 129, 136, 141, 267, 277
Communism
  Abraham Vereide and, 48–49
  Billy Graham and, 35–36, 38, 61
  Cecil B. DeMille and, 140
  Christian Anti-Communism Crusade (CACC), 149, 151, 154, 156, 158–161
  Fred Schwarz's anticommunism efforts, 148–161
Compassionate conservatism, 287
Congressional prayer breakfast meetings, 44–45
Continental Can Company, 85, 254
Connally, John (politician), 51
Constitution
  Christian amendment proposal, 95–98, 100
  First Amendment (*see* First Amendment)
  James W. Fifield and, 11
  prayer amendment and, 203–237
Constitutional Prayer Amendment, Inc., 211–212
Constitutional Prayer Foundation, 212, 222, 227
Cook, George T. (minister), 210
Cook, Robert A. (minister), 200, 221
Coonley, Howard (NAM leader), 44–46
Corporations, advertising by, 130–138
Cowling, Donald J. (college president), 11
Cox, Harvey (minister), 256
Crane, Edward (Cato Institute leader), 284
"The Credo of the American Way," 70–71
Cronkite, Walter (news anchor), 110, 255
Crystal Cathedral, 287

Cushing, Richard (Catholic archbishop), 200

Daiker, Bertram (school board counsel), 177
Daschle, Tom (senator), 289
Dateline Disneyland (TV special), 127
Davis, Elmer (radio commentator), 92–93
Decker, R. L. (NAE director), 90–91
Declaration of Independence, 27–30, 33–34, 56, 67, 90–92, 106, 141, 171, 176–178, 182, 189, 268, 289–290
Deism, ceremonial, 99–100, 113, 124, 169, 176, 182, 293
DeMille, Cecil B. (filmmaker), xv, 9, 33, 41, 140–148, 161
DeMille Foundation for Political Freedom, 141–142
Dent, Harry (Nixon aide), 252–253
Deering-Milliken Company, 158–159
Democratic National Conventions, 5, 152, 290
Depression. *See* Great Depression
Desmond, Charles S. (judge), 175
Detroit Edison Company, 30
Dickinson, Alfred (minister), 179
Dillon, Read & Company, 85
Dirksen, Everett (senator), 228–237
Dirksen Amendment, 229–231
Discharge petition, 209–212, 224
Disney, Walt (executive), 28, 69, 127–130, 155
Disneyland, 127–130, 152
Docherty, George M. (minister), 104–107, 109–111, 140
Dodd, Thomas J. (senator), 153–154, 157
Dole, Bob (senator), 281, 284
Douglas, William O. (justice), xv, 98–99, 176, 178–179, 182–183, 196, 199
Douglass, Walter (developer), 41
Drinan, Robert (dean), 231–232
Duffy, John E. (chaplain), 73–74
Dukakis, Michael (governor), 282–283
Dulles, John Foster (secretary of state), 67, 82–83, 85, 113

DuPont (E. I. du Pont de Nemours and Company), 4, 18, 225
Durkin, Martin (secretary of labor), 85

"E Pluribus Unum" motto, 121, 123–124
East Room, religious services in, 249–257
Eastern Airlines, 28
Eastland, James (senator), 185, 228
Eberharter, Herman (representative), 118
Eisenhower, Dwight D. (president)
    Advertising Council support, 134
    "America on Its Knees" (painting), 77
    "Back to God" program, 74–75
    baptism of, xii, 72–73
    Billy Graham and, x, 58–64, 72
    cabinet meetings opened with prayer, xii, 81–84
    Camp David, 92–93
    Constitutional Prayer Amendment, Inc. endorsed by, 211
    corporate elite in cabinet, 84–86
    "The Credo of the American Way," 70–71
    on *Engel* decision, 185
    Frank Carlson and, 76
    Freedoms Foundation and, 69–72
    "In God We Trust" on stamps and currency, 113–115, 118, 120
    inauguration (1953), ix–xii
    at Lincoln Sunday service (1954), 105, 107
    National Day of Prayer, 92
    National Prayer Breakfast, 78, 80–81
    Pledge of Allegiance, 110
    presidential campaign (1952), 59–62
    public prayer and, 36
    Richard M. Nixon's inauguration, 244
    Ronald Reagan's support for, 276
    religious themes, 60, 67–69, 72, 75, 78, 87, 293
    religious upbringing, 57–58
    Sid Richardson and, 58–59
    Statement of Seven Divine Freedoms, 88
    welfare state and, 86–87

Elson, Edward L. R. (minister), 73, 139, 197
Engel, Steven (parent), 174
Engel v. Vitale, 174–190
    Frank Becker and, 207
    Hugo Black and, 179–182, 185–186, 188
    reaction to decision, 183–189
    religious supporters of decision, 188–190
Ervin, Sam (senator), 236
Estrich, Susan (campaign manager), 283
Evans, Rowland (columnist), 204, 222
Everson v. Board of Education, 180

Faith and Freedom (publication), 23–27, 63, 69
Falwell, Jerry (minister), 277–278, 281, 291
Federal Marriage Amendment, 290
Federal Trade Commission, 130
Ferguson, Homer (senator), 109–110, 117
Fifield, James W., Jr. (minister)
    attacks on, 11, 21
    Cecil B. DeMille and, 141–142
    Don Belding's praise of, 69
    Faith and Freedom (publication), 24–27
    First Congregational Church, 8–12
    The Freedom Story (radio program), 22–23
    "Freedom Under God" celebrations, 34
    J. Howard Pew and, 16–17
    at NAM annual meeting (1940), 3, 6–7
    Spiritual Mobilization, 11–15, 18–27
    theology of, 10–11
    wealth of, 10, 21
Finkelstein, Louis (rabbi), 252
Firestone, Harvey (executive), 15, 28
Firestone Tire and Rubber Company, 15, 20
First Amendment, 100
    Bible readings in schools, 193
    establishment clause, 181, 182, 196, 198

free-exercise clause, 198
    religious groups support of, 214, 219, 220, 223
    school prayer and, 175, 179, 181–183, 206
    separation of church and state, 98–100, 105–106, 141, 147–148, 167–169, 180–184, 197
    Southern Baptist Convention and, 237
First Congregational Church (Los Angeles), 8–12, 15, 18, 141, 146, 149
Flag Day, 110–111
Flag "desecration," 283–284
Flaherty, Vincent (columnist), 154
Flanders, Ralph (senator), 96
Fleischer, Ari (Bush press secretary), 289
Flynt, Wayne (historian), 179
Foundation for Economic Education, 18, 23, 28
Frady, Marshall (author), 243
Frankfurter, Felix (justice), 178–179
Fraternal Order of Eagles, 145–148
Frawley, Patrick (executive), 152–154, 156, 264
Free enterprise
    advertising and, 130–132
    Billy Graham and, 37–38, 51
    Fred Schwarz and, 150, 152
    Freedoms Foundation and, 69–70
    James W. Fifield's defense of, 6–7, 14
    NAM promotion of, 4
    Spiritual Mobilization and, 28, 32, 37
    Walt Disney and, 129
    See also Capitalism
The Freedom Story (radio program), 22–23, 27, 70, 92
"Freedom Under God" celebrations, 27–34, 56, 73, 88, 92, 102, 129, 136, 141, 251, 272
"Freedom Under God" idea, xiv, 26–27, 34, 63, 88, 109, 146, 149, 293
Freedoms Foundation, 28, 69–72, 77, 86, 141, 151
Friberg, Arnold (painter), 144
Frost, Robert (poet), 184
Frum, David (author), 287

Fry, Franklin Clark (minister), 190
Fulbright, William (senator), 119

General Electric, 3, 132, 254
General Foods Corporation, 85
General Motors Company, 3, 4, 13, 17,
    18, 20, 26, 28, 84, 85, 134, 142,
    254, 264
Gibbons, James (Catholic archbishop),
    216
Gideons International, Inc., 165–169
"God Bless America," Reagan sign-off,
    275–276
Goldberg, Arthur (justice), 196, 199
Goldwater, Barry (senator), 87, 148, 150,
    185
Goodwill Industries, 39–40
Goodyear Tire and Rubber Company,
    254
Gore, Al, Jr. (senator-vice president), 286
Gore, Albert (senator), 261
"Government Under God" theme, xii,
    78, 79, 81, 83, 87, 92, 108
Graham, Billy (minister)
    "Christ for Greater Los Angeles"
        campaign, 36
    communism and, 35–36, 38, 61
    crusades, 49–50, 53–55, 59–60, 104,
        141, 149, 242–243, 260–263
    Dwight D. Eisenhower and, 58–64,
        72
    on Engel decision, 188–189
    film production company, 51
    Fred Schwarz and, 149
    free enterprise and, 37–38, 51
    George H. W. Bush and, 281
    Harry S. Truman and, 52–54, 56, 61
    Honor America Day, 263, 265–269
    Hour of Decision (TV show), 53, 139
    National Day of Prayer, 55–57
    National Prayer Breakfast, 78, 80,
        248–251
    political connections, 52, 54, 58–64
    at Republican National Conventions,
        242, 275
    Richard M. Nixon and, 242–244,
        246–247, 252, 260–263
    Sid Richardson and, 50–51, 54

    White House church service, 249,
        254–255
Grant, George (representative), 184
Graves, John Temple (journalist), 63
Great Depression, 4–5, 8, 10, 40, 80,
    130, 273, 275, 292
Greater New York School of
    Anti-Communism, 160–161
Gulf Oil, 20, 28

Haake, Alfred (economist), 17–18, 24
Hagerty, Jim (Eisenhower press secre-
    tary), 73, 81
Haldeman, H. R. (Nixon chief of staff),
    250–251, 260, 263–265
Halverson, Richard (minister), 252
Hargis, Billy James (evangelist), 204
Harlan, John Marshall II (justice), 179,
    196, 199
Harlow, Bryce (Eisenhower aide), 120
Harris, Frederick Brown (chaplain), 78
Harrison, Benjamin (president), 101
Harte, Mary (school board member),
    173–174
Hartke, Vance (senator), 228
Hawkes, Albert W. (executive-senator),
    9, 15, 18
Hayakawa, S. I. (college president), 254
Hayek, Friedrich (economist), 19
Haynesworth, Clement (judge), 255
Hearst, William Randolph, Jr. (pub-
    lisher), 183, 212
Hennings, Thomas (senator), 121
Herberg, Will (sociologist), 68
Herrick Union Free School District,
    173–174
Heston, Charlton (actor), 146–147, 282
Hiat, Philip (rabbi), 190
Hill, E. V. (minister), 281
Hilleboe, Guy (superintendent of
    schools), 167
Hilton, Conrad (executive), 28, 76–77,
    81, 212
Hobby, Oveta Culp (secretary of health,
    education and welfare), 83, 85
Hocking, William (philosopher), 11
Hoffman, Julius (judge), 255
Holiday Inn, 37

Holland, Spessard L. (senator), 123
"Hollywood's Answer to Communism,"
    154–156, 158
Honor America Day, 263–273
Hoover, Herbert (president), 12–14, 19,
    28, 70–71, 185
Hope, Bob (entertainer), 263–266, 271
Hopper, Hedda (columnist), 129
Hour of Decision (TV show), 53, 139
House of Representatives
    code of ethics, 117
    discharge petition, 209–212, 224
    hearings on prayer amendment, 206,
        212–224, 226, 228, 230–231
    "In God We Trust" motto displayed
        in, 185
    prayer amendment and, 207–224
    prayer breakfast meetings, 44–45
    Un-American Activities Committee,
        129, 140, 149
Howard, Irving (minister), 25
Howes, Robert (priest), 212, 221–222
Hruska, Roman (senator), 232
Hughes Aircraft Company, 28
Humphrey, George (secretary of the
    treasury), 84, 118
Humphrey, Hubert (senator), 242
Hunt, H. L. (oilman), 50, 86
Hunter, David (priest), 232–233
Hutchinson, B. E. (executive), 28, 225
Hutton, E. F. (stock broker), 28, 69

"In God We Trust" motto, 99–100,
    293–294
    classroom placement of, 191
    on coins, 112
    courtroom display of, 175
    House of Representatives display of,
        185
    as official national motto, 121–124
    origin of, 111–112
    on paper currency, 116–121, 125
    on stamps, 113–116, 125
Independence Day, framed as religious
    event, 27, 30–34, 56, 91–92
Ingalls, E. K. (parent), 167
Ingebretsen, James (Freedom Under
    God organizer), 32–33

Ingersoll, Roy (executive), 46
Inouye, Daniel (senator), 228
International Business Machines (IBM),
    45
International Council for Christian
    Leadership (ICCL), 48, 62, 96,
    117–118, 149
International Peace Garden, 146–147
Ivins, Molly (columnist), 285

J. Walter Thompson Company, 33,
    131–132, 136, 138, 251, 263
Jackson, C. D. (publisher), 155–158
Jaeger and Jessen Company, 91
Jefferson, Thomas (president), xiii, 180
Jepsen, Roger (senator), 279
John Birch Society, 155–156, 158, 205,
    240
Johnson, Lyndon B. (president), 50, 110,
    217, 228, 246, 249
Johnson, William (editor-journalist),
    23–24
Johnston, Olin (senator), 49
Judd, Walter (representative), 134,
    153–154, 157

Kehr, Ernest (columnist), 112–113
Kelley, Dean (minister), 188, 213–214,
    216, 218, 224, 226
Kemp, Jack (representative), 281–282
Kennedy, John F. (president), 184, 249
Kennedy, Robert (attorney general-
    senator), 159, 228
Kent State shootings, 257, 259, 266
Kerpelman, Leonard (attorney), 196
Kerry, John (senator), 290
Kertzer, David (anthropologist), 284
Khrushchev, Nikita (Soviet premier),
    152
King, Martin Luther, Jr. (civil rights
    leader), 267–268
Knight, Goodwin (governor), 127–128
Knights of Columbus, 102–104, 207,
    239–240
Knowland, William (senator), 110
Kraft Foods, 44, 285
Krauthammer, Charles (columnist),
    291

LaGuardia, Fiorello (mayor), 43
Lane, Rose Wilder (author), 24
Langlie, Arthur (mayor-governor), 42, 60–61
Lantry, Walter (longshoreman), 239–241
Latta, Del (representative), 218
Leaming, Charles (minister), 212, 221
Lecoque, Ralph (parent), 168
Leedom, Boyd (judge), 244
Lefkowitz, David Jr. (rabbi), 74
Lerner, Monroe (parent), 174
LeTourneau, R. G. (executive), 47
Lewis, Anthony (columnist), 213
Lewis, Hobart (publisher), 264
Lichtenstein, Dan and Ruth (parents), 173–174
Lincoln, Abraham (president), 55, 96, 104–105, 112, 153
Lippmann, Walter (columnist), 64
Long, Huey (senator), 204
Lord, John Wesley (Methodist bishop), 219
Luccock, Halford (minister), 139
Luce, Henry (publisher), 28, 49, 242
Lyons, Lenore (parent), 173–174

MacArthur, Douglas (general), 28, 61
MacKenzie, Aeneas (screenwriter), 142–143
A Man Called Peter (film), 104, 140
Manion, Clarence (radio host-author), 23–24, 30
Mansfield, Mike (senator), 113, 236
March of Freedom, 88, 90–92
Mark A. Hanna Company, 84
Marriott, J. Willard (executive), 244, 264–266, 273
Marshall, Fred (representative), 185
Marshall, Peter (minister), 104, 140
Martin, William (religious scholar), 244
Marshall Field and Company, 28, 45, 264
Massachusetts Citizens for Public Prayer, 212, 221
Matthews, Billy (representative), 218
Maytag, Inc., 28, 69

McBain, Hughston (executive), 28, 45
McCain, John (senator), 291
McCarthy, Joseph (senator), 95
McCormack, John (representative), 52, 56, 185
McGrory, Mary (columnist), 273
McIntire, Carl (minister), 200, 204–205, 233–234
McIntyre, James Francis (Catholic archbishop), 200
McWilliams, Carey (journalist), 21
Memorial Day Massacre (1937), 21
Meyer, Bernard (judge), 175
Meyer, Frank S. (editor), 151, 161
Miller, Edward O. (minister), 188
Miller, William Lee (theologian), 67–68, 116, 171
Milliken, Roger (executive), 158–159
Minton, Sherman (justice), 47
Monroney, Mike (senator), 119
Monsanto Chemical Company, 130
Moody, Dwight (evangelist), 57
Moore, Art, Jr. (representative), 219
Moral Majority, 277, 279, 281
Morrison, William A. (representative), 219
Morse, Wayne (senator), 119–120, 228
Mosk, Stanley (California attorney general), 160
Multer, Abraham (representative), 118–119
Mundt, Karl (senator), 61
Murphy, George (senator), 154–155, 157–158
Murray, Madalyn (parent), 194, 197, 211, 239
Murray v. Board of School Commissioners of Baltimore City, 194–195, 198–199

National Association of Evangelicals (NAE), 88–91, 120, 200, 221, 232
National Association of Manufacturers (NAM), 3, 6–7, 16–17, 44–46, 69
National Association of Religious Broadcasters (NARB), 279
National Conference of Christians and Jews (NCCJ), 111

National Council for Christian Leadership (NCCL), 46
National Council of Churches (NCC), 74, 82, 114, 199, 210, 213–214, 218, 220, 225, 232–235, 286
National Day of Prayer, 55–57, 92, 176
National Flag Conference, 102
National Labor Relations Board, 79, 159, 244
National Lay Committee, 225
National Prayer Breakfast, xii, 75–81, 184, 248–249, 266, 278, 284, 286–288
National Presbyterian Church (Washington, D.C.), 73, 197
National Reform Association, 96, 98
New Deal
    advertising industry and, 130
    Cecil B. DeMille and, 140
    clergy support for, 5–6
    Dwight D. Eisenhower and, 86–87
    J. Howard Pew and, 16
    James W. Fifield's attacks on, 6–7, 11–14
    NAM and, 3, 4
    Ralph Flanders and, 96
    Social Gospel and, 5–6
    Spiritual Mobilization and, 19, 24, 28
New Testament, Gideon Bibles and, 165–169
New York Avenue Presbyterian Church (Washington, D.C.), 104–105, 140
New York Board of Rabbis, 172
New York Board of Regents, 170–172, 189
Newdow v. Elk Grove Unified School District, 289
Niebuhr, Reinhold (theologian), 62, 103, 189, 256
Nixon, Richard M. (president)
    "Back to God" program, 74–75
    Billy Graham and, 242–244, 246–247, 252, 260–263
    campaign donors, 254, 264–265
    church services inside the White House, 244, 249–257
    construction workers support, 259
    Earl Warren and, 246–247
    Honor America Day, 271–272
    "In God We Trust" stamp, 114
    inauguration, 244–248
    meeting antiwar protesters, 258
    National Prayer Breakfast, 80, 248–249
    polarization of public religion, 294
    Statement of Seven Divine Freedoms, 91
    University of Tennessee appearance (1970), 260–263
Noerdlinger, Henry (researcher), 143
North American Aviation, 84
Novak, Robert (columnist), 204, 222

Oakman, Charles (representative), 108–109
Obama, Barack (president), 290–291
Olsen, Alec (representative), 212
"One Nation Under God" banners, 239–240
"One nation under God" motto, 99–100, 107, 109, 111, 124, 170, 273–274, 288–289, 294
"One Nation Under God" postcards, 240–241
Opinion Research Corporation, 85–86
Opitz, Edmund A. (minister), 225
"Our American Heritage" campaign, 131

Pacific Mutual Life Insurance Company, 9
Paper currency, "In God We Trust" motto, 112, 116–121, 124–125
Paramount Pictures, 107, 145
Parochial schools, xvi, 99, 103, 180
Paschall, H. Franklin (SBC president), 234
Pastore, John (senator), 115–116
Patriotism, piety and, 130, 135, 153, 169, 206, 241, 243, 277, 286, 290
Patterson, J. Renwick (minister), 98
Peabody, Stuart (Advertising Council chairman), 132
Peale, Norman Vincent (minister-author), 14, 27, 45, 74, 139, 245, 247, 250

Pearson, Drew (columnist), 52, 224
Pendergrast, J. Gilbert (judge), 194
Penney, J. C. (executive), 28, 45
Pentagon, religious practices at, 83
PepsiCo., 254
Percy, Walker (novelist), 243
Perot, H. Ross (executive), 265
Pew, J. Howard, Jr. (executive), 16–17,
    20–22, 28, 46, 103, 225, 252, 264
Pew, Joseph Newton, Jr. (executive), 46
Pfeffer, Leo (lawyer), 168
Philbin, Philip J. (representative), 118
Phillips, John (representative), 48
Piety, patriotism and, 130, 135, 153, 169,
    206, 241, 243, 277, 286, 290
Pike, James A. (Episcopal bishop), 189,
    212
Pledge of Allegiance
    celebrations of new, 110–111
    George H. W. Bush's use as partisan
        issue, 282–283
    George M. Docherty and, 105–107
    music, 111
    as official pledge, 102
    original, 100–102
    required recitations in schools, 288
    "under God" inserted into, 102–104,
        106–110, 116, 124, 169, 178, 186,
        272, 293
Pollock, Channing (author), 15
Potter, Charles (senator), 113
Powers, James E. (American Legion
    commander), 210–211
Prayer
    cabinet meetings opened with, 81–84
    corporate, 190
    First Amendment and, 175, 179, 181,
        182
    John F. Kennedy's comments on,
        184–185
    National Day of Prayer, 55–57
    in political life, 47, 98
    in public schools, 170–190, 205
    at Republican National Convention,
        275
    See also Public prayer
Prayer amendment, 203–237
    hearings in the House, 215–224

    in House of Representatives,
        207–224
    opposition to, 206–207, 213–215,
        217–221, 223, 225–226, 231–234
    in Senate, 227–237
    separation of church and state, 209,
        224–225
Prayer breakfast meetings, 36, 41–45,
    79–80, 278–279
Precision Valve Corporation, 264
Prentis, H. W. (NAM president), 6, 15
Project Prayer, 222, 231
Protestant Council, 172
Protestants and Other Americans
    United for the Separation of
    Church and State (POAU), xvi,
    99, 123, 240
Proudly They Came . . . To Honor America
    (album), 272–273
Public prayer, 75, 98
    national heritage of, 175
    Nixon inauguration, 244
    as political development, 36
    popularization of, 38–39
    school prayer amendment, 203–237
Public relations
    Advertising Council and, 131
    faith emphasized in campaigns, 6
    National Association of Manufactur-
        ers (NAM), 4, 6
    piety and, 251
    prayer and, 37
Public service campaigns, 131
Publishing, religion in, 138–139
Puder, Glen D. (minister), 128

Quaker Oats Company, 46

Rabaut, Louis C. (representative),
    102–104, 108–111, 113–115
Racial segregation, 95, 184, 205
Randolph, William (representative), 185
Rayburn, Sam (representative), 50, 54,
    102
Reagan, Ronald (president), xiv, 28,
    275–281
    Committee to Proclaim Liberty and,
    28

Disneyland dedication, 127–128
Fred Schwarz and, 148
"God Bless America" phrase use,
    275–277
"Hollywood's Answer to Commu-
    nism" and, 155
National Affairs Briefing of the
    Religious Roundtable, 278
National Association of Religious
    Broadcasters (NARB) address,
    279
National Prayer Breakfast, 278
renomination as president, 280–281
at Republican National Convention,
    275–276
sacralization of state by, 278
school prayer amendment, 278–279
at Southern California School of
    Anti-Communism, 153–154
"Regents' Prayer," 171–173, 175,
    177–179, 182–183, 185
Reitman, Alan (ACLU official), 123
Religion
    in politics, 124, 130, 244, 255, 280,
        286
    in popular culture, 130
    in public life, 82, 166, 190, 206, 237,
        244, 292–294
    in public schools, 165–201
    "Religion in American Life" (RIAL)
        campaign, 132–138
Religious revival
    "Back to God" movement, 73–75
    Eisenhower administration and,
        87–88, 96, 100, 130, 293
    March of Freedom and, 90
    Nixon administration and, 247
    postwar, 68, 112, 176
    Reagan administration and, 276–277
    "Religion in American Life" (RIAL)
        campaign and, 134
Religious heritage
    generalizations about, 172
    Hugo Black and, 180
    public prayer, 175, 178
    school prayer and, 170, 172, 180
Religious nationalism, 161, 169,
    241–242, 246, 273, 292

Religious Observance Committee,
    244–245
Religious right, 277–279, 281, 287, 290,
    293
Republic Steel Corporation, 20, 21, 23,
    28, 69, 254
Republican National Conventions, ix,
    46, 59, 60, 62, 153, 216, 224, 242,
    275–276, 282, 285, 288
Reston, James "Scotty" (journalist), 60
Reuther, Walter (labor leader), 103, 160
Rhodes, Fred (lay preacher), 252–253
Richards, Ann (governor), 282
Richardson, Sid (oilman), 50–51, 54,
    58–59, 64, 69, 84, 87
Richfield Oil Company, 130, 153,
    156–159
Ridgway, Matthew (general), 33
The Road to Serfdom (Hayek), 19
Robb, R. E. (columnist), 97
Roberts, Cliff (investment banker), 72
Robertson, A. Willis (senator), 47, 54
Robertson, Pat (evangelist), 47, 277, 278,
    279, 282, 285, 291–292
Robinson, Claude (Opinion Research
    president), 86
Romney, George (governor), 247
Romney, Mitt (governor), 292
Roosevelt, Franklin D. (president), 4–8,
    11–14, 16, 28, 39–40, 89, 128,
    140, 275
Roosevelt, Theodore (president), 112
Ross, Roy (minister), 114
Rostow, Eugene (dean), xv, 98–99, 176,
    293
Roth, Larry (parent), 174–175
Rove, Karl (Bush strategist), 290
Rovere, Richard (writer), 159
Rucker, Allen W. (author), 26
Ruegemer, E. J. (judge), 145–147
Rushdoony, R. J. (missionary), 26
Russell, Henry Edward (minister), 253
Russell, Richard (senator), 253

Safire, William (Nixon speechwriter),
    284
Salit, Norman (Synagogue League of
    America president), 114

San Diego Gas & Electric Company, 29–30

Sawyer, Henry (attorney), 195

Schempp, Edward (parent), 193, 197–198

Schempp, Ellory (high school student), 192–193

Schick Safety Razor Company, 152, 156, 158

Schools
  Bible readings in, 190–201, 205
  Engel v. Vitale, 174–190
  Gideon Bible distribution to, 165–169
  "In God We Trust" motto placement in classrooms, 191
  parochial, xvi, 99, 103, 180
  Pledge of Allegiance required recitations, 288
  prayer amendment and, 203–237, 278–279
  prayer in public schools, 170–190, 205

Schools of Anti-communism, 150–153, 158, 160–161

Schuller, Robert (minister), 287

Schulz, Charles (cartoonist), 187

Schwartz, Herman (rabbi), 167

Schwarz, Fred (doctor-activist), 148–161
  attacks on, 155–157, 160
  C. D. Jackson and, 155–158
  Christian Anti-Communism Crusade (CACC), 149, 151, 154, 156, 158–161
  congressional testimony, 149–150
  "Hollywood's Answer to Communism," 154–156, 158
  on *Meet The Press* (1962), 161
  Patrick Frawley and, 152–154
  Roger Milliken and, 158–159
  Schools of Anti-communism, 150–153, 158, 160–161
  You Can Trust the Communists (. . . To Do Exactly as They Say), 150, 157

Scott, Bob (governor), 249

Scott, Hugh (senator), 228

Sears, Roebuck, 3, 105

Seaton, Fred (secretary of the interior), 138

Seattle Gas Company, 43

Seldes, Gilbert (dean), 159

Senate
  prayer amendment and, 227–237
  prayer breakfast meetings, 44, 45, 47, 76, 79, 96, 278–279

Separation of church and state
  Everson v. Board of Education, 180
  Gideons International and, 166–169
  Hugo Black and, 179–182
  John F. Kennedy and, 184
  prayer amendment and, 209, 224–225
  in public schools, 166–169, 179–182
  religious organizations support of, 218–219
  Thomas Jefferson and, xiii, 180
  Tudor v. Board of Rutherford and the Gideons International, 168

Shales, Tom (media critic), 275

Sheen, Fulton (Catholic bishop), 92, 139, 221, 270

Shepherd, David R. (author), 280

Sherwin Williams Company, 69

Silent Majority, 241, 260–261, 263–267, 270

Skelton, Red (comedian), 271–272

Skousen, W. Cleon (author), 151, 152, 154

Sloan, Alfred (executive), 26

Slosser, Bob (author), 280

Smith, Gerald L. K. (activist), 204

Smith, Howard W. (representative), 184

Snyder, Murray (Eisenhower deputy press secretary), 120

Social Gospel, 5–7, 25, 108, 273

Society of Christian Socialists, 100

Sollitt, Kenneth W. (minister), 32

Southern Baptist Convention (SBC), 226–227, 234, 252–253, 278

Southern California Edison Company, 27

Southern California School of Anti-Communism, 152–154, 158

Soviet Union, 22, 35–36, 49, 109, 152
  See also Cold War; Communism

Spellman, Francis (Catholic archbishop), 114, 189, 212
Spiritual Mobilization
   attacks on, 21
   Cecil B. DeMille and, 141–142
   "The Christian's Political Responsibility," 63
   clergy recruitment by, 12–14, 16–21, 24–25
   Committee to Proclaim Liberty, 27–34
   Don Belding and, 69
   Faith and Freedom, 23–27, 63, 69
   founding, 11–12
   The Freedom Story, 22–23, 70, 92
   "Freedom Under God" celebrations, 27–34, 73, 92
   funding of, 15, 18–22
   J. Howard Pew and, 16–18, 20–22, 28
   James W. Fifield and, 11–15, 18–27
   minister-representatives, 18–19
   pledge, 14
   publications, 14–15, 23–27
   sermon competitions, 20, 30–32
St. Clair, William (executive), 41
St. George, Katharine (representative), 78
Stamps, "In God We Trust" motto on, 113–116, 125
Standard Oil Company, 3, 164
"The Star-Spangled Banner," 111–112, 121
Stassen, Harold (Eisenhower assistant), 81
Statement of Seven Divine Freedoms, 88–89, 91
Stennis, John (senator), 47
Stephens, R. G. (representative), 212
Stevenson, Adlai (governor), 61–62, 63
Stewart, Jimmy (actor), 33, 155, 272
Stewart, Potter (justice), 177, 179, 181–183, 196
Stone, I. F. (journalist), 243
Strauss, Bob (party chairman), 283
Strikes, labor, 13, 21, 37–38, 40–41, 128
Strout, Richard (journalist), 85, 160
Student protests, 254, 257–259, 262
Sullivan, Amy (journalist), 290

Sun Oil Company, 16, 20, 225
Sun Shipbuilding Company, 46
Summerfield, Arthur (postmaster general), 85, 113–114
Sumner, Charles (senator), 96
Sunday Evening Club, 9, 141
Supreme Court, U.S.
   Abington School District v. Schempp, 194–195, 198–199
   Brown v. Board of Education, 95
   Engel v. Vitale, 176–190
   Everson v. Board of Education, 180
   flag desecration statutes, 283–284
   Murray v. Board of School Commissioners of Baltimore City, 194–195, 198–199
   Tudor v. Board of Rutherford and the Gideons International, 168
Synagogue Council of America, 200, 220
Szilagyi, Stephen T. (minister), 258

Talmadge, Herman (senator), 185
Taylor, Clyde (NAE official), 88
Technicolor Corporation, 154, 156, 158
Television, religious programming on, 139–140
Teller, Edward (physicist), 153, 159
Ten Commandments, 7, 19
Ten Commandments monuments, xv, 145–148
The Ten Commandments (film), 140, 142–145
Thomas, Cal (Moral Majority spokesman), 279
Thurmond, Strom (politician), 49, 160
Timmons, Bill (Nixon aide), 253
Todt, George (columnist), 154
Truman, Harry S. (president), 22, 26, 28, 52–54, 56, 61, 102, 185
Tudor, Bernard (parent), 168
Tudor v. Board of Rutherford and the Gideons International, 168
Tuller, Edwin H. (minister), 218–219
Tydings, Joe (senator), 233–234

Un-American Activities Committee, 129, 140, 149

Union Carbide and Carbon Corporation, 69, 132, 264
Unitarian Ministers Association, 107
United Airlines, 28
US Chamber of Commerce, 6, 9, 14, 28, 33, 37, 51, 136, 273
US Rubber Company, 69
US Steel Corporation, 13, 20, 28, 264
Utah Power & Light Company, 30

Van Deerlin, Lionel (representative), 212
Vereide, Abraham (minister), 36–37
    Billy Graham and, 53
    business and, 37, 40–49
    charity work, 39–40
    communism and, 48–49
    Dwight D. Eisenhower supported by, 62–63
    Franklin D. Roosevelt and, 39–40
    Fred Schwarz and, 149
    International Council for Christian Leadership (ICCL), 48, 62, 96, 117
    National Council for Christian Leadership (NCCL), 46
    political connections, 43–49
    prayer breakfast meetings, 36, 41–45, 78–80
Vietnam War, 240–241, 257, 262, 266, 284
Vinson, Fred (justice), x, 47, 78–79
Vitale, William J., Jr. (school board president), 174
von Mises, Ludwig (philosopher-economist), 23, 26

"Wake Up America!" rally, 266
Walker, Ronald (Nixon aide), 265
Wallace, DeWitt (publisher), 264
Wallace, George (governor), 205, 241–242
Ward, Philip (lawyer), 195
Warren, Earl (governor-justice), 34, 79–80, 95, 177, 179, 196–197, 246–247
Warner Bros. Pictures, 155
Washington, George (president), 137
Washington Pilgrimage of American Churchmen, 104, 111

Watkinson, M. R. (minister), 112
Watson, Albert (representative), 253
Watson, Allan (minister), 253
Watson, Thomas (executive) 45
Wayne, John (actor), 154–155, 160
Weeks, Sinclair (secretary of commerce), 84–86
Welch, Robert (John Birch Society founder), 155–156
Welfare state, 5–7, 24, 26, 32, 53, 61, 86–87, 89, 108, 153
Wells, Kenneth (Freedoms Foundation president), 151
Weyerhauser, F. K. (executive), 46
White, Bryon (justice), 196
White, Charles (executive), 21–22, 69
White, K. Owen (SBC president), 226–227
White, Theodore (journalist), 50
Whittaker, Charles Evans (justice), 178
Wicker, Tom (journalist), 247–248, 258
Wiley, Alexander (senator), 78
Williams, John B. (chaplain), 74
Wills, Garry (writer), 257, 260–261, 285
Wilson, Charles (representative), 214
Wilson, Charles E. (General Electric executive), 132
Wilson, Charles E. (General Motors executive), 28, 83–84
Winchell, Walter (columnist), 161
Winchester, Lucy (Nixon social secretary), 257
Winegarner, Charles W. (Citizens Congressional Committee official), 203–204, 222
Woll, Matthew (labor leader), 28
Wright, Jeremiah (minister), 291
Wright, Jim (speaker of the House), 283

Yardley, Jonathan (writer), 287
Yorty, Sam (mayor), 153
You Can Trust the Communists (. . . To Do Exactly as They Say) [Schwarz], 150, 157
Young, James Webb (advertising executive), 131

Zorach v. Clauson, 98

Etta Recke

Kevin M. Kruse is a professor of history at Princeton University and the author or coeditor of four books, including the award-winning *White Flight*. He lives in Princeton, New Jersey.